Four Generations of Hoopers & Sturgises

THE FIRST GENERATION

Robert Hooper m. Mary Ingalls
1741–1814, merchant   1740–1807

six children

William Sturgis m. Hannah Mills
1748–1797, merchant   daughter of the
Rev. Jonathan Mills

Hannah   William

THE SECOND GENERATION

John Hooper m. Eunice Hooper
1776–1854, banker   1781–1866, daughter
of Samuel Hooper,
John's third cousin

Eunice   John   Anna   Robert   Francis
Mary   Elizabeth   Samuel   Nathaniel

William Sturgis m. Elizabeth M. Davis
1782–1863, sea captain   daughter of
and merchant   Judge John Davis

William   Anne   Mary
Ellen   Caroline   Susan

THE THIRD GENERATION

Robert William Hooper m. Ellen Sturgis
1810–1885, doctor   1812–1848

Ellen Sturgis   Edward William   Marian

THE FOURTH GENERATION

Ellen (Nella) Hooper m. Ephraim Whitman Gurney (no children)
1838–1887   1829–1886, Harvard professor

Edward (Ned) Hooper m. Fanny Hudson Chapin
1839–1901, lawyer, Harvard official   1844–1881

Ellen   Louisa   Mabel   Fanny   Mary

Marian (Clover) Hooper m. Henry Adams (no children)
1843–1885   1838–1918, historian

For Helen
Merry Christmas
and Much Love
JHS.

1979

ALSO BY OTTO FRIEDRICH

THE POOR IN SPIRIT

THE LONER

DECLINE AND FALL

THE ROSE GARDEN

BEFORE THE DELUGE: A PORTRAIT OF BERLIN
IN THE 1920'S

GOING CRAZY

CLOVER

Clover

BY

OTTO FRIEDRICH

SIMON AND SCHUSTER · NEW YORK

DESIGNED BY EVE METZ
PICTURE EDITOR: VINCENT VIRGA
MANUFACTURED IN THE UNITED STATES OF AMERICA

1 2 3 4 5 6 7 8 9 10

LIBRARY OF CONGRESS CATALOGING IN PUBLICATION DATA

FRIEDRICH, OTTO, DATE.
CLOVER, A LOVE STORY,
BIBLIOGRAPHY: P.
INCLUDES INDEX.
1. ADAMS, MARIAN HOOPER, 1843–1885.   2. UNITED
STATES—BIOGRAPHY.   3. ADAMS FAMILY.   4. ADAMS, HENRY,
1838–1918.   I. TITLE.
CT275.A34F73   973'.07'2024 [B]   79–12165

ISBN 0-671-22509-X

FOR PRISCILLA

CONTENTS

CONTENTS

Book IV: The Knot of Existence

Epilogue

I had a farewell letter from Henry James. . . . He wished, he said, his last farewell to be said to me as I seemed to him 'the incarnation of my native land'—a most equivocal compliment coming from him. Am I then vulgar, dreary, impossible to live with?
                                                        CLOVER ADAMS

James knows almost nothing of women but the mere outside; he never had a wife.
                                                        HENRY ADAMS

1

PROLOGUE

THE STATUE IN ROCK CREEK CEMETERY

AT A PAUSE IN THE MILD SLOPE of a Washington hillside, shadowed now by the holly trees that bar the dying sun, there sits the enigmatic figure of a woman in bronze. She is of heroic size, more than six feet tall, and anyone who comes to look at her must look upward, as though from the position of a kneeling supplicant. Her metallic face seems utterly impassive, blackened by almost a century of wind and rain. Her eyes are downcast, perhaps in sorrow, perhaps in resignation. Her head is covered with a bronze shroud —rusted green by now—"so that it throws the face in shadow," as her creator said, "and gives a strong impression of mystery." In her lap lie a few holly leaves that yellowed and fell here during the previous winter.

All around this statue, in Rock Creek Cemetery, the traditional gravestones preserve the names of the dead. Here lies Bernard Nailor, 1856–1906, and his wife, Minnie, and a fallen army of respectable citizens with names like Kennard and Harris and Henderson. Here lies Anne May, wife of George A. Gustin, who died on September 4, 1881, at the age of thirty-two, and here lie her children, Alfred Francis, dead on August 11, 1875, at the age of one year and seven months, and Anne Violet, dead on January 21, 1877, at the age of four years and three months. The bronze woman offers no such testimony. There is no statement that this is the grave of Clover Adams, born Marian Hooper, who killed herself on December 6, 1885, at the age of forty-two. And no statement that her husband, Henry Adams, having declared that "life was complete," encouraged someone to return here on every anniversary of Clover's death—"my haunting anniversary," he once called it—to place on her grave a bouquet of her favorite flowers, white violets.

In a way, the anonymity is appropriate, since the woman in bronze is not Clover Adams at all. She represents an approximation of Kwannon, the Buddhist goddess of compassion, whom Henry had seen at the Japanese imperial shrine of Nikko. Clover was small and sharp and funny and by no means a goddess. "She is certainly not handsome; nor would she be called quite plain, I think . . ." Henry once wrote to a friend about the young Miss Hooper, whom he had recently discovered in Cambridge. "She knows her own mind uncommon well. Her manners are quiet. She reads German—also Latin—also, I fear, a little Greek. . . ." Henry James was less academic in his appraisal. Writing to his brother William in 1870, when he and Clover were both twenty-seven, he complained of a certain deficiency in the brittle conversation of the young ladies of London. "They are well enough," he said, "[but] I revolt against their dreary, deathly want of—what shall I call it?—Clover Hooper has it—intellectual grace. . . ."

The bronze woman in Rock Creek Cemetery is rather different—stately, serene, not quite human—and many strangers who never knew much about Clover have come to this cemetery to admire this statue as one of the finest creations of Augustus Saint-Gaudens. In *A Modern Comedy*, for example, John Galsworthy sent the villainous Soames Forsyte to sit on the encircling brown granite bench, designed by Stanford White, and to reflect that Saint-Gaudens' statue was "the best thing he had come across in America: the one that gave him the most pleasure, in spite of all the water he had seen at Niagara and those skyscrapers in New York." Alexander Woollcott, a sort of American cousin of the philistine Forsytes, made a similar voyage to Rock Creek Cemetery and proclaimed Saint-Gaudens' work "the most beautiful thing ever fashioned by the hand of man on this continent."

But this is a sentimental hyperbole from a sentimental age. Not many people make the pilgrimage to the Adams memorial nowadays. "I don't even know where that cemetery is," says the Washington taxi driver, a white-haired man wearing a green knitted cap on his head in the 80-degree heat, and sucking on an unlit cigar butt that he holds between his toothless gums—a survivor, possibly, from the days when the shriveled figure of the octogenarian Henry Adams still walked the shaded fringes of Lafayette Square. Only with a map can the taxi driver find Rock Creek Cemetery, and only after protracted circling can he find Clover's grave. Parked on the slope, then, he shuts off his engine and applies a match to the sodden cigar butt and waits, indifferent, waits for his passengers to finish their rituals of search and recognition.

If the woman in bronze is not Clover, then it can only be an image, like so many other images in her life, of what other people thought she represented. Henry Adams himself proposed his idea to Saint-Gaudens in abstractions. "Mr. Adams described to him in a general way what he wanted," said the artist John La Farge, who was present at the meeting, "going, however, into no details, and really giving him no distinct clew, save the explanation that he wished the figure to symbolize 'the acceptance, intellectually, of the inevitable.' " Saint-Gaudens responded by adopting a pose that represented what he thought Adams wanted.

"No," said Adams, "the way you're doing that is a Penseroso."

Saint-Gaudens tried several more poses until Adams agreed to one of them. Then, instead of going to find an appropriate model, Saint-Gaudens simply called out to an Italian boy who was mixing clay for him, ordered him to sit still, and draped a blanket over his head. (Many years later, Adams disputed the idea that the figure was a woman at all. Saint-Gaudens wanted an expression "a little higher than sex can give . . ." he wrote to Theodore Roosevelt. "The figure is sexless.")

"Now that's done," said Adams. "The pose is settled. . . . I don't want to see the statue until it's finished."

As for all the details, Adams subsequently wrote to a friend that he had told Saint-Gaudens that he should be "absolutely free from interference." Such an absolute freedom is hard to imagine, for either the writer or the sculptor. From Saint-Gaudens' own correspondence, we learn that he wrote inquiringly to Adams: "Do you remember setting aside some photographs of Chinese statues, Buddha, etc., for me to take away from Washington? I forgot them. I should like to have them now. Is there any book *not long* that you think might assist me in grasping the situation?"

Who but a sculptor could make such a suggestion? That the husband of a dead woman might know of a book—*"not long"*—that might illuminate some photographs—*"etc."*—that might provide the materials for a statue. Adams' response was his traditional recourse: silence. So when Saint-Gaudens asked Adams to come and see his clay model of the future statue—hoping, presumably, for the approval that every artist wants of his unfinished work—Adams refused even to look at it. That was apparently his idea of "freedom from interference." Saint-Gaudens, however, was apprehensive. "The face is an instrument on which different strains can be played," he wrote to Adams, "and I may have struck a key in a direction quite different from your feeling in the matter." Adams gave way only to the extent of asking his friend La Farge to look at the clay model. La Farge apparently approved, but then Adams took him off on a lingering tour of the South Seas. From places like Samoa, Adams began complaining about Saint-Gaudens' delays. "At times I begin to doubt if Saint-Gaudens will ever let the work be finished," he wrote to a friend in 1891. "I half suspect that my refusal to take the responsibility of formally approving it in clay frightened him. Had I cared less about it, I should have gone to see it as he wished. . . ."

Actually, of course, Saint-Gaudens was laboring away—always seeking new commissions, always falling behind his promised deadlines—at his cluttered studio on New York's upper west side. In due time, he finished the hooded figure that is perhaps his masterpiece, finished it and installed it and waited for the taciturn historian to come and inspect it. The historian, having paid something on the order of $20,000 for the monument, was deeply impressed. "Naturally every detail interested him," he subsequently wrote in *The Education of Henry Adams*, "every line; every touch of the artist; every change of light and shade; every point of relation; every possible doubt of Saint-Gaudens' correctness of taste or feeling; so that, as the spring approached, he was apt to stop there often to see what the figure had to tell him that was new; but, in all that it had to say, he never once thought of questioning what it meant."

Clover herself might have been more skeptical. Nowadays, having been educated to the visions of a Mondrian or a Kandinsky, we

14

are not likely to ask what any work of art "means," but in that era of new railroad lines and electric lights, when the Philadelphia Centennial Exposition of 1876 had proudly exhibited not only the newly completed forearm of Frederic Bartholdi's Statue of Liberty but also a classical head of Iolanthe sculpted in butter and a Liberty Bell made of tobacco plugs—in such an era, the meaning of any monument was as much a part of the public domain as its height or tonnage. Mark Twain was apparently the first to give Clover's memorial one of its most familiar names: Grief. Adams himself wrote to a friend: "My own name for it is 'The Peace of God.' " But as he sat on the brown stone bench that still confronts the statue, he was surprised to hear other visitors argue over its meaning, and even more surprised to hear various clergymen denounce it. "One [minister] after another brought companions there," he observed, "and, apparently fascinated by their own reflection, broke out passionately against the expression they felt in the figure of despair, of atheism, of denial. Like the others, the priest saw only what he brought. Like all great artists, Saint-Gaudens held up the mirror and no more."

Adams professed to believe that the meaning of the statue would have been perfectly obvious to anyone who lived outside the American struggle for money and power and position. "He [Adams, himself] supposed its meaning to be the one commonplace about it —the oldest idea known to human thought," he wrote in the *Education*. "He knew that if he asked an Asiatic its meaning, not a man, woman, or child from Cairo to Kamchatka would have needed more than a glance to reply." Perhaps, perhaps—but why is it, then, that when Saint-Gaudens held up his mirror, we can see all of American culture in the Gilded Age, and yet we cannot catch even a glimpse of Clover herself?

"You're really going to write a whole book about Clover Adams?" the woman asks, a nice woman, sensible, intelligent, a reviewer of cultural events for *The New York Times*, and we are drinking cheap red wine amidst the debris of somebody else's dinner party. In another room, guests are watching a private showing of a film about R. D. Laing. "After all, what did she ever *do?*"

"Nothing special, but it's a different way of looking at the Adamses' Boston and the Adamses' Washington and the Adamses' friends and the Adamses' marriage—"

"Oh, that—that's all mystery. I once spent a lot of time—and suffered a lot of scraped knees—looking for that statue in Washington."

"Why did you do that? I mean, why so much effort in the search for Clover Adams?"

"Well, partly because Henry Adams never once mentioned her in his whole autobiography."

It is, of course, true. The twentieth chapter of the *Education* is entitled "Failure" and dated 1871, the year before Adams' marriage to Clover. The next chapter is entitled "Twenty Years After," and dated 1892. During those missing years, Henry and Clover were generally thought to be enjoying an idyllic marriage. They went riding together every morning in the woods along the Potomac, and they argued all the tumultuous issues of the day, from the rise of Social Darwinism to the corruption of the civil service, and they maintained the most fashionable salon in Washington, with dinner guests as diverse as General Sheridan and Henry James (Clover would not, however, admit the scandalous Oscar Wilde to her house). Indeed, James confided to his *Notebooks* in 1884 that he would like "a chance to *do* Washington, so far as I know it, and . . . I might even *do* Henry Adams and his wife." When he did finally do the Adamses, in a story entitled "Pandora," he portrayed a couple of such social distinction that the husband, Alfred Bonnycastle, a man who "was not in politics, though politics were much in him," could propose to his wife a truly omnivorous party at the end of the social season: "Let us be vulgar and have some fun —let us invite the President."

How strange indeed that Henry Adams never spoke of those thirteen happy years as part of his education, never spoke of them, in fact, at all.

The house where Clover killed herself, one Sunday in December, one cold, bleak Sunday morning in December, is gone now, vanished, destroyed. And so is the nearby house that she was in the process of moving into, the house that had been designed as a medieval fortress by Henry Hobson Richardson, who designed virtually all of his houses as medieval fortresses, rich in turrets and battlements and buttresses and stained glass—that is gone, too, also destroyed. And such is the state of impermanence of American building that the new stone hotel that now stands on this corner of Lafayette Square has itself become a kind of antique, destined either for destruction as an anachronism or for preservation as a monument.

"Is there anybody here who can tell me about the history of this place?"

"It's all over there," says the gray-haired man behind the reception desk, "over there on that plaque behind that pillar."

The plaque is obscure enough. It provides a photograph of Richardson's turreted château. Then it adds, with all the artificial language of artificial inevitability: "When the old houses disappeared and the hotel rose on the site it was only natural that it should be named the Hay-Adams House."

Everything is oak and walnut paneling here, as though to appease the watching ghosts of John Hay and Henry Adams (note the sequence of names—Hay, the Secretary of State under McKinley and Roosevelt, was once far more celebrated, by Washington standards, than his friend and next-door neighbor). But a table beneath the plaque is laden with complimentary copies of *The Iran Times*, a propaganda paper that emblazons its front page with portraits of the President and the visiting Shah and describes itself as "an independent newspaper for the Persian-speaking community of the United States and Canada." And as one looks up from this heap of generally ignored newspapers, one realizes that the whole dark lobby is full of Iranian officials and merchants, suavely outfitted in gray suits with flared trousers, representatives of the new power of Middle Eastern oil, and they are here to savor the consequences of that power.

And somewhere not far from here, unmarked, is the exact spot where Henry Adams, on climbing the vanished stairs of the vanished house to ask Clover whether she wanted to receive any visitors on that December day, "was horrified," according to the account in the *Washington Critic*, "to see her lying on a rug before the fire, where she had fallen from a chair. He hastened for assistance, after placing her on a sofa, and . . . the physician stated that she was dead. . . ."

"How often we have spoken of Clover as having all she wanted, all this world could give, except perhaps children." That expression of bewilderment, written shortly after the suicide by Mrs. Alexander Whiteside, was the common view among Clover's friends. Her marriage, her entire life, had seemed such a paradigm of what a well-bred and well-educated Boston woman of the period might properly consider happiness that nobody seemed able to offer any explanation for the sudden act of self-destruction. The only acceptable answer was that Clover, like another Ophelia, had fallen into a profound melancholia over the death of her father, Dr. Robert William Hooper, in April of that same year. And that this melancholia, perhaps exaggerated but at least comprehensible, had driven her to desperation. Even in our own time, such a traditionalist as Samuel Eliot Morison has written of Clover's suicide that it would be "futile to hunt for hidden motives."

On reflection, though, it is difficult to accept such a simple explanation. Ophelia is a literary creation, after all, and even she was further afflicted by the disappearance of her brother and the apparent madness of her lover. Could even the most self-effacing of Victorian daughters, then, have been so frail of spirit that the unavoidable death of a septuagenarian father would have led inexorably to suicide? Or are there other reasons, less obvious and perhaps less acceptable, for Clover's death?

Maybe there are clues to be found in the vast archive known as the Adams Papers. The building that houses the Massachusetts Historical Society, at 1154 Boylston Street in Boston, is worthy of its name and address. It is a monolithic structure of granite blocks and yellow bricks, fluted pillars and black iron balconies. A buzzer opens the heavy door to the empty foyer, where marble busts and muted paintings gaze blindly at the intruder. Here lie the Adams Papers, more than 300,000 pages of them, a collection that reflects the family's intense determination to commit its views to paper and to save all that paper as evidence for the judgments of history. The journals and letters and documents range from John Adams' Promethean warnings to the future ("Posterity! You will never know how much it cost the present generation to preserve your Freedom!") to Henry's bemused contemplation of the past ("I have been amusing myself with constructing genealogical tables of my own and my wife's ascendants to the eighth generation, at which stage not less than 128 grandfathers and grandmothers have to be waved on in a straight line.")

Scholars have been working over these papers for more than twenty years. More than 600 reels of unedited microfilm copies have been distributed to other libraries around the country. More than twenty volumes of the most important papers have already been published by Harvard's Belknap Press. (The recent Volumes V and VI of the *Diary of Charles Francis Adams*, at $20 a volume, record the future diplomat's activities only from the ages of twenty-six to twenty-nine, thus promising many future volumes for his seventy-nine years of life.) Over all this scholarly industry the Adams family still keeps a watchful eye. Until recently the president of the historical society was Thomas Boylston Adams, a member of the sixth generation descended from John and Abigail. "The fight never stops," according to Adams, who campaigned unsuccessfully for the Senate as an anti-Vietnam-War candidate in 1966. "There'll always be an establishment and the rebels. I hope our family will always be on the side of the rebels."

It is a hope that might have surprised Clover, who, as an Adams in-law, earned the right to have her surviving letters maintain a small place among the 300,000 pages. In contrast to Henry, who wrote straight up and down and formed each fat, round letter with meticulous neatness, Clover scrawled letters that look bold and agitated, even a little violent. She began every t with a decisive downward slash and crossed it with a stroke as long as an entire word. There may be assertiveness in that handwriting, but the extent of the Adams family's rebelliousness during the last year of Clover's life consisted largely in their voting for the Democratic presidential nominee, Grover Cleveland, against the extravagantly corrupt Senator James G. Blaine. In the penultimate letter of the series that she wrote to her father almost every Sunday for thirteen years, Clover began by reporting from her house on Lafayette Square that "Grover Cleveland is safely installed over the way." Once again, therefore, and for the last time, Clover seized the opportunity to watch history on parade. "This entire city looked like a gigantic tulip bed" as she rode her horse, Daisy, to a special vantage point near the military reviewing stand for the inauguration. "The colored regiments were very fine—" she continued, "one especially in high bearskin caps. . . . One band would pass playing 'Dixie' and the next playing 'The Union Forever,' 'Huzzah, Boys! Huzzah!' and 'Marching through Georgia' and everyone looked gay and happy and as if they thought it was a big country and they owned it. . . ."

The first Democratic President in twenty-four years was supposed to bring reconciliation and reform, and Clover's last letter to her father is full of the Adamses' reborn hopes for political influence. The new Secretary of the Navy, William C. Whitney—"tall, dark, good-looking [with] a keen, intelligent, very ambitious face" —has just been to the house to drink tea and admire the watercolors. And so has Jim Stetson, "one of Cleveland's bosom cronies, a clever young New York lawyer. They had just come from the White House. . . . The old party hacks are so full of wrath at the mugwumpish tendencies of appointments that it makes one hopeful. . . ." But she ends by saying, "Take care of yourself. We both are awfully used up—with colds and can't get rid of them." Within a few days of that last letter, Doctor Hooper's angina pectoris became sharply worse, and Clover went to Boston to nurse her father through his last month.

The few remaining letters in which Henry describes Clover's state of mind after her father's death display a laconic tone that might be attributed either to his sense of privacy or to his unawareness of the depths of her misery. To Sir Robert Cunliffe, during Clover's last month, he wrote mainly about politics but added: "My wife, who has been as it were a good deal off her feed this summer, and shows no such fancy for mending as I would wish, joins me in sending warm love." And to John Hay, during that same month: "We are still in poor state and unfit for worldly vanities. I see little or no one." The only known letter that Clover herself wrote during her last days, destined for her sister Ellen but never sent, absolves Henry of any responsibility for her sadness and yet implies a despair and self-abnegation far deeper than the sorrow over her father's death. "If I had one single point of character or goodness I would stand on that and grow back to life," she wrote. "Henry is more patient and loving than words can express. God might envy him—he bears and hopes and despairs hour after hour. . . ."

Many years later, when one of Henry Adams' friends was writing a sonnet about the Saint-Gaudens statue, the historian quoted to him two sentences from the Book of Ezekiel: "Son of man, behold, I take from thee the desire of thine eyes at a stroke yet shall thou neither mourn nor weep, neither shall thy tears run down. So spake I unto the people in the morning: and in the evening my wife died."

If the letters in the archives do not surrender their secrets easily, are there at least a few portraits to be studied?

"I know of only one surviving photograph," says one of the stately librarians who guard the Adams Papers, "though Mrs. Adams herself was a gifted photographer and took many portraits of her family and friends."

"You mean that one of her on the horse?"

"Yes, in the collection of her letters."

It is a tintype that dates from 1869, when Clover was twenty-five. It shows a small (she was only five feet two) and rather dour looking woman sitting sidesaddle on a horse. Her dark dress extends from her tightly buttoned white collar down to a point well below her feet. A white hat shaped like an inverted pie pan tilts forward over her face so that nothing can be seen except two short tufts of dark-brown hair, a straight nose, and a thin, unsmiling mouth.*

"But that's a terrible picture. You can hardly tell what she looks like at all."

"Perhaps that is why it has survived," the librarian says.

There is another archive, however, an archive that has never been catalogued or microfilmed or subsidized by charitable foundations. It was accumulated over the course of many years and passed from hand to hand, and now it lies in the attic of a country house. There is a crib in this attic, and some sturdy children's chairs, and a pride of boxes—stout wooden chests built to with-

---

* A member of Clover's family disputes this description of the portrait, arguing that the taking of a photograph in 1869 was so prolonged that even the most cheerful people rarely smiled during the process. "I commend to you," she added, "Lewis Carroll's 'Photographing of Hiawatha' with its delicious refrain:

> *"But the picture failed entirely,*
> *Failed because he moved a little,*
> *Moved because he couldn't help it!"*

stand rough handling and long sea voyages, boxes filled with the family papers, yellowed and faded letters sealed with daubs of purple wax, crumbling journals held together with bow-tied ribbons, memoranda and documents of events that took place long before Clover was even born. Here, for example, is the program for the graduation ceremonies at Boston Latin School on July 3, 1824, informing us that William Watson Sturgis, Clover's uncle, won a first prize for declaiming a speech by Patrick Henry. He was to die two years later, at the age of sixteen, in a sailboat accident. Captain Sturgis, Clover's grandfather, refused for years to let the boy's name be mentioned in his presence.

Clover herself suddenly appears in a chocolate-colored photograph. A chubby girl of about seven, her brown hair parted in the middle, she stares straight into the camera, her large eyes set wide apart, her head tilted a bit to one side, as though she were listening to one of the talkative older Sturgises tell stories. Her first letter dates from that same period. It is a small piece of blue notepaper, folded three times, bearing only a small domestic announcement to her Aunt Eunice: "I began my slipper Wednesday, and used those colors that you told me first. . . ." Somewhat later, she writes again to Aunt Eunice to tell her of a blackberrying expedition on which she filled a quart-sized basket. She adds a note of jubilation: "I got my dress stained a great deal which I was glad of because it looked as if I had been berrying." She ends on a note of childish confidence: "Don't show this."

Then there are Clover's things. Clover's copy of *Robinson Crusoe* in French, dated 1854, when she was eleven, Clover's *Tanglewood Tales* and *Faerie Queene*, and *Greek Syntax* by James R. Boise, and a two-volume Greek edition of *The Iliad*, which Henry Adams carried off to the South Seas after Clover's death and inscribed, "Tahiti, 1891." And Clover's Civil War pictures, gory panoramas of Confederate corpses sprawling in their muddy trenches, all recorded on film by Brady & Co. and mounted on cardboard and sold to the crowds during the victory parades through Washington, to be shown at home later on the family stereoscope. And Clover's bouquet holder, a horn-shaped device of gray steel mesh, with a delicate chain on one end. It lies on a red velvet setting inside a green brocaded box, and on the bottom of the box, a shaky hand has written: "Miss Clover Hooper with G. Griswold Gray's love." The guardian of the private archive at the house in the country smiles as she reads the inscription. "Isn't that a *gage d'amour?*" she remarks.

And Clover's dresses. The guardian of the private archive unwraps the tissue paper and gently lifts them from their cardboard boxes. One is of Burgundy velvet, the other gold brocade and moss-green velvet, both still bearing the label of M. Worth. Clover once wrote to her father about the interview that was to lead to the gold and green dress. It occurred during her stay in Paris at the end of 1879. "Yesterday I went to consult Mr. Worth about a gown to go with my Louis XIV lace, which he admired extremely, as I knew he would. He was standing pensively by the window in a long puce-colored dressing gown with two exquisite black spaniels —twins—sitting on two green-velvet chairs. This is what he wants me to have: the main dress gold colour, the velvet only to lay the lace on and at the bottom in front. I have become bored with the idea of getting any new gowns, but Henry says, 'People who study Greek must take pains with their dress.' "

Now the guardian lifts up the dress and holds it against herself. It looks a little too small for her—Clover was tiny—but she savors the richness of the material and the labor that has sewn the buttons on the front, the bows at the throat, the fringed tassels at the waist. "What a *swell* dress," she says. She holds out one side of it to demonstrate the effect of a bustle at the back. And the stiff white lace at the bottom.

"What's that for?" asks the voice of ignorance.

"That's a—I can't quite think of the name," the guardian says. "It's supposed to drag along on the ground when you walk. A dust ruffle, that's what it's called."

Nor must we forget the matching slippers, one pair green and one purple. They are very small, about seven inches long and two inches wide. They might fit Cinderella.

"There's the label there," says the guardian. "Alexander Sulker, *cordonnier* to Her Majesty the Queen of Saxony. And there: 'Mrs. H. Adams.' That's how we knew for sure that the dresses belonged to Clover Adams."

That's how we knew. That's how we knew who had once worn the gold brocade and purple velvet, who had danced and laughed and boasted of her latest acquisitions, who had been so intensely alive until that gray December day when her husband found her by the fireside, alive no longer.

BOOK ONE

𝔄 𝔅oston

𝔈ducation

It is a vulgar error that love, a love, is to woman her whole existence. She is also born for Truth and Love in their universal energy.

MARGARET FULLER

2

A DREAM OF BEAUTY

CLOVER ADAMS acquired and kept and left behind her a surprising number of bibles, more of them than one might expect of an intellectual Bostonian of the last century. Or perhaps the multiplicity implies a restless inability to find an answer in any one of them. The last of four bibles preserved at the private archive in the country is inscribed in Henry Adams' hand on the occasion of his honeymoon trip up the Nile—Cairo, 5 March, 1873—and one can only wonder what might have inspired the newly married voyagers to buy a bible at such a time in such a place. Perhaps a still-undeciphered hieroglyphic that Clover wrote inside the back cover after her first breakdown: P. 16.8 E. 19. 18.

Clover's real bible, though, was the one that she was given at the age of thirteen. Its dark brown cover is badly cracked by now, and the binding has split, and only an old purple ribbon still holds the remnants together. It is the King James edition, published at Oxford in 1850, "translated out of the original tongues, and with the former translations diligently compared and revised by his majesty's special command. . . ." Inside the front cover, an aged and unidentifiable hand dedicated the bible to Clover with a rather grim quatrain: "Teach me to feel another's woe; / To hide the fault I see; / That mercy I to others show, / That mercy show to me." And beneath that, in the same script: "Blessed are the pure in heart —for they shall see God." But a different hand, possibly that of the young Clover, copied inside the back cover a poem that begins:

I slept and dreamed that life was Beauty,—
I woke, and found that life was Duty. . . .

The resolutely Puritan couplet still shines, through more than a century, with the same kind of luster that Henry James once perceived when he wrote of a character in *The Bostonians* that "she was heroic, she was sublime, the whole moral history of Boston was reflected in her displaced spectacles." The poem* first appeared, actually, in the inaugural issue of a stout, blue-covered quarterly magazine, dated July 1, 1840, and named *The Dial*. Founded by the Transcendental Club, *The Dial* was jointly edited by Ralph Waldo Emerson, who called it "a bold Bible for Young America," and his friend Margaret Fuller, who proclaimed her own goal to be "stimulating each man to think for himself, to think more deeply and more nobly." By cajoling their spiritual neighbors to contribute literary works (without payment), they had acquired for their first issue Theodore Dwight's analysis of Transcendentalism, *The Divine Presence in Nature and the Soul*, William Henry Channing's views of Rome, a poem by Thoreau, and the poetic reflections on duty by one of Margaret Fuller's friends, Ellen Sturgis Hooper.

Mrs. Hooper was then twenty-eight, just three years married and the mother of two children—her third, whom she was to call Clover, had not yet been born. It is quite possible that the rearing of two children may seem to require a life devoted to Duty, but it is more likely that Clover's mother acquired her stern principles from her own sternly principled parents. She was, as her daughter was to be, a Sturgis—a name that rings almost as resonantly in Boston as does that of Adams. Indeed, about two years before the first Henry Adams arrived from Sommersetshire in 1636 with his wife and nine children, Edward Sturgis had already settled on a grant of four acres in Charlestown, just across the Charles River from Boston. Even then, it was a venerable name, for the family tradition claims descent from a William de Turgis whose name appears on legal documents in Northamptonshire in 1293. Edward Sturgis soon moved to Yarmouth, where he was "lycensed to keep an ordinary and draw wyne." He was also elected a constable, and

---

* By one of those odd coincidences that are better left unanalyzed, virtually identical lines flowed many years later from the pen of the Bengali poet Rabindranath Tagore: "I slept and dreamt / That life was joy / I awoke and saw / That life was duty / I acted and behold / Duty was joy."

made surveyor of highways, and chosen to represent the town in a dispute with nearby Indians. He moved again to the Cape Cod fishing village of Barnstable, where, after rearing eight children and celebrating his fiftieth wedding anniversary and finally burying his loyal wife, Elizabeth, he married once again, in his eightieth year. He lived to be eighty-three.

Of Edward Sturgis' eight children—there may have been more who died in infancy—one son, Thomas, married a Lothrop and had ten children. One of these ten, also named Thomas, married a Russell and had eight children. One of these eight, also Thomas, married a Paine and had nine children. One of these nine, William, married Sarah Burdick and had a daughter, Sarah, and then married again, to Hannah Mills, daughter of the Reverend Jonathan Mills, a graduate of Harvard, and had a second daughter, Hannah, and a son, William. The elder William was a sea captain, and he died at the hands of pirates in the West Indies. Young William Sturgis, then fifteen, determined to follow his father to sea and there to make his fortune. . . .

These Sturgises had as a poor relation—a remote and complicated in-law relationship—the Spanish philosopher George Santayana. They helped to support him during a relatively impoverished boyhood in Boston, and he later wrote somewhat derisively of "the not too brilliant intellect of the family." He nonetheless saw the value of "the Sturgis mind," which "was straightforward, believed in what it saw, and in what sounded right." There was value, too, in "the good looks, affability . . . and kindness common to the whole family." Beyond that, the Sturgises of the early nineteenth century had arrived at just the time when a certain kind of wealth could be acquired. They were, as Santayana wrote in *Persons and Places*, "the Great Merchants: a type that in America has since been replaced by that of great business men or millionaires, building up their fortunes at home; whereas it was part of the romance and tragedy of these Great Merchants that they amassed their fortunes abroad, in a poetic blue-water phase of commercial development that passed away with them, and made their careers and virtues impossible for their children."

William Sturgis, who was Clover's grandfather, had first left home at the age of fourteen to work in the counting room of his uncle, Russell Sturgis, already a successful fur trader. The murder of William's father in the following year inspired him to ship out for seven dollars a month as a cabin boy aboard the *Eliza*, a 135-ton schooner bound for the Northwest Pacific Coast and China. He was an eager adventurer. He not only studied Ossian in his cabin and kept a diary of everything he saw but also practiced navigation and learned the languages of the fur-trading Pacific Indians. When the *Eliza* encountered another ship that had been crippled by a mutiny, Sturgis was offered the chance to serve aboard it as a mate. On his next voyage, as a mate, the captain fell ill and died. Sturgis took command. He was nineteen.

There were great fortunes to be made in the China trade, but not without danger. In 1809, Sturgis sailed to China as captain of the *Atahualpa*, carrying no less than $300,000 to be invested in Chinese cargo. He arrived at Macao Roads and anchored overnight in a dead calm. Early in the morning, he saw twenty-one junks rowing toward his ship, and although he suspected no danger, one of his passengers expressed alarm. Sturgis' ship carried four small cannon, so he fired one of them across the bow of the leading junk. "But the junks were upon her," according to one of the Sturgis family chronicles, "and from the first of them the swarming savages tried with long poles and the pilot's hook to catch the end of her spanker boom, and only just failed. Then at close quarters the captain worked his four small cannon and every musket on board; while the pirates crowded about his ship with fearful yells, firing jingalls and fire balls upon her deck. The cruelty of these Chinese pirates was well known, and Captain Sturgis had a barrel of powder ready with which he told his crew he would blow them up if the pirates once got possession of the ship." The pirates succeeded in setting the *Atahualpa* afire, but a breeze had sprung up, and that enabled Sturgis to sail slowly toward the shore until he came within range of Macao's coastal batteries. After about an hour of battle, the batteries combined with Sturgis' own cannons to drive off the pirates. "The great number of men on board their vessels induced a belief that many men have been killed," Sturgis later reported back to a Boston newspaper. "Fortunately, not one of [us] was wounded, though many shot struck in almost every part of the hull, and our sails and rigging were much cut to pieces."

By this time, Sturgis was thinking of settling down and getting married, to Elizabeth M. Davis, daughter of Boston Federal District Judge John M. Davis. "The opportunities I have had of observing the sweetness of disposition, ingenuousness of mind, and many amiable traits of character you constantly display, have ripened [my] partiality into a tender, sincere and lasting attachment," he wrote to her. "Will you, my lovely girl, consent to unite your fate with mine, entrust your future happiness to my keeping?" Two days later, she rejected him. "I must ever consider myself unfortunate," she wrote, "in awakening in your bosom any other sentiment than that of esteem." There apparently was considerable opposition from the Davis family. One letter from Sturgis refers to "the persecution you have suffered on my account." But he persisted ("You well know how troublesome I am when a favorite point is to be gained") and after more than a year of courtship, they became engaged. "Amongst all our acquaintances," Sturgis wrote, "none, my Eliza, has a fairer prospect for happiness than ourselves."

In the year of his marriage, 1810, the twenty-eight-year-old Captain Sturgis retired from the sea and joined John Bryant in founding the trading partnership of Bryant and Sturgis. He was to become immensely successful, immensely rich. It has been estimated that between 1810 and 1840, fully half of all trade between the United States and the Pacific Coast and China was handled by the firm of Bryant and Sturgis. Mere wealth was not enough for Captain Sturgis, however. He yearned, as fiercely as any Adams, for the torments of public service. He spent much of the next thirty years representing the city of Boston in the state legislature, representing it, that is, as much as a Sturgis could represent anything so unlike himself. "He was not, and from his nature would not be, popular in political life," as one of his friends later wrote, "nor fitted to succeed as an aspirant for political preferment, even if his taste or inclination had pointed in that direction. He was altogether too independent and self-relying, and too single-minded in his conception of duty, to enter into the compromises required of the leaders of a political party."

One senses a love of controversy, not simply rhetoric or the expression of social prejudice but a Johnsonian appetite for disputation. In 1843, the year in which his granddaughter Clover was born, Captain Sturgis embroiled himself in the case of Midshipman Philip Spencer, who was later to become the prototype for Herman Melville's Billy Budd. In defiance of the general approval of Spencer's execution for mutiny, Sturgis' long articles in the Boston *Courier* excoriated Commander Alexander S. Mackenzie of the *Somers* for his haste and severity in imposing punishment. That was only one instance. As Boston struggled with its conscience on the issue of slavery, Captain Sturgis refused to allow the claims of commerce to impose silence. On one typical occasion in the late fifties, according to a contemporary chronicle, "some disturbance arose" from hecklers trying to prevent a speech by the abolitionist Wendell Phillips. Although Captain Sturgis "was probably as decidedly opposed to the orator's peculiar sentiments as any person in the room," the chronicle continues, he "immediately stepped forward upon the platform, and, appealing to the sense of propriety and the self-respect of the audience, secured the meeting from further interruption."

There is one photograph of Captain Sturgis in this period, growing bald now, with a few tufts of gray hair flying around his ears like ocean spray. The nose is thick and strong, the blue eyes shrouded by heavy brows. The whole expression is proud, but not haughty. He betrays a faint smile, the kind that a venerable merchant might show after having posed an exasperating riddle for his granddaughter. They were, in fact, the best of friends. They told jokes and made up stories and went to the circus together. "Of Clover I can truly say that she is 'good as pie,' " the captain wrote to her mother one spring Sunday in 1848, "as hearty as a North Carolina pig (that eats more than it earns) and as healthy as a young Indian. Her round, red cheeks exceed anything you ever saw among the aristocratic portion of society and are quite equal to an Irish child that eats everything it gets hold of and sleeps on the soft side of a board. I have never heard an unpleasant sound from the child since you left. She and I have become so intimate that you may find it somewhat difficult to get her from me. She is certainly *the best child in the world.*"

Clover was then four, the captain sixty-six. He had stayed home from church that day to write about "my little charge" to her mother. "Clover has just come in from church," the letter continues, "and says she must sign her name 'this minute.' " There follows then the four-year-old's scrawled self-proclamation: CLOVER. "There you have it," the captain happily adds, "—her own signature made by herself." And so the letter rambles on, the doting grandfather scribbling away, the child tugging at his sleeve to interrupt, the grandfather perhaps helping to guide her chubby hand. "Clover persists in adding another word—she is just boasting that she 'has just learned to write'—DEAR FATHER I LOVE YOU—CLOVER. . . ."

The reason for this correspondence was that Dr. Hooper had taken his wife to Georgia for a few weeks in an effort to escape the tuberculosis that was killing her, and would indeed kill her before the year was over. The doctor wrote optimistically back to Boston: "I perhaps deceive myself, but if I do not, Ellen is better than when we left home. I heard her say a few minutes ago, on putting down a novel and then laying herself down, 'This indolence is a luxury!' " Ellen herself wrote a typically flowery postscript: "Change of air does wonders! I find here a taste of what I have long coveted—the dignity and repose of the vegetable kingdom. Not that part of it which has to keep up to spring expectations . . . but of that humble lichen tribe, the Chinese of the soil."

Ellen Hooper's optimism was not characteristic. She had lived all her life under the shadow of illness. Even as a young schoolgirl, she suffered a severe attack of what her mother called "lung fever," and she had to be bled and blistered. "Heaven only knows the result of this sickness . . ." Mrs. Sturgis wrote. "The language of my life (oh that it may be that of my heart) is 'Thy will be done.' " As Ellen grew up, the result of her sickness began to appear increasingly ominous. The first of her poems that is anchored by a date (1835) is a cry of protest: "Oh, melancholy liberty, / Of one about to die— / When friends, with a sad smile, / And aching heart the while, / Every caprice allow, / Nor deem it worthwhile now, / To check the restless will / Which death so soon shall still!" Another poem, also bearing the date 1835, is even more anguished: "Not as the Pagan lays / His hopeless head and his death-stricken heart / Upon the pile, impatient of delay, / Not so do I depart. . . . This life is yet as new / In hope and joy as when it first was mine, / Thy gifts as precious—help me to resign / All—all—thy will to do."

The tone of these poems—posthumously and privately printed by Clover's brother Ned—is rather artificial, and yet they do express a genuine desperation. The year 1835 must have marked the point at which Ellen Sturgis learned that her chest pains and her weariness and her attacks of coughing were symptoms of consumption. She was then twenty-three, still single, still at the beginning of life, and, as her poems try to say, very unwilling to accept the doctors' verdict. Like many a Jamesian heroine, Ellen Sturgis regarded her wintry surroundings and cried out for warmth. "Oh God, who framed this stern New-England land, / Its clear cold waters, and its clear, cold soul, / Thou givest tropic climes and youthful hearts / Thou weighest spirits and dost all control— / Teach me to wait for all—to bear the fault / That most I hate because it is my own, / And if I fail through foul conceit of good, / Let me sin deep so I may cast no stone."

In that same year of Ellen Sturgis' apparent sentencing, 1835, there returned to Boston from Paris—like a more genial and more prosperous Merton Densher ready to marry the dying Milly Theale in *The Wings of the Dove*—Dr. Robert William Hooper. He was then twenty-five years of age, and "one of the pleasantest fellows," according to his friend Oliver Wendell Holmes. Holmes and Hooper had gone to Harvard Medical School together and then voyaged to France for the more sophisticated medical training available in Paris. Holmes pursued this two-year training with a passion (no other student, he wrote to his parents, has "sought knowledge so ardently and courted pleasure so little"), Hooper somewhat less so. He went off on jaunts to Holland, Germany, Italy. His diary is full of dinner parties and trips to the theater, and once a week the most convivial of Boston students gathered for food and wine at the *Trois Frères*.

Though little is known of the courtship of Doctor Hooper and Ellen Sturgis—no flashes of Hooper's characteristic cheerfulness brighten the threnodies of her poetry—perhaps Holmes sketched the scene in the closing pages of his first novel, *Elsie Venner*. When the young hero finishes his medical studies, his professor jovially exhorts him to practice among the rich. "Take care of all the poor that apply to you," he says, "but go for the swell-fronts and south-exposure houses; the folks inside are just as good as other people, and the pleasantest, on the whole, to take care of. They must have somebody, and they like a gentleman best. Don't throw yourself away, but have a good presence and pleasing manners. . . . You have all the elements of success: go and take it." The young doctor protests his indifference to social distinctions and his desire to "be useful to his fellow-beings," but he does as the professor orders and soon is seen "looking remarkably happy and keeping step by the side of a very handsome and singularly well-dressed young lady."

Now it happened that Dr. Hooper's older brother, Samuel, had married, three years earlier, Anne Sturgis, aged nineteen. Samuel became a partner in the family business of Bryant and Sturgis (and eventually went into politics, serving six terms in Congress). So what could be more natural than for the youth newly returned from Paris to be seen keeping step by the side of the sister of his newly acquired sister-in-law, the pale, gifted, and very intense Ellen Sturgis? Captain Sturgis had no need to investigate the Hoopers' background, for they were as well established, if not as rich, as the Sturgises. There had been Hoopers in Massachusetts since 1635, and back in the mists of English genealogy, when a William de Turgis was roving about in thirteenth-century Northamptonshire, a William le Hopore could be found in thirteenth-century Dorset. The Hoopers even had their own family martyr, John Hooper, bishop of Gloucester, a Puritan of Zwinglian persuasion, who was stripped of his offices and burned at the stake in 1555.

The first Hooper to come to Massachusetts, in 1635, was a humbler sort, a youth named William, aged eighteen, apparently a weaver. But the tribe had prospered, most recently in the person of John Hooper, born in Marblehead in 1776 and destined to become rich. He was for many years the president of the Marblehead Bank, a man described as "of great business energy and shrewdness, combined with much regard for equity and public spirit." He built a mansion on the northern side of the Marblehead Common, and there he lived with his wife, Eunice, who was also a Hooper, the daughter of his third cousin. And there they reared nine children, of whom the seventh, born in 1810, was Robert William,* destined for Harvard and a Beacon Street practice and a marriage, just two years after his return from Paris, to a Sturgis.

Captain Sturgis lived in a handsome but austerely furnished mansion at 52 Summer Street, on Church Green, facing the octagonal church that had been designed by Bullfinch and equipped with a bell by Paul Revere, so it seemed fitting for him to help his

---

* His college friend Holmes referred to him as "Bob," but after his marriage, he appears in the Hooper family correspondence as "William," possibly another sign of Captain William Sturgis' remarkable domination of his family.

new son-in-law establish himself in a home nearby. That was the way fathers provided for their daughters in those days; Doctor Hooper himself would later provide much the same kind of establishment for Clover and Henry Adams. The newly married Hoopers acquired a house at 44 Summer Street, which was then a most elegant little street just a block east of the Common. Governor Edward Everett lived there; Queen Victoria's father, the Duke of Kent, attended a wedding there, and Daniel Webster entertained the Marquis de Lafayette when the aging French hero came to Boston to dedicate the Bunker Hill Monument. Webster's house on Summer Street had recently been sold, however, to Boston's greatest millionaire, Peter Chardon Brooks, whose daughter Abigail had married Charles Francis Adams, the son of the President.

Even in the Hoopers' days, the area was changing rapidly. The Webster house was torn down in 1867 to make way for one of the new stores that were sprouting along Summer Street, and Bullfinch's church was demolished two years later, partly because so many of its parishioners were moving to the new housing developments known as Back Bay. The Hoopers duly left 44 Summer Street and moved to a narrow brownstone house at 107 Beacon Street, and then, a few years later, across the avenue to a new brownstone at 114 Beacon. Then, on the night of November 9, 1872, a boiler fire went out of control in the basement of the Tebbetts, Baldwin & Davis building at the corner of Summer and Kingston Streets, and within less than twenty-four hours, the blaze destroyed about sixty-five acres of Boston's commercial district. Today, Summer Street is a rather dark and narrow lane dominated by its giant department stores. Where the Hoopers once lived stands a gray five-story building containing a moderately large jewelry store named Thomas Long, its windows stripped bare every weekend so that nothing on the felt-topped display stands can tempt a thief to throw a rock. Directly across the street stands the brick fortress of Jordan Marsh Co., occupying the whole block between Washington and Chauncy Streets. Its brightly lighted windows advertise "The look of leisure," as demonstrated by a series of male mannequins outfitted in emerald-green terrycloth bathrobes and white parkas with scarlet trim. They also have bottles of suntan lotion and spray cans of deodorant.

Here, in 1838, the year after her marriage, Ellen Hooper gave birth to her first child, and named her Ellen, and then the following year came her only son, Edward, and then four years later, Clover. And throughout these years, she never really escaped from her illness. "I am not well enough or in sufficiently good spirits to lay claim to much enjoyment anywhere," she wrote to her sister Caroline in the summer of 1840, long before Clover was even born. "If I come [to visit you] I should be so much fettered by the children that I should be unable to abandon myself to the spirit of the place. I live bolt upright. . . . I have now, I fear, little elasticity of spirits. I do not know whether I shall overcome life or it shall overcome me. Still, self-trust . . . will not permit me to yield to the latter belief."

Captain Sturgis took command of this situation by buying an abandoned hotel at Horn Pond, near Woburn, and refitting it as a summer headquarters for his five daughters and their various husbands and children. "It is a pretty place—a sheet of water in front, low pine in rear," Ellen wrote to a friend in Chicago, enclosing a sketch of the massive building and its two outlying wings. And again: "It is a very pleasant home for us, our children, horses and dogs, of all of which we have plenty." The captain loved to take his grandchildren out rowing on the still waters of Horn Pond, or simply out walking in the woods, and Aunt Carrie once wrote that if she ever chose "to pop in suddenly some morning," she could expect to find "Clover meandering about like a little brook." And then there were the tales that the captain told to his grandchildren, about his boyhood adventures among the Indians of the far northwest. "After frolicking with them in their childhood games," according to one friend of the family, "he would yield to their solicitations for some stories about the Indians. Such narratives, beginning in the twilight on the piazza, were sometimes protracted into late evening."

Ellen Hooper was more literary than her father. She and her sister Caroline regularly attended the "Conversations" that Margaret Fuller began organizing in 1839 in the parlor of Elizabeth Peabody on West Street. Miss Fuller's topic that first year was Greek mythology and its Transcendental implications. The following year, she devoted herself to the fine arts. All the most interesting ladies in Boston attended—Mrs. George Bancroft, Mrs. Josiah Quincy, Mrs. Theodore Parker, and the three Peabody sisters, who were destined to marry Horace Mann, Nathaniel Hawthorne, and (almost) William Ellery Channing. But among all these, Margaret Fuller said of Ellen Hooper, "I have seen no woman more gifted by nature than she." So when Ellen Hooper occasionally wrote about her children, she wrote about them as Transcendental objects, symbolic personifications of the *Ding an sich*. And yet there occasionally burst forth from the philosophical cobwebs an impassioned sense of her prospective loss. "I give thee all, my darling, darling child, / All I can give—the record of good things, / All maxims, truths in memory's storehouse filed, / And point thee to a rest 'neath angel wings—I give thee counsel from a mother's heart, / Bread earned with tears. I lay my page of life / Unrolled with bitter shame before thine eyes / That thou mayest shun or better share the strife— / All this is thine—and prayers to speed thee on, / And patience, which would wait th'appointed hour, / But oh, my child, example ask thou not,—Thy mother's life shows not the ripened flower—"

And Ellen's mother, the captain's wife, could not stand it, absolutely could not bear it. Shattered some years earlier by the death of her only son, who had drowned in a boating accident, the grief-ridden Elizabeth Sturgis withdrew ever more deeply into herself and her tormented yearning for God. Her brother-in-law, the Reverend Ezra Styles Goodwin, tried to persuade her to moderate her devotions. "It may seem singular advice for a minister to give," he told her, "that you allow the things of Earth to interest you deeply [but] I do not think it is the best advice I can give. Interest yourself freely in your house, its arrangements and preparations . . . reserving only the supreme affection for God."

Mrs. Sturgis apparently tried to follow his suggestions, but her anxieties and her sieges of depression were too powerful. A few years later, in 1831, she suddenly departed from Captain Sturgis' house and took refuge with her sister Ellen and the Reverend Goodwin in the Cape Cod village of Sandwich. The captain wrote stately and stoical pleas for her to come home: "I indulge the hope, my dear wife, that you will return so improved in health and spirits that you will be able to resume your place in the family, to get along easily in *a quiet way*. . . ." In vain. More than a year later, the captain officially wrote to her that he proposed to send her $1,000 a year, and would send more if she wanted it, and he added "the assurance I have made before, that whenever you feel able and willing to return home, assume the place in your family that belongs to you, and live with me on friendly terms, you will be received with kindness."

He sent the money through Ellen, then twenty, the oldest of his five daughters, and she seems to have acted as a regular intermediary. To her, Mrs. Sturgis wrote confusedly of returning home. "I have no choice for myself. I wish to be in whichever place is on the whole thought best. . . . I care not. . . . That course which will be the greatest relief for others, that course will best suit me." She seems, then, to have returned to Boston, but not permanently. In still later letters, she wrote to the captain that she no longer needed his money, that her father could provide her with enough for herself and "my religious association," and that it was "ever painful to a truthful, just nature to be constantly receiving where naught can be done in reciprocation." And Ellen herself wrote to her younger sister, after an absence, that she would soon be seeing her mother, and then she added: "Caroline, how pitiable her life is. What a mystery of sorrow. I do not wonder that she cannot shake off the sadness now. She has lost the energy of youth. . . . The accumulation of years of suffering is too mighty. I am appalled to think how well I can understand her suffering."

The worst of these afflictions, Ellen's own illness, came to appear in Mrs. Sturgis' eyes like a trial of her religion. In that same April of 1848 when Captain Sturgis and Clover were writing their joint letter to Ellen Hooper in Savannah, Mrs. Sturgis was writing to her husband that Ellen's condition was simply an element in God's purpose. "I believe it to be the constant design of Divine Providence (now more *clearly* manifested) to bring all into the true harmony which is in the heavens. May a realizing sense of this blessed truth be with us all." A little later, she tried to explain her feelings more explicitly: "The long decline of Dear E was more than I was supported thro' for my faith was weak. . . . To have smoothed her pillow, and nursed her as I can nurse, could have been a precious boon. . . . I took not up this cross! but as in prison awaited the event. . . ."

Hooper cheerfully wrote home from Georgia about his wife's progress. "We make frequent excursions in the saddle and I think that at each successive one Ellen goes further and returns less fatigued than at the preceding." Ellen agreed. "I cough hardly at all, and I hope to throw off the remnant. I am satisfied it was best to come—'an ounce of prevention is worth a pound of cure,' as I think Susie said." Far from home, though, she suffered stabs of longing for her youngest child. "Kisses for Clover on her eyes and ears and lips and the tip of her little nose," she wrote. And to Clover herself: "My precious silver gray, You know I love you as much as ever. I see your little stems of legs trotting up and down stairs. . . ." And then to the captain: "Dear little Clover! She evidently thinks we suffer now the consequences of our mistake in leaving her. . . . I think Clover a very good child—particularly as she has always been a pet. . . ."

When Ellen Hooper got back to Boston, she began, in her way, to prepare for her death. She had a number of meetings with the Reverend Ephraim Peabody, who had presided at her marriage eleven years earlier, and they talked about God's plans in the ordering of lives. "With all her wit, her sense of the ridiculous, her keen and quick perceptions, her almost morbid delicacy of taste . . ." Peabody later wrote to a friend, "she had the most genial, kind, excusing, sympathetic, tolerant judgment that I ever knew." She worried, specifically, about her children, all still small and coltish, only partly formed. She had hoped and expected so much for them. A month before her death, she talked to Peabody about "the way in which our Saviour judged men. He did not, as the world commonly does, condemn men for single actions. The denial and falsehood of Peter, the woman taken in adultery, how kind the judgment of them. He knew that one wrong act did not imply depravity of character."

But what was to become of Ned and Nella and Clover? Ellen Hooper knew that she could no longer control their destiny. "A man starts in life with the idea that he will bring up all his children on one model, and cannot endure any departure," Peabody quoted her as saying in this last talk. "But one child goes in one direction, another in another, and the parent's heart must follow all. He at length sees that goodness may manifest itself in different ways. . . ." But then comes the guillotine, or rather, in God's judgment on Ellen Hooper, the garrote, the coughing and spitting and gasping and the slow strangulation. The Reverend Peabody's letter continues: "A short time before her death, nearly or quite her last words, as I have been told, she said feebly, 'Patience! Patience!' Her husband said, 'Cannot you go to sleep?' seeing her weariness and exhaustion. She said, 'It is not time yet.' In half an hour, the worn body was at rest, and the spirit had awakened to the peace of a higher life. . . . Today I read beside her coffin, amidst her mourning friends, the words of Christ, 'I am the resurrection and the life.' "

Ellen Hooper died in Boston on November 4, 1848. And Captain Sturgis never wanted to return to Horn Pond again, and so he sold the old hotel there. And Mrs. Sturgis began to have visions of her daughter's return to earth. "I'm sure hers is a medium through which I constantly receive instruction and consolation," she wrote to the captain. "She came back Saturday night just before day-break. . . . I must never turn from such manifestations. They are imperative. . . . I talked with her and was permitted to recollect all that had passed and sometimes it was too evanescent, being too spiritual for the life of the body. . . . We were in a beautiful open place—not an apartment—I saw her quite near on the right—in a simple white dress such as I made for her when a child, with a cambric frill around the neck. I said Ellen dear is that your heavenly garment? No matter! I am to have it tomorrow, those mysteriously beautiful lucid eyes as when in life fixed on mine—"

At that point, Mrs. Sturgis' letter simply breaks off.

"Was thy dream then a shadowy lie?—" continues the poem that was so carefully inscribed in the back of Clover's bible. "Toil on, poor heart, unceasingly. / And thou shalt find thy dream to be / A truth and noonday life to thee."

3

TURTLES WERE EVERYWHERE

ABIGAIL ADAMS, who never learned to spell very well, often blamed
her shortcomings on a lack of formal education, and her complaints
have echoed through the years as a cry of oppressed womanhood.
Feminist ideologists still like to cite her charge that "it was fashionable to ridicule female learning," and to quote her couplet grumbling that "the little learning I have gained / Is all from simple
nature drained." In reality, Abigail Adams was kept home mainly
because of her fragile health, and at home in the parsonage of the
Reverend William Smith, she was encouraged to read Virgil,
Shakespeare, Molière, Locke, and *The Spectator.* Indeed, one of the
reasons that John Adams married her was that he thought her the
most intelligent and educated girl he knew.

The whole question of the education of women in past centuries
is confused by our image of powerful universities barring their
doors to legions of underprivileged genius. At the time of America's
Declaration of Independence, however, the colonies contained only
seven pitiful little church schools that called themselves colleges.
Anyone who wanted academic training in medicine or law had to
go to England (most people with such ambitions, including more
than a few women, stayed home and served an apprenticeship with
some practicing professional). Even as late as 1800, the entire Harvard faculty consisted of the president, three professors, and four
tutors.

The vast majority of people, men and women alike, worked on
farms and knew no need for any education beyond the fundamen-

tals of reading and arithmetic and the Bible. In contrast to our time, there was no thought that a man (or woman) should acquire a certificate attesting to a knowledge of Social Relations or The American Novel as a prerequisite to working in a store. Those who had intellectual ambitions usually derived those ambitions from their parents, and so they learned, like Abigail Adams, what their parents taught them. Louisa May Alcott, for example, was reared on dinner-table discussions of Plato, and Emily Dickinson's stern father filled her mind with Shakespeare before sending her off to the Amherst Academy and Mount Holyoke. Margaret Fuller, to take a more severe example, had to begin Latin lessons with her father at the age of six. At seven, she was being drilled in Virgil, Ovid, and Horace. Unlike Abigail Adams, she remembered the intellectual rigors of childhood as the cause of "continual headaches, weakness and nervous affections, of all kinds."

A Boston girl might also aspire to formal schooling on a level higher than what is generally available today. When Captain Sturgis and his wife ran aground, they sent their oldest daughters to a school in Hingham, and so we learn, in the homesick letters of Clover's mother, something of the curriculum provided for ten-year-old girls, not the least part of that curriculum being an exquisite penmanship, worthy of the cloister. Ellen Sturgis was learning, among other things, Latin, French, chemistry, and astronomy, but her favorite subject was Greek history. "We are studying about the war between the Thebans and Spartans at the time when Thebes was contending for the empire of Greece," she wrote. "I want the Thebans to beat. I like Epaninondas better than Agiselaus. We read the other afternoon the life of Solon (written by Plutarch)." Despite her interest in the Thebans, Ellen kept pleading for letters from her parents, but Mrs. Sturgis wrote back in a magisterial tone that hardly conforms to the tradition of females denied an education: "You are deprived, for a time, of the enjoyment of *home;* but are, doubtless, fully convinced of the judiciousness and kind arrangements made for your best good. You are with teachers as well as with intelligent instructors, and will find another *home* as well as a *school* under their roof. I shall be happy to receive a line from each of you, occasionally and repeatedly, as proves to be convenient. . . ."

Schooling for girls had indeed been primitive during the colonial era, but so had life itself. At the dawning of independence, an American's life expectancy was about thirty-five years (a bit more

for women than for men); the city streets were seas of mud, and
one mansion in Maryland contained the only indoor toilet in all of
the colonies. Most towns had what were known as "dame schools,"
where impecunious women provided shelter and rudimentary lessons to any child who could pay a tuition fee of about three pence
a week. By the time Clover was born, however, public primary
schools for both boys and girls were fairly common throughout the
East. In addition, the increasing prosperity at the turn of the century brought forth an army of itinerant schoolmasters who established scores of little academies that would teach anything that
anyone wanted to learn for anything that anyone could afford to
pay. Among the topics offered in New York City, according to one
account, were Latin, Greek, Low Dutch, merchants' accounts, surveying, navigation, and midwifery. Also enameling, japanning,
and the creation of artificial fruits and flowers. The list may sound
frivolous, but it could probably be duplicated in many suburban
high schools of the 1970's. Then as now, a girl was free to learn, or
not learn, what her parents wanted her to learn.

The general purpose of this learning, undeniably, was not to
create a generation of female astronomers or riverboat captains.
Some of the textbooks of the period make that quite clear. *The
Matrimonial Preceptor*, for example, was an anthology that contained
some domestic excerpts from Ovid, Pope, and Richardson, along
with a variety of anticipatory essays, *The Folly of Precipitate Matches*
and *The Duties of a Good Wife*. It is common nowadays to see oppres-
sion in the nineteenth-century assumption that girls were destined
—if they were lucky—to spend much of their lives in raising families. In fact, the nineteenth-century boy was taught much the same
thing, that the function of his education, if any, was to enable him
to earn enough money to support his wife and children. The idea
that education should represent some kind of "self-fulfillment" remained largely unknown, to boys and girls alike.

There was a certain amount of discrimination, of course, in the
education and training of American children, but it was based less
on gender than on caste. Revolutionary America had needed and
used women to operate its smithies and slaughterhouses. Post-Rev-
olutionary prosperity made that less necessary. Women continued
to do heavy work on the frontier that kept moving westward, but
in the East, more and more of them hoped to become ladies, leaving
the labor to the servants. Becoming a lady might limit one's options

toward politics or war or even commerce, but the limitations were relatively pleasant. It is reasonable to suppose that eighteenth-century women were quite willing to put aside their axes and shovels and listen to their nineteenth-century daughters practice Chopin waltzes. Unschooled Abigail Adams, who called herself a "farmeress" and really did manage John Adams' farm, rarely traveled with less than two personal servants; Clover Adams, who learned Greek, usually kept six.

Among the letters that survive from Clover's childhood is one in which the ten-year-old gloats to an aunt about the harvest she had received at Christmas. "I had sixteen Christmas presents. Father gave me a lovely topaz breastpin set with pearls. Grandmother gave me a silver napkin ring. Uncle Robert gave me a pair of porcelain birds. . . . I am writing this at school instead of composition."

From this we learn, aside from the early view of Clover's lifelong love of finery, that she attended some school where intellectual development was encouraged and discipline was mild. We know little more about her elementary schooling—no class records, no report cards. What we do have, however, stored away in those wooden boxes at the archive in the country, are the books that Clover acquired as a child. They bear witness to the kind of girl she was and to the kind of people in charge of her upbringing.

The earliest one is *The Black Aunt Stories and Legends for Children*, translated from the German by Charles A. Dana. It contains instructive tales with titles like "The Inkstand" and "How Two Finches Got Married." It was presented to Clover when she was five, "with Aunt Mary's love," for Christmas of 1848, just six weeks after her mother had died.

Then *The Golden Legend*, by Henry Wadsworth Longfellow, published in 1852. Clover was nine by now, and she was given this book by Captain Sturgis.

The study of history began early. A small, fat red volume is entitled *Historical Tales and Sketches from Real Life for the Instruction and Improvement of Youth*. An anonymous work, it portrayed a diverse collection of heroes: Oliver Cromwell, Thomas à Becket, Blanche of Castille, Walter Raleigh, Alexander the Great, Robin Hood. It was inscribed by Aunt Fannie on December 25, 1853, Clover's tenth Christmas.

Then *Robinson Crusoé*, inscribed in Clover's own hand: Marian Hooper—44 Summer Street—1854. So she must, at the age of eleven, have been studying fairly advanced French, for this is a translation described on the title page as "par Daniel Foé."

Then *Select Works of the British Poets*, by a Dr. Aiken, inscribed once again by Clover herself: Marian Hooper, 1856. This is only the first volume of a ten-volume set, but it indicates that at the age of thirteen Clover had at least been introduced to Milton's *Paradise Lost* and a broad selection from the plays of Ben Jonson.

Then a thin blue volume in a state of ruin that could indicate either heavy reading or simply poor printing and binding: John Keats's *Eve of St. Agnes.* Clover's Uncle Sam Hooper, the Congressman, gave it to her for Christmas of 1857, when she was fourteen. By then, she was already enrolled at Elizabeth Agassiz's new school for young ladies on Quincy Street in Cambridge, the model for the institution that was later to be known as Radcliffe.

Education is not just a matter of books, of course, but also of studying one's elders and learning their rules and their values. For girls, this traditionally means studying one's mother, and Clover's mother had died when she was five. There are always other models, though. The most flamboyant of the women in Clover's childhood was undoubtedly her aunt Caroline Sturgis Tappan, the ardent pursuer of Transcendentalism, friend and correspondent to Ralph Waldo Emerson, composer of endless unpublished poems about the inscrutability of God. Aunt Carrie often invited Clover out for summer visits in the Berkshires, where, with grudging payments from Captain Sturgis, she was building a hillside mansion named Tanglewood. From the beginning, she envisaged a center for visiting artists. Among them was one of Transcendental Concord's most distinguished figures, Nathaniel Hawthorne, whom Carrie Tappan invited to stay in a nearby red cottage— hence *Tanglewood Tales.* The temperamental novelist and his temperamental hostess quarreled bitterly, however, about the division of the apple crop, and Hawthorne may have had Carrie Tappan in mind when he wrote angrily about the prevalence of a "damned mob of scribbling women." And again: "I wish they were forbidden to write, on pain of having their faces deeply scarified with an oyster shell."

Aunt Carrie's papers are preserved by the hundreds in the hushed sanctity of Harvard's Houghton Library, but next to nothing is known about the person who had the most constant influence on Clover, Betsy Wilder. Betsy was the Hoopers' housekeeper, a servant of the kind that used to cook meals and sweep floors and walk the children to school and listen to their problems and, if necessary, help deliver the Irish setter's puppies under the back porch. Betsy appears fleetingly as early as 1848 in a letter from Mary Louisa Sturgis to her sister, Ellen Hooper—"Clover never seemed so sweet as she does now and looks particularly pretty . . . and Betsy like an attendant mentor"—and she keeps reappearing just as fleetingly in many of Clover's later letters home: Love to Betsy or Tell Betsy about this or that. Only after Clover began taking photographs, late in her life, do we finally see Betsy, a thin, wrinkled, disapproving figure of perhaps seventy, sitting on the porch of Dr. Hooper's house at Beverly Farms. Her head is encased in a beribboned bonnet; her body in a stiff, dark taffeta Sunday dress that falls to her toes. Her eyes, behind thick-rimmed spectacles, concentrate on the knitting in her lap. Betsy came from somewhere to help Ellen Hooper with the three children, and when Ellen died, Betsy stayed on to raise the children, and even after they had all grown up, she stayed on to take care of Dr. Hooper for the rest of his life, and only after his death, after forty years of service, was she pensioned off. She was a servant. She left no papers to be preserved.

Even though Clover's mother died when she was five, Dr. Arnold Gesell of Yale has demonstrated that every child's character is quite solidly formed by that age, its basic education completed before the official process of education begins. In this formation of character, and attitude, and cast of mind, the influence of the failing, coughing, dying Ellen Hooper must have been one that haunted Clover's half-forgotten memories for all of her life. Ellen Hooper had strong ideas about how she wanted Clover to be reared. "One thing I beg," she wrote to Captain Sturgis during her useless flight to Savannah in 1848, "that no one will attempt to correct her English and impose pronunciation on her, and I shall be very sorry to find her precocious in that respect when I return."

Ellen Hooper was what we now call a feminist, but feminism is too mild a word to convey her desperate passion. "I read books of women's rights until I feel like the down-trodden women," she wrote to her younger sister, Susie, "and equalize things by curtailing William or distributing wrongs proper for men's use." The new war against Mexico struck her as a typical male blunder. "I had an impression that wars were solemn concerns," she wrote to Carrie, "and it seems that . . . men shuffle into great events as they do into little ones." She even made fun of Carrie's greatest hero, Ralph Waldo Emerson. Taking as her text the sage's statement that "dry light makes the best souls," she wrote a poem addressing him as "Dry-lighted soul." She promised him a laurel wreath "for the victories / Which thou, on Thought's broad, bloodless field hast won," but she added a malicious suggestion that "Bacchus, at thy birth, forgot / That drop from out the purple grape to press / Which is his gift to men, and so thy blood / Doth miss the heat which oft-times breeds excess."

When her sister Susie suggested that women limit themselves to "women's sphere," Ellen was contemptuous. "I am thankful one woman is in her sphere (as you seem to believe you are) and only wish a visiting committee for the nations may be appointed to ascertain its exact circumference. A woman's sphere seems to me just what she can fill and I don't see why Charlotte Corday had not as good a right to the dagger as Brutus, although I have no doubt she may have been missed in the kitchen." Ellen must have hoped that somehow she could infuse these passions in her younger daughter, but the child was still too young for disputations. To Susie, then, Ellen interrupted her argument to write: "My beloved Clover—I wanted you to see her tonight, denuded—previous to her bed operations, on the full trot, a misshapen monster, all stomach, a little head, no legs. . . ."

The best place to send girls to school in the Boston of the late 1850's, the place to which Dr. Hooper sent both Nella and Clover, was the third floor of Elizabeth Cary Agassiz's house on Quincy Street in Cambridge. Elizabeth Cary had been born to one of Boston's best merchant families. Her grandfather, Colonel Thomas Handasyd Perkins, was among the city's richest men. The education of Colonel Perkins' daughters and granddaughters was such that Mollie Cary married Cornelius Felton, professor of Greek at Harvard, and since Mollie liked to sing duets with her younger

48

sister Lizzie, it was only a matter of time before Lizzie met and captivated Felton's friend, Louis Agassiz.

Once the penniless son of a Swiss pastor, Agassiz was already an international institution, "a broad-featured, unctuous man," as Ralph Waldo Emerson rather maliciously noted in his journals, "fat and plenteous as some successful politician." King Frederick William IV of Prussia had sponsored Agassiz's first scientific exploration of America, some 5,000 Bostonians had crowded his first Lowell Lecture, Harvard immediately granted him a chair in zoology and geology, and Emperor Napoleon III vainly offered him $20,000 a year to return to France as director of the *Jardin des Plantes*. Having left a wife and three children back in Switzerland, Agassiz remained in Cambridge not only because he was engrossed in collecting new specimens but because he saw the possibility of erecting his own museum of natural history. It would be, he said, with typical grandiloquence, "a library of the works of God," a library that would some day be "as complete as it is humanly possible to make it."

When his wife died, Agassiz stayed on, by now one of Cambridge's pets, a genial man, full of enthusiasm and affection. Lizzie Cary married him, and sent for his three children, Alexander, Ida, and Pauline, so that she could make a home for them in Cambridge. It was also a home for an arkful of Agassiz specimens. He was going through a period of fascination with turtles, and one of his students, Theodore Lyman, recalled that "turtles were everywhere, some in jars, some dried on shelves, then living ones in all directions. Many little terrapins hid under the stairs, and soft shelled turtles inhabited [bath]tubs." Out in the garden, Agassiz kept, at various times, a "small alligator" in a tank, a cage for eagles, a family of opossums, and a bear. Mrs. Agassiz once went to put on a pair of shoes for church and, as she later wrote, "caught sight of a good-sized snake which was squirming among the shoes. I screamed in horror to Agassiz, who was still asleep, that there was a serpent in my shoe closet. 'Oh yes,' he said sleepily, 'I brought in several in my handkerchief last night—probably they must have escaped. I wonder where the others are.'"

Despite Agassiz's fame, and the support of various millionaires, his explorations and his laboratory expenses kept him constantly in debt. Even his acquisition of his new house on Quincy Street—a three-story white clapboard structure on the site where the Fogg Art Museum now stands—required Harvard to take out a large mortgage on it. He worried so much about his debts and his expenses that his wife finally decided that a school for girls would help pay the bills. She feared that Agassiz might not approve of his wife's attempting such a commercial venture, but he was delighted. So just three years after the new house had been built, she borrowed $2,000 from her father and began tearing out partitions in the attic so that the whole third floor could be turned into one large classroom.

Agassiz was not only delighted at the prospect of his wife earning money; he was equally delighted to take over the intellectual direction of her school. He dictated to her the institution's first prospectus: "I myself superintend the methods of instruction . . . and while maintaining that regularity and precision in studies so important to mental training, I shall endeavor to prevent the necessary discipline from falling into a lifeless routine, alike deadening to the spirit of teacher and pupil." Agassiz himself gave a lecture every morning on whatever scientific topic interested him, a range that included, according to his wife's subsequent memoirs, "physical geography and paleontology, zoology, botany, coral reliefs, glaciers, structure and formation of mountains, geographical distribution of animals . . . philosophy and nature etc."

This may sound rather lordly and overbearing, but Agassiz was apparently a great teacher, richly able to convey his own enthusiasm about the most arcane subjects. "It was a wonderful gift of his," said one of his pupils, Georgina Schuyler, at a commemorative meeting at Radcliffe a half-century later, "to keep a classroom of girls alert and interested while describing the structure of a jelly-fish, the distinction between Discophora and Ctenophora . . . 'What I wish for you,' I can hear him say in his clear tones, 'is a culture that is alive, active, susceptible of further development. Do not think I care to teach you this or the other special science. My instruction is only intended to show you the thoughts in Nature which Science reveals, and the facts I give you are useful only, or chiefly, for this object.' "

One of Louis Agassiz's male students at about this same time was no less admiring. "The only teaching that appealed to his imagination," Henry Adams, Class of 1858, was to write in the *Education*, "was a course of lectures by Louis Agassiz on the Glacial

Period and Paleontology, which had more influence on his curiosity than the rest of the college instruction altogether." If Agassiz awakened such interest among his pupils, Henry Adams and Clover Hooper alike, then perhaps it mattered relatively little that he was less than infallible. On the most important scientific controversy of the day, in fact, Agassiz argued vehemently against the Darwinian theory of evolution. "The resources of the deity," he declared, with a logic that might have pleased his long-dead father, the Swiss pastor, "cannot be so meager that, in order to create a human being endowed with reason, he must change a monkey into a man."

Agassiz's friends on the Harvard faculty were brought in from the beginning to teach Mrs. Agassiz's girls (as they were to be brought in during the first days of Radcliffe). The distinguished mathematician Benjamin Peirce provided puzzles for the arithmetic class, and the classicists Cornelius Felton and Ephraim Whitman Gurney both taught Greek. The Agassiz children helped, too. Alex, by now twenty, newly graduated from Harvard, was assigned to teach Latin and mathematics, while the eighteen-year-old Ida taught German and French, the latter being the official language of the school. The real manager of the institution, however, was Elizabeth Agassiz, who shepherded the girls through their classes, tutoring some who were laggard in their French, and often warming the tardy commuters with bowls of mutton broth. Unlike most academies, the Agassiz school gave no marks in deportment, since Mrs. Agassiz had only one rule: "I expect you to behave as you would in your mothers' drawing-rooms." As Georgina Schuyler was to recall, "She had it so at heart, that we girls should get the benefit of our teaching, that we should see and appreciate what was given us, that, unconsciously, perhaps, she made us feel it. Above all, we were *trusted*."

The Agassiz school soon attracted the daughters of many of Boston's best families. Lodges, Shaws, Eliots, Appletons, Russells, Lymans, and Bigelows all came trekking to the house on Quincy Street. So did girls from as far away as New York and Buffalo and even St. Louis. "I only wish I were a little girl and were to be sent to Mrs. Agassiz," wrote Professor George Ticknor, the celebrated author of the *History of Spanish Literature*. "In time . . . I should come to something."

The easygoing atmosphere of school life in Cambridge is perhaps best conveyed by a series of chirping letters that one of Clover's

51

schoolmates, Sarah Ellen Browne, wrote to her mother in Salem: "Prof. and Mrs. Agassiz were standing at the head of the stairs to receive us, they seemed very glad to see the scholars. Our school is *crowded* this year. Some sit at tables and on the lecture benches. I do not know the number of scholars but there are *thirty* in our French class. We are to study 'Fables de Florian'. . . . I am to study German, French, Latin, Geology, Mackbeth, Arithmetic, History. . . . Tomorrow there is to be a Fair in Cambridge to help a poor colored man, who wishes to buy his children from slavery. If I learn my lessons early I shall go in the evening with Miss Mary. . . . I went up to Fresh Pond with a large skating party. We rode up on the cars as far as Fresh Pond Lane, then walked to the pond. After we had been there a little while it began to rain quite fast. Sallie Howe fell down and got very wet. . . . On Friday afternoon Prof. Peirce was skating on the pond, [and] he got in up to his neck. . . . I went to Bible class. He read the ninth chapter of John. When the class was over Pauline Agassiz walked home with me, she told me how much she enjoyed the classes. I *love Pauline* very much. . . . We played cards in the evening, 'Old Maid' twice, for Miss Ida's benefit, as she can play no other game with cards. I love Pauline *so much!* . . . Last evening, Lizzie and Sally, Albert and I went to [Sigismond] Thalberg's concert. I could see his fingers very well, they moved as if by magic. . . . We all went up to Fresh Pond and staid there until almost dark. I had a delightful time, there were nearly two thousand people on the pond. The ice was smooth as glass, and it was *black* ice which is always the best. . . . Last evening I went with Mr. Howe, Miss Sarah and Lizzie to hear Mr. Cabot of Boston read the 'Merchant of Venice.' He read very finely. . . . Prof. Agassiz, his wife and Pauline sail this morning for Europe. So many people wished to go down to the steamer with them, they thought it best to give up school until tomorrow. . . . A week from tomorrow is the last day of school! What shall I do? I wish the week to be as long as possible. It will be *very hard* for me to part from all the girls."

The Agassiz school was a great success from the start, partly because there was no other prestigious academy for adolescent girls anywhere around Boston. Mrs. Agassiz charged $150 per year (about what a working man might earn in the same period) and immediately acquired some sixty pupils. A chartered coach drawn by four horses brought the Hooper sisters and the other girls from

Beacon Street across the Charles every morning; Emerson's daughter and several of her friends had to catch an early train from Concord; girls from farther away were placed in rented rooms around Harvard Square. Mrs. Agassiz made a profit of about $2,000 a year during the nine years of the school's existence, enabling Agassiz to pay for his turtles, and to refer to the school as his "milk cow."

Although the school closed in 1863, the idea survived. Mrs. Agassiz, widowed in 1873, was working on a biography of her husband when she was approached by a neighbor, Arthur Gilman, who wished she could revive her school for the sake of his daughter Grace. In 1879, Mrs. Agassiz agreed to head a committee that became known as the Society for the Collegiate Instruction of Women by Harvard Professors, then as the Harvard Annex, and finally as Radcliffe, of which she was the first president. Among those most actively involved in Mrs. Agassiz's work was Clover's sister Ellen, who hoped that Clover might help with fund-raising in Washington. Clover sent $50 but added: "It's no use to expect anything from 'Washington nabobs.' . . . No one here cares for higher education—for women or men either." As for Grace Gilman, she never actually attended the institution created for her.

Since Clover lived at home, and regularly saw most of her friends and relatives, there are only occasional letters providing occasional glimpses of adolescent life. Thus Clover at thirteen, having been caught lying in an effort to avoid going to someone's party: "I have come to the conclusion that whoppers are indispensable, though I have not told more than one. . . ." And Clover at sixteen, writing to Nella about the sadness that was to afflict her all her life: "The dark clouds which settled on my horizon have not yet lifted, and I don't see any prospect of their so doing. I thought of you, last night at tea, riding through the Cotuit woods, and longed to be in your shoes. . . . You are now I suppose sitting in the church and they are just singing the hymns before the sermon. Do you know, I think it is rather nice to feel melancholy."

The most interesting document of Clover's school years is a strange account of her own death. It was apparently addressed to her cousin, Annie Hooper, but it was written in the form of a parody of a will, including detailed instructions for the funeral.

53

Since Clover was always much preoccupied with clothes, it even contained a tassel of blue-green fringe, which it described as "a pattern of blue for her funeral riggings, that color being most becoming to her style of beauty."

It would be a mistake to exaggerate the implications of such self-derision, but it would also be a mistake to ignore them. We cannot know exactly what was in Clover's mind when she was jocularly describing her death at the age of thirteen, but since she did ultimately kill herself, we must consider her "will" in terms of Freud's thesis that every joke has a very serious meaning, that the language of humor is one of the secret and symbolic languages of the unconscious.

Having bequeathed a ring and a tea caddy to Annie, Clover began this suicidal fantasy: "On the night of the 6th of January, 1857, she passed the evening at Number 56, Beacon St. Her house was at 107, the same street. It was a bitter cold night and the wind howled most fearfully. As the time drew near for her departure, she felt a presentiment of death stealing up on her, and was loth to depart, but at last summoning up all her courage, she set forth, attended only by one of the masculine tribe. She had passed in safety the three first crossings below Charles Street when arriving at the last crossing a sudden gust of wind caught her nose—that being the most prominent feature of her body—and whirling her through the air dashed her upon the frozen waters of Back Bay. The servant was seized by a contrary wind and drowned in the waters of the River Charles. A milkman riding in from the country on Wednesday morning discovered her body laying upon the ice. On looking at the face, he discovered that it was minus a nose and whilst returning in perplexity to the land he perceived a nose minus a head. . . . A coroner's inquest will be held upon the body this afternoon at 3 o'clock precisely. Price of tickets 25 cts children half price viz 12 cts. . . . A customary speech of hers was it's a weary world we live in, and her last speech just before reaching the 4th crossing was changed to it's a windy world we live in."

4

THE HOUR OF THE BRAVE
AND THE TRUE

HENRY ADAMS, who went to Washington in 1860 as private secretary to Congressman Charles Francis Adams, subsequently offered
the judgment that "not one man in America wanted the Civil War,
or expected or intended it." To even the most bloodthirsty parti-
sans of union or secession, the winter and spring of 1860–61
seemed primarily a time for intrigue. The Republicans gloated over
Lincoln's victory in the November election. The Democrats, still
in office, many of them Southerners, talked darkly of preventing
the new President from ever being inaugurated. When Lincoln did
finally arrive in Washington at the end of February, he hardly
seemed a commanding presence. Frederick Law Olmsted, the landscape architect, passed him in the street and observed that he
"looked much younger than I had supposed, dressed in a cheap and
nasty French black cloth suit. . . . Looked as if he would be an
applicant for a Broadway squad policemanship." The young Henry
Adams was hardly less contemptuous. At the inauguration ball, he
viewed the new President as "a long, awkward figure; a plain,
ploughed face; a mind, absent in part, and in part evidently worried
by white kid gloves."

   That very day, Lincoln had promised to respect slavery and to
enforce the fugitive slave laws, but he had also declared that "in
contemplation of the universal law and of the Constitution, the
union of these states is perpetual." It was not self-evident. Almost
a month had passed since the first seven seceding states had assembled in Montgomery to form the Confederate States of America;

yet another month passed before the Charleston shore batteries opened fire on Fort Sumter. Until then, even Boston had been reluctant to fight. A well-dressed crowd shouted down Ralph Waldo Emerson as he tried to speak at a meeting commemorating the death of John Brown. But the news of Fort Sumter set off what Emerson called "a whirlwind of patriotism." Walt Whitman heard the drums:

> *Beat! beat! drums!—blow! bugles! blow!*
> *Through the windows—through doors—burst like a ruthless force,*
> *Into the solemn church, and scatter the congregation,*
> *Into the school where the scholar is studying. . . .*
> *Mind not the timid—mind not the weeper or prayer,*
> *Mind not the old man beseeching the young man,*
> *Let not the child's voice be heard, nor the mother's entreaties.*

"Never in my whole life have I seen anything approaching in the slightest degree to the excitement and enthusiasm of the past week," one young Bostonian, Henry Lee Higginson, wrote to his brother. "Everything excepting the war is forgotten, business is suspended, the streets are filled with people, drilling is seen on all sides and at all times. . . . You should have seen the troops, Jimmy: real, clean-cut, intelligent Yankees, the same men who fought in '76, a thousand times better than any soldiers living. . . . *Everyone* is longing to go."

Dr. Johnson declared on some occasion that every man who had gone to war would remember the experience forever, and that every man who had not gone would always wonder what it was like, and how he would have met the test. Clover's whole generation was thus marked throughout its time. It was not quite true, though, that everyone was longing to go. Only one member of the Harvard faculty answered President Lincoln's call for 75,000 volunteers, and that one a German immigrant. The Harvard students, however, were more emotional, and these were Clover's friends and neighbors and relatives. "I wish that every man in the country would enlist," the girl at the Agassiz school wrote to a cousin. Her stationery displayed the Stars and Stripes and the motto "Stand by the flag." Young Henry Higginson, who had dropped out of Harvard and wanted to become a musician, was suffering from a sprained foot but he soon won a lieutenant's commission in the 2nd Massachusetts Infantry Regiment—"the dear old Second," as Clo-

ver later called it, an almost legendary regiment destined for Antietam, Gettysburg, and the conquest of Atlanta. Among their escort
troops in the Fourth Battalion of Massachusetts Volunteer Militia
was a twenty-six-year-old lawyer, Charles Francis Adams, Jr. "Not
to [enlist]," he wrote in his journal, "would be to incur lasting
disgrace, in comparison with which the hardship and boredom and
danger of a campaign would be a festive pastime." One of his first
duties on his arrival at Boston's Fort Independence was to partici-
pate in the firing of a salute to honor the departure of the new
ambassador to London, Charles Francis Adams, Sr., who was taking with him as private secretary his third son, Henry.

Oliver Wendell Holmes was shepherding through the presses of
The Atlantic Monthly the last installments of *Elsie Venner*, that
strange allegory of a girl who was partly a snake, when the firing
on Fort Sumter inspired him to turn to patriotic verse: "Listen
young heroes! your country is calling! / Time strikes the hour for
the brave and the true! / Now, while the foremost are fighting and
falling, / Fill up the ranks that have opened for you." And again:
"O, Lord of Hosts! Almighty King! / Behold the sacrifice we
bring!" Among those being offered as a sacrifice was the poet's
twenty-one-year-old son, Oliver Wendell Holmes, Jr. A senior at
Harvard, Holmes had just taken Hobbes' *Leviathan* out of the Atheneum library, and he was walking down Beacon Street with the
book under his arm, "when as I passed the State House someone
told me that the Governor had commissioned me in the 20th Mass.
[Regiment]. I returned the book and went off . . . to the war."

And Henry James' younger brothers, Wilky and Bob, abandoned their studies at the Sanborn school in Concord and enlisted.
Wilky, at seventeen, was the first to go. He joined the 44th Massachusetts Infantry Regiment and then transferred to the 54th,
which was to win the distinction of being the North's first black
regiment. It was trained and commanded by Clover's second cousin, Colonel Robert Gould Shaw, and it also included Shaw's sister's new husband, Charles Russell Lowell, the nephew of the poet,
James Russell Lowell, who was later to describe the youth, dead,
as "the best thing we had."

Colonel Shaw was only twenty-six, a slender figure with long
blond hair, and much of Boston turned out to watch him ride
through the streets at the head of his departing troops. On Essex
Street, he paused to salute the two abolitionist leaders, William

Lloyd Garrison and Wendell Phillips, standing together on the balcony of Phillips' house. Tears were streaming down Garrison's cheeks. As Shaw passed his own family's house, at 44 Beacon Street, he raised his sword and kissed it. His younger sister Ellen thought at that moment that "his face was as the face of an angel and I felt perfectly sure he would never come back." James Green-leaf Whittier saw a similar vision: "The very flower of grace and chivalry, he seemed to me beautiful and awful, as an angel come down to lead the host of freedom to victory."

Henry James, already invalided by his "obscure hurt," lay ill that day, but he nonetheless fretted in his memoirs over his brother's departure with Colonel Shaw, "to great reverberations of music, of fluttering banners, launched benedictions and every public sound." William James, equally invalided by a variety of nervous afflictions, was to return, many years later, to the scene of Colonel Shaw's march up Beacon Street and to speak at the dedication of Saint-Gaudens' powerful monument portraying that march.

Within a week after the firing on Fort Sumter, Massachusetts was ready to send five regiments of infantry, one battalion of riflemen, and one battery of artillery. But in the evil-smelling mudflats along the Potomac, where the thousands of new recruits began pitching their tents, virtually no measures whatever had been taken for the housing and feeding of an invading army. There were no movable hospitals, not even latrines. A number of women's groups in New York organized the Women's Central Relief Association to provide medical supplies and services, but the Army Medical Department regarded their efforts with disdain. Surgeon General Thomas Lawson was over eighty, a veteran of the War of 1812, and not of a mind to listen to criticisms or even suggestions. It was not specifically that the critics were women; they were civilians, and civilians' views were not welcomed. The women of New York turned to Henry Whitney Bellows, the popular minister of the First Unitarian Church, and persuaded him to persuade President Lincoln to authorize the creation of a national Sanitary Commission. Its only purpose was to let the women provide what the government itself had notably failed to provide: hospital beds, uniforms, bandages, food. The President only reluctantly agreed.

"On Nov. 28, 1861," according to the final report in 1865 by the Supply Department of the New England Women's Auxiliary Association, "a few ladies met in a private parlor in Boston, to listen to a request made then and there by Dr. Bellows, president of the Sanitary Commission, that a New England branch might be formed. . . . On Dec. 13, 1861, we opened our office at 22 Summer Street, and made our arrangements for an easy work, to last, possibly, several months; for the war was then hardly more than a skirmish. . . . Before a week was over, we discovered it was no mere holiday pastime in which we were engaged."

This was what Clover Hooper did during the Civil War, Clover and her sister Ellen, and Julia Ward Howe and Amelia Holmes and all the other spirited women of Boston—and, for that matter, Mrs. March, the mother of Louisa May Alcott's "little women." It was perhaps not a "mere holiday pastime," but the work was not unbearably strenuous either. Clover was seventeen when the war started, and toward the end of that year, she wrote to her father that she had been to "the sanitary rooms" of Dr. Gridley Howe, the head of the Perkins Institute for the Blind and husband of Julia Ward Howe, "and stamped blankets, towels, etc. from 1 o'clock til 4½. The store was cold and dark, and though it was hard work we liked it." The following summer, while staying with Ida Agassiz at Nahant, she wrote to her sister Nella that the Sanitary Commission work had become a kind of game. "We have a Sanitary bee every Wednesday and Saturday from 10 to 1, and Hamilton James reading aloud from 'Vanity Fair.' " Later that summer, "having a gulluptious time" while staying near Aunt Caroline in the Berkshire resort of Lenox, she began to feel guilty. "What fearful times we are living in!" she wrote. "I try to, but can't, realize it at all. Nothing but disaster and excitement on all sides. I really feel ashamed to be having such a good and jolly time." Almost everyone she knew had a son or husband involved. "Only think of poor Henry Russell in a cell, on bread and water. I should think the family would be desperate. . . ." Then she noted that a young officer named Charles Mills was "bidding me goodbye and begging for a photograph. He leaves on Thursday; has a commission in the 2nd. What a fearful loss that regiment have had. . . ." Mills was indeed destined to die soon afterward. Clover's letter ended on a note of guilt suppressed, or partly suppressed. "I hope there will be a killing amount of work at the Sanitary all winter."

A stronger involvement sent stronger women toward the battle-fields. "I've longed to be a man," Louisa May Alcott wrote not long before she went to Washington to start nursing the wounded,* "but as I can't fight, I will content myself with working for those who can." Mary Edwards Walker, the only woman in the class of 1855 at the Syracuse Medical College, treated the wounded on the bat-tlefields of Virginia, won a commission in the army, spent four months in a Confederate prison, and won the Congressional Medal of Honor (until it was mysteriously stripped from her in 1917). And when Sanitary Commission Secretary Frederick Law Olmsted guided the commission's first hospital ship into the carnage of the second siege of Yorktown, four female volunteers stood on the deck and sang hymns. "In June [of 1862]," the Boston report continues, "the floating hospital, Daniel Webster, brought to Boston its living freight of wounded and sick men. It was our privilege to refit and dispatch her again on her errand of mercy. . . ."

The less heroic women, like Clover, simply went on working. But how they worked. By the end of the war, the Boston branch of the commission had raised $314,874.04 for the cause and spent all but $6,462.14. Overall, 7,000 chapters raised $50 million. The women of Boston had sent to Washington a mountain of supplies, including, among other things, 112,886 cotton shirts, 125,536½ pairs of stockings, 151,180 handkerchiefs, 14,540 quilts, 545 crutches, 2,537½ pounds of bandages, 33,017 pounds of jellies and preserves, 18,919 quarts of pickles, 115,036 pounds of dried fruits, 46 quarts of vinegar, and 21,913 fans.

Almost thirty years later, Henry James' younger sister Alice, dying, wrote in her diary: "I always sympathized so with Ellen [Hooper] Gurney when she told me of how she ran and slammed the drawing room door when she heard, in the old war days, her brother Edward's voice suddenly in the hall downstairs, he having come home unexpectedly, as they always did in those days."

Ned Hooper, who was twenty-one when the war started, re-mained at the Harvard Law School long enough to get his degree

* Miss Alcott fell ill with typhoid pneumonia after only three weeks' duty. She was treated with calomel, a mercury compound then highly regarded by doctors as a cure for a wide variety of infections. It also caused chills and trembling, loss of teeth and hair, and hallucinations. Miss Alcott had visions of a Spanish grandee in black velvet who leapt through windows in pursuit of her. She was finally cured by a female mesmerist.

that spring and then won a commission. He was not destined for the firestorms of Antietam and Fredericksburg, but for one of the more peculiar corners of the battlefield.

The Union Navy needed a base from which to maintain its blockade of the Southern coast, and it soon settled on Port Royal Sound, a natural harbor and a cluster of prosperous islands roughly halfway between Charleston and Savannah. The harbor was protected by two stout forts, but the Navy assembled at Hampton Roads an armada of seventy-four steam frigates, steam sloops, coal-carrying schooners, gunboats, and transports laden with 12,000 seasick troops. On November 7, 1861, the warships' cannons smashed the two forts into submission. The landing parties found them deserted except for a flock of turkeys. Pressing onward, they discovered many nearby cotton plantations inhabited only by some 10,000 abandoned slaves. "Nearly all the Negroes left on the islands were in densest ignorance," wrote one arriving officer, Captain Hazard Stevens, son and aide to General Isaac Ingalls Stevens of the Second Brigade, "some of the blackest human beings ever seen, and others the most bestial in appearance. These ignorant and benighted creatures flooded into [the town of] Beaufort . . . and held high carnival in the deserted mansions, smashing doors, mirrors, and furniture and appropriating all that took their fancy."

The view of the local commander, General David Hunter, was that all able-bodied black males should be recruited into uniform, so he brusquely ordered them rounded up and assigned to basic training. In Washington, however, civilian officials reminded the Army that slavery was still perfectly legal, and that the abandoned slaves of Port Royal were simply contraband property, to be returned to work on the plantations. The Treasury Department assumed the responsibility for making the ownerless plantations profitable, and it assigned a young Harvard Law School graduate named Edward L. Pierce to take charge of the problem. To Northern abolitionists, on the other hand, the sudden acquisition of some 10,000 slaves seemed not a problem but an inspiring opportunity for education and missionary work. The abolitionists began organizing—the Port Royal Relief Association in Philadelphia, the Education Committee in Boston—and in March of 1862, the first boatload of forty-two male and twelve female missionaries arrived on the scene to do good works. One of them, Susan Walker, considered it "most delightful" to be rowed across the harbor by six "stalwart Negroes [who] sing, as they row, their own songs—some impromptu and all religious—about the Savior and the Kingdom," and to be accompanied on this idyllic boatride by "our escort, Mr. Hooper."

The whole atmosphere at Port Royal was idyllic. Even as early as March, the orange trees were white with blossoms, and the yellow jasmine was in full bloom. Lieutenant Ned Hooper, who had last been in this region when his mother took him south in the year of her death, now wrote home regularly about the acres of corn, the turkeys and pheasants, the "finest blackberries in abundance," and "water melons and fresh figs in profusion." "They talk of the horrors of war; we have made them a jest—so far," observed Charles Francis Adams, by now a first lieutenant in the First Massachusetts Cavalry, also assigned temporarily to the Port Royal islands. "Talk of luxury—you should see our tents. Here on my table is a bundle of flowers. . . . I write on a mahogany table and behind me is a looking glass and a sofa."

Adams was to move onward, to Antietam and Gettysburg, but his future in-law remained on the coastal islands as a manager of the army-occupied plantations. Some 5,000 acres of cotton had been planted, along with 5,000 acres of corn, and nearly 1,000 acres of sweet potatoes. "The welfare of the laborers required that they should have regular work and that they should be made a self-supporting people," Ned wrote back to Boston. "After this we have made teaching a prominent thing. I think most people in the North would be surprised to see how quickly these people, old as well as young, learn to read. They are all very eager to learn."

Doctor Hooper worried about his son's health on the malarial islands, but Ned repeatedly reassured him that he was taking quinine every day. He thanked the doctor for sending him a parasol and a new saddle, and a case of used clothes for the black field hands. He continued to puzzle over his charges. "They are humble, feel their inferiority to white men as to education and probably even as to capacity. It is very easy for a white man to bully them, and yet I think it would be very difficult to make them slaves again."

On January 1, 1863, President Lincoln decreed all slaves in the Confederacy (and only in the Confederacy) "shall be, then, thenceforward, and forever free." At a Jubilee Concert at the Music Hall in Boston, Ralph Waldo Emerson declaimed a poem written for the occasion: "Today unbind the captive / So only are ye unbound; / Lift up a people from the dust, / Trump of their rescue, sound!" Then they played Beethoven's violin concerto. "After that," according to Fanny Chapin, a pretty eighteen-year-old student who had gone to join the celebrations, "somebody announced that the President's Proclamation was coming over the wires and then everybody cheered and waved their handkerchiefs till it seemed as if the walls must shake with enthusiasm. . . . Then somebody cheered for Garrison and the most enthusiastic followed his example, but some people hissed. . . . The tears would come to my eyes and heart to think that the curse of slavery had been removed from America. . . . After the Concerto came Dr. Holmes' 'Army Hymn' . . . and then the Fifth Symphony. The glorious Fifth! It never sounded so exquisite before. . . . And when the Hallelujah Chorus was sung, everybody stood, which made it very impressive."

The bloodshed was often less heroic. Tens of thousands of ill-trained and ill-led young soldiers slashed at each other in hayfields and scrubby crossroads that barely had names. Like Aldie Gap, outside Aldie, Virginia. "My poor men were just slaughtered," said Charles Francis Adams of the First Massachusetts Cavalry, "and all we could do was to stand still and be shot down while the other squadrons rallied behind us. The men fell right and left and the horses were shot through and through. . . ."

Henry Lee Higginson, who had left Harvard to become a pianist, was there, too, at Aldie Gap. "We rode down another very steep hill, and at the bottom they caught us, and we had a little shindy," he later wrote back to Boston. By "shindy," he meant hand-to-hand combat, on horseback. Higginson lunged out with his saber and knocked one of the Confederates from his horse, then lunged again and found himself lying in the road. "Over me was standing [the] man whom I had unhorsed, and who struck at my head." The saber tip slashed open Higginson's cheek, and as he writhed in the dirt, he felt a strange sensation in his back, put a hand there, and felt a bloody hole where a bullet had hit him. The Confederate soldier "proposed to take me prisoner, but I told him

I should die in a few minutes [so] he took what he could get of my goods and rode off, leaving my horse, which had been shot with four bullets. In five minutes the shindy was over. . . . I crawled along to a brook, where I lay down and drank a pailfull of water, then crossed the brook and got up into a wood. . . ."

Young Oliver Wendell Holmes had hardly reached the Potomac when his 20th Regiment was ordered to cross the river and seize a plateau known as Ball's Bluff. From behind a row of trees, the Confederates charged. Holmes was down on one knee, taking aim, when a bullet pierced his chest. "Perhaps the first impulse was tremulous—" he later wrote, "but then I said—by Jove, I die like a soldier anyhow—I was shot in the breast doing my duty up to the hub—afraid? No, I am proud. . . ." But he was not dying, simply bloody and helpless. Others dragged him off to an improvised hospital and cleansed the wound and let him recover a bit. (Surrounded by pictures of Boston girls. "He declared," according to one comrade, "that to look at the portrait of Miss [Ida] Agassiz was like having an angel in the tent.") To that same hospital they brought golden-haired Willie Putnam, one of Ned Hooper's college companions, the only son of James Russell Lowell's sister Mary. Willie had last been seen leaping to the aid of a fallen adjutant, and now the doctors could not save him. And in Amherst, Massachusetts, a recluse named Emily Dickinson noted that a young man with the same name, Francis H. Dickinson, had been killed at Ball's Bluff, the town's first battle casualty, and began writing a poem: "When I was small, a Woman died— / Today—her Only Boy / Went up from the Potomac / His face all Victory. . . ."

Holmes returned home to Charles Street and, as his father put it, played Othello to "a semicircle of young Desdemonas"—Ida Agassiz, for one, and Ellen Hooper, whom Holmes described as "one of my particulars." Then back to the 20th, battling through the muddy fields of McClellan's Peninsular Campaign. At Antietam, a bullet hit Holmes in the side of the neck, just missing the jugular vein, then passing out the back, just missing the spinal column. This time, the first message to Boston said nothing more reassuring than that the wound was "thought not mortal," so Dr. Holmes set out to find his son. It was one of the peculiarities of that war—or perhaps it just seems peculiar because we have become accustomed to sending our troops to fight far from home— that every battle was followed by a swirl of parents in rented carriages and muddy boots all searching for their wounded children. It took Dr. Holmes a week of wandering through the confusion before he found his object. Their encounter was ineffably Bostonian. "How are you, Wendell?" said the searcher. "How are you, father?" answered the son.

And then Gettysburg, and three whole days of slaughter, and Pickett's relentless line of bayonets charging up the ruined slopes of Cemetery Ridge, and General Armisted, with his cap on the tip of his sword, hurtling over a stone wall to lead the doomed vanguard of about 100 Confederate infantrymen across the unconquerable Union line. When the news reached Boston, Dr. Hooper, who had not really practiced medicine for years, felt that he had to do something, whatever he could, to help. He went forthwith to the governor's office and got himself assigned to the battlefield.

"Up to this place in a cattle car," he wrote to his daughter Nella in a weary letter that is dated "Friday, I believe." Before even finding a place to stay, he set about his task. "I received from farmers' wagons a large number of wounded men, fed them and dressed their wounds and shipped them off in a train for their homes or the hospitals in the Philadelphia–Baltimore area. . . . They were grateful for our attention and when we had lifted them into the cars and carefully packed their wounded limbs, they cheered and waved their caps at us on starting. Many of them were straight in from the woods and swamps where they had got no attention and some were washed out by the heavy rains, some even drowned, unable to get away from the rising waters. . . ."

As soon as Dr. Hooper finished with one batch of wounded men, he sent for more. "When I see a knot of idlers, men who came here to stare about and pick up bullets, I order them to work and never fail to get them for they don't know what might be the consequences of a refusal. . . . As I wear only a gray suit without waistcoat, a blue flannel shirt and no shoulderstraps, they cannot tell what my rank is. I may be a Grand Mufti in disguise."

Dr. Hooper considered himself "as independent as a hippopotamus," and he portrayed himself "wallowing about this fearful mud with pockets full of bandages and coat collar bristling with pins." He was delighted to report that these medical materials were the very ones that the women of the Sanitary Commission had produced. "It was good to see the bandages that our friends have been rolling come to good use. We covered a good many bare legs with nice flannel drawers and backs with shirts."

Two days later, he was still working, under great pressure. "I am very busy looking after the wounded and shipping them off," he scribbled in a note to Nella. "Cannot tell when I can get away. There seems no end of wounded men, rebels and ours. I am writing this under very difficult auspices. I have not had my clothes off but for a moment this morning. Slept on the floor. But never felt better. It is very hot and muggy and the smell of the battlefield is disagreeable. . . . You can hardly conceive of the horror of a late battlefield —and this has been a fearful one."

On the last day of May, 1897, a light rain was falling, and a crowd gathered across from the gold-domed State House for the dedication of the Saint-Gauden monument commemorating Colonel Shaw's assault on Fort Wagner. This was, perhaps, the last occasion on which Boston could reverently celebrate what it had once been. Colonel Shaw was an embodiment of the dying idea that there were causes holier than life itself, causes to which life could be sacrificed without question, with pride. William James, by now fifty-five, gray and gaunt, looked back across three decades and imagined the doomed attackers, "their eyes fixed on the huge bulk of the fortress looming darkly . . . against the sky, and their hearts beating in expectation of the word that was to bring them to their feet and launch them on their desperate charge. . . ."

Even on the remote island near Port Royal, where Shaw had prepared his black troops for the attack on Fort Wagner, the abandoned slaves had been "advised" by their new military masters that they should contribute their pennies to this monument. Such a suggestion, Ned Hooper wrote home, would be "a good rallying point for them and their children." In Boston itself, the wartime fund-raising reached a total of $3,161, and then the fund-raisers, thinking that sum unworthy of the hero, invested it in the nation's growing industries. And so perhaps the Irish and the Poles who swung the sledgehammers that laid the railroad lines, and perhaps also the farm girls who hunched over the stitching machines in the brick factories of Lawrence and Lowell, perhaps all of them contributed to the remarkable growth of the Shaw Memorial Fund, which rose to $7,000 by 1876, and to $17,000 by 1883, and to $23,000 by 1897. The sum was just barely enough to cover the fee for Saint-Gaudens and the cost of all that concrete and bronze. By now, thirty-four years had passed since Colonel Shaw had died, and James Russell Lowell had written the poem that was to be inscribed on the monument:

> *Right in the van*
> *On the red rampart's slippery swell,*
> *With heart that beat a charge, he fell*
> *Foeward, as fits a man. . . .*

Does it ever really happen like that? Shaw and his black troops had been in action throughout most of the previous day and night. They must have been exhausted, grimy, hungry. Fort Wagner, guarding the harbor at Charleston, could be conquered only by an uphill charge, across two dry moats and over a revetment of palmetto logs, but the Northern commanders thought that the 600 men of Shaw's 54th outnumbered the defenders by two to one. In fact, the ratio was just the opposite. There were not 300 defenders but 1,700. And although the Northern forces spent all day inflicting on Fort Wagner one of the heaviest artillery barrages of the war, they failed almost totally in the effort to destroy the defenders' batteries of 32-pounders. So when Colonel Shaw ordered the advance, his outnumbered men had to charge not only uphill but into an inferno of cannon fire.

"Just before nightfall the attack was made," William James said to the hushed crowd gathered before the Saint-Gaudens monument, trying to make them see, as he himself saw, the blond youth leading his black troops up that fire-swept hill. "Shaw . . . briefly exhorted them to prove that they were men. Then he gave the order: 'Move in quick time till within a hundred yards, then double quick and charge. Forward!' and the 54th advanced to the storming, its colonel and the colors at its head. On over the sand . . . and up the rampart; with . . . Fort Wagner, now one mighty mound of fire, tearing out their lives. Shaw led from first to last. Gaining successfully the parapet, he stood there for a moment with uplifted sword, shouting 'Forward, 54th!' and then fell headlong, with a bullet through his heart."

The battle raged on for two hours, but the Confederate defenders could not be conquered. They killed more than half the men of the 54th before compelling the rest to retreat back down the hill. The next day, they buried the dead in a mass grave.* This end of Colonel Shaw roused William James to a new fervor. "His body, half stripped of its clothing, and the corpses of his dauntless Negroes were flung into one common trench together, and the sand was shoveled over them, without a stake or stone to signalize the spot. In death as in life, then, the 54th bore witness to the brotherhood of Man."

Such, in any case, is the rhetoric of Man. The Shaw women spoke less exaltedly of their losses. When Ned Hooper went to visit the family on Staten Island shortly after Colonel Shaw's death, Mrs. Shaw gasped at the sight of her son's friend, then tried to stifle her misery. "I never could see why mothers made such a fuss about their children dying," she said. Her pregnant daughter Effie, newly married to Charles Russell Lowell, showed the same desperate stoicism the following year when she learned the news of the Battle of Cedar Creek. "Mrs. Lowell was embroidering him a pair of shoulder straps when she heard of his death," one of her friends wrote later, "and she finished them for his funeral."

Once again the fathers journeyed to the battlefield to search for their sons. One of them was the father of Cabot Jackson Russel, who had been killed on the slopes beneath Fort Wagner. In the course of his sad search, Russel came upon the dying figure of his son's best friend, Wilky James, wounded in the side and ankle. Determined to bring some good out of the carnage, Russel packed Wilky onto a boat and then escorted the stretcher directly to the James home in Newport. For days, Wilky lay just inside the door, too sick to be moved, while the doctors came to treat him (among them was Dr. Hooper of Beacon Street), and the family fluttered. William drew a sketch of the stubble-cheeked invalid, and Henry composed a short story about a wounded soldier being brought home. "Poor Wilky cries aloud for his friends gone and missing,"

---

* During the war, Bostonians proudly spread the legend that the Confederate commander, General Johnson Hagood, had said of Shaw, "We have buried him with his niggers." On subsequent investigation, it turned out that the only source for this famous statement was a captured Navy surgeon, John T. Luck, who quoted Hagood somewhat differently: "I shall bury him in the common trench with the Negroes that fell with him." On still further investigation, Hagood said he could not recall ever having said anything of the sort.

his father wrote to a colleague, "and I could hardly have supposed he might be educated so suddenly up to a serious manhood altogether as he appears to have been."

Charles Francis Adams, Jr., who seems to have genuinely enjoyed the years of wartime combat, showed a perverse pride in having fallen asleep in the midst of the Battle of Antietam, and again at Gettysburg. On both occasions, he was exhausted, trapped in an obscure corner of the battlefield, and numbed by the roar of cannon. And so, "while the fate of the army and the nation trembled in the balance, at the very crisis of the great conflict, I dropped quietly asleep. It was not heroic; but it was, I hold, essentially war, though by no means war as imagined in the workroom of the theoretic historian."

It was "essentially war" that less than half of the Union dead (140,000 out of 360,000) were killed in combat. The rest fell prey to the traditional scourges of infection and disease. Adams, by now a colonel in command of the Massachusetts Fifth Cavalry, slowly succumbed throughout 1865 to a combination of dysentery, jaundice, and malaria, hardly improved by regular doses of quinine and opium. "True, I had the satisfaction of leading my regiment into burning Richmond, the day after Lee abandoned it, [but] I was then a mere wreck—pitiably reduced and weak."

Malaria also felled Ned Hooper, even in the sanctuary of Port Royal. He had several attacks of chills and fever in 1863 and several more in the following year. Quinine did not help, the doctors advised him to avoid "much exercise of any kind," and so he resigned in May of 1864. "I am of little use now and should be worse than useless probably in the warmer weather," he wrote his father.

Ned had another good reason to want to leave the Army. He planned to get married that summer to Fanny Chapin, the effervescent young music student whom we last saw applauding Beethoven on the occasion of the Emancipation Proclamation. Ned was a friend of the whole Chapin family, and when he suddenly arrived at their home in Brookline during a short leave in late August of 1863, Fanny professed total surprise at his proposal. "I was so astonished yesterday afternoon," she wrote to a friend. "I never once dreamed I was anything to him. . . . Oh, I am too happy; it seems too good to be true."

"Mr. Chapin was most surprised and Fanny next," observed their minister, the celebrated Reverend James Freeman Clarke. "But Fanny seemed perfectly prepared to love him and did not make him wait a minute! Dr. Hooper came out the next day to see her—kissed her and called her Fanny. . . . Old Captain Sturgis, 80 years old, showed himself quite grandfatherly on this occasion and came out to the carriage and kissed Fanny. Fanny was particularly gratified by being kissed by Dr. Hooper and Capt. Sturgis —though in my opinion, the benefit of such an operation must accrue far more to them than to her. Nobody needs to hesitate a moment about kissing Fanny."

So it was done, Captain Sturgis must have felt, and there would be a new generation at last. He, the only son of his murdered father, had lived through the anguish of burying three of his six children, and of observing his wife's unfathomable misery, but now there were seven grandchildren near the age of marriage, including his beloved Clover. Her brother Ned, bright and handsome in his blue captain's uniform, was to be, in the midst of this terrible war, the first to marry and to bring him great grandchildren. And in that state of satisfaction and anticipation, Captain Sturgis suddenly fell victim to the plagues that await any man who has passed the age of eighty. He kept to his room for two or three days and then felt a little better and planned to go out on the morrow for a walk around Church Green. "He died somewhat suddenly," according to the *Boston Evening Transcript*, "while sitting in his chair."

A century later, he still maintains a deathly rule over his family. In the rather cluttered tranquillity of Mt. Auburn Cemetery, the final destiny of nineteenth-century Cambridge, not far from the modest tombstones of Agassiz and Holmes, of Julia Ward Howe and Winslow Homer, not far from the heavy sphinx that commemorates the Union dead, not far from the Halcyon Lake and the pillared temple that marks the last protest against death by Mary Baker Eddy—here, in the shade of a massive gray beech tree, (*Fagus Grandifolia*, says the neatly printed sign), lies Captain Sturgis, surrounded by many of those whom he treasured most.

It is not an easy grave to find. There is no family nameplate, only a hillside row of small white gravestones marked with initials and dates of death. *W.S. 1863*. That is all that remains of Captain

Sturgis, prince of the China trade. To his right, just a foot away, lies the beloved son who was killed while sailing—*W.W.S. 1827*—and just beyond that, the maddened wife—*E.M.D.S. 1864.* To Captain Sturgis' left, in a double grave, lie his oldest granddaughter, Ellen, and her husband, Ephraim Whitman Gurney, and beyond that, the son-in-law, Dr. Hooper, *R.W.H. 1885.* There are thirteen graves in all—Carrie Sturgis Tappan too, and her daughter Mary—all neatly identified by their initials and their dates of death, all reflecting a Boston family's sense of coherence and of privacy. The only one missing is Clover.

> *The ship is anchored safe and sound, its voyage closed and done,*
> *From fearful trip the victor ship comes in with object won. . . .*
> *Walt Whitman*

A month after Lincoln's assassination, Clover read in the newspapers that Grant's triumphant Army of the Potomac was to pass through Washington in review. "Then and there," she wrote to her cousin, Mary Louisa Shaw, "I vowed to myself that go I would." Her father, naturally, "hooted at the idea of such a thing," and a cousin whom she asked to escort her "jeered, manlike." Clover, undaunted, "stamped for an hour or two; said all the naughty words I could think of—then put on my most festive bonnet and went forth to seek a man." She soon found one, of course, the father of a friend, who agreed to escort four Boston girls to Washington.

There was no room in the hotels—people were even renting benches in streetcars for the night—but Clover commandeered some space in the attic of her uncle, Congressman Sam Hooper, where, as it happened, President Johnson had been living since the assassination. Then off to see the sights—"a lovely summer afternoon—blue sky overhead—roses everywhere—bands playing." She went to visit the house where Lincoln had died, and where "the pillow is soaked with blood . . . a painful sight, and yet we wanted to see it, as it is an historical fact." She even squeezed into the courtroom where the conspirators were being tried. "Mrs. Suratt only shows her eyes, keeping her fan to her face. All the men except Paine have weak, low faces. Paine is handsome but utterly brutal . . . his great gray eyes rolling about restlessly."

Clover had come to see the parade, however, so she negotiated with her uncle for a seat in the Congressional reviewing stand.

Then "up at five-thirty, the most perfect day I ever saw. . . . The platform covered with Stars and Stripes, gay flags; between the pillars pots of flowers—azaleas, cactus and all in full bloom. . . ." At about nine-thirty, the band struck up "John Brown's Body," and General Meade came riding past the stand. All his officers "had their hands filled with roses, and many had wreaths around their horses' necks." There was a pause, and then a lone horse galloped past "with a hatless rider, whose long golden curls were streaming in the wind; his arms hung with a wreath. . . . It was General Custer." When Custer regained control of his horse, he went back and resumed the lead of his 10,000 cavalrymen, each of whom wore a scarlet scarf "with the ends hanging half a yard long."

"Among the cavalry," Clover wrote to her cousin, "came the dear old Second, Caspar Crowninshield looking splendidly on his war horse—then came artillery, pontoon bridges, ambulances, army wagons, negro and white pioneers with axes and spades, Zouave regiments, some so picturesque with red bag trousers. . . . And so it came, this glorious old army of the Potomac, for six hours marching past, eighteen or twenty miles long, their colors telling their sad history. Some regiments with nothing but a bare pole, a little bit of rag only, hanging a few inches, to show where their flag had been . . . all the rest shot away. It was a strange feeling to be so intensely happy and triumphant and yet to feel like crying."

5

TIME FOR SOME OF US
TO GET MARRIED

HENRY ADAMS' engagement book for Wednesday, May 16, 1866, indicates that the American minister's young secretary had dinner at home with, among others, Lord and Lady Baconworth, Lord and Lady Stanley, Sir Robert and Lady Philimore, Sir Robert and Lady Palmer, General and Mrs. Bartlett, Sir C. and Lady Lyell, and Dr. and Miss Hooper.

That appears to have been Clover's first meeting with her future husband. Dr. Hooper had taken Clover on a tour of Europe in the postwar spring of 1866, and the American Legation in London was a natural meeting place for visiting Bostonians. Perhaps Adams was impressed by the young Miss Hooper, then twenty-two, not a beauty but full of gaiety and energy. Perhaps they exchanged clever remarks about the new comedy at the Haymarket. More likely not. It often happens that first meetings are inconclusive, too tangential to disturb the self-preoccupations of the future lovers. No trumpets sound.

Adams, growing bald at twenty-eight, was more self-preoccupied than most, ill at ease, and enough of a snob to concentrate his attentions on the higher-ranking guests. Ever since he had arrived in England in 1861, he had suffered from a yearning for social eminence, and from having to deny that yearning, having to recognize that the English simply didn't take American social pretensions seriously. "He was, like all Bostonians, instinctively English," he wrote, and he quaked with anxiety on first being presented, in his naval blue coat and gold eagle buttons and knee breeches and white silk stockings, to Queen Victoria. Indeed, he wrote later that he was "frightened to death" that his chronic dyspepsia might cause a "relapse" in the midst of the ceremony. Even among lesser aristocracy, on which he danced attendance, he experienced the anguish of being an awkward outsider. "His little mistakes in etiquette or address made him writhe with torture," he still recalled a half-century later in the *Education*. "He never forgot the first two or three social functions he attended: one an afternoon at Miss Burdett Couts's in Stratton Place, where he hid himself in the embrasure of a window and hoped that no one noticed him. . . . Still another nightmare he suffered at a dance given by the old Duchess Dowager of Somerset, a terrible vision in castanets, who seized him and forced him to perform a Highland fling before the assembled nobility and gentry. . . ."

There were compensations, however, in the weighty talk of the Liberal and pro-Northern intellectuals who frequented Adams' legation off Portland Square—John Stuart Mill, Thomas Huxley, Robert Browning, Leslie Stephen. The Sir C. Lyell who appeared at dinner on the same evening as Clover and her father was the eminent geologist Sir Charles Lyell, whose *Antiquity of Man* (1863) had provided powerful support to the new theories of his friend Darwin. Adams was deeply impressed. "I tell you these are great times," he wrote to his brother Charles. "Man has mounted science and is now run away with. . . . Some day science may have the existence of mankind in its power, and the human race commit suicide by blowing up the world."

Adams' own intellectual ambitions were more modest. He had just begun working on his first serious historical article, a deflation of the myth of Captain John Smith and Pocahantas. It brought him little satisfaction. "In spite of determination to be actual, daily and practical," he wrote in the *Education*, "Henry Adams found himself, at twenty-eight, still in English society, dragged on one side into English dilettantism, which of all dilettantism he held the most futile: and, on the other, into American antiquarianism, which of all antiquarianism he held the most foolish."

He was perhaps a little bothered, too, by a sense of isolation. Charles Francis, Jr., whom he had always looked up to, had just gotten married the previous year to a Boston girl named Mary Ogden. Henry shied away from such a prospect. "Charles and his wife are so happy [honeymooning] in Italy that I could envy them," he wrote to a friend, "if it were not for that 'something ere the end,' that undiscovered country from whose bourne no bachelor returns makes me rather 'accept the ills I have, than' the rest—Hamlet's logic is good for more cases than suicide."

It was traditional to believe that young men struggled to avoid marriage and that girls yearned for it. Clover, in any case, had the matter on her mind even before Ned Hooper's wedding to Fanny Chapin. "Clover suggested in her last letter," Ned wrote to Nella in the spring of 1863, "that it was time for some of us to get married." Perhaps it was the sense of uncertainty caused by the continuing bloodshed. If the outbreak of war brought a momentary sense of unity, of coherence and crusade, that eventually gave way to a sense of restlessness and disintegration, a need to confront postponed emotions. Or perhaps it was simply a matter of youth. Clover was twenty-one when the war ended, and that was considered a rather advanced age at which to remain single, an age at which to begin wondering whether one might be doomed to the pitiable state of rejected and ignored spinsterhood.

Many of Clover's friends from school days were beginning to parade to the altar. Ida Agassiz, for example, the older of Louis Agassiz's two daughters, the chief of staff at Clover's school on Quincy Street, was being offered by the matchmakers of Cambridge, to Francis Parkman. The greatest of Boston's Romantic historians, having already written *The Oregon Trail* and *The Conspiracy of Pontiac,* Parkman was also a victim of insomnia, arthritis, heart disease, partial blindness, and one of those nineteenth-century forms of madness that often afflicted the Boston sensibility. If he read or even thought for more than five minutes at a time, he began to feel an iron band around his forehead, crushing him. He sat in the dark, behind curtains, with his eyes bandaged, dictating for a few minutes or writing by means of a machine of his own invention, a wooden square with horizontal wires to guide the pencil along each line. "I am no better off than an owl in the twilight," he wrote. He was already a widower of forty, some fourteen years older than Ida Agassiz, and yet he still thought of her as "a most exceptional person," and he wrote to a friend that "for a year or two, my dearest wish has been to make her my wife."

There is some higher force, however, that saves girls like Ida

Agassiz from men like Francis Parkman and bestows them on simpler souls like the wounded cavalryman Henry Lee Higginson. Ida seems to have needed someone to nurse, and Higginson, unlike Parkman, was curable, not exceptionally intelligent but good-hearted and full of incompetent charm. The marriage took place in the Harvard College Chapel, and Ida wore white silk with a lace veil. From London, Henry Adams wrote to the groom a remarkable outburst of what he considered wit: "I consider him who marries to be an unmitigated and unmitigable ignoramus and ruffian. In your particular case, however, I incline to the opinion that there are palliating circumstances. I have not the honor of knowing Miss Agassiz, though I have an indistinct recollection of once seeing her somewhere. But I have heard a great deal about her, from an early youth, and this has induced me to believe that she is a person whom weakminded men like you and me instantaneously, profoundly and irredeemably adore. Probably I shall have some occasion to tell her so some day, if ever a misguided Providence permits me to go home. Meanwhile I only hope that your life won't be such an eternal swindle as most life is."

Henry Lee Higginson was too innocent ever to regard life as a swindle. Casting about for something to do with himself after the war, he remembered those bucolic plantations along the Carolina coast, where he had encountered Ned Hooper in the midst of the government's experiment of paying abandoned slaves to grow cotton. With two other equally guileless veterans, Channing Clapp and Charles Morse, Higginson invested $27,000 of the family fortune in a 7,000-acre plantation about thirty miles south of Savannah. The three entrepreneurs soon learned that the previous proprietor owned less than half of the land that he had sold them, and that the railroad by which the cotton was to be shipped out had never been repaired since General Sherman's troops had destroyed it, and, finally, that the freed slaves were unaccustomed to Boston ways. "They know it is wrong to steal and lie," Ida wrote, "but they do it continually."

The Higginsons planted 400 acres in cotton and persuaded themselves that a crop of 32,000 pounds would bring $32,000. They soon lowered their hopes to 25,000 pounds, and the price was already dropping from a dollar a pound to eighty cents, and then came "insects," and then "continual rains," and Higginson wrote back to Boston that "we found quite a lot of cotton beaten out and lying useless in the sand. . . . [The] rain has cut off all our profit, I fancy." He was still too optimistic. Having borrowed almost $10,000 from his father for the first year's expenses, he now had to admit that the utopian plantation would not break even. Malaria made its annual visit, and whooping cough swept through the schoolroom where Ida dedicated herself to teaching reading and religion. Three of her fifteen pupils died. When a further $20,000 invested in 1866 yielded a return of only $10,000, Higginson and his friends finally gave up. The plantation was sold for $5,000, an overall loss of about $60,000.

His father, George Higginson, a businessman of sorts, was hardly shrewder. He took the inheritance that he received in 1867 and proceeded to invest it in some obscure Michigan copper mines named Calumet. The copper stock, which had been issued at $12.50, soon sank to $5. The family, like so many Boston families that had been trained only in propriety and rectitude, faced destitution. And then, one fine day, Higginson's brother-in-law, Alex Agassiz, a Harvard graduate but a Swiss by birth, rebelled against the whole tradition of genteel incompetence. He dreamed of sailing through the Pacific to study coral reefs, but he hated his father's dependence on the charity of Boston businessmen. In an encounter on a Boston street corner with Charles W. Eliot, the future president of Harvard, who was then an unknown chemistry professor at M.I.T., Agassiz burst forth with his plan: "Eliot, I am going to Michigan for some years as superintendent of the Calumet and Hecla mines. I want to make money. It is impossible to be a productive naturalist in this country without money. I am going to get some money if I can and then I will be a naturalist. . . ."

Alex Agassiz went to Michigan, where he found the Calumet and Hecla mines to be a buried mountain of copper, but in a state of dilapidation that amounted almost to ruin. He had to bring in the timber to save the mine shafts from collapse. He had to build a private railroad line to get the copper to the lake shore, and when the locomotive arrived and proved to be one inch too narrow for the track, he had to rip up and re-lay the whole railroad line, and he had to finish it before the winter blizzards swept in. Work, struggle—despite what Professor Agassiz might preach against Darwin, the younger generation believed in the new creed of evolution and survival of the fittest, and in postwar America their beliefs could make them rich. When Agassiz returned from his labors in Michigan to resume his study of coral, he urged Calumet and Hecla shares on friends and neighbors like the Shaws and Adamses, and stocks that had once sold for $5 eventually soared to a peak of about $1,000. Alex himself had almost 8,000 shares. Henry Lee Higginson had about 5,000. He used the wealth that Alex had brought him to found the Boston Symphony Orchestra and to pay all its deficits, usually at least $20,000 a year, for the rest of his long and tranquil life.

We have few traces of the Hoopers' travels in Europe in the spring of 1866, but since they encountered Oliver Wendell Holmes, Jr. at a London dinner, it is possible to conjecture that they saw similar sights and received similar impressions. Though Holmes was much impressed by the nightingales and mossy lawns at the Thames-side estate of the banker Russell Sturgis, a distant relative of Clover's, he displayed a characteristic American dislike of English social pretensions. "Everybody tries to be a swell," he wrote in his diary, "[but] few of the gentlemen [are] real ones." It was quite probably on this first visit to London that Clover acquired her unconquerable dislike of the English. Perhaps she felt a residue of resentment for the recent British support of the Confederacy, or perhaps she simply sensed that ineffable air of superiority that expressed the standard British view of all foreigners. She was later to write of Matthew Arnold that he was "as big a snob as any Britisher," and that he "brings vividly home the deep saying of R. W. Emerson that 'every Englishman is an island.' " And on leaving London, after a later stay, she was to write that "our own land is gayer—lighter—quicker and more full of life."

Beyond the Bostonian social scene in London, it is even further conjecture to wonder where Dr. Hooper escorted Clover on the continent. There are only a few later references to their having gone to Paris, but what could be more likely than for the middle-aged doctor to revisit all the places he had enjoyed when he and young Holmes' father had been medical students—Italy, Germany, the Low Countries. That was, to an increasing extent, the American style. In contrast to the pre-war merchants who had bustled across the Atlantic in search of business, more and more Americans now had the money, the leisure, and the social ambitions, to take their families sight-seeing. Henry James recorded the scene in myriad variations, thus creating the legendary character of the American girl on tour—high-spirited and headstrong, carefree and often rather spoiled. As Daisy Miller, "dressed in white muslin, with a hundred frills and flounces," she would insist on clambering about in the Colosseum by the light of the moon. As Maggie Verver, in *The Golden Bowl,* she would feel it perfectly proper for her father to buy her a prince for a husband, and yet to believe, as Mrs. Assingham put it, that she "wasn't born to know evil."

While James was the subtlest of reporters of these transatlantic searchings, Henry Adams described the American tourist more succinctly: "Bored, patient, helpless; pathetically dependent on his wife and daughters; indulgent to excess, mostly a modest, decent, excellent, valuable citizen; the American was to be met at every railway station in Europe, carefully explaining to every listener that the happiest day of his life would be the day he should land on the pier at New York."

Back in Boston, there was the Boston routine. Dr. Hooper had been living since 1862 in a new house at 107 Beacon Street, at the edge of the new development of the Back Bay. Today that narrow five-story brownstone overlooks the oncoming rush of traffic debouching from the superhighway called Storrow Memorial Drive; a century ago, it undoubtedly enjoyed a peaceful view of the Charles. Clover helped keep house for the widowed Dr. Hooper, making sure that the servants kept the silver brightly polished and set out the roses properly. Aunt Eunice Hooper, who lived a few doors down Beacon Street, came to dinner from time to time, as did the Shaws and the Higginsons and other old friends.

Both Clover and her sister Nella liked to go to balls at the dancing academy on Tremont Street operated by the dashing Count Lorenzo Papanti, who, in 1834, had joined Mrs. Harrison Gray Otis in performing the first waltz that Boston had ever seen. But Boston was a serious place, and the Hoopers were serious people. It was only a few windswept blocks along the Common to the hushed corridors of the Atheneum. Dr. Hooper, like all the best Bostonians, was a shareholder; Clover a dedicated reader.

And the horse cars still heaved across the Charles to Cambridge every hour. Clover regularly went on long walks with her friend Wendell Holmes. What did they talk about? Cambridge talk is as

79

fugitive as the yellowed elm leaves that blow across the Yard, but Cambridge people, even more than Boston people, are apt to write things down as a statement of principle, and Holmes was no exception. He had written an article, a few years earlier, outlining his precociously judicious views. "The highest conversation," he declared, "is the statement of conclusions, or of such facts as enable us to arrive at conclusions, on the great questions of right and wrong, and on the relations of man to God. And so we all know the difference, in our various associates, between him who lives only in events, and can relish nothing but the college gossip of the day, and him who feels . . . that he can find higher food for thought."

It was the fate of the Cambridge woman—to some extent, it still is—to listen. Holmes required a lot of listening, somewhat too much for his own father, who also required a lot. The elder Holmes, by now dean of the Harvard Medical School, went calling on the elder Henry James, who had moved his household to Quincy Street so that the family could remain together while William and young Henry pursued their studies. Dr. Holmes had an interesting question. Did James find, he inquired, that his sons "despised" him? The Swedenborgian sage considered the matter with his customary serenity. No, he said, he was "not bothered in that way."

It would probably never have occurred to Holmes to ask James about the views of his daughter, for as young Henry later wrote to a niece, "in our family group girls seem scarcely to have had a chance." Alice James, who was never to marry, began in about 1867 to give in to her madness, to what she called "violent turns of hysteria," turns that left her "prostrate after the storm, with my mind luminous and active, and susceptible of the clearest, strongest impressions." It was a madness fairly typical for Boston girls of the period, a madness savage but silent, turned inward. Alice James' father imagined very little of what was happening to her. "As I used to sit immovable," she wrote some years later, "reading in the library, with waves of violent inclination suddenly invading my muscles, taking some one of their varied forms, such as throwing myself out of the window or knocking off the head of the benignant Pater, as he sat, with his silver locks, writing at his table, it used to seem to me that the only difference between me and the insane was that I had [not] only all the horrors and suffering of insanity, but the duties of doctor, nurse, and strait-jacket imposed on me too. Conceive of never being without the sense that if you let yourself go for a moment, your mechanism will fall into pie, and that at some given moment you must abandon it all, let the dykes break and the flood sweep in. . . ."

Alice asked her father, eventually, whether it was a sin for her to feel "very strongly tempted" to commit suicide. The philosopher reflected gravely on this and then gave her his permission to "end her life whenever she pleased." He asked only that she "do it in a perfectly gentle way in order not to distress her friends." James believed he had judged his daughter shrewdly: "Now [that] she could perceive it to be her *right* to dispose of her own body when life had become intolerable, she could never do it; that when she felt tempted to it, it was with a view to break bonds, or to assert her freedom."

It was a peculiarly Yankee view—that suicide was an assertion of freedom, and that freedom, once granted, precluded suicide. It did not acknowledge that freedom itself could lead to the despair that leads to suicide. It did not acknowledge that a devoted daughter, reading in the library, could ever think of beating her father to death.

Effie Shaw Lowell, Clover's cousin, who was embroidering some shoulder straps for her new husband when she heard that he had been killed at Cedar Creek, gave birth to her baby and wanted only to die. "Oh, it was so heart-rending," said Fanny Hooper, who sent Ned to the Shaws' house on Staten Island with a basket of white jasmine, white roses, and carnations. "Mrs. Shaw said she grows sadder every day. She hardly goes downstairs and sees almost no one. . . . Mrs. Shaw said Effie wept bitterly when she saw it was a girl. Mr. and Mrs. Lowell cried and I believe Mrs. Shaw herself." Fanny could not help adding: "I think that part of it is positively wicked. . . . She is a splendid-looking child, large and strong-looking. Isn't it a mercy babies are unconscious when they first come?"

The strong-looking child grew, and was named Bonny, and Effie Lowell slowly recovered, and three years later the two of them came to visit Clover in Boston. "Which has been a great spice for the family," the cheerful Fanny reported. Effie "looks tired and worn all the time" but "is lovely with Bonny, who is very much interested in everything going on—so much so that she never has any playthings." Clover decided to give a party for the child, a traditional Boston children's party, then found that Bonny represented a new generation. "Clover . . . thought she must have nothing but bread and milk and sponge cake," Fanny wrote, "but Mrs. Lowell assured her that Bonny would be contented with nothing short of ice cream and flowers on the table."

Clover and Effie decided to go out one evening, by themselves. Dr. Hooper fretted at their lack of an escort, and as a farewell jibe at their independent manner, he humbly said, "I'll stay at home and take care of the baby." They considered that perfectly appropriate, for they were off to attend the latest women's convention.

The women's movement had run aground during the Civil War. There had not even been a meeting between 1860 and 1866, for the large majority of reformers believed that all efforts should be devoted to winning the war and freeing the slaves. The National Woman's Loyal League, established in 1863 and headed by Elizabeth Cady Stanton and Susan B. Anthony, took little more than a year to collect 400,000 signatures for the Thirteenth Amendment, abolishing slavery. Reformers like Charles Sumner and Wendell Phillips then began working for a Fourteenth Amendment to grant the freed slaves equal rights, but when Mrs. Stanton first saw the proposed draft, she was appalled to see that, for the first time in any Constitutional amendment, the rights were being granted specifically to "male citizens." "We must not trust any of you," cried Mrs. Stanton, for, as she later wrote in her autobiography, "it is impossible for the best of men to understand women's feelings or the humiliation of their position." Sumner, who was by now the Republican leader in the Senate, insisted that it would be "most inopportune" for the women to interfere with black suffrage by demanding their own rights at the same time. Sojourner Truth, on the other hand, could and did speak as both a black and a woman when she protested in 1867: "If colored men get their rights, and not colored women theirs, you see the colored men will be masters over the women, and it will be just as bad as it was before."

There is no evidence that Clover was ever a dedicated feminist, and by the standards of her time, she had no strong reasons to feel oppressed. If she could not go to Harvard like her brother Ned, she was not one whit less well educated at home, and if she could not vote for Grant or Horatio Seymour in the new elections of 1868, she was nonetheless born rich, and that gave her far more freedom and independence than could be enjoyed by any Irish workman standing in line at the polling station. Still, there was, as Mrs. Stanton said, "the humiliation of their position," and none of the Hooper women or the Sturgis women was of a sort to accept humiliation.

We can still hear the echoes of female protest in some of the writings of Clover's aunt, Carrie Tappan, now tenderly preserved in the muffled reliquaries of Harvard's Houghton Library. One brief poem, for example, is entitled simply "Disenfranchised": "Standing like statues, ever in one place, / When every man a citizen shall be, / But I and all my sisters long must wait, / Enforced obedience our childish fate." Although she had the freedom of wealth, Carrie Tappan felt bitter about her inability to influence the political uses of that wealth. In a letter to a woman who had petitioned the state legislature against female suffrage, she tartly recalled an example of discrimination: "Several years since, the town in which I live became involved in a wild-goose scheme which I considered worse than useless and likely to fail. It failed, a heavy debt was incurred and I judge by looking over the assessors' book that I am forced to give more money towards the payment of this debt than any other person in the town. When I first heard of this scheme, I wished to remonstrate against it, but I have no place in the town meetings, no power of voting for town officials. I am helpless as a babe in the cradle and you ask the state to keep me, all my life, in this helpless condition. I have stated to the legislature that I desire to vote in my town; what right have you to beg it to ignore my wish?"

In the attic of the Hoopers' private archive, too, there lies an unsigned poem, faded ink on heavy blue paper, that sounds a more general complaint and sounds unmistakably like Aunt Carrie. *Any Woman to Any Man* is its title. "Because I am a woman you disdain me," it begins, "Pass careless by, or speak some trivial word / The silence of your heart is all you deign me / The speech of mine is not one moment heard. / You think my life is all of trifles made, / Of dress and etiquette and pretty pleasures / Alas if so, 'tis that I have obeyed / The destiny that man for me still measures. . . ."

So Clover and Effie Shaw went to the women's convention, and perhaps Fanny went too, for hers is the only account that we have,

83

and it sounds like that of a reluctant witness. "They signed a paper petitioning for suffrage," Fanny wrote to a friend, "but some of the strong-minded females made themselves so obnoxious that they must have injured the cause. Mrs. [Julia Ward] Howe said she had hitherto held aloof from the 'woman' question, she had even written many ingenious poems to prove that suffrage was out of a woman's sphere—'She had not wished to hear her Father, Grandfather and Great Grandfather abused, nor ever to hear her husband condemned as a Satan behind the scenes,' which was a hit at Mrs. Lucy Stone, who thought it degrading to take her husband's name and who went to hotels with her husband and registered her maiden name under her husband's. Clover and Mrs. Lowell . . . returned at eleven o'clock without an escort. . . ."

Of all the weddings that took place in this postwar marriage season, the one that made the deepest impression on Clover was undoubtedly that of her sister Ellen—kindly, sensible Nella—to one of the teachers at the Agassiz school, Ephraim Whitman Gurney. He was something of a Cambridge institution, one of those mild, soft-spoken men who seem unable to part from the shadowing elms, the brick sidewalks, and the company of eager youths. His father had been superintendent of Massachusetts General Hospital, and he himself was Phi Beta Kappa in the Harvard Class of 1852. He thought of becoming a minister, but teaching was clearly his vocation. He taught at a boys' school in Boston, then returned to Cambridge to start a school of his own. Visits to Agassiz were a natural addition. His return to Harvard was inevitable. He began in 1857 as a tutor in Greek and Latin, became an assistant professor of philosophy, then shifted to classical history. Ultimately, he was to become the first dean of the faculty and a major figure in Charles William Eliot's transformation of the university.

But not a bureaucrat. A beaming, bespectacled figure with a long, thick beard, he liked to tell his Latin pupils not just about verb endings but also about social life on the Aesquiline, and one of them summed up his rare quality by saying that he "actually liked college boys." He lived for many years in a single room on Dunster Street, where both students and other teachers gathered regularly for tea and talk. Some of them grieved over Gurney's departure into marriage—on October 3, 1868, when he was already thirty-nine years of age—but he and Nella walked directly from the Boston church back over the bridge to their new house near the Cambridge Reservoir and threw open the doors. "The Gurneys' house," said Henry Lee Higginson, "became . . . a place that young students could go to. . . . To go to that home was a liberal culture."

But the marriage of the Gurneys was more than a mere alliance. It was a revelation to two shy and inhibited Bostonians that they could find riches in each other. Ellen bloomed. "She is so supremely happy," Fanny Hooper wrote to a friend. "Mrs. [Ida] Higginson says she has 'rounded' since it was settled; her eyes are twice as large as before." The transformation seemed almost scandalous. The Hooper girls' aunt, Mary Shaw, declared that Ellen "should be ashamed to walk the streets with such a happy face without a veil." Ellen, who was already thirty, affected the role of Gurney's pupil, and Gurney was delighted to oblige her. "Ellen studies with him and wants to know as much as he does," Fanny reported, "and they have three lessons a day together and Ellen says she wakes him up in the night to ask him questions. He follows her everywhere, makes morning calls with her and has I believe never been in town but once without her since they were married."

Ellen's marriage, and her happiness in marriage, had a stunning effect on Clover, for it represented a kind of permission. It meant that she too could get married—indeed, must get married, and must find in marriage the kind of happiness that Ellen had found. Four years later, when she did finally get engaged to Henry Adams, Clover wrote to Ellen of "a horrid dream" that she had had. "I dreamt that for ever so many years you and I sat side by side with a high wall of ice between us, and very often when I tried to look through it I saw something in you that was so like myself, that it made me cold all over; and I think it was the same with you. About four years ago the sun began shining so on your side of the wall that it began to thaw, and then I looked over and saw you and Whitman and began to have a nice time with you. But there I was without the sun and my ice couldn't thaw. . . ."

It was unthinkable, of course, for well-bred girls like Ellen and Clover to go out and search for whatever it might be that could thaw the ice that surrounded them. They could only keep whirling from tea to dinner and hope some day to discover the sun. "Thursday went to a charming dinner at Ida's with Prof. and Mrs. Agassiz, Tom Appleton and Mr. Gay," Clover wrote to a friend early in 1871. "We had much festive talk, politics largely. Mr. Ag thinks the cause of civilization is set back thirty years by the triumph of Prussia. I think that his judgment in many things is as valuable as a pussy cat's, and yet he is quite eloquent. . . ."

These were the days in which the supposed empire of the supposed Napoleon III was crumbling under the hammer blows of Bismarck and Moltke. Postwar Boston disapproved, for it had just finished celebrating five years of peace. A gigantic Peace Jubilee Colisseum had been built in what is now Copley Square, and President Grant himself had come to attend the jubilee in June of 1869. The highlight was a performance of the anvil chorus from *Trovatore* by 1,000 musicians, 10,000 singers, a battery of electrically controlled cannon, and 100 Boston firemen beating on anvils with sledgehammers. On a smaller and lighter scale, too, Bostonians liked to devote their evenings to concerts. "Thursday evening went to a musical party at Mrs. Bell's," Clover wrote to a friend. "Small and pleasant—Mr. Leonard played enchanting things and Sebastian sang. . . . Next Thursday a great ball at Papanti's. I accepted and sent Papa with an olive branch in his hair. You can't think how sweetly becoming it was to him. . . . The public excitements are raising money for a vessel of flour to send to France. $40,000 or more have been raised in the past four days."

And again, a dinner at the Gurneys', where Clover sat between the distinguished historian Francis Parkman and the no less distinguished clergyman Phillips Brooks. "And found Mr. Brooks very unclerical and jolly and full of talk. He told me interesting things of Paris in September, and I think him much nicer out of the pulpit than in. I've heard him preach twice, but each time neither heart nor brain got any food. . . . The news of peace is very cheering tho' those unhappy Gauls seem to be wobbling in a mire of incapacity and dissension. What can come of it all? Aren't you glad the Germans went into Paris? If they hadn't, the French would never have realized how utterly beaten they are. There is an excitement among the feminine portion of this community as to the French fair. I think sending a vessel of food, for which $80,000 was raised in 20 days, was very nice. . . ."

This was all very interesting—Boston society was dedicated to being interesting—even, to use its favorite word, "amusing"—but what was to become of a single woman of twenty-eight, a woman with charm but no suitors, with intelligence but no vocation? Clover did not know. Perhaps she did not need to know. "I'm so happy sitting on the floor," she wrote to a friend one Sunday morning in March of 1871, "with my back against the window and hot sun going through me bringing a prophecy of spring and summer and green things. . . . It seems a fitting time for a friendly chat when the gay church bells have rung the good white sheep into their respective fields and left the naughty black ones to enter sunshine and quiet."

That was enough for a Sunday morning in spring but not enough to satisfy Clover's restless spirit indefinitely. She suddenly decided, for want of anything else, to learn Greek. It had been taught at the Agassiz school, but she had never mastered it, and there was something about its resonant complexities that challenged her. Perhaps because it was the ultimate mark of intellectual aristocracy, the language not only of Homer and Thucydides but also of Emerson and Longfellow, a language to which the Sturgises and Hoopers could only bow with the deference that commerce owes to culture. Perhaps, on the other hand, she had no reasons so elaborate as that. Perhaps she simply wanted something to occupy her mind, or to impress the people she met at dinner parties. Perhaps she simply wanted to keep up with her older sister Ellen in Ellen's persistent interrogations of her new husband, the professor of classical literature.

In any case, Clover began, in 1871, a regular course of studies in Greek. She appeared at her brother-in-law's house twice every week to begin declining nouns—*o anthropos, too anthropoo, ton anthropon.* . . .And since Professor Gurney now taught not just the classical languages but classical history as well, it was inevitable that Clover should encounter, one of these days, the clever young man she had once met at the American Legation in London, the brilliant Washington journalist, the new professor of medieval history, the timidly arrogant genius she was destined to marry.

BOOK TWO

The House of Adams

*If I had not been an Adams I would have kneeled at
your feet . . . and kissed your hand. . . . Do not pity
me, no do not pity me, I am an Adams and not
pitiable. . . .*

GERTRUDE STEIN,
The Mother of Us All

6

ABIGAIL'S LATCHSTRING

PAST THE SOUTH SHORE Television and Colman's Sporting Goods
and Vincent's Barber Shop, past the Ray-Kal Appliance Servicen-
ter and Alfredo's Cocktail Lounge and the Hancock Tire Company, the elephantine green bus carries us back to the small red
wooden house where the story of the Adams family begins. At 133
Franklin Street, Quincy, Massachusetts, the old house stands only
a few feet from the rumbling of the trucks along what was once the
Old Shore Road to Boston. Once this was all farmland. Once the
old house governed about 200 acres. That was before the Quincy
hills were torn apart for their granite, leaving what Charles Francis
Adams, Jr., called "an abomination of desolation." Quincy is now
the last stop at the southeastern end of the subway that connects
Harvard Square to Park Street in downtown Boston, but in the
days when Quincy was relatively remote, Henry Adams' earliest
memories defined the differences between country and city: Boston
"was restraint, law, unity"; Quincy "was liberty, diversity, outlawry, the endless delight of mere sense impressions." The strongest of the senses, he still recalled in his seventies, was that of smell
—"smell of hot pine-woods and sweet-fern in the scorching summer noon; of new-mown hay; of ploughed earth; of box hedges; of
peaches, lilacs, syringas; of stables, barns, cow-yards; of salt water
and low tide on the marshes. . . ."

Deacon John Adams, farmer and shoemaker, constable, select-
man and officer of the North Precinct Church, had bought the old
house, in what was then part of Braintree, in 1720, when he was

91

twenty-seven. And there his wife, Susanna Boylston Adams, daughter of one of the most prominent physicians in the colony, gave birth to their first son, John, on October 19, 1735. John was a pudgy baby, willful, proud, ordained to be the founder of the dynasty, to the extent that anyone can found a dynasty without his father having been the founder before him. "My father," John wrote later, "had destined his first born, long before his birth, to a public education and I was taught to read very early." Taught to read and taught to compete and ultimately sent to Harvard, where, according to the tradition of ranking by social standing, he stood fourteenth in a class of twenty-four. When the deacon died in 1761, he left his farm to his second son, Peter, who had not been sent to Harvard, and left to John a second little house that he had built nearby (a third son inherited a smaller tract but died of dysentery during the Revolution). It was here that John brought, in 1764, his beguiling bride, the former Abigail Smith, and here that she bore her first son, John Quincy Adams.

The clanging succession of Presidents Adams is what brings tourists on the green bus to these two little houses on the edge of Franklin Street, but inside, it is the spirit of Abigail Adams that dominates the hearth. Perhaps this is partly the predilection of the elderly guide, who takes the tourist's dollar and leads him out to the kitchen. "That is Abigail's latchstring," she observes, gesturing at the door, "so that she could decide whether she wanted to let a visitor into her kitchen. And over here is Abigail's buttery. If you'll step inside for a moment, you can see how she kept her food cool, by using that grill in the floor to the cellar. . . ."

Perhaps, then, the long tradition of regarding the Adamses as Presidents and Presidents *manqués* is a tradition that underestimates their lives at home in Quincy, where they were first of all sons and husbands and fathers. The tradition also underestimates the series of sharp-witted and often unhappy women who undertook the difficult task of becoming Adamses by courtship and by law, the series of women who, generation after generation, kept altering the bloodline, so that the Adamses who kept calling themselves Adamses were actually commingled with the Boylstons and the Smiths and the Johnsons and the Brookses and God knows how many other stout, sturdy, stolid New England families who were not, whatever else they might be, Adamses. And perhaps, finally, the presidential tradition most sadly falsifies history in ignoring all those Adamses who failed to live up to their fathers' incessant instruction—ignoring John's alcoholic son Charles, for example, and John Quincy's eldest son George, who apparently committed suicide in a state of paranoid hallucination.

A streak of nervous disorder ran through the family from the beginning. Describing the establishment of Deacon Adams, the young John wrote: "Passion, accident, freak, humor, govern in this house." And of himself, when he began keeping a diary, he was equally observant: "My brains seem constantly in as great confusion and wild disorder as Milton's Chaos. I have never any bright, refulgent ideas. Everything appears in my mind dim and obscure, like objects seen thro' a dirty glass or roiled water. . . . Vanity I am sensible is my cardinal vice and folly, and I am in continual danger, when in company, of being led into an *ignis fatuus* chase by it, without the strictest caution and watchfulness over myself."

This youthful conflict between the urgings of passion and the sense of a need for caution was to tear at Adams throughout his long life. He was proud of his great abilities but felt guilty about that same pride. He spoke bluntly to others but dreaded criticism. He also dreaded conflict, yet tended to regard every compromise as a threat to his integrity. He was hot-tempered, and in his explosions of temper one sees evidence of a deep rage, only with difficulty restrained. Restraint puffed him up, made him solemn and slightly ludicrous (as Vice-President, he insisted on wearing a ceremonial sword to the Senate), yet there is something endearing about his agonized awareness that people laughed at him and called him "The Duke of Braintree." Thomas Jefferson was more charitable when he wrote to James Madison that Adams was "vain, irritable and a bad calculator of . . . the motives which govern men," but also "profound in his views [and] so amiable I pronounce you will love him if you ever become acquainted with him."

Self-discipline and self-improvement, those were the rules. In his early twenties, John Adams was already writing in his diary: "I am resolved to rise with the sun and to study the Scriptures. . . ." At seventy, he was still rereading Thucydides and vowing to learn both Chaldean and Chinese. For his sons, too, he was determined to apply the same regimen: early rising and regular exercise, systematic study of the Bible and the classics, endless self-analysis in the endless pages of a journal. "There," says the guide in the little red farmhouse on Franklin Street, "is where John Quincy kept his books." The visitor is invited to inspect an enormous cupboard in a corner of a second-floor bedroom and to imagine the studious youth's accumulation of Plato and Milton and Montesquieu. John Quincy ultimately learned to read ten languages and left behind a library of 12,000 volumes, which his own son Charles Francis entombed at Quincy in a library built entirely of stone. "I must study politics and war that my sons may have liberty to study mathematics and philosophy," John wrote to Abigail with prophetic grandiloquence. "My sons ought to study mathematics and philosophy, geography, natural history, naval architecture, navigation, commerce and agriculture, in order to give their children a right to study painting, poetry, music, architecture, statuary, tapestry and porcelain."

When it came to applying these grand principles, Adams relied heavily on his wife. "It is time, my dear," he confidently wrote to Abigail at one point, "for you to begin to teach them French." And again: "Cultivate their minds, inspire their little hearts, raise their wishes. Fix their attention upon great and glorious objects. . . . Weed out every meanness, make them great and manly." Abigail was ready. Independent, intelligent, assertive, self-reliant, Abigail was ready for anything. She had borne five children in seven years, and now she was ready to teach them, to work, to write, to keep accounts, to stay home in Quincy and be a "farmeress," or to set sail for Europe to rejoin the man she called her "dearest friend." The Adamses were separated for years on end, while John served as minister to Paris and London and The Hague, and yet they continued to write impassioned love letters to each other. "Could you . . . be satisfied with my telling you that I was well . . . &c. &c.," Abigail cried in one outpouring. "By Heaven . . . you could . . . have changed hearts with some frozen Laplander." And again: "I have seen near a score of years roll over our heads, with an affection heightened and improved by time—nor have the dreary years of absence in the smallest degree effaced from my mind the image of the dear untittled man to whom I gave my heart."

Abigail has attracted considerable attention in recent years as a pioneer in the campaigns over women's rights. "In the new code of laws which I suppose it will be necessary for you to make," she wrote her husband in 1776, "I desire you would remember the ladies and be more generous and favorable to them than your ancestors. . . . Remember all men would be tyrants if they could. If particular care and attention is not paid to the ladies, we are determined to foment a rebellion. . . ." Much attention, too, has been paid to Adams' answer, rebuking Abigail for being "saucy," and adding that "we know better than to repeal our masculine systems." It is not so often noted, in these ideological times, that Adams' letter went on to argue that "our masculine systems" are "little more than theory." He added: "In practice you know we are the subjects. We have only the name of masters."

Abigail seems not to have cared very much about political power, or even about women's suffrage (the vast majority of men couldn't vote either), but she did care strongly about her own concept of equality. "I will never consent," she wrote in old age to her sister Eliza Peabody, "to have our sex considered in an inferior point of light. Let each planet shine in their own orbit. God and nature designed it so—if man is Lord, woman is *Lordess*—that is what I contend." And John, though he never doubted that it was Abigail's function to keep house and raise children, not only listened to her views on politics and diplomacy and life in general but insisted that she organize those views and write him about them. "I must entreat you," he said, "to take a part with me in the struggle." She was determined to do so, and yet she begrudged him the sacrifices. Looking back, once, she wrote that she considered "his honors as badges of my unhappiness."

The struggle ended in 1796, as Abigail probably was sure it would, with John Adams becoming the President of the United States. He did not campaign for the position; he gave no speeches, issued no statements, made no promises to the various factions. Such activities, in the comparatively serene early days of the Republic, were considered inappropriate. Just as Adams felt entitled by experience and seniority to become Washington's Vice-President, so he felt equally entitled to become his successor, and most of the electors in Philadelphia agreed. The only omen of the difficulties ahead was Alexander Hamilton's maneuver in supporting another candidate, Thomas Pinckney, in order to reduce Adams' mandate. In a field of five, Adams defeated Jefferson by only three votes out of 239.

Having become President, Adams seemed to have no systematic plans for his country, no policy except to maintain order and avoid war with either Britain or France. His restricted view of the presidency, combined with his prickly character, made him less a leader than an administrator. He declined to replace Washington's cabinet even though several of its members were openly antagonistic. Undercut by Hamilton on the one side and Jefferson on the other, he fussed and sulked and began to suffer a series of maladies. Benjamin Franklin Bache sneered at him, in his *Aurora*, as "old, querulous, bald, blind, crippled, toothless Adams." The press had indeed become so ferociously partisan that Adams approved the imprisonment of some of his more virulent critics under the Alien and Sedition Act of 1798. So did Abigail. She wrote in praise of the government's right "to punish the stirrer up of sedition, the writer or printer of loose and unfounded calumny."

At sixty-three, Adams was hardly a Methuselah, but Bache's description was not wholly inaccurate. Adams was undeniably bald, and had recently lost a number of teeth, and suffered from periodic eye trouble, and from a palsy so severe that he had difficulty in writing. More sinister was a mysterious kind of nervous affliction that sometimes overwhelmed him in periods of political crisis. He had first suffered from this combination of anxiety, depression, and physical exhaustion while defending the participants in the Boston Massacre in 1771 ("God grant, I may never see such another night," he wrote after the crisis had passed). A far worse attack struck while he was serving in Holland. He went into a coma for almost a week and nearly died. He thereafter referred to such difficulties as "the Dutch complaint," or, in milder episodes, simply as "the fidgets." And Abigail was sick, too, with rheumatic pains and a series of fevers, which she dosed three times a day with mixtures of nitre, calomel, and tartar emetic. After becoming President, the harassed and unhappy Adams cited general reasons of health as an excuse to avoid the capital entirely. From April to October of 1799, he simply stayed home in Quincy, occasionally threatening to resign, and insisting that he could handle all affairs of state by corresponding with his cabinet. One day when three associates rode out to see him, he sat sullenly reading a newspaper until they departed again.

When Adams finally did return to the presidency, he found

himself embroiled not only in political intrigues but also in the difficulties of his children. His oldest daughter, Abigail, had married a handsome ne'er-do-well named William Smith, who was constantly speculating and in debt. A far worse fate had befallen his second son, Charles, who was sinking rapidly into alcoholism. Adams could not understand it. Charles had been so bright and eager. "He is a delightful little fellow," John had once written to Abigail. "I love him too much." Adams had sent the boy to Harvard, seen him established as a lawyer, approved his marriage to Sally Smith, and now Sally told him that Charles had disappeared on another drunken spree, leaving her destitute. "I renounce him," John wrote bitterly to Abigail. "King David's Absalom had some ambition and some enterprise. Mine is a mere rake, buck, blood, and beast."

Abigail was a bit more lenient. She went to New York and found Charles with a consumptive cough, a liver infection, and "his mind at times deranged thro his sufferings." "The poor child is unhappy, I am sure," she wrote to John Quincy. "He is not at peace with himself; and his conduct does not meet my wishes." She had to add that Charles had appropriated some of John Quincy's savings to rescue their brother-in-law Smith from bankruptcy, and now that money, more than $5,000, was also gone. Abigail sweetened the news by assuring John Quincy that he was her favorite. "How sharper than a serpent's tooth it is to have a graceless * child, may you, my dear son, never experience. Blessed be God, I have those in whom I can rejoice." Scarcely a year later, in the midst of the voting for presidential electors, almost at the very moment in which Adams learned that he had lost South Carolina and thus the White House, he also learned that Charles had died of cirrhosis at the age of thirty. "Oh!" he wrote to his youngest son, Tom, "that I had died for him if that would have relieved him from . . . his disease."

Adams affected stoicism at his humiliating political defeat. "All my life I have expected it," he wrote. But he was bitterly hurt, and bitterly resentful of the triumphant Jefferson. Avoiding the victor's inauguration—he may not have been invited—he left early in the morning to make his way back to his sanctuary in Quincy. There

---

* Assuming that Abigail knew she was quoting from one of King Lear's tirades against Goneril, it would be interesting to know how she happened to change Lear's adjective from "thankless" to "graceless."

97

stood the small but handsome clapboarded house that Adams had bought on his return from London in 1787. He had tried to name it "Peacefield," but ultimately it came to be known simply as "the old house." It had been built in 1731 by Major Leonard Vassall, a West Indian sugar planter who had imported mahogany from Santo Domingo for the paneling in his study. Adams was proud to buy the seven-room house from the major's grandson, but Abigail loftily remarked that it "feels like a wren's house," and so the expansions and elaborations began.

John Adams built a large gabled ell that included a long living room and an upstairs study; John Quincy was to add a passageway along the north side of the house; Charles Francis contributed servants' quarters over the kitchen and the stone library out in what had been Abigail's garden. Henry Adams was to remember that "the old house at Quincy was eighteenth century. What style it had was in its Queen Anne mahogany panels and its Louis Seize chairs and sofas. . . . Bathrooms, water-supplies, lighting, heating, and the whole array of domestic comforts were unknown at Quincy." But in the pantries and cupboards that were eventually refurbished by Charles Francis, the trimly uniformed federal guide now shows us rack upon rack of "Abigail's Meissen" and "Abigail's Waterford," and in the kitchen stands "Abigail's grandfather clock, which dates from 1690 and still keeps perfect time."

Even Abigail's garden is still here, with Abigail's box hedges, smoky green and shiny and slightly redolent, as always, of cats. John Quincy was an avid gardener, too, and so was the younger Abigail, Charles Francis' wife, who codified the various species to be planted within the rectangular framework of the hedges, and so they still bloom, on sunny June afternoons, in neatly restrained profusion: white roses and iris, poppies, bachelor's buttons, and snapdragon. And inside the cool, dark house (Major Vassall wanted to escape the memory of the Caribbean sun), the guide leads the way past the "long room," where John Quincy entertained forty guests on his eightieth birthday, and up the stairs to the study that John Adams built for himself, to write his memoirs and his journals and the noble letters that finally made peace with Jefferson. "This is where the President died, on July 4, 1826, exactly fifty years after the Declaration of Independence," the guide says proudly. "He was sitting right in that chair over there when he said his last words, 'Thomas Jefferson still survives.' Of course, he couldn't know that Jefferson had died just a few hours earlier that same day."

It was here, in the perfect time of Abigail's grandfather clock, that John Quincy Adams brought home to his parents his miserably unhappy wife, Louisa. Old John Adams approved, for Louisa was very beautiful, with curly red hair and large, watchful eyes. Abigail made it clear that she thought her brilliant and beloved oldest son might have done better than this alien and timorous girl. "Do what I would," Louisa later recalled in an autobiographical sketch that she entitled *Adventures of a Nobody*, "there was a conviction on the parts of others that I could not *suit.*"

Louisa Catherine Johnson was the second of seven daughters of a Maryland merchant named Joshua Johnson, who lived in France during the American Revolution and eventually acquired the position of U.S. consul in London. Louisa, raised in a French convent, was seventeen years of age before she was ever permitted to remain alone in the same room with a young man. The first young man to undergo this experience was John Quincy Adams, then the U.S. minister to Holland. John Quincy had only recently been in love with a girl in Boston, Mary Frazier, but his own poverty, and his mother's warnings, had forced him to abandon her. Now that he encountered the wealthy Miss Johnson, he wrote her glowingly about "taking you as the companion for the remainder of the journey or voyage and of my life." Louisa felt herself unworthy. "I am so miserably dull, stupid, and wan," she wrote him, "that I have gained the appellation of the nun."

John Quincy duly proposed and was accepted. Louisa wanted to get married at once, but John Quincy pleaded affairs of state. He returned to Holland and wrote long letters instructing Louisa how to improve her mind. Louisa was so terrified that she asked her governess to write her answers. When John Quincy finally reappeared in London a year later, he did not come to Louisa's house until the following day, and Louisa felt a "mortified affection more bitter than I could express." John Quincy's diary entry for July 26, 1797, is remarkably dispassionate: "At nine this morning I went, accompanied by my brother, to Mr. Johnson's, and thence to the Church of the parish of All Hallows Barking, where I was married to Louisa Catherine Johnson."

Two weeks after the marriage, Louisa suffered a tormenting embarrassment. Her father, swindled by a business partner, went bankrupt, and Louisa became convinced that people would think she had married Adams for financial reasons. President John Adams did subsequently appoint Johnson superintendent of the stamp office in the Treasury Department, and several of the Johnsons repeatedly approached the Adamses for various favors, but that hardly justified Louisa's belief that the bankruptcy had, as she put it, "prostrated my pride, my pretensions, I will say my happiness forever." Aside from her pride and pretensions, Louisa was sickly, and she underwent a devastating series of miscarriages, at least three of them, or perhaps it was the miscarriages that made her sickly. One was caused by her shock, while standing at her window in Berlin, where Adams had newly become the U.S. minister, at seeing a child run over by a cart. She fainted and fell to the floor, and then the hemorrhaging started. Young Queen Louisa of Prussia liked her American namesake, and pitied her pale fragility. When she gave Louisa Adams a box of rouge, John Quincy forbade her to use it. When she tried it anyway, he washed it off. The Adamses, Louisa said many years later to her son Charles Francis, on the occasion of his engagement, were "peculiarly harsh and severe" to their women.

Louisa's first son was born in Berlin, in 1801, under dreadful conditions. A drunken midwife treated her so roughly that she couldn't walk for more than a month. John Quincy decided to name the boy George Washington Adams. "I know not whether . . . it be wise to give a great and venerable name to such a lottery-ticket as a new-born infant," he observed, "but my logical scruples have in this case been overpowered by my instinctive sentiments." And Louisa remained sickly. Her doctors thought she had tuberculosis. The following year she could barely manage to accompany John Quincy back to the United States, where he dabbled briefly in law and then became a state senator. Louisa's debt-ridden father died shortly afterward, and Louisa was heartbroken. Her state of illness seemed almost continuous. Shortly after Adams was elected to the U.S. Senate in 1803, she became pregnant again, suffered from fainting spells, and from a loss of feeling in her hands. Her doctors instructed her to have her hands tied up in laudanum poultices.

Her apparently imperturbable husband was hardly less tormented, particularly when his stubborn refusal to follow Federalist policies led the party to force him out of the Senate. His "dreadful restless anxiety made me almost crazy," said Louisa. "It was too distressing to see him at such times for he could not control his feelings." It was the Adams sense of duty that drove John Quincy to distraction. "I am forty-five years old," he wrote in his diary. "Two thirds of a long life have passed, and I have done nothing to distinguish it by usefulness to my country and to mankind. . . . Passions, indolence, weakness and infirmities have sometimes made me swerve from my better knowledge of right and almost constantly paralyzed my efforts of good."

"What has preserved this race of Adamses," John once wrote, "in all their ramifications, in such numbers, health, peace, comfort?" His own answer was that it was religion, "without which they would have been rakes, fops, sots, gamblers, starved with hunger, frozen with cold, scalped by Indians, etc., etc., etc." The pious John Quincy could subscribe to that, but he also felt the scourge of his father's insistence on learning. As a boy, he had once written to his father a schedule of his daily activities: "Make Latin, explain Cicero, Erasmus; pierce Phaedrus; learn Greek racines; Greek grammar, geography, geometry, fractions. . . ." Now, in the discontents of middle age, he concentrated his passion for instruction on his firstborn son, George Washington Adams. And George Washington Adams, as a boy, seemed prepared to accept his destiny. When he was six, he fell out of a swing and broke his collarbone, and a doctor had to set it, and Grandfather John Adams, who doted on the boy, gave him a quarter for being brave, and George ran out to buy gingerbread for his friends, saying to one of them: "When I am President, I will make you Secretary of State."

John Quincy left George behind when he went off to become minister to Russia in 1809—he never consulted Louisa about the move, either, simply announcing that she should leave the two older boys at home and prepare to sail with the baby, Charles Francis—but he sent back endless instructions to his brother Tom about George's education. Not only must the boy rise early to study his Bible and his Greek, but he must also practice fencing, and "be encouraged in nothing delicate or effeminate. . . . If he goes into Boston to see a play, let him walk." Tom and old John Adams were to interrogate the boy at least once a month in Latin and Greek. "If I could inspire the souls of my three boys with the sublime Platonic idea of aiming at ideal excellence," John Quincy wrote. "If I could persuade them to soar for the standard of emulation to the lofty *possible* instead of crawling upon the ground with the dirt-clogged *real*—But I have not the time."

John Quincy never had enough time. In April of 1814, on being informed that he had been appointed to the diplomatic team assigned to arrange a peace treaty with Britain, he simply departed for the negotiations in Ghent, leaving Louisa and Charles Francis to fend for themselves in St. Petersburg. (A daughter had also been born there, and died at the age of one in what Louisa called the "inhospitable clime.") And when the peace treaty was settled, almost a year later, John Quincy abruptly wrote to Louisa to close down their house, sell the furniture, and set out across the midwinter snowdrifts to rejoin him in Paris. The ailing Louisa (who would live to be nearly eighty, just like her equally ailing and grumbling mother-in-law, Abigail) did exactly as she was told. She managed to lose her way at night; the carriage wheels broke; ruffians menaced her; and finally, in the midst of Napoleon's triumphant return from Elba, she was engulfed by swarms of riotous soldiers who threatened to kill her, until she agreed to shout *"Vive l'Empereur!"* John Quincy, as she wrote after they were finally reunited in Paris, "was perfectly astonished at my adventure."

Boston's pro-English Federalists had driven Adams from the Senate because of his support of the nationalistic policies of Jefferson and Madison, but those same idiosyncrasies won him the appreciation of the White House. After the Treaty of Ghent, Madison made him minister to London, and Monroe made him Secretary of State, an office that traditionally led to the White House. And Louisa rather enjoyed the social aspects of Washington. It was still, to be sure, a pigsty of a town, with its muddy streets unpaved, its garbage lying in heaps. Most of the Congressmen lived in cheap boardinghouses and spent their evenings on cheap whiskey and cheap cigars. The office of Secretary of State paid only $3,500 per year (increased by Congress to $6,000 in 1819), and John Quincy's expenses in his first year in Washington were more than $11,000, but his brother Tom had managed his property so well that he possessed by now a fortune of about $100,000.

He bought a handsome three-story house on F Street. It had a ballroom, and Louisa liked to entertain. She was "at home" every Tuesday to between fifty and one hundred people. For one of her greatest extravaganzas, to celebrate the anniversary of Andrew Jackson's victory at the Battle of New Orleans, she invited five hundred guests. John Quincy ordered pillars installed to brace up the floors. Nearly one thousand people came. There was dancing on the ground floor and dinner on the third. Louisa, according to *Harper's Bazaar*, wore "a *suit* of *steel*." Her dress was "composed of steel llama; her ornaments for head, throat and arms were all of cut steel, producing a dazzling effect. General Jackson was her devoted attendant during the evening." We can see her loveliness even now in a portrait painted by Charles Bird King in 1824. At forty-nine, Louisa was still very handsome, stately, robust, her flowing white Grecian robe cut low across the bosom. In her right hand, she clutches a harp; in her left, a music book opened to Thomas Moore's song, "Oh, Say Not that Woman's Heart Can Be Bought."

General Jackson won the election of 1824 with 153,544 votes against 108,740 for Adams, 47,136 for House Speaker Henry Clay, and 46,618 for Treasury Secretary William H. Crawford. But since no candidate had a majority, the election was carried to the House, and the negotiation began. Adams and Clay, whom Adams had only recently described as having "a mind very defective in elementary knowledge, and a very undigested system of ethics," made a deal. We do not know to this day what they promised each other —only that the deal made Clay the Secretary of State, and Adams a minority President, tainted and even ludicrous in his uncompromising insistence on his principles of rectitude. Once he was inside the White House, he was its prisoner. He himself later referred to his presidency as "a four years' martyrdom."

Louisa, too, came to feel imprisoned. Despite her fondness for parties, she disliked official ceremony. She preferred to play the piano or to work at her writings and to entertain only her family and friends. One of her dramas, which may well have been acted by her relatives, was entitled *The Wag, or Just from College: A Farce in Three Acts*. Another, dealing with the Greek struggle for independence, was *The Captives of Scio of the Liberal Americans: A Melo-Drame*. The family audience was a large and constantly shifting group, not just the three Adams boys but three orphaned children of Louisa's sister, Mary, Johnson, and Thomas Hellen. The two boys were scapegraces—Thomas dropped out of Harvard and

Johnson ran off with a White House maid—and Mary flirted with all three of the Adams boys. The oldest of them, George Washington, proposed to her and was accepted, but John Quincy demanded an engagement of four or five years and sent George back to Harvard, then to study law in the Boston office of Daniel Webster, then to win a seat in the Massachusetts state legislature. He began to drink. A gentle and nervous youth, George had hoped to study art and literature, but he was the beloved favorite of his grandfather in Quincy, and it was clearly his mission to become President. He once had a dream that he was making love to a girl, and his father appeared in the dream and said, "Remember, George, who you are and what you are doing."

John Quincy's second son, John, had a less illustrious destiny. The President was so appalled to learn that John stood 45th in his Harvard class of 85 that he forbade the boy to come home to Washington for Christmas. "I could feel nothing but sorrow and shame in your presence until you [have] made large progress in redeeming yourself from that disgraceful standing," he wrote. John did improve somewhat, but John Quincy refused to attend his graduation unless he became one of the five top students in his class. Instead, he was expelled for taking part in a student rebellion, and it was not until 1873 that the rebels were belatedly awarded their degrees. In disgrace, John returned to Washington, where, with uncharacteristic leniency, John Quincy took him in, gave him secretarial work to do, and began teaching him the inevitable family profession of law.

Mary Hellen, meanwhile, began spinning a new web for her absent fiancé's younger brother. "She has some alluring ways which are apt to make every man forget himself," the youngest brother, Charles, wrote in his diary. "George would be in a perfect fever and sickness if he was to imagine that she had encouraged me in the least." And again: "Mary has been behaving unworthily to George. . . . I am sorry for John, who, I understand, is the victim of her arts." John and Mary were privately married in the Blue Room of the White House in February of 1828, and George, who did not attend, sank deeper and deeper into alcoholism and madness.

His health had already broken down during the previous summer in a series of fevers and abscesses. Louisa journeyed to Boston to nurse him. She wrote back to the White House that he was "constantly acting like one divested of understanding," but she eventually restored him to being "the same old exaggerated conceited timid enthusiastic negligent cold and eccentric being that he has been since he was born." John Quincy, too, as he neared the end of his "four years' martyrdom" in the White House, began suffering various miseries—the digestive trouble that seemed chronic among the Adamses, and a persistent cough that disturbed his sleep, and cramps in his side, and profound depression, "a sluggish carelessness of life, an imaginary wish that it were terminated."

John Quincy sent George $1,000 to pay off his various debts, and insisted that he keep a diary, "one of the best preservatives of morals," and even asked that George send him excerpts of the diary for his inspection. "Time was," he wrote to his son, "when I took it for granted that your life was sober, regular, and industrious, now I need weekly assurance." He also urged that George join the Boston Society for the Suppression of Intemperance in order to save himself from the "insatiable and all devouring calamity" of alcoholism. George tried and failed and tried again and failed again. When John Quincy was driven from the White House by the triumphant forces of Andrew Jackson, he wrote to George to come to Washington and help the retiring first family return to Quincy. George went into a profound funk. Perhaps he was terrified that his father would discover his new debts, or his involvement with a chambermaid named Eliza Dolph, who was already making demands on behalf of their illegitimate child, or perhaps he simply could not bear any confrontation with his awesome father, the defeated President. "He complains of dejection, low spirits, and inability to occupy himself," Charles observed "and this acts upon reflections of a melancholy kind in regard to Father and himself."

John Quincy insisted, and so George went to Providence and boarded the steamer *Benjamin Franklin* for New York. He complained of a headache and said that he could hear the ship's engines talking, repeatedly saying, "Let it be! Let it be!" He claimed that other passengers had broken into his room, but a search showed nothing missing. He went to bed, then got up again. He accused another passenger of spreading stories about him. He got a candle and routed several other passengers out of bed, then gave up and returned to his own cabin. About three A.M. he went to Captain E. S. Bunker and asked to be put ashore. He said that the other passengers had been laughing at him. Before Captain Bunker could settle the matter, he was suddenly called away on other business, and shortly after that, George Washington Adams mysteriously fell overboard. His body washed up near City Island two weeks later.

Louisa's reaction to the news was, in John Quincy's words, "not to be described." She began suffering a raging fever and a wracking cough. John Quincy, too, felt a grief that "I never knew before. . . . My sensations . . . were agonizing. The power of prayer alone is left." Prayer, yes, but Louisa's prayers were lacerations. "God almighty forgive me!" she wrote of having left the child in Quincy during her diplomatic wanderings. "I was not worthy to keep [him] and my sin was visited on [him]." And she never forgave John Quincy his sterile yearning to be the President. Even when George was still alive, she had once written: "In this agony of agonies can ambition repay such sacrifices? Never."

Under a cloud of bitterness and desperation, John Quincy returned to his father's old house near the sea, and he planted walnut trees and read the Bible and worried about his catarrh and his lumbago, and then, scarcely more than a year after his retirement, he was asked if an ex-President would consent to fill a mere Congressional seat. Louisa complained of his "insatiable passion" for politics, but John Quincy was adamant. "I must fulfill my Destiny," he said. His destiny, finally, was to speak out again and again on what he called "that outrage upon the goodness of God, human slavery." The Adamses have often been derided for being out of tune with their times, and this was certainly true on the question of slavery. Slavery was the issue on which all great statesmen, from Jefferson to Webster, equivocated and compromised, and to be a successful politician in the early nineteenth century meant collaboration and acquiescence. In the case of John Quincy Adams, on the other hand, the very qualities that made him an unsuccessful President made him a brilliant opponent of slavery: he was stubborn, moralistic, uncompromising, indifferent to popularity, quite willing to stand alone for what he conceived to be right. In this combat, he was so isolated that at the age of seventy he looked back over his lifetime and observed, "I can scarcely recollect a single instance of success in anything that I ever undertook." Yet he absolutely would not give in. He was to serve seventeen proud years in the House, until, on February 21, 1848, in the middle of a vote to award medals to several generals in the Mexican War—Adams had just voted "No"—he collapsed. His last words, that evening, were "This is the end of earth, but I am composed."

Louisa was to live on for another four years, "thoroughly weary," as her grandson later wrote in *The Education of Henry Adams*, "of being beaten about a stormy world." In her weariness, though, she too finally reached a kind of serenity. "To the boy," Adams wrote, "she seemed singularly peaceful, a vision of silver gray . . . ; an exotic, like her Sevres china; an object of deference to everyone . . . but hardly more Bostonian than she had been fifty years before, on her wedding day, in the shadow of the Tower of London. [Adams] never dreamed that from her might come some of those doubts and self-questionings, those hesitations, those rebellions against law and discipline, which marked more than one of her descendants."

Charles Francis Adams, named for the wastrel uncle who had died of cirrhosis, seemed to be stillborn at birth. He lay silent for five minutes before showing any sign of life. It was an appropriate beginning for this most staid and silent of the Adamses. "Grave, sober, formal, precise and reserved" were the words he later used to describe himself, adding, in his diary: "A man's heart should be known only to his Maker." When Charles was four, he encountered the Emperor Alexander out on a stroll in St. Petersburg, and since he shyly said nothing, the emperor asked what languages he knew. English, French, German, and Russian, said John Quincy, who was supervising his education. "*Une jeune homme très éclairé*," said the emperor. His grandmother Abigail agreed. "A thinking boy," she called him.

Like his older brothers, George and John, Charles Francis went to Harvard; like them, he was unhappy there and did not do well. He confessed that he was "addicted to depraved habits," specifically "billiards, drinking, parties and riding." "Preserve your morals pure and let your scholarship be as it pleases heaven," John Quincy scolded him. "If I must give up all expectations of success or distinction for you in this life preserve me from the harrowing thought of your perdition in the next." Like his brothers, Charles proceeded to the study of law and nourished a modest but unformed desire to write (the traditional image of the Adamses as frustrated politicians is misleading; they were generally more successful as politicians than as writers). What markedly differentiated Charles Francis from his brothers, aside from a more stable and stolid character, was that he encountered an immensely rich girl named Abigail Brooks. He soon began to love her, as, he said, "a woman ought to be loved—sincerely, fervently, and yet with purity and respect."

Abigail was the daughter of Peter Chardon Brooks, perhaps the richest man in Boston. (At his death in 1849, he left an estate of $2 million.) Son of a minister, orphaned at fourteen, Brooks had found work as a clerk to a marine insurance firm that operated out of the Bunch of Grapes Tavern on State Street. He worked long hours, rose in prosperity, and married well, to the daughter of Nathaniel Gorham, a delegate to the Constitutional Convention of 1787 and an investor with vast holdings in the wilderness of western New York. Brooks was prepared to bestow a fortune on his daughter, and he was dismayed to find that Abigail had agreed to marry a young man who, though undeniably the son of the President, was only nineteen years old, knew no profession, and had no income except an allowance of $1,000 per year. Such an engagement, Brooks wrote to the White House, was "not a thing to be spoken of." John Quincy, thus challenged, stopped his customary harassment of his sons and rose to the defense. Despite Charles's youth, he said, he had agreed to the engagement because Charles was "sedate and considerate; his disposition studious, and somewhat reserved; his sense of honour high, and delicate—his habits domestic and regular." Besides, Charles and Abigail had agreed to wait two years before getting married. Brooks thereupon agreed to let his daughter Abby "act at her pleasure," and he expressed regrets if his previous objections had caused "a moment's pain . . . to anyone."

Gore Vidal has used the term "hypergamy" to describe this persistent Adams custom of marrying well, "that obligatory act of all families destined to distinguish themselves." This was not true of all the Adamses, of course, but it seems to be generally true that those Adamses who married well prospered, and those who married badly failed. Starting with Deacon John Adams' marriage to Susanna Boylston, daughter of a distinguished physician, the Adamses who married well acquired from their wives not only money but a higher social position, for though the women of the eighteenth and nineteenth centuries could not make independent use of their wealth and position, they could be remarkably important as vehicles for the transmission of family wealth from generation to generation.

Even when engaging in "hypergamy," however, the Adamses had a deplorable tendency to analyze their acquisitions. Charles Francis was not so blunt as John had been in his letters to Abigail, nor so malicious as Henry was to be in his letters about Clover, but he nonetheless recorded in his diary a rigorous examination of the young Abigail Brooks. Her education was "faulty," he wrote, and she had a tendency to indulge in "hasty errors" and "unmeaning and loud nonsense." She was not beautiful, he decided, but her face was "expressive," and there was "a frankness, a simplicity about her manner" that he preferred to "the studied elegance of an accomplished belle." Perhaps there was an element of guilt in those stern judgments. To a modern observer who can view the young Abigail only in the portrait by William E. West, she looks rather luscious, with full lips and large brown eyes. She also has, however, a certain look of conventionality, like those Bachrach girls once known as debutantes who still stare prettily from the society pages of *The New York Times* but now report that they are studying psychology.

Marriage to such a girl freed Charles Francis from the need to struggle with the law. He became, instead, a gentleman of leisure. He wrote articles for the Boston newspapers. He managed his father's confused financial affairs and restored him from near-bankruptcy to prosperity (John Quincy, typically thankless, told him that property was no longer "of value to him"). And there came children. Two years after the marriage, in 1831, Abigail gave birth to Louisa, and then followed, with remarkable regularity, John Quincy II in 1833, Charles Francis, Jr., in 1835, Henry Brooks in 1838, and Arthur in 1841. By then, the family needed a new house, so Peter Chardon Brooks bought them one at 57 Mt. Vernon Street, on Beacon Hill. It had, according to the bitter recollections of Charles Francis, Jr., only one large and sunny room on the second floor, which "my father fixed on for his library regardless of other considerations." The house, he went on, an old man by then, "threw a shadow across my whole early life. . . . And when, forty-seven years later—my mother having died and the house having been emptied of everything—I crossed the threshold for the last time, and turned the key in the door, I walked away with a distinct sense of relief. . . . I have not a single pleasant recollection associated with No. 57 Mt. Vernon Street. There hangs about it, stretching through a memory covering long years, a monotonous atmosphere of winter gloom."

But summer, too, still returns to Mt. Vernon Street, and only an Adams could fail to enjoy the house at Number 57. About a block east of Louisburg Square, it is a five-story red-brick building, built early in the nineteenth century. It is a very simple house, square and sober, without even shutters on the plain windows. The only gesture of frivolity is an iron grillwork porch on the second floor. Out in front stands a giant chestnut tree that must have sheltered Charles Francis' sons throughout their childhood. All of this is protected now by its designation as a National Landmark, and it needs protection of a sort that Charles Francis Adams never anticipated. A few doors up the street on the way to the State House, at Number 47, a similar brick building has become the headquarters of the Suffolk University College of Business Administration, and a hand-lettered sign in the window says: "Do not park motorcycles on sidewalk."

7

DISTINCTLY BRANDED

THE TRIUMPH of Henry Adams' *Education* was that it convinced the
world that the self-portrait was a true one, that Adams had been,
all his long life, even in his infancy, a tiny, wizened old man,
snapping and wheezing at the futility of existence. "He seemed to
know nothing—to be groping in darkness—to be falling forever in
space," this highly cerebral historian wrote, "and the worst depth
consisted in the assurance, incredible as it seemed, that no one
knew more." It was the triumph, in turn, of Adams' principal
biographer, Ernest Samuels, to convince us that the *Education* is a
masterpiece of disguise and deception. "As students of Adams
know," he wrote with a stern invocation of academic consensus,
"the *Education* not only distorts and suppresses many of the facts of
his life, but it often falls into plain factual error." Far from being a
querulous cynic, Samuels demonstrated, the young Henry Adams
was, as he put it, "a very human and ardent idealist," a youth
dedicated to the application of moral purpose and the politics of
reform. But it is the triumph of the artist, finally, to outlast his
critics and biographers. Even after we have been persuaded that
the white-bearded wit who wrote the *Education* distorted his portrait of his own youth, we nonetheless turn back to that portrait to
see how Adams chose to imagine that youth.

The very first note, characteristically, is one of infantile helplessness. "Under the shadow of the Boston State House," Adams begins, "[in a] little passage called Hancock Avenue [on] February 16,
1838, a child was born, and christened later by his uncle, the

minister of the First Church after the tenets of Bostonian Unitarianism, as Henry Brooks Adams." There immediately follows, with a touch of the antisemitism that occasionally stained Adams' later writings, the confession of inadequacy: "Had he been born in Jerusalem under the shadow of the Temple and circumcised in the Synagogue by his uncle the high priest, under the name of Israel Cohen, he would scarcely have been more distinctly branded, and not much more heavily handicapped in the races of the coming century." In Adams' case, of course, the brand consisted of being the son of a very rich statesman, the grandson and great grandson of presidents, and when he contemplated this circumstance a bit further, the handicap seemed somewhat less onerous. "Probably no child, born in the year, held better cards than he," he observed, though he added an immediate touch of suspicion as to "whether life was an honest game of chance, or whether the cards were marked and forced." And then the final self-judgment on this accident of birth: "As it happened, he never got to the point of playing the game at all; he lost himself in the study of it, watching the errors of the players."

The most vivid passages in these early pages of the *Education* are not these self-judgments, however, but rather the evocations of the senses. His first recollection, he said, was one of color, the color yellow. He was three years old, in the family house in Quincy, when he suddenly "found himself sitting on a yellow kitchen floor in strong sunlight." And then the sense of taste. Shortly before his fourth birthday, he developed scarlet fever, and lay for several days "as good as dead," but all he subsequently remembered of that illness was the arrival of an aunt in the sickroom, "bearing in her hand a saucer with a baked apple."

Quincy represented a "drunken" sense of "liberty, diversity, outlawry," but every winter the family moved back to Mt. Vernon Street, which represented not just "restraint [and] law" but also the modern age of technology. The house on Mt. Vernon Street "had already a bathroom, a water-supply, a furnace and gas. The superiority of Boston was evident, but a child liked it no better for that." The differences between Boston and Quincy were also embodied in the child's two grandfathers. Peter Chardon Brooks presented to each of his grandchildren, at birth, a silver mug. From the other grandfather, John Quincy Adams, each child received a

Bible, with "the proper inscription" on the flyleaf "in the President's trembling hand."

Brooks is a shadowy specter, hardly mentioned in the *Education* as other than "amiable and sympathetic." The contrasting figure of John Quincy Adams, aged seventy-one when Henry was born, now living the crabbed life of an elder statesman in permanent opposition to the rest of the world, looms like a giant, a wizard, an object of wonder. The boy crept about in his grandfather's study, searching for foreign coins, playing with the old man's sword cane, keeping watch on the row of inverted tumblers where the former President tried vainly to supervise the transformation of caterpillars into moths. John Quincy Adams still rose every morning at dawn, lit his fire with flint and steel, and went out to survey the progress of the peach trees that he had grown from pits. And then to make notes, and keep journals, and write to his friends in far places. His grandson remembered him hunched over his desk for hours, his fingertips perpetually stained with ink.

And then the unforgettable scene of young Henry's noisy refusal, one day, to go to school, until the door to the ex-President's library opened and the old man silently marched down the steps. "Putting on his hat, he took the boy's hand without a word, and walked with him, paralyzed by awe, up the road to the town." For a mile, under a hot sun, the ex-President led the unruly schoolboy to his class, and then silently went home again. "He had shown no temper, no irritation, no personal feeling, and had made no display of force. Above all, he had held his tongue . . . ; he had uttered no syllable of revolting cant about the duty of obedience and the wickedness of resistance to law; he had shown no concern in the matter; hardly even a consciousness of the boy's existence."

The old man, as Henry later reflected on the scene, was probably thinking much less about his grandson than about "the iniquities of President Polk," for all Adamses, when expelled from the halls of power, were inclined to look back on their successors as usurpers. "As for the White House," Henry wrote, "all the boy's family had lived there, and, barring the eight years of Andrew Jackson's reign, had been more or less at home there ever since it was built. The boy half thought he owned it, and took for granted that he should some day live in it."

Perhaps Charles Francis Adams unconsciously thought the same thing, though he had no specific plan to fulfill the unspoken wish. He met in his study from time to time with a few worthy and like-minded Bostonians, notably Richard Henry Dana and the future Senator Charles Sumner, to decry the general decline of public spirit and the inexorable spread of slavery. The only result, in his son's recollection, was that all such troublemakers were "socially ostracized."

Just three months after the death of John Quincy Adams in 1848, the Whigs convened in Philadelphia, ignored the protestations of the antislavery forces, and awarded the presidential nomination to General Zachary Taylor, a Virginia slaveholder and a hero of the Mexican War. The "Conscience Whigs" from eighteen states promptly bolted the party and called a convention in Buffalo to nominate an antislavery candidate, perhaps someone as high-principled and impractical as the Massachusetts Delegate Charles Francis Adams. The most popular leader they could find, however, was the rather unprincipled former President Martin Van Buren, and so, in one of those deals characteristic of American politics, they nominated Van Buren for President and Adams for Vice-President. Adams himself had publicly condemned Van Buren as a man who made "a trade of public affairs" and was loyal to no philosophy "but his own interest." Just as John Quincy had made a deal with Clay to win the White House, however, Charles Francis now persuaded himself that Van Buren had reformed, and that the only purpose of the Buffalo convention was "to effect high ends without a whisper of bargain and sale." The new coalition against the westward expansion of slavery called itself the Free Soil Party, with the slogan: "Free soil, free speech, free labor, and free men."

Zachary Taylor easily defeated the Democrats' Lewis Cass. The Free Soilers won about ten percent of the vote but carried not a single state and won no electoral votes. Adams professed himself content. He felt "perfect satisfaction," he wrote in his diary, "in the idea that my duty has been honestly done."

Henry Adams often wrote of his youth as though he had been an only child. In fact, the house was always full of rambunctious children, and their leader was Henry's older sister Louisa. She was seven years older than he, and he adored her. She was quoted in later family chronicles as saying that she would marry an African to get away from Quincy, but she ended by marrying a wealthy Philadelphian named Charles Kuhn and going to live in Italy. When Henry went to Berlin after Harvard and tried halfheartedly to study civil law, she rescued him and carried him off to the South. "She was the first young woman he was ever intimate with," Henry later wrote, "—quick, sensitive, willful, or full of will, energetic, sympathetic and intelligent enough to supply a score of men with ideas."

Then came John Quincy II, who took his name seriously enough to become a lawyer and to run for political office. Indeed, he ran for governor half a dozen times, but always as a Democrat in a Republican era, and thus doomed to defeat. But cheerfully doomed. His greatest passion was to go fishing. And then Charles Francis, Jr., the cavalry colonel, who decided after the war that the future lay not in politics but in business, specifically in railroads, and so, like an Adams, he maneuvered his way into the presidency of the Union Pacific, and, again like an Adams, was driven from office by the forces of Jay Gould. "I have known, and known tolerably well, a good many 'successful' men . . . during the last half-century," he observed in his old age, when he had rededicated himself to the writing of history, "and a less interesting crowd I do not care to encounter . . . either in this world or the next."

And then, after Henry, the babies, Arthur, and Mary, and Brooks. Mary stayed close to her increasingly invalid mother until she finally went off to marry Dr. H. P. Quincy, and then only Brooks stayed on in the old house until 1927, cranky, irascible Brooks, who once confessed that "people don't like me and have no patience with me; they won't even listen to what I say." What he had to say, once, at a dinner party, was a marriage proposal, and when he was rejected, he could only offer the ultimate Adams retort: "Why you damned fool!"

Of these younger Adams children, the mysterious one is Arthur. He was born in 1841, when Henry was three, and he died in 1846, when Henry was eight. According to the traditional views of historians and biographers, Henry Adams is important as a thinker, and his thought begins only with his entering Harvard. So none of the biographies devotes more than a sentence or two to the brother who died at the age of five. Arthur left no precocious journals, and we know very little about him. Yet in the journals of Charles Francis Adams, there is a cry of anguish at the sudden attack of croup that began choking his youngest son.

"*Monday, Feb. 2, 1846:* . . . The night was much broken by uneasiness on account of the sickness of one of the children, Arthur. *Feb. 3:* . . . Arthur seemed relieved this morning although his attack was a fierce and unusual one. . . . *Feb. 4:* . . . Arthur's case resolved by the physicians into cough and seizure. Much alarmed about him. *Feb. 5:* . . . Night passed in watching him with great anxiety. *Feb. 9:* What need of a detail of the agony of this interval of time. . . . My poor, beautiful boy, Arthur, expired at a quarter past six o'clock this day, having carried on a most terrible contest with this arch disease. Stunned by this blow and exhausted by watching and attendance night and day during the whole period, I could do little else than rest my swimming head and yielding limbs upon my bed, where I soon forgot my woes in sleep." Arthur's grandparents were equally stricken. "He [has] passed away, like a delightful vision," John Quincy wrote in his journal, "and leaves a memory of blighted hopes and blasted prospects, for which there is no consolation to his bereaved parents or to me." And Louisa wrote that if it was God's will "thus to try you, and to take from you this lovely blossom of great promise; bow down with humility to him who knows what is best for us." But Charles Francis could only groan. "There is not an hour passes in which we do not miss that cheerful, noisy voice and those pattering feet, and that inquisitive eager mind and those speaking eyes, which made the house a living and a breathing symbol of himself."

Henry never mentioned Arthur in the *Education*—but then he never mentioned Clover either—so it is impossible to determine the effects of Arthur's death. It is difficult to believe, though, that an eight-year-old boy would not be powerfully impressed by the week-long death throes of a younger brother and the prostration of his parents. We can best imagine his reaction to the disaster by observing the depths of his anguish at the subsequent fate of his sister Louisa, who, as he wrote, "faced death, as most women do, bravely and even gaily, racked slowly to unconsciousness, but yielding only to violence, as a soldier sabred in battle."

The schooling of Henry Adams, to be distinguished from the education, was an unhappy affair. "In any and all forms," he later wrote, "the boy detested school." The first form he encountered, when he was about ten years of age, was the classroom of David B. Tower, who operated a private school in the basement of the Park Street Church, just across the Common from the Adams house on Mt. Vernon Street. Charles, who had gone to the same classes a few years earlier, remembered Tower as "a very portly, good-natured man . . . and a good teacher," but Henry's judgment was less amiable. "He hated it because he was here with a crowd of other boys and compelled to learn by memory a quantity of things that did not amuse him. His memory was slow, and the effort painful."

Customarily, the Adams boys proceeded to Boston Latin to prepare for Harvard, but the school was beginning to balk at accepting pupils from families that didn't pay Boston taxes. Charles Francis Adams, who considered his Quincy taxes good and sufficient, sent Henry to a new school founded at 20 Boylston Place by Epes Sargent Dixwell, longtime master of Boston Latin. There the drilling continued: Latin, Greek, mathematics, history, geography, composition, and rhetoric. Henry remained hostile: "He always considered his school days, from ten to sixteen years old, as time thrown away."

Then Harvard, fair Harvard. "No one took Harvard seriously," Henry later observed. "All went there because their friends went there. . . . It taught little, and that little ill, but it left the mind open, free from bias, ignorant of facts, but docile." Adams' biographers have demonstrated that he was being somewhat malicious in this withering judgment of his college. He actually learned a good deal, and enjoyed it. He was inspired not only by the lectures of Louis Agassiz but by those of James Russell Lowell, who had just succeeded Henry Wadsworth Longfellow in the Smith professorship of modern literature. Besides, one of the main functions of Harvard—perhaps of any university—is to permit the students to teach one another, and themselves. Adams walked the Yard with students like Oliver Wendell Holmes, Phillips Brooks, and Henry Hobson Richardson, and he read widely in Emerson, Thackeray, Carlyle.

And he wrote. He began keeping a daily diary, as his father had long urged him to do—a diary that he was to destroy after Clover's death—and from these regular orderings of his thoughts came a series of essays in the new *Harvard Magazine*, his impressions of Holden Chapel and of his rooms in Hollis Hall ("the coldest, dirtiest and gloomiest in Cambridge)." In an essay on "Reading in College," he came to a rather sentimentally valedictorian conclusion that "the most vulgar mind and the poorest understanding must be somewhat elevated and instructed by two years of contact with what is better than itself." In a similar spirit, he wrote a Bowdoin Prize essay on Seneca and St. Paul (he won second prize, $30) and challenged his readers to "say if they can that the world is not infinitely better than it was." And in this same spirit, finally, on a hot day in June of 1858 the black-gowned young Adams rose to speak as the Class Day orator and told his audience that "this nation of ours furnishes the grandest theatre in the world for the exercise of that refinement of mind and those high principles which it is a disgrace to us if we have not acquired."

There is something touching about the arrogant idealism of Henry Adams at twenty, but the old man was probably right when he dismissed these youthful declarations as "thin, commonplace, feeble." The same adjectives might just as well apply to the college that had trained him in such oratory. It was, still, a glum sort of place, summoning its students to prayer every morning at seven, and again at dusk. It graded every action—eight points for a perfect recitation in Greek, 48 points for a sophomore English composition, minus eight points for oversleeping, minus 16 points for playing a musical instrument during study hours. Adams' academic work was erratic, and disciplinary demerits came frequently, for smoking in the Yard, for cutting classes in philosophy, for "calling up to a college window under aggravating circumstances." He ended with a rank of 44th in a class of 89. Looking back on his graduation, he observed that "as yet he knew nothing. Education had not yet begun."

His older brothers had both gone on to law school, and so Henry stumbled into the idea of going to Berlin to study civil law, learning only upon his arrival in the German capital that he didn't know enough German to study anything, much less civil law. He hated that too, for "Berlin was a poor . . . provincial town, simple, dirty, uncivilized, and in most respects disgusting." He tried to learn

German, first by taking lessons, and then by the odd device of enrolling as a pupil in a local high school. He found his fellow students "rather sympathetic" but regimented and oppressed beyond the imaginings of mere Puritanism. "The German high school," he later wrote, "was something very near an indictable nuisance." And he was miserably lonely. "Fellows who can live on music or art or women are all very well here," he wrote to Charles, adding cryptically: "The first two are good. The last is a damned humbug."

When April brought the first wan sun to Berlin, Adams fled southward with three Harvard friends—Ben Crowninshield, James J. Higginson, and John Bancroft—on one of those traditional walking tours through the woods of Thuringia. Adams stayed for a time in Dresden, pretending to renew his study of law, but actually devoting more time to Schiller's *Thirty Years' War* and to such novelties as *Rienzi* and *Tannhäuser*. That summer, the wandering continued, across Bavaria and Switzerland to join forces with Louisa and undertake a tour of northern Italy. Returning to Berlin in the fall, he found it a "cold, unfriendly, wet, soulless town," and so he again retreated to Dresden. There, while still struggling over German irregular verbs, he spent three mornings a week learning to fence. He was boarding at the home of a botanist, Heinrich Reichenbach, and he became rather attached to Reichenbach's daughter, Fräulein Augusta, who had "a will of her own and gives me the most immense delight." To his mother, however, he wrote that Augusta "might be dangerous if—well, if it only weren't that to me she isn't. I don't know why. One can't explain these things."

Springtime lured him to Italy again, to Rome, "seductive beyond resistance," and to the steps of Santa Maria di Ara Coeli, where, as Gibbon had recorded, "the idea of writing the decline and fall of the city first started to my mind." Adams reverently sat in Gibbon's place, "curiously wondering that not an inch had been gained by Gibbon—or all the historians since—towards explaining the Fall." Seduced but baffled by Rome, Adams wandered southward, for he was planning to write a series of impressionistic "letters" for the *Boston Courier*, and in Naples he heard the first rumors of an impending invasion of Sicily by the guerrilla forces of Giuseppe Garibaldi. Some odd instinct, some need to move toward the center of things, inspired Adams to visit the U.S. consul and have himself assigned as a courier bearing official dispatches to Palermo. In Palermo, by now in the hands of the insurgents, he coolly marched into the Senatorial Palace and interviewed Garibaldi. The Italian leader "had his plain red shirt on, precisely like a fireman," and Adams was able to boast to the readers of the *Courier*, "Here I was at last, then, face to face with one of the great events of our day."

In Boston, of course, the only event of the day was the threat of civil war, which was passing very rapidly from threat into reality. Charles Francis Adams, the onetime Free Soiler, had finished editing his grandfather's papers and then recaptured in 1858 the Congressional seat once held by his father. Re-election in the 1860 campaign of Abraham Lincoln was simple enough. Adams, however, was a supporter not of Lincoln but of Senator William Seward of New York, an old friend of the family, "a slouching, slender figure," as Henry was to describe him, "a head like a wise macaw; a beaked nose; shaggy eyebrows . . . and perpetual cigar." In that treacherous "secession winter" of 1860–61, Senator Seward, with Congressman Adams at his side, repeatedly preached a mild doctrine of conciliation and thus helped to avert the danger of a Southern *coup* until Lincoln could be inaugurated. Lincoln knew and disliked the fragility of his authority. He installed his rival Seward as Secretary of State and permitted Seward to insist on Adams as minister to London.

Adams was not particularly pleased. The announcement, according to the diary of his son Charles, "fell on our breakfast table like a veritable bombshell, scattering confusion and dismay. . . . My mother at once fell into tears and deep agitation; foreseeing all sorts of evil consequences and absolutely refusing to be comforted." Despite Mrs. Adams' unhappiness, Adams felt that he could not decline the position. He journeyed to Washington, presented himself to Seward, and was ushered into the White House, a place which, as Charles Francis, Jr., later recorded, "Mr. Adams associated most closely with his father, and his father's trained bearing and methodical habits." A door opened, and in came "a tall, large-featured, shabbily dressed man of uncouth appearance [wearing] much-kneed, ill-fitting trousers, coarse stockings and worn slippers." The newly appointed minister expressed his gratitude to President Lincoln for his assignment. "Very kind of you to say so, Mr. Adams," said Lincoln, "but you are not my choice. You are Seward's man."

Then, leaning back in his chair and folding his hands behind his head, Lincoln made it clear that all such decisions were simply part of the vast system of patronage. "Well, Governor," he said to Seward, "I've this morning decided that Chicago post-office appointment."

Adams was hurt, pained, as he was presumably intended to be. "He never recovered from his astonishment," the younger Charles later recalled, "nor did the impression then made ever wholly fade from his mind." He took his own peculiar revenge. Appointed on March 20, he dawdled for six weeks to await the marriage of his oldest son, John Quincy II, to Fanny Crowninshield (when Henry married Clover, by contrast, Adams didn't make any effort to attend at all). Not until May 1 did he set sail with his wife and his three youngest children, Henry, Mary, and Brooks. When he made his belated appearance in London, he discovered that the British government had just declared its neutrality in the Civil War, thus implying that both sides were equal. Charles Francis Adams delivered a protest. It was ignored.

Despite that unpromising start, Adams was well suited to his new position. Intelligent, meticulous, aloof, he was an imposing figure. Charles, Jr., for one, disliked the element of icy rectitude in that character—"hereditarily warped," he said of his father—but Henry came to admire this same quality. "Charles Francis Adams," he wrote, "was singular for mental poise—absence of self-assertion or self-consciousness,—the faculty of standing apart without seeming aware that he was alone,—a balance of mind and temper that neither challenged nor avoided notice, nor admitted question of superiority or inferiority, of jealousy, of personal motives, from any source, even under great pressure."

Acting as the legation's unpaid private secretary, Henry was awed at the sight of his father in action, for though we may now devalue the role that Adams played, he did fulfill an important function in keeping Britain neutral and restraining London's covert support of the Confederacy. His father's successes not only renewed Henry's somewhat dissipated sense of the Adams tradition but filled him with a lifelong belief in the efficacy of diplomacy among the great powers. He tried, with limited success, to convey his new perceptions in a series of anonymous dispatches to *The New York Times*—"American Topics in England," "Affairs in London," and so on. The main purpose was to support his father's diplomacy by preaching moderation and dissuading Americans from wild thoughts of seizing Canada. But his social pretensions and his instinct for gossip inevitably got him into trouble. After a journey to Manchester to inspect the cotton factories, he wrote for the *Boston Courier* an informal article contrasting the friendliness of Manchester society to the arrogance of London. "In Manchester, I am told, it is still the fashion for the hosts to see that their guests enjoy themselves," he wrote with some bitterness. "In London the guests shift for themselves, and a stranger had better depart at once as soon as he has looked at the family pictures. . . . In Manchester it is still the fashion to finish balls with showy suppers. . . . In London one is regaled with thimblefulls of ice cream and hard seed cakes." It remained only for the editor of the *Courier* to announce proudly Adams' authorship of the originally anonymous article, and for that announcement to drift back to the London press. *The Times* of London delightedly urged Adams to "persevere in frequenting *soirees* and admiring family pictures . . . and we shall not despair." The *Examiner*, on the other hand, warned all London hostesses "to be more careful of their cakes, the softness and the seeds thereof." Crushed and humiliated, Henry dreaded the possibility of being further exposed as the anonymous special correspondent of *The New York Times*, from which he now resigned, but nobody seemed to make that connection. Not even Charles Francis Adams, who shared a study with his son. Indeed, it was a measure of Charles Francis' peculiar character that he never once mentioned that son's public discomfiture.

Henry tried to settle down to the diplomatic routine—"private secretary in the morning, son in the afternoon, young man about town in the evening"—but he found that "for him nothing whatever could be gained by escorting American ladies to drawing-rooms or American gentlemen to levees at St. James' Palace, or bowing solemnly to people with great titles, at Court Balls, or even by awkwardly jostling royalty at garden parties; all this was done for the Government." Adams himself found much greater pleasure in meeting people like the young Swinburne, and "listening to the rush of Swinburne's talk. . . . the best talking of the time," or hearing the stoutly independent M.P. John Bright declare that "We English are a nation of brutes, and ought to be exterminated to the last man." But as he circled about London, Adams was continually embroiled in petty controversy with the legation's official secretary,

Benjamin Moran, who felt that his duties were being usurped by the minister's son. Adams "is very conceited," Moran recorded in his diary, "and talks like a goose."

When the war finally ended, Charles Francis Adams duly returned home, in 1868, bringing with him a son who felt himself lost in a nation he had not seen for almost a decade, "an estray, a flotsam or jetsam of wreckage, [as out of place as] the Indians or the buffalo, who had been ejected from their heritage by his own people." There remained, as a refuge, only the press, that "last resource of the educated poor. . . . Any man who was fit for nothing else could write an editorial." Adams was glacially condescending when he described journalism as a way to "work off on a helpless public . . . the enormous mass of misinformation accumulated in ten years of nomad life," and he was never more glacial than in his assessment of a Washington correspondent's need for highly placed sources of information. "The first step, of course, was the making of acquaintance," he observed in the *Education*, "and the first acquaintance was naturally the President, to whom an aspirant to the press officially paid respect." Adams already knew the Attorney General, William Evarts, so Evarts took him to the White House to meet Andrew Johnson. "The interview was brief," Adams recalled, "and consisted in the stock remark common to monarchs and valets, that the young man looked even younger than he was."

Despite the valetudinarian tone of his memoirs, the Henry Adams who arrived in Washington at the age of thirty was assertive and aggressive and quite determined to save the nation from its new rulers. Senator Sumner's private secretary, Moorfield Story, was to remember the newcomer at a Washington dinner as "a strange young man there who was monopolizing the conversation, as it seemed to me, and laying down the law with a certain assumption." The law was that of reform, both political and social—civil-service reform, meaning the abolition of the spoils system of political patronage; tariff reform, meaning the abolition of protective rates for every lobby that could influence Congress; currency reform, meaning the redemption of the wartime "greenbacks" in gold. Beyond such specific measures, though, reform meant a new and rather arrogant high-mindedness. "We want," as Henry wrote to his brother Charles, "a national set of young men like ourselves

or better, to start new influences not only in politics, but in literature, in law, in society, and throughout the whole social organism
of the country—a national school of our own generation."

Charles was already at work on an effort to expose the malefac-
tions and inefficiencies of the railroads, and Henry, despite his later
affectation of helplessness, quickly made arrangements to write
Washington articles for *The Nation* and the *New York Post*. "I want
to be advertised," he wrote to a friend, "and the easiest way is to
do something obnoxious and to do it well." His basic plan was to
work at a level between that of the journalist and that of the historian. Specifically, he wanted to write for *The North American Review*, a small but distinguished Boston quarterly of perhaps 1,000
readers, an annual assessment of the government at work, to be
called, each year, "The Session." His first attempt, published in
April of 1869, opened fire with a fine youthful indignation. Although he conceded that most Congressmen "are not venal," he
went on to assert that "a network of rings controls Congress," and
that the party organizations "have no decency and no shame." And
again: "We submit that Government is wrong in plundering the
people in order to support party organizations. . . ." Exaggerations, perhaps, but people paid attention, and Adams was delighted. "For once, I have smashed things generally," he wrote to
a friend, "and really exercised a distinct influence on public opinion
by acting on the limited number of cultivated minds. . . . If the
future goes straight, I will make my annual 'Session' an institution
and a power in the land."

The election of General Grant seemed, at the start, a sign of
renovation. Adams voted for him, and he nourished hopes that the
incoming administration would encourage such reformers as the
new senator from Missouri, Carl Schurz, and such young profes-
sionals as John Hay, onetime secretary to Lincoln and now an
envoy to Madrid. "The new president had unbounded popular
confidence," Adams wrote in his second (and last) "Session," in a
tone that so many hopeful journalists have applied to so many new
Presidents. "He was tied to no party. He was under no pledges.
He had the inestimable advantage of a military training, which,
unlike a political training, was calculated to encourage the moral
distinction between right and wrong." Unfortunately for Adams'
high hopes, of course, Grant had no intention of asserting his executive powers, for reform or anything else. All power devolved

onto the highly corruptible legislators, about whose susceptibilities Adams later quoted a cabinet member: "You can't use tact with a Congressman! A Congressman is a hog! You must take a stick and hit him on the snout!"

Years afterward, as he looked back on his disillusionment with Grant's inability to control his political subordinates, Adams still puzzled over the General's intellectual efforts, observing him as though he were some kind of turtle. Grant's colleagues, Adams concluded, "could never follow a mental process in his thoughts. They were not sure that he did think." Almost as bad, to the fastidious historian, was the President's version of social discourse, "as when he seriously remarked to a particularly bright young woman [perhaps Clover?] that Venice would be a fine city if it were drained." Such awkwardnesses might have been tolerable if an Adams could accept the general principle of human fallibility, but Henry was looking, like a Teilhard de Chardin poking at the bones of Peking Man, for evidence of Darwinian improvement. "That," as he began one of the most passionate sentences in the *Education* —"That, two thousand years after Alexander the Great and Julius Caesar, a man like Grant should be called—and should actually and truly be—the highest product of the most advanced evolution, made evolution ridiculous. . . . The progress of evolution from President Washington to President Grant was alone evidence enough to upset Darwin. . . . [Grant] was archaic and should have lived in a cave and worn skins."

General Grant appears to have been innocent of corruption, but the men around him were shameless. The Secretary of War, General William W. Belknap, took thousands of dollars to make an appointment in the Indian trade. The St. Louis "whiskey ring," which defrauded the government of millions of dollars in taxes, enjoyed the patronage of Grant's personal secretary, General Orville E. Babcock. The Navy Department, the Interior Department, the Post Office—everything was for sale. Focusing on perhaps the worst example of corruption in Grant's Washington, Adams raked in the outrageous details of Jay Gould's attempt to corner the gold market in September of 1869.

Gould, who was later to defeat Charles Francis, Jr., in a protracted struggle for control of the Union Pacific Railroad, impressed Henry as the embodiment of all the powers that he himself lacked. "His nature suggested survival from the family of spiders,"

Adams wrote in *The New York Gold Conspiracy*. "He spun webs, in corners and in the dark. His disposition to subtlety and elaboration of intrigue was irresistible. He had not a conception of moral principle." He was, in his way, a natural partner for Jim Fiske. "One was slight in person, dark, sallow, reticent and stealthy . . ; the other was large, florid, gross, talkative and obstreperous." The key figure in Gould's conspiracy, however, was Abel Corbin, Grant's brother-in-law. Gould bought him, and thus bought access to the President, and that access, no matter how innocently granted, made the gold corner feasible. Gould could learn in advance whatever the President planned, and with that knowledge he could begin bidding up the price of gold. He pushed it from $134 up to $162, and only then, when the bubble burst, did Fiske learn that Gould had betrayed him by secretly selling out; Fiske himself survived only by betraying his own supporters. Both men then retreated to their offices in a marble theater, where, as Adams observed, "few men cared to face Fiske's ruffians in order to force an entrance."

Adams could describe such scandals with both wit and contempt, but the political effect of his attacks was absolutely nil. The vast corruption of the Gilded Age was enveloping everyone. The gold conspiracy scandal, Adams declared, "smirched executive, judiciary, banks and corporate systems, professions and people, all the great active forces of society, in one dirty cesspool of vulgar corruption." Yet that scandal was a mere beginning. "Grant's administration outraged every rule of ordinary decency," Adams still raged in the *Education*. "Every hope or thought which had brought Adams to Washington proved to be absurd. No one wanted him; no one wanted any of his friends in reform; the blackmailer alone was the normal product of politics as business."

If this was the reality of postwar America, then, Henry Adams decided to escape "out of the dust and dirt of politics," as he wrote to a friend, and back to the leisurely pleasures of Europe. He had hardly arrived in England in that prewar June of 1870, however, before he received word that his sister Louisa was desperately ill in Italy. It had all happened suddenly, a violent and absurd event. Louisa had been riding in a horse cab in Bagni di Lucca, and there had been a collision. She was thrown from the cab and bruised her foot, nothing more than that. Then tetanus set in. Henry arrived at her bedside and found her "as gay and brilliant in the terrors of lockjaw as she had been in the careless joy of 1859." The sensuous surroundings made her condition all the more macabre. "The hot Italian summer brooded outside," he recalled years later, "over the marketplace and the picturesque peasants, and, in the singular color of the Tuscan atmosphere, the hills and vineyards of the Appenines seemed bursting with mid-summer blood. The sick-room itself glowed with the Italian joy of life. . . ." In a letter to a friend, Adams tried to speak lightly about the disaster: "Her talking is only a growl between her teeth and even this is quite often inarticulate, but we have learned to understand it pretty well." But the end was inevitable: "Hour by hour the muscles grew rigid, while the mind remained bright, until after ten days of fiendish torture she died in convulsions."

To lure Adams back to Cambridge was the ambition of Ephraim Whitman Gurney, newly appointed dean of the faculty at Harvard. "One of the most astute and ideal administrators in the world," as Adams later described him, Gurney had started that spring by offering Adams his own position as editor of *The North American Review*. Adams was reluctant to leave Washington and declined the offer, though keeping open the possibility of becoming the *Review*'s political editor. That summer, in Europe, Adams received a letter from Harvard's new president, Charles William Eliot, offering him an assistant professorship in medieval history. Once again, he declined. "Having now chosen a career," he said, "I am determined to go on in it as far as it will lead me."

Dean Gurney, who seems to have guided all the discussions of Adams' appointment, was not to be dissuaded. He approached Charles Francis Adams, who had declined the Harvard presidency in 1869, thus opening the way for Eliot, and who still remained a powerful member of the Board of Overseers. So when Henry returned from Europe after the Franco-Prussian War got under way in the fall of 1870, he found President Eliot, Dean Gurney, and the entire Adams family all prepared to insist on his new career. There occurred, then, the memorable scene that Adams eventually recorded in the *Education:* " 'But, Mr. President,' urged Adams, 'I know nothing about Mediaeval History.' With the courteous man-

Captain William Sturgis, c.1855.
He became immensely rich in the
China trade, doted on his grand-
daughter Clover. "The best child
in the world," he once called her.
Photograph by Josiah Hawes.
*Courtesy of the Massachusetts Histor-
ical Society.*

Clover Hooper at age of eight or
nine. Photograph by Southwork
and Hawes. *Courtesy of the Massachusetts Historical Society.*

Clover took this photograph of her father, Dr. Robert William Hooper, going out for
a drive at Beverly Farms, just a few years before his death shattered her life. *Courtesy of
the Massachusetts Historical Society.*

The parlor at Beverly Farms. Photograph by Clover. *Courtesy of the Massachusetts Historical Society.*

Clover's beloved brother, Ned Hooper, taken in 1859. Ned was the strong member of the family: a lawyer, Harvard treasurer, and art connoisseur. *Courtesy of the Harvard University Archives.*

Afternoon tea was one of Clover's rituals, so she posed her three terriers, Possum, Marquis, and Boojum, taking part in the same ceremony. *Courtesy of the Massachusetts Historical Society.*

Clover's portrait of Betsy Wilder, who reared all three Hooper children during the forty years she worked for the family. "An attendant mentor," Clover's aunt Carrie once called her. *Courtesy of the Massachusetts Historical Society.*

The Hooper cousins at Beverly Farms. Photograph by Clover. *Courtesy of the Massachusetts Historical Society.*

(*Left*) Abigail Smith Adams. *Courtesy of the New York Public Library.* (*Right*) John Adams. *Courtesy of the Granger Collection.*

(*Left*) John Quincy Adams. *Courtesy of the Library of Congress.* (*Right*) Louisa Johnson Adams. *Courtesy of The White House.*

Charles Francis Adams and his wife, Abigail, disapproved of Clover, who took this photograph of their disapproval. *Courtesy of the Massachussetts Historical Society.*

Clover's photograph of Henry Adams communing with Marquis. *Courtesy of the Massachusetts Historical Society.*

Louis Agassiz, "a great teacher, richly able to convey his own enthusiasm about the most arcane subjects," was the only lecturer whose teaching appealed to Henry Adams. Both Clover and her sister attended Agassiz's school. *Courtesy of the Library of Congress.*

A photograph of the Civil War, taken by Mathew Brady, whose work was an inspiration to Clover. *Courtesy of the Library of Congress.*

Clover was twenty-one when she watched Grant's victorious parade through Washington. "It was a strange feeling," she wrote, "to be so intensely happy and triumphant and yet to feel like crying." *Courtesy of the Library of Congress.*

Saint-Gaudens' sculpture of Colonel Shaw leading his black regiment off to war. "He seemed to me beautiful and awful," wrote James Greenleaf Whittier, "as an angel come down to lead the host of freedom." *Courtesy of the Library of Congress.*

For their honeymoon, the Adamses voyaged up the Nile. This is Clover's photograph of Henry in the stateroom of the *Isis. Courtesy of the Massachusetts Historical Society.*

(*Opposite*) Clover at twenty-six. The only known adult portrait. *Courtesy of the Massachusetts Historical Society.*

The *Isis* (*right*) at Philae. Clover was fascinated, but the strains of the voyage apparently brought on a crisis. *Courtesy of the Massachusetts Historical Society.*

A bold and assertive handwriting marked Clover's weekly letters to her father. Clover's sketch shows the Adamses lying seasick on their honeymoon trip to Europe. *Courtesy of the Massachusetts Historical Society.*

Clover is at the right and Henry is standing at the left at Wenlock Abbey. With them are Lady Pellington, Lady Cunliffe, Charles Milnes Gaskell, Sir Robert Cunliffe, and Lord Pellington. *Courtesy of the Massachusetts Historical Society.*

View of the Capitol at about the time the Adamses moved to Washington in 1877. Mark Twain called the vista of Pennsylvania Avenue "mean and cheap and dingy," but Adams regarded Washington as "the only place in America where society amuses me." *Courtesy of the Library of Congress.*

(Left) James Russell Lowell, who after thirteen years of teaching literature at Harvard sailed with the Adamses to Europe at the age of fifty-three to discover whether he was really a poet. *Courtesy of the National Portrait Gallery, the Smithsonian Institution.* *(Right)* Clarence King, noted geologist and member of "The Five of Hearts," the Adamses' elite group. Henry Adams predicted King would become "the richest and most many-sided genius of his day." *Courtesy of the Library of Congress.*

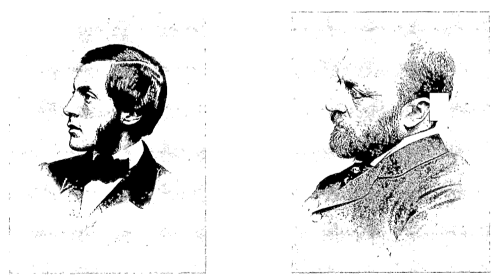

(Left) Charles William Eliot, once an unknown chemistry professor at MIT, became President of Harvard and hired Henry Adams to come and join him in revolutionizing American education. *Courtesy of the National Portrait Gallery, the Smithsonian Institution.* *(Right)* Henry James, the novelist, who admired Clover's "intellectual grace" and called her "a perfect Voltaire in petticoats." In his farewell letter to her he said she seemed to him "the incarnation of my native land." *Courtesy of the Granger Collection.*

Aunt Eunice, Dr. Hooper's elder sister, was a lifelong friend to Clover, who took this photograph of her. *Courtesy of the Massachusetts Historical Society.*

Saint-Gaudens' sculpture of William Dean Howells and his daughter Mildred. Henry gave Howells' *Their Wedding Journey* to Clover on the day they became engaged. *Courtesy of the National Portrait Gallery.*

The Adamses' new house under construction in December of 1884 on Washington's H Street. "We know just what we want," Clover wrote. *Courtesy of the Massachusetts Historical Society.*

John Milton Hay, Adams' best friend, photographed by Mathew Brady when Hay was private secretary to Abraham Lincoln. *Courtesy of the Granger Collection.*

Clover's portrait of Henry Hobson Richardson, the architect of the Adamses' house. *Courtesy of the Massachusetts Historical Society.*

Portrait of a Lady (and detail), by Anders Zorn, thought to be a painting of Elizabeth Cameron. *Courtesy of the National Collection of Fine Arts, Smithsonian Institution.*

The finished house typifies the massive Richardsonian style that Clover called "neo-Agnostic." The Hay-Adams Hotel now stands on the site. *Courtesy of the Library of Congress.*

Saint-Gaudens' sculpture over the Adamses' graves in Washington's Rock Creek Cemetery. Its creator wanted it to give "a strong impression of mystery." *Courtesy of the Library of Congress.*

8

THE ICE MELTS

IN THE LOBBY of a grimy concrete building on Manhattan's West Side, an old Fox Movietone News studio at the corner of Tenth Avenue and 54th Street, they have installed new dark-blue wall-to-wall carpeting and little globular lights that glow at the end of long rods, and the black receptionist with the turquoise scarf over her head ignores the babbling television set. That is how we can always tell when we are in the land of television: the TV set never stops, and nobody ever watches it.

The studio upstairs is one enormous room, perhaps 40 feet wide and 100 feet long. The floor of white plastic tiles has measurements built into it, so that it looks like a grid of measuring tapes, and no matter where we stand, we know exactly how far we are from one another. Overhead, the fluorescent lights inflict a relentless glare.

"Henry James?" someone calls out. "Where's Henry James?"

A fat man in a purple shirt responds to the call and joins in a hushed consultation at the row of plywood tables that form a kind of command post along one side of the studio. Here, surrounded by two dozen aides and adjutants, sits the producer, Virginia Kassel, a stocky woman in her forties, wearing a flowered dress. She seems cheerful but obviously worried. There have already been reports that her budget is crumbling before a tidal wave of unexpected production costs. Next to her sits Fred Coe, the director, looking very *sportif* in a tan windbreaker, and Sam Hall, the scriptwriter, masked by sunglasses. One of the assistants calls everyone to attention. The final rehearsal of Part XII of *The Adams Chronicles* is about to begin.

It is a dramatization of the romance between Henry Adams and Clover Hooper, and since recorded history provides virtually no details of this romance, we might as well watch to see how television imagines the event. There are no cameras involved at this point. The actors are simply reciting. Henry Adams is declared to be working in the Harvard Library. Clover appears and starts rummaging around on one of the shelves. She drops a book. He picks it up.

Henry: Miss Hooper!

Clover: Good morning, Mr. Adams. (Laughs) You look surprised.

Henry: At the sight of a woman in Harvard Library, yes. But I certainly don't object. (He looks at her book.) Plato! In the original!

Clover: Well, I don't like translations.

Henry: How wise of you.

Clover: So Dr. Gurney is going to teach me to read the language . . . (Pause).

Henry is an actor named Peter Brandon, fortyish, slender, bony, red-cheeked. He wears a faded maroon track jacket. Clover is played by an imposing actress named Gilmer McCormick, perhaps thirty, tall and strong. She has twisted her thick reddish-brown hair into a braid and wrapped it around her head. The script calls for her to be demure.

Clover: . . . Are you enjoying your professorship?

Henry: More than I ever thought possible. It's incredible what the students are teaching me.

Clover: Do you always deprecate yourself, Mr. Adams?

Henry: I beg your pardon?

Clover: Well, you did when we met at dinner last week. Is it a habit of yours? Or an affectation?

Henry: I never thought about it. A habit, undoubtedly. A subtle warning to strangers not to expect too much.

Clover: What a pleasant surprise. My first impression was wrong. Good morning, Mr. Adams.

Henry: Have a pleasant day, Miss Hooper.

(Music swells)

This implausible little scene appeared on millions of American television sets in the spring of 1976, near the end of the thirteen hour-long dramatizations that made up *The Adams Chronicles*. A five-year project timed for broadcasting on educational television stations during the nation's bicentennial celebrations, the series was subsidized by $5.2 million in grants from the National Endowment for the Humanities, the Mellon Foundation, and the Atlantic-Richfield Corporation. Then, through a series of union conflicts, deadline pressures, and general confusions, the series cost about $1.5 million more than had been budgeted. The result, with all its 250 settings and 3,000 costumes, managed to be showy, superficial, and unconvincing, and everybody loved it. Critics chorused praises, public television ratings soared, and more than 300 colleges scheduled the shows for their history classes. So no matter what one may think of *The Adams Chronicles*, the series of broadcasts and rebroadcasts will affect for many years the popular view of the Adams family.

The Adams scholars at the Massachusetts Historical Society had to approve each script, not for quality and not even for complete accuracy but rather to restrain the scriptwriters' imaginations within the limits of the innocuous. So not long after Henry and Clover have met, he takes her to a New Year's Eve party.

Clover: I've been reading as many of your articles as I can find. You could be a very *important* man.

Henry: You insult me, Miss Hooper. I think I am.

Clover: Important in a different way than you are. . . .

As they part, Adams asks, "Shall I see you soon?" Clover answers, after a weighty pause, "Whenever you like—*Henry.*" Two scenes later, Henry is already talking to his father of his hopes of getting married. "In short, sir, I'm in love. I don't know why. She respects me. She has the taste to admire my opinions, my skills, such as they are. I don't think until recently she's thought about marrying, perhaps because she didn't expect to find anyone who appreciates her as much as her own family does. But I do, you see."

In a parallel scene, Clover is shown talking to her own father.

Clover: He's a brilliant man, Father. Dr. Gurney says he has revolutionary methods for teaching history.

Dr. Hooper: How do you *feel* about him, Marian?

Clover: I *think* about him, father. He could be the most notable Adams of them all. . . .

The patterns of the script are simple. They portray a Clover excessively attached to her father, marrying Henry Adams not for love but to satisfy her intellectual ambitions. That neatly prepares the way for the suicide that will follow Dr. Hooper's death about forty-five minutes later.

Is that conventional explanation all that is necessary to account for Clover's desperate end? Sam Hall thinks so. He is a friendly, cherubic man, mostly bald, with long white sideburns. At home now, he wears a yellow shirt and dark slacks and black suede shoes with a piece of gold across the instep. He lives in comfort in an apartment on Seventh Avenue. It has pillars in the hall doorway and a fireplace in the living room and a parquet floor and a grand piano.

"I became very interested," says Sam Hall, "with that generation of the Adams family in terms of—they really were desperately trying to live up to these mythic characters from their family's past, and there was no way that they could do it. And then I read the wife's letters to her father. There was an ever-present incestuousness in their relationship. I mean, not physical incestuousness, but as I saw her, she had this enormous crush upon the man, without realizing it, and there was a reason that she was twenty-eight or whatever it was when she married.

"I thought that she was fascinating, as someone to think about and try to make some sense out of. She was very ambitious. She drove Henry. She was the one who organized all the soirées and kept the salon. She would have liked very much to have been the wife of a major novelist, or a major historian. She wanted *more* than she had. There's no doubt about that. But Henry was much more passive than she was. I don't think he was very—he must have been quite asexual. But that's only hinted at. . . .

"The original script had them meet at a dinner party at Dr. Gurney's, and I said to Fred [Coe], 'It's going to be so boring if we have to sit through so much ritual shit with numerous extras saying, "Isn't the lamb overdone?" while these two ogle each other.' I said, 'Let's get them into the Harvard Library, and he's astonished at a woman being there.' And Fred said, 'Fine.' Anything to avoid a dinner party. Of course, they did actually meet at the Gurneys', so for the historians' sake, we added a line that this was not the first time they'd met. But it was the first time they'd ever really connected."

A Cambridge courtship in the early 1870's was probably somewhat less feverish than the modern imagination suggests. It could flower in leisurely strolls along the Charles, in recitals of Chopin waltzes and nocturnes at the Music Hall, in dinner-table conversations about the strange new fantasy entitled *Through the Looking Glass* or the news of Stanley finding Dr. Livingstone in darkest Ujiji. The main cultural event being organized in the spring of 1872, actually, was the arrival of Johann Strauss to direct 100 sub-conductors and 20,000 musicians at the Peace Jubilee Colosseum, in a spectacular performance of his waltz "The Blue Danube." In general, however, social life was fairly tranquil. Henry James, back in Cambridge on a visit, provided a glimpse of the scene in a letter to his friend Grace Norton in Florence. After lunch at the Norton establishment at Shady Hill, he wrote, "the grass was all golden with buttercups—the trees all silver with apple blossoms, the sky a glorious storm of light, the air a perfect hurricane of zephyrs. We sat (Miss C. Hooper, Miss Boott* &c.) on a verandah a long time immensely enjoying the fun. . . . Mesdemoiselles Hooper and Boott talked of Boston, I thought of Florence. . . ."

Professor Henry Adams was undoubtedly engaged in similar rituals, for he described himself in one letter of 1872 as "a social butterfly," adding that he felt "a contemptible weakness for women's society and blush at the follies I commit." The only such folly that he recounted, with some twittering, was a luncheon at his Harvard rooms, "at which I had the principal beauty of the season and three other buds, with my sister to preside; a party of eleven, and awfully fashionable and larky. They came out in the middle of a fearful snowstorm, and I administered a mellifluous mixture known as champagne cocktails." Despite his tone of delighted wickedness, Adams added the observation that Boston girls were lively but chaste. "In this Arcadian society sexual passions seem to be abolished," he wrote. "Whether it is so or not, I can't say, but I suspect both men and women are cold, and love only

* Elizabeth Boott was to serve as the model for Pansy Osmond in *Portrait of a Lady*.

133

with great refinement. How they ever reconcile themselves to the brutalities of marriage, I don't know."

How two such prisoners of their own refinement could ever have fallen in love remains a mystery, as always, but perhaps we can reconstruct the scene by turning to *Esther*, the novel that Adams so clearly based on his family and friends. Esther Dudley, the very image of Clover, says to the celebrated minister, Stephen Hazard, that she is planning to go to Europe. "Take me with you!" cries Hazard. "What shall I do without you! I love you with all my heart and soul. . . . ! You are the only woman I ever loved! Ah! You must love me!" Whether or not Adams ever made such a declaration, it was presumably an approximation of what he thought appropriate to the situation. In the novel, at least, it had an effect. "Esther, trembling, bewildered, carried away by this sudden and violent attack, made at first a feeble effort to withdraw her hand and to gasp a protest, but the traitor within her own breast was worse than the enemy without. For the moment all her wise resolutions were swept away in a wave of tenderness. . . . She shut her eyes and found herself in his arms. Then in terror at what she had done, she tried again to draw back.

" 'No, no!' she said rapidly, trying to free herself. 'You must not love me! You must let me go!'

" 'I love you! I adore you! I will never let you go!'

" 'You must. . . . ! I am not good enough for you. You must love someone who has her heart in your work. . . . I shall ruin your life! I shall never satisfy you!' "

The only reference to such a scene in Clover's letters came just after Henry had finally proposed, when she wrote to Elly Shattuck Whiteside, "Tell your family . . . and Fred that he nearly stopped all this, that if he had sat one hour longer that fatal Tuesday P.M. this might never have come to pass. . . . Henry outstayed him and vows he will never go away." Henry himself was equally oblique. On March 3, 1872, he started a letter to his younger brother Brooks with yet another reference to his lunch with "the young buds" of "the ultra-fashionable set," and only on the next page did he add that he himself, at the age of thirty-four, was finally planning to join in what he had called the "brutalities" of marriage. "And now prepare yourself for a shock. I am engaged to be married. There! What do you say to that? I fancy your horror and incredulity. . . ." Adams' letter indicates that Clover was neither the only possibility nor the inevitable choice. "Try to guess the person. Who do you say? Clara Gardner? No! Nanny Wharton? No. It is, however, a Bostonian. You know her, I believe, a little. You are partly responsible, too, for the thing, for I think you were the first person who ever suggested it. I remember well that in our walks last spring you discussed it. Yes! It is Clover Hooper. . . .

"The truth is, though I didn't think it worthwhile to confide in mankind, that I have had the design ever since last May and have driven it very steadily. On coming to know Clover Hooper, I found her so far away superior to any woman I had ever met, that I did not think it worth while to resist. I threw myself head over heels into the pursuit and succeeded in conducting the affair so quietly that this last week we became engaged without a single soul outside her immediate family suspecting it. . . . I'm afraid she has completely got the upper hand of me, for I am a weak-minded cuss with women, and the devil and all his imps couldn't resist the fascination of a clever woman who chooses to be loved. Such is your brother's fate!"

This sounds like love, as much as an Adams would ever sound that way, and yet the process of analysis never stopped. We have already noted a few lines from the letter in which Adams wrote to a friend that his fiancée was "certainly not handsome" but did read German, Latin, and "also, I fear, a little Greek." In that letter to Charles Milnes Gaskell, the infinitely patronizing Adams now continued: "Through her mother, who is not living, she is half Sturgis, and Russell Sturgis of the Barings is a fourth cousin or thereabouts. Socially the match is supposed to be unexceptionable. . . . She talks garrulously, but on the whole pretty sensibly. She is very open to instruction. We shall improve her. She dresses badly. She decidedly has humor and will appreciate our wit. She has enough money to be quite independent. She rules me as only American women rule men, and I cower before her. Lord! how she would lash me if she read the above description of her!"

Adams' letter is evidence of the gap that lay, perhaps was always to lie, between him and his future wife. Clover was considerably less formidable, considerably more vulnerable, than Adams jocularly supposed. When her sister, Ellen, congratulated her on her engagement, she described her recent life in terms of "a horrid dream" in which she and Ellen had both been imprisoned by a wall of ice. Ellen had been freed by her marriage to Gurney, Clover wrote, and only now could she herself see an escape from the ice. "This winter when the cold weather came the sun began to warm me, but I snapped my fingers at it and tried to ignore it," she wrote. "By and by it got so warm that I tried to move and I couldn't, and then last Tuesday, at about sunset, the sun blinded me so, that in real terror I put my hands up to my face to keep it away. And when I took them away, there sat Henry Adams holding them. And the ice has all melted away, and I am going to sit in the sun as long as it shines. . . ."

Oliver Wendell Holmes to Charles Francis Adams, March 14, 1872:
"My dear Sir,
"My son's engagement having only just come out yesterday morning, I was so full of it today that I talked of nothing else and forgot to congratulate you on the engagement of your son to the daughter of an old friend of mine.
"I am sure you cannot but be made happy by the prospect of receiving Miss Hooper, whom we have found and you will find so worthy of love and esteem, into your family. It was with the greatest interest that we all heard of an engagement which everybody seems to be delighted with and which those who know the young people best feel sure will be very happy for both and for all who love them. I know your son only through others, but with what they tell me, and the name he bears and the stock he comes from, I consider my young friend Miss Hooper very fortunate in the prospect of having him as the companion of her life."

On the day of their engagement, Henry Adams gave Clover a copy of William Dean Howells' new novel, *Their Wedding Journey*. It still lies in the attic of the private archive in the country—among the bibles and the Greek grammars and the childhood copy of *Robinson Crusoe* in French—inscribed in Clover's bold hand: "Henry Adams & Clover Hooper—Feb. 27th, 1872."

Their Wedding Journey is a rather pale travelogue, a thinly fictionalized account of Howells' own trip from Boston to New York to Niagara Falls to Montreal and Quebec, redeemed only by the fledgling novelist's gently humorous style and by his talent for portraying the ordinary ("Ah! poor Real Life, which I love, can I make others share in the delight I find in thy foolish and insipid face?"). Adams and Howells were cordially acquainted, fellow editors both brought to Harvard by the new Eliot regime, and Adams wrote a lordly but sympathetic welcome to the new book in *The North American Review*: "If extreme and almost photographic truth to nature, and remarkable delicacy and lightness of touch can give permanent life to a story, why should this one not be read with curiosity and enjoyment a hundred or two hundred years hence? Our descendants will find nowhere so faithful and so pleasing a picture of our American existence, and no writer is likely to rival Mr. Howells in this idealization of the commonplace. . . ."

The review makes Howells' book sound like a mildly appropriate present for Clover's betrothal, but there are darker undercurrents in *Their Wedding Journey* ("Quarrels from beginning to end, just the way it would be," as Theodore Dreiser later wrote). Howells and his hero, Basil March, adopt from the beginning an amiably condescending attitude toward Isabel, the new Mrs. March. "Like all daughters of a free country, Isabel knew nothing about politics," Howells observes, for example, and "his wife, as a true American woman, knew nothing of the history of her own country." The ignorant Isabel appears to be all simper and squeal and twirling parasols, but when she eventually provokes a quarrel over nothing, and then compels Basil to give in, "she met his surrender with the openness of a heart that forgives but does not forget."

The Marches proceed to Niagara, and there Isabel undergoes a strange kind of crisis. She and Basil venture out from Goat Island over a series of "pretty suspension bridges" to three smaller islets that perch at the edge of the abyss. For a time, Isabel gives "fearful glances at the heaving and tossing flood beyond, from every wave of which at every instant she rescued herself with a desperate struggle." Then she suddenly collapses. "Without the slightest warning she sank down at the root of a tree, and said, with serious composure, that she could never go back on those bridges; they were not safe. He stared at her cowering form in blank amaze. . . . Isabel burst into tears. . . .

" " 'I never can go back by the bridges, never.'
" 'But what do you propose to do?'
" 'I don't know, I don't know!' "

Isabel's absurd terror is cured by an absurd turn—another woman tourist arrives by the bridges and Isabel is ashamed to be found cringing in terror, so she simply walks ashore. Thereafter, however, March "treated Isabel . . . with a superiority which he felt himself to be very odious, but which he could not disuse."

Niagara Falls, which the Indians had once considered a holy place, was to be important in Clover's destiny. Toward the end of her life, she went there with Henry and stayed for a time at the edge of the swirling waters, and stared into the mist and foam. She, too, may have experienced a moment of panic. That, at any rate, was the scene of the final crisis in *Esther*. And *Esther* was to be, for Clover, a confirmation of everything that she dreaded.

The Adamses were somewhat divided in their feelings about Henry's betrothal. His mother favored the match, and even before Henry had proposed, she once burst forth with her opinion: "Henry, I do wish you would marry Clover Hooper." Henry's older brother Charles, who later recorded the scene, was violently opposed. "Taken by surprise and suspecting nothing," he wrote, "I exclaimed, 'Heavens!—no—they're all crazy as coots. She'll kill herself, just like her aunt!' "

Charles was presumably referring to Ellen Sturgis Hooper's youngest sister, Susan Sturgis Bigelow, who, while pregnant with her second child, at the age of twenty-eight, took arsenic. (She now lies in Mt. Auburn Cemetery, next to her mother.) But there seem, judging by Charles' outburst, to have been widespread rumors of madness in Clover's family—rumors that may, however, have been based on nothing more demented than the eccentricity of Aunt Carrie's poetry. Henry, presumably aware of the eccentricities in his own family, may have been referring to the rumors about the Sturgises when he wrote to Brooks, "I know better than anyone the risks I run. But I have weighed them carefully and accept them."

Madness in the family was a rather commonplace affliction in the nineteenth century—as it is today, though no longer condemned as a collective responsibility—and even the proudest of the Adamses could hardly have forgotten the fates of Uncle Charles and Uncle George. Indeed, Henry in this season of romance wrote to his father, absent in Geneva to negotiate the United States claims against England for its involvement in the depredations of the Confederate cruiser *Alabama*, that his mother was suffering from what he called "nervous prostration." This was not, in those days, a condition for which doctors were invoked. It was simply part of everyday life, particularly for New England women. Mrs. Adams' chief symptom, apart from her rheumatism, seems to have been a chronic anxiety and a compulsion to talk endlessly about trivia. "Mamma has her good days and her bad days," Henry wrote to his father with an affectation of unconcern, "but her best days are by no means gay, and her worst are very bad. I am tolerably well accustomed to her, and all her troubles do not alarm me very much, but to persons who have had no experience with her, the effect is startling, especially as they see her when she is most upset and uncontrollable. . . . I tried to make her promise not to talk with others while in these nervous moods, but she can't help it and I can't control her. . . . Nothing can be done because there is really nothing the matter. . . . Her difficulty is in having nothing to oc- cupy her mind, to counteract the influence of unpleasant ideas. Hence the merest trifle upsets her, and a wakeful night seems to her a lifelong calamity."

Henry went on to talk about the intolerable pressures on his younger sister Mary, "who has to bear the heaviest part of the work," and to urge that both his mother and sister rejoin Adams in Geneva. Adams wrote back that he was returning home for profes- sional reasons. There was a break in the Geneva negotiations, and Adams wanted to consult with the State Department. There was also a presidential campaign approaching, and it might be the last chance for John Adams' grandson to fulfill the family destiny by recapturing the White House.

In retrospect, it is easy to see that nothing could have prevented the re-election of General Grant. Not only did the commercial powers cherish his lenient rule but the ordinary people still loved their wartime hero. At the time, however, the ineptitude of Grant's first administration seemed to demand a replacement. The party of Lincoln, as Senator James W. Grimes of Iowa wrote, had become "the most corrupt and debauched political party that has ever ex- isted."

Into this confusion marched Victoria Woodhull, née Claflin, a rather stocky but magnetic young woman, a spiritualist medium who had heard in a trance the voice of Demosthenes telling her that she must make her fortune by moving to a certain address in New York. Following Demosthenes' instructions, she soon found that one of her new neighbors was the recently widowed Commodore

Cornelius Vanderbilt, aged eighty-four. Mrs. Woodhull helped the Commodore to communicate with long-dead friends, while her younger sister Tennessee used the dubious methods of magnetic healing to treat the aches of Vanderbilt's old age. The Commodore gave his protégées tips on the stock market, then helped them to become the first female stockbrokers on Wall Street and the publishers of *Woodhull & Claflin's Weekly*. In that paper, in 1870, Victoria Woodhull announced her candidacy for the presidency on a platform of women's rights and free love.

Some of the most dedicated suffragettes were appalled. Susan B. Anthony described Mrs. Woodhull as "a lady quite déclassée in any society." Elizabeth Cady Stanton, on the other hand, argued that "If Victoria Woodhull must be crucified, let men drive the spikes and plait the crown of thorns." The House Judiciary Committee solemnly accepted Mrs. Woodhull's petition that women be allowed to vote, summoned her to testify on the matter, and then filed the petition away. Mrs. Woodhull took to the lecture circuit. At Steinway Hall in New York, someone asked the twice-married candidate whether she herself engaged in free love. "Yes!" she cried. "I am a free lover! I have an inalienable, constitutional, and natural right to love whom I may, to love as long or as short a period as I can, to change that love story every day if I please! And neither you nor any law that you can frame have the right to interfere!"

People disapproved. Mrs. Woodhull and her sister were evicted from their house. Their brokerage business and their newspaper suffered. Mrs. Woodhull fretted over the hypocrisy of New York society, typified in the plans to celebrate the twenty-fifth anniversary of Henry Ward Beecher's installation in the pulpit of the Congregational Plymouth Church of Brooklyn. Beecher, the brother of Harriet Beecher Stowe, preached mellow sermons every Sunday on the beauties of virtue, but Mrs. Woodhull knew, as did many of Beecher's parishioners, that he was a philanderer. She was in Boston, addressing the annual convention of the National Association of Spiritualists, of which she was president, when she felt, she later said, a supernatural force compelling her to tell the assembled spiritualists about the Reverend Beecher's adulteries.

The newspapers at first declined to publish her revelations, for fear of libel suits, so Mrs. Woodhull published them herself. "Believing in the right of privacy and the perfect right of Mr. Beecher socially, morally, and divinely to have sought the embraces of [any] woman whom he loved and who loved him," she wrote, "I still invade the most secret and sacred affairs of his life, and expose him to the opprobrium and vilification of the public." While Beecher and his followers tried vainly to buy and burn all copies of *Woodhull & Claflin's Weekly*, Anthony Comstock of the Young Men's Christian Association got the sisters arrested on a charge of sending obscene literature through the mail. Bail was set at $8,000. "The women's rights people have made themselves so odious that I think we are rid of them forever," Henry Adams wrote to a friend in England. "And I assure you that this is a joyful riddance."

Respectable citizens in that election year of 1872 inclined to favor the nomination of Charles Francis Adams. He had, after all, served an appropriate apprenticeship in Congress and in the diplomatic service. More important, perhaps, he represented a kind of old-fashioned probity and honor that began to seem increasingly attractive in the scandalous age of Grant. Two leaders of the liberal Republicans, Senator Carl Schurz and Governor B. Gratz Brown, tried to organize all opponents of Grant by summoning a Liberal Republican convention in Cincinnati on May 1. The basic platform would include civil service reform, free trade, and amnesty for the South. Adams had widespread support, including such influential newspapers as the *Springfield Republican* and the *Louisville Courier-Journal*, even though he himself refused to campaign at all. Not only did he refuse to campaign but he refused to authorize anyone else, even his sons, to organize support on his behalf. Not only did he refuse to campaign or to authorize a campaign but he refused even to remain in the country. Having completed his discussions at the State Department, he gathered up his wife and sailed off, just a week before the Cincinnati convention, to resume the *Alabama* negotiations in Geneva. Not only did he refuse to campaign, not only did he leave the country, but he wrote a letter to one of his supporters, David A. Wells, an economist and leader of the free-trade movement, expressing the Adams family's traditional disdain for party politics. He did not particularly want the nomination anyway, he wrote, and if it had "to be negotiated for" with any kind of "assurances given," then he preferred to have his name withdrawn "out of that crowd." On the other hand, if the delegates

really felt a "need of such an anomalous being" as he was, and if
they decided to issue an "unequivocal call" for his nomination—
then he would consider it.

This bleak letter was duly published, and even that failed to
shrivel the reformers' enthusiasm for a third Adams as president.
"As yet my father commands much the most powerful support for
the nomination, and it is not improbable that all parties may combine on him . . ." Henry wrote to a friend, adding, a little dis-
ingenuously, "I have found myself comparatively little disturbed
by the infernal row which is going on. That one's father should be
president is well enough, but it is as much as his life is worth, and
I look with great equanimity upon the event of the choice falling
on some other man. . . . My fiancée, like most women, is desperately ambitious and wants to be daughter-in-law to a President
more than I want to be a President's son. So we are altogether in a
chaotic condition."

Adams ran well ahead on the first ballot, with 243 votes to 147
for the voluble publisher of *The Tribune*, Horace Greeley, but there
were three other candidates to divide the vote. Greeley's candidacy
was an eccentric one. Though he had been a founder of the Republican Party and an early supporter of Lincoln, his various causes
ranged from teetotalism to high tariffs, the latter representing the
exact opposite of the reformers' platform. The delegates were divided and subdivided in a number of ways, however, and so they
began the very kind of bargaining that Adams had deplored. On
the second ballot, one candidate dropped out and Greeley gained a
two-vote lead over the absent Adams. On the third ballot, Adams
recaptured the lead by six votes, and on the fourth, he was ahead
by 279 to 251. Then, for reasons that have never been fully explained, the delegates stampeded to Greeley and nominated him
by 309 to 258.

"Odd," Charles Francis Adams wrote in his journal when the
news of Greeley's nomination reached him in London. "My first
sense is one of great relief in being out of the mêlée." He predicted
that Greeley's actual election was "out of the question," and, of
course, he was right. The American people, once again, wanted
Grant. They re-elected him by an overwhelming 3.6 million to 2.8
million for Greeley. Exhausted by the campaign, and then by the
lingering death of his wife, Greeley went into delirium and died at
the end of that same month of November. Victoria Woodhull, who

was in jail on election day, duly emerged, ran for the presidency four more times with equally little success, married a rich English banker, lived on to be almost ninety, claiming to the end that it was she who won the vote for American women.

June 27, 1872, was the day set for the wedding, and still Henry Adams kept analyzing the incredible prospect. "In fact it *is* rather droll to examine women's minds," he wrote to his friend Gaskell on May 30. "They are a poor mixture of odds and ends, poorly mastered and utterly unconnected. But to a man they are perhaps all the more attractive on that account. My young female has a very active and quick mind and has run over many things, but she really knows nothing well, and laughs at the idea of being thought a blue. . . . I think you will like her, not for beauty, for she is certainly not beautiful, and her features are much too prominent; but for intelligence and sympathy, which are what hold me." And again: "If it weren't that I am such a sceptical bird I should say that we two were a perfectly matched pair and that we were sure to paddle along through life with all the fine weather and sunshine there is in it, but perhaps when one is in the lover's stage, it is safest not to look at the future."

"Gay as a lark," Adams described himself in the week of the wedding, a ceremony that he had organized to suit his own tastes. "For once I am to carry out the idea of my most cherished prejudices, and have a wedding which is absolutely private. It is to be performed here [in Beverly Farms] in my bride's house, at noon. The clergyman is a very jolly young fellow of our set, intimate with me and my fiancée, and ready to do all we wish in the way of cutting down the service. Only brothers and sisters are to be present, eight in all, besides the papa [Dr. Hooper], so that the whole party will be only ten or eleven. . . . Luckily for us, no one dares interfere. Relatives submit like lambs to being left at home, and we are treated beautifully by everyone. When you know my young woman, you will understand why the world thinks we must be allowed to do what we think best. From having had no mother to take responsibility off her shoulders, she has grown up to look after herself and has a certain vein of personality which approaches eccentricity. This is very attractive to me, but then I am absurdly in love. . . ."

The very day after the wedding, Clover began writing to her father the letters that were to record the thirteen years of her marriage. "We think our wedding and the lunch went off charmingly, thanks to your cheerfulness and care," she began, "and we shall always remember how you did everything in your power to make our engagement and marriage smooth and pleasant. It seems to me more than I deserve to go from the care of such a kind father to a good husband, and I am very grateful." There followed, then, a postscript from Henry: ". . . I wish it were in my power to make the loss of Clover less trying to you, but I know no other way of doing it than by making her as happy as I can."

BOOK THREE

Young
Mrs. Adams

Oh, you dear good father!" cried Mary, putting her
hands round her father's neck . . . "I wonder if any
other girl thinks her father the best man in the world!"
  "Nonsense, child; you'll think your husband better."
  "Impossible," said Mary. . . . "Husbands are an
inferior class of men, who require keeping in order."
                                    GEORGE ELIOT,
                                      Middlemarch

9

TEMPLES DO BEGIN TO PALL

IMMEDIATELY after the wedding, the Adamses went to spend a two-week honeymoon at a nearby cottage that Clover's Uncle Sam owned at Cotuit Point. Everything was perfect, according to Clover's first letters to Dr. Hooper. "We jog on peacefully and happily . . ." she wrote. "We had a charming sail in the *Maud* yesterday, and the day before I caught eleven blue fish and Henry four, and blistered my hands, and our noses are like scarlet geraniums."

Here too, presumably, Henry finally introduced Clover—or vice versa—to what he had called "the brutalities of marriage." Because of the outcome of this marriage, there has been speculation that something was wrong from the start. Among the various television people who had assembled to make *The Adams Chronicles*, for example, it was widely suspected that Adams was a repressed homosexual, or, as one of them remarked, "it was alluded to that Henry was bisexual." There are other theories as well. The late Professor Samuel Eliot Morison of Harvard, who had publicly warned against all hypotheses on the cause of Clover's death, suggested in private that Adams might have been impotent.

It seems likely, however, that the twentieth century is once again casting the shadows of its own morbidity back across the nineteenth. Not that the nineteenth century lacked morbidity, as anyone can determine from the works of Krafft-Ebing, or, for that matter, the mystery of Jack the Ripper. Still, despite all the turbulent undercurrents, the Victorian Era did impose a certain reticence not only in speech but in behavior. Jane Carlyle is said to have been a virgin after fifteen years of marriage, and John Ruskin seems to have gone to his death in that same unhappy condition. There is no evidence that Henry James, the master of conjugal intrigues, ever engaged in sexual relations with anyone at all. And when Edith Wharton actually did get married, she was so dismayed by the revelations of her wedding night ("For heavens sake, don't ask any more silly questions," her mother had told her) that she avoided any possibilities of a repetition for the next twenty years. What, then, of Henry and Clover, both so chaste, so nervous, so uncertain, so self-deprecating—how must they have experienced that moment of confrontation? With, one suspects, acute embarrassment. Tortured embarrassment. Then perhaps a timorous curiosity, perhaps a timorous pleasure. Perhaps even surprise. Perhaps, after all, relief. As one of Stendhal's heroines said after her first experience, *"Ce n'est que ça?"*

At the end of two weeks, it came time to set out on the voyage for London, a voyage that Adams planned to extend from a honeymoon into a full year of wandering and reflecting on his new profession of historian. He had bought tickets on the steamer *Siberia*, which was to prove, in a small and Bostonian way, a ship of fools. "We are to have a pleasant party. . . ." Adams wrote to a friend. "My *confrère*, James Russell Lowell and his wife, Professor Francis Parkman,* our best American historian and a very agreeable man, are on board. We are all professors and friends. . . ."

While Henry and Clover were just beginning to explore their life together, Parkman, at forty-nine, was already embarked on a somewhat more desperate exploration. Having failed in his hope of marrying Ida Agassiz, he had turned to his flower garden as a means of combatting the crippling nervous attacks that he called "the enemy." With characteristic diligence he eventually assembled about one thousand different varieties of roses in his garden. (His *Book of Roses* [1866] soon became a standard manual.) His specialty, however, was the lily. He was the first to bring the *Lilium auratum* to flower outside the newly reopened Empire of Japan, and with an

---

* Adams sometimes addressed Parkman as "cousin," for the two historians were related. Adams' millionaire grandfather, Peter Chardon Brooks, had a younger sister named Joanna, whose daughter Caroline married the Reverend Francis Parkman and became the mother of the future historian.

aristocratic passion for the crossbreeding of new varieties, he combined two Japanese strains to create the *Lilium parkmani*, which he sold to an English connoisseur for $1,000.

Parkman had even become a professor of horticulture at Harvard in 1871, but he still clung to the more ambitious goal that he had conceived as an undergraduate, to chronicle the entire history of the struggle between France and Britain for the domination of the American wilderness. Though he had been forced to give up virtually all writing for fourteen years, and though now, in his near-blindness, he had to have documents read to him until he could memorize them and then dictate from his scribbled notes, despite all this he was absolutely determined to pursue his work to the end. He had already made half a dozen forays to Canada, ranging over forgotten frontier battlegrounds as far away as Cape Breton Island, and now he was on his second journey to Paris to dredge from the Archive de la Marine et des Colonies the secrets of his grandiloquent and half-demented hero, Count Frontenac.

A no less troubled search had brought Adams' old teacher, James Russell Lowell, to the *Siberia*. After thirteen years of teaching literature at Harvard, and lately co-editing *The North American Review* with Adams, Lowell felt that he had "suffered a professor change . . . too deep for healing." That is, he felt he could no longer write poetry, or rather, he felt dissatisfied and unhappy about the poetry that he did write. "The fountain is still flowing," he observed to a friend, "but it will not be dipped by any but the golden bowl of leisure." After three years of brooding about how to escape from the duties of the classroom, he finally sold a large piece of land adjoining his house, which brought him an income of $4,000 a year. This enabled him to resign from Harvard—"I have gone over to the enemy and become a capitalist," he wrote—and to sail for Europe, at the age of fifty-three, to discover whether he was really a poet.

And John Holmes, who had long ago discovered that he wasn't really anything, boarded the *Siberia* just for his own amusement. The younger brother of Oliver Wendell Holmes—"the best and most delightful of men," according to Lowell—had never married, never found an occupation. He lived quietly in the Appian Way in Cambridge, so quiet a place, he said, that when two cats crossed the street, all the neighbors rushed to the windows. When he spoke of going "across the water," he ordinarily meant going not to En-

gland or France but across "the dreary waste of waters to Boston."
Holmes' chief amusement was to play whist with Lowell, Estes
Howe, and John Bartlett, the Little, Brown editor who was already
famous for his compilation of *Familiar Quotations*. Henry James was
to describe him as "the most unassimilable" New Englander in
Europe, and when he reached Venice, he visited one intersection
every day solely because it reminded him of the intersection of
Broadway and Cambridge Street in front of Memorial Hall.

The S.S. *Siberia* must have had elements of a Platonic academy,
but the most powerful influence on the assembled sages was sea-
sickness. "H. and I lie and gaze at each other," Clover wrote in a
shipboard journal. "Wonder if life has anything in store for us.
Swallow beef tea. Think it may have. Struggle on deck at two.
. . . Mr. Parkman confesses he has been happier; Mr. Lowell
quotes Shelley. . . ." Henry's contribution to the journal was
equally glum: "Wish I were dead! Wish I'd never been born!" Not
until they had been at sea for nearly a week did they begin to
recover. Henry noted a "nice chat with Messrs. Lowell and Parkman."

Although the surviving letters provide no details of these "nice
chats," it is not unreasonable to suppose that Clover and Parkman
had some sharp exchanges on the much-discussed question of
women's suffrage. Parkman believed with great fervor that there
are so many "differences of nature and function" between the sexes
that "it may be doubted if men and women can ever understand
each other." Parkman did not deny the benefits of reciprocity, but
he insisted that women, with their "more delicate sensitivities [and
their] passivity of temperament," should confine themselves to their
domestic functions. "It is among women who have no part in the
occupations and duties of the rest of their sex," he observed, "that
one is most apt to find that morbid introversion, those restless
cravings, that vague but torturing sense of destinies unfulfilled. . . ."

If these "restless cravings" ever took the form of casting ballots,
Parkman foresaw a "parade of imaginary horribles" ranging from
the matron "outvoted in her own kitchen" by her own servants to
the Army sent off to fight some unjust war by a "government
subject to female suffrage." Parkman was to formulate all these
grim views in "The Woman Question," published in *The North
American Review* in 1879, after Adams had abdicated the editorship
and moved to Washington, and Clover resented Parkman's procla-

mations. Having visited North Africa that year, she suggested to Dr. Hooper that Parkman's "ideal woman is found in perfection" behind the purdah of Morocco. "If I talked much with him," she added, "I should take the stump for female suffrage in a short time."

Most of the time aboard the S.S. *Siberia*, however, seems to have been devoted to the pastimes of convalescence amid the rolling seas of the North Atlantic. Clover noted that "Mr. Grahame, manager of the Boston Museum, gave a Shakespearean reading in the saloon." Adams said of his bride that she "grumbles at the feed," while he himself challenged his older colleagues at shuffleboard. "Parsons and I beat Lowell and Parkman," he wrote. "Beautiful!"

Their first destination in England was Wenlock Abbey in Shropshire, the home of Adams' lifelong friend, Charles Milnes Gaskell, son of James Milnes Gaskell, M.P. It was to Gaskell that Adams had written those callow letters describing Clover as "certainly not handsome" and mocking her intelligence for "really knowing nothing well." Clover reported to her father no judgment on Gaskell other than that he was "most cordial," but she was greatly impressed by his house. "Such an ideal place as this is! The ruins of an immense abbey, ivy-covered. . . . The garden is full of roses, white lilies and ferns, with close-shaven lawn. . . . The drawing room where I am now sitting [is] long, 35 feet high, with an elaborate ceiling of oak beams, black with age, polished oak floor, jet black, with an immense Persian rug which would fill Ned's soul. . . . I feel as if I were a 15th century dame and newspapers, reform, and bustle were nowhere."

That Sunday, they caught the express train from Liverpool to London and visited some of Adams' friends, notably Frank Palgrave, art critic of *The Saturday Review* and compiler of the famous *Golden Treasury of English Songs and Lyrics*. One of the purposes of the wedding journey was to shop for the furnishings of the house that the Adamses would someday acquire, and Palgrave had a born teacher's eagerness to help. He gave them as a wedding present a pen-and-ink drawing by William Blake, which prophetically portrayed Ezekiel mourning over his dead wife, and then he took them out to inspect some art galleries. They considered a Rembrandt drawing, a chalk sketch by Van Dyke, a "very spirited figure" by

Hogarth, but the prices dismayed them. Clover found twelve Blake illustrations of Milton "very curious" but hardly worth one hundred pounds. (She also saw at the new Royal Academy in Piccadilly a portrait by James Whistler of his mother, "the whole picture in black and gray, interesting, but affected, it seemed to us.")

Pictures were only a beginning, for the London of 1872 was the shopping center for almost everything. Henry bought "a photographic apparatus" for the trip up the Nile that he was already planning for the following winter. Clover concentrated on the unseen house. "We explored china shops pretty thoroughly," she wrote to Dr. Hooper. "The tiles I did not like; some of Minton's vases are very handsome. . . . We saw some pretty Danish ware which next spring we may buy—a delicate blue pattern on white ground; a full dinner service costs about £12. We searched for Morris and Rossetti [wallpapers], but in vain; and I want you before April to send me their address. . . ."

After a week in London, where Clover began reading a fashionable new novel entitled *Middlemarch*, the Adamses proceeded to Antwerp ("more modern and Frenchy than I hoped"), and then to the Hague ("bright and entertaining"), where they were rather grimly welcomed by John Lothrop Motley, the distinguished historian of the Dutch Republic, now at work on his biography of John Barneveld. Motley had only recently been made minister to London, then mysteriously dismissed within a year by President Grant, and Adams heard, and couldn't resist repeating, "that Grant took a dislike to Motley because he parted his hair in the middle." Now, Clover recorded, "we dined and breakfasted with them, heard all their grievances rehearsed till we were fairly exhausted." Then on to Bonn and Cologne, where Clover found the cathedral "extremely ugly" but was rather impressed by "an old church where 11,000 virgins were killed and their bones are stuck all over the walls, their skulls decorating every nook and corner."

The Adamses had planned to proceed to Berlin "and get through with Henry's business there," but Brooks Adams wrote to them from Geneva that the reparations conference was breaking up and the older Adamses were planning to return home. Henry took Clover directly to a family reunion in Geneva, where they found the American delegation euphoric at having won an arbitration award of $15,500,000 in gold for the British support of Confederate sea raiders. The first night, there was a dinner for fourteen; then came a dinner for thirty. "I think a dinner of thirty is rather a bore . . ." Clover complained. "I had a headache and cold and so went to bed. . . . I fancied it was so quiet from Mrs. Adams' letters that I left my wedding gown in London and my wardrobe is hardly prepared for such a strain. Tell Betsy I miss her hourly and don't look half as nice as when I had her to take care of me."

Clover's letters often expressed homesickness. From Dresden, she asked Dr. Hooper to send her "a bright red maple leaf," and from Berlin she wrote: "What a nice time you seem to be having in that dear old place which is worth all Europe put together." In a way, this was perfectly natural, even on a honeymoon. Clover was deeply attached to the routines of the Hooper household, to Ned and Ellen, to Betsy and the horses, the regular moves between Beacon Street and Beverly Farms. She had never before been separated for long from all the secure rituals, and the separation from all that she depended on cannot have been easy.

More than homesickness, though, the letters disclose an aching sense of absence from her father, and this sense reverberates through many of the letters that she wrote almost every Sunday morning for the next thirteen years. She saved none of the letters that he wrote back to her every week, and so he remains a silent partner in this remarkable correspondence. We do not know how he addressed her or what kind of tone animates his letters, but from the tone of hers we can imagine the intimacy and dependence on both sides. Clover usually addresses him as "Dear Pater," sometimes "Dear Papa," and once "My Angel Pa." She often signs herself "lovingly" or "always lovingly." Sometimes, she sounds comradely—"It is always pleasant to sit and chat with you"—but sometimes she becomes quite emotional. In Venice, the magical city, she was still thinking of Boston. "I miss you very, very much," she wrote, "and think so often of your love and tenderness to me all my life, and wish I had been nicer to you. But I'll try to make up my shortcomings when I come home, and you must keep my place open and let me come into it again." Though we do not know Dr. Hooper's answers, he must have written to her in a similar spirit, for on another occasion, Clover wrote: "I am glad, though, that you miss me because I long to see you, and it wouldn't be nice to have it all on my side."

Henry's "business" in Berlin was to meet a number of prominent historians, and that was much helped by the fact that the U.S. minister was George Bancroft, whose nine-volume *History of the United States* was a monument to both his erudition and his amiable optimism. An ardent liberal and a former Secretary of the Navy, Bancroft had served in Berlin since 1867, and he had become both a friend and a supporter of Bismarck, whom he regarded as a force for progress. The Chancellor and the white-bearded American regularly went riding together in the Tiergarten, talking of the ambitions of Napoleon III or the latest opera by Meyerbeer. When there were rumors that the new Grant administration wanted to replace Bancroft, Bismarck even wrote a letter to Motley, then the U.S. minister in London, asking him to intervene. "I learn from Paris," he wrote, "that they want to take Bancroft away from us on the pretense that he does not represent America in a dignified manner. No one in Berlin would support that assertion. . . . Bancroft is one of the most popular personalities in Berlin."

Bancroft was also a distant cousin of Clover Adams, a relationship of which he seemed only dimly aware. Perhaps he was also only dimly aware that Henry had snapped at him in *The North American Review* for the "peculiarities of his style." As soon as Henry arrived in Berlin, Bancroft invited him to dine that same evening at the ministry on the Regentenstrasse, overlooking the Tiergarten, and to meet the most celebrated historians from the University of Berlin. "When [Henry] said he must go back to dine with his wife, and explained who that was," Clover wrote home with some asperity, "George was very much excited and pretended I was his dearest friend and insisted that I must come too. So, at an hour's notice, scrambled into a gown, not knowing whether it was a big affair or not. The guests were: Professor Mommsen, whose history [of Rome] Ida [Agassiz] and I plunged through. . . ."

Mommsen had become an institution. Mark Twain was much impressed at meeting the great man. He saw him once at a public dinner and saw everyone rise at his entrance. "Rose and shouted and stamped and clapped and banged their beer mugs," Twain wrote. "Just simply a storm! Then the little man with his long hair and Emersonian face edged his way past us and took his seat. I could have touched him with my hand—Mommsen—think of it!" Clover was quite aware of the man's prestige, but she simply went on with her list: There was also Ernst Curtius, "who has written a great book on Greece," and Hermann Grimm, a professor of art and son of one of the famous brothers, and a Belgian journalist and a French diplomat. "As I was the only lady," Clover went on, "I went in with the host and Mommsen sat on my right. He speaks English but not very easily, French better, German like a mill wheel. He is full of fire and fun and cut across people's bows with great vigour. . . ."

Partly with Bancroft's help, Adams also met a number of other German historians—Germany being at that time renowned for its archival scholarship—Henrich von Sybel, an expert on the Crusades and editor of the *Historische Zeitschrift*, Heinrich Rudolph von Gneist, a scholar specializing in Germanic legal institutions, George H. Pertz, editor of the *Monumenta Germaniae Historica*. (The following year, Adams was to visit Oxford on a similar mission, to interrogate Sir Henry Maine, whose text on ancient law was required reading in Adams' seminar, and William Stubbs, who was at work on his constitutional history of England.) Adams wrote rather nonchalantly about these encounters, remarking only that he had "pumped" Von Gneist for an entire evening, and that in general he "did the historians very satisfactorily." It seems clear, however, that he was trying to work out a more complete concept of his new profession, to clarify in his own mind what it meant to be a historian and to seek the meaning of the past.

His most detailed account of that search appears somewhat obliquely in a series of letters he wrote to his pupil, Henry Cabot Lodge, who had graduated from Harvard the previous year and was engaged in a similar search. Lodge had "never really studied anything," by his own account, until he "stumbled into the course in mediaeval history given by Henry Adams." Lodge originally had no more than "a vague curiosity" about the romantic tales of popes and emperors, but Adams somehow "roused the spirit of inquiry and controversy in me." Lodge was so aroused that he wanted to emulate his teacher, so he wrote to inquire about the prospects of becoming a historian. Adams' answer, just a few weeks before his marriage that June, sounds so cynical, so stridently ambitious, that one would like to suspect him of simply playing the role of a very worldly adviser.

"The question," he wrote, "is whether the historic-literary line is practically worth following, not whether it will amuse or improve you. Can you make it *pay?* either in money, reputation, or any other solid value." His own answer was that the profession could be made to pay quite well. "No one has done better and won more in any business or pursuit, than has been acquired by men like Prescott, Motley, Frank Parkman, Bancroft, and so on in historical writing; none of them men of extraordinary gifts, or who would have been likely to do very much in the world if they had chosen differently." Anything they had accomplished, Adams continued, could be equaled by others. "Boston is running dry of literary authorities. Anyone who has the ability can enthrone himself here as a species of literary lion with ease, for there is no rival to contest the throne. With it, comes social dignity, European reputation, and a foreign mission."

Adams conceded that such a success would require patience, hard work, and perseverance, but he added that Lodge could learn these by studying "the Germans [who] have these qualities beyond all other races." In this, at least, he was not being ironic. Having followed his own advice by making his own tour of Germany, he wrote again to tell Lodge to learn German and the German strategy, "to master the scientific method, and to adopt the rigid principle of subordinating everything to perfect thoroughness of study." The Germans need not be his only model, Adams went on, but they "have the great merit of a very high standard of knowledge." He provided lists of books for study, not for the subject so much as for the technique: Friedrich Thudichum's *Gau und Markverfassung*, Heinrich Brunner's *Entstehung der Schwurgerichte*, Georg von Maurer's *Einleitung zur Geschichte der Mark-, Hof-, Dorf-, und Stadt-Verfassung*. Back in Boston, the prospect of becoming a literary lion began to strike Lodge as chimerical. Having followed Adams into the thickets of Germanic law, he later recalled, "I certainly could not have found drier reading than the latest and most authoritative German writers of that day. . . . The work was not inspiriting, it was in fact inexpressibly dreary."

But not to Henry Adams, who was amusing himself by reading aloud with Clover from Schiller's account of the Thirty Years' War as they rattled across Germany on Bismarck's new railroads. Indeed, he delighted in acquiring "a small library of books which I carry about with me." And to Lodge he wrote, once again, that he was studying Anglo-Saxon and finding it "quite amusing." He tried to cheer up his protégé by reminding him that any new subject of study usually fills the student with "a very helpless feeling," but that "patience is the salvation of men at all such emergencies." And he kept insisting that even if Lodge's goal remained uncertain, his principal purpose should be to learn an intellectual method. "I have, no doubt, more respect for knowledge, even where knowledge is useless and worthless, than for mere style, even where style is good," he wrote, "but unless one learns beforehand to be logically accurate and habitually thorough, mere knowledge is worth very little. At best it can never be more than relative ignorance, at least in the study of history."

But there was a goal, Adams finally disclosed to Lodge. In the most casual way, he reported that he had spent his honeymoon in "accumulating notes upon some points of early German law," that he expected "in time" to turn them into "a pamphlet or small book," and that "if you like," he would turn over his notes to Lodge, and "we will proceed to work the subject up together." The study of Anglo-Saxon tribal law might be, as Lodge originally thought, "inexpressibly dreary," but Adams saw in it an element that inevitably fascinated him. Long before there were parliaments or even governments, he believed, "the centre of early law" was that passion of the Adamses, the family. "To study the Family therefore . . . was the natural course to follow," he wrote to Lodge. "The organisation of the Family, the law of inheritance, of testaments, of land tenure, of evidence and legal procedure, the relations of the Family to the community, in its different forms of village, county and state, as well as many other parallel lines of study lay open before me. . . ."

But *Middlemarch!* What must Clover have thought as she began reading of young Dorothea Brooke, who was "regarded as an heiress" and "usually spoken of as being remarkably clever," and whose style of dress "gave her the impressiveness of a fine quotation from the Bible?" And who thought that "the really delightful marriage must be that where your husband was a sort of father and could teach you even Hebrew if you wished it?"

Perhaps nothing.

But when Dorothea married a gray-haired dotard of forty-five, Mr. Casaubon, because he was writing a history of mythology and had "a great soul," and marrying him would be "like marrying Pascal"? And when, on their honeymoon in Rome, which Mr. Casaubon devoted largely to the study of Vatican archives, Dorothea found that marriage to a theologian was less inspiring than she had once imagined? That, in fact, Mr. Casaubon's "way of commenting on the strangely impressive objects around them had begun to affect her with a sort of mental shiver"?

Perhaps nothing.

"How was it," George Eliot remorselessly continued, "that in the weeks since her marriage Dorothea had not distinctly observed but felt with a stifling depression that the large vistas and wide fresh air which she had dreamed of finding in her husband's mind were replaced by anterooms and winding passages which seemed to lead nowhither?"

Five years later, at the withered age of thirty-nine, Adams would jocularly observe that he had "always felt myself like Casaubon in *Middlemarch*." But not yet, not yet. This was the honeymoon, and Clover was not Dorothea Brooke, and Henry was not Mr. Casaubon.

The Adamses were just about to sail from Brindisi on their long-planned voyage up the Nile when they heard of the disaster that had befallen their native city—"this dreadful news," as Clover wrote, "of the fire which has desolated Boston." She first feared that it might be a repetition of the great Chicago fire of 1871, but she soon learned that the blaze had been confined within the business district. Still, that was where she had been brought up—the fire had started on Summer Street—where she had first gone out for walks in the Common, first gone to church at Trinity, first gone to supper at Captain Sturgis' house on Church Green. Virtually all of those scenes of childhood were now destroyed. "We long to hear from you," Clover wrote to Dr. Hooper, "and yet we fear it may be so many weeks before we shall get your letters. I feel anxious about Fanny and Annie Lothrop,* for the shock must have been fearful. . . ."

The shock was indeed fearful, for Boston had never accepted its vulnerability. Washington had been burned by the British, and New York by the draft rioters, but Boston still felt secure and serene. Henry Cabot Lodge was reading in his library when he heard the first warning bells, "thought nothing of it," then heard a general alarm and sauntered forth to see what was happening. "After leaving my house," he recalled later, "I crossed the Common and walked down Summer Street. The fire had then made but little progress, comparatively speaking, and was raging in the lower part of the street just in the neighborhood where I was born. I went from point to point and watched the fire spread, which it did with terrifying rapidity. I saw tall buildings catch in their roofs like huge matches and blaze up, I saw walls falling and stone crumbling in the heat, and in a short time I realized that the fire was far beyond control. . . ." Francis Parkman too was watching the catastrophe, with a kind of awe. "The flames spread with incredible speed and fury," he wrote to a friend back in France. "The steam pumps threw in torrents of water to no effect. Banks, stores, and business offices were devoured by dozens. . . . The spectacle was at the same time sublime and frightful. Huge solid buildings of granite or sandstone seemed to melt as if in a furnace. . . .

Boston's financial leaders worried not only about their buildings but about the papers within that certified their wealth. Harvard University, for example, owned a lot of property along Franklin Street, which succumbed to the fire at about midnight, and President Eliot began to wonder what would happen if the flames reached the commercial centers of State Street, only four or five blocks to the northeast. Harvard had stored securities with a book value of $2,508,254. Eliot consulted with the university treasurer, Nathaniel Silsbee, and another member of the Harvard Corporation, Francis B. Crowninshield, and then decided to rescue the treasure. "We packed all the securities into an old-fashioned carpet bag made of carpet and leather, which stood nearly three feet high

* Fanny Hooper, Ned's wife, was in an advanced state of pregnancy and did indeed give birth to her first child on November 12, just three days after the fire started. It was named, like its aunt and its grandmother, Ellen Sturgis Hooper. Annie Lothrop, the daughter of Clover's Uncle Sam Hooper, did not have her child until November 23.

when placed on its end," Eliot recalled later. "No private carriage or other convenience was procurable. We decided to carry the bag through the streets to Bowdoin Square, and there take a horsecar to Harvard Square. I carried the bag. Mr. Silsbee walked beside me on my right, and Mr. Crowninshield followed with his right hand holding a pistol in the pocket of his coat. In about three quarters of an hour we had the satisfaction of depositing that bag in the Charles River Bank."

Others, of course, had similar ideas. "I hovered 'round the safety vaults in State Street, where I had a good deal of destructible property of my own and others, but no one was allowed to enter them," Oliver Wendell Holmes wrote to Motley. "So I saw the fire eating its way straight toward my deposits and millions of others with them and thought how I should like it to have them wiped out with that red flame that was coming along clearing everything before it. . . ." Henry Lee Higginson, by now a partner in the brokerage firm of Lee, Higginson & Co., was one of those who maintained order on State Street. "A crowd of men kept trying to have the vaults opened," he said afterward, "and I was continually fending them off."

The main problem, however, was to fight the fire itself. The fire department was hampered by an illness among its horses, by exhaustion and some drunkenness among its men, and by panic and confusion among its leaders. Higginson and several others went to the mayor to insist that a number of buildings in the path of the flames be blown up to create a gap. "I found a covered wagon open at the sides," he said, "got it to the end of Long Wharf, and loaded some thirty kegs of powder on it and drove up State Street, which was full of engines pumping, and sparks were flying in every direction." No sooner had Higginson started to put his gunpowder in place, however, than an alderman ordered him arrested. Higginson then had to go and get new authorization from the military authorities. The blasting "struck me as a horrible thing to do, but there was nothing else to be done . . . and I did it," Higginson said. Even that proved ineffectual, however, and after two days of destruction, the fire finally died out, because, as Higginson put it, "there was not much more to burn."

To the Adamses, of course, the fire seemed little more than a baleful glow on the horizon. They could only fret about their friends and their fortunes—the overall property damage was estimated at $100 million. And even as they set off for Egypt, they were followed by reverberations of distant ruin. "I long to hear from you about the fire, which we only got news of in English papers," Clover wrote anxiously to her father from Alexandria. "We are curious, too, as to how it may affect our income, as we can change our plans in any way after the Nile." When she did receive an account of the disaster from her sister, Nella, she wrote back that it was "perfectly disheartening. . . . What is the use of building up cities if a few hours' fire sweeps them away?" And when the Adamses finally returned to Europe and learned from Ned Hooper that their loss had been $10,000, Clover kept mulling over her vulnerability. "Is it a dead loss? We've no right to growl when we have enough to eat, but I'd rather have money run away with than burnt up, 'cos then someone enjoys it. I'm going to buy a big Japanese teapot and put everything in it—a fireproof one."

At the beginning, there was nothing ominous about the trip up the Nile. It seemed almost a vacation within a vacation. Henry was "utterly devoted and tender," Clover wrote to her father, and the weather was "beautiful, warm as June, roses and jasmine in bloom. We saw the most beautiful of all mosques brilliantly illuminated the other night, and spinning and howling dervishes to make it complete."

There were reports of cholera on the upper Nile that year, but a voyage through Egypt was nonetheless very much the fashion for Americans of means. The Khedive, Ismail Pasha, had finally opened the Suez Canal (to the strains, somewhat later, of Verdi's *Aida*), and he was eager to enrich his principality with such western novelties as the railroad and the post office. Definitely a place worth inspecting. So Ralph Waldo Emerson, for example, nearing his seventieth birthday and a bit dotty by now, unable to remember words and sometimes repeating whole pages in the lectures that still attracted throngs—stricken, then, by a fire that suddenly engulfed his house in Concord, a fire that prompted a worldwide outpouring of donations, including $5,000 from Carrie Sturgis Tappan and $1,000 from George Bancroft—Emerson was urged to recuperate in Egypt, and there was such a deluge of funds that Ellen Emerson was able to lead her father onto the S.S. *Wyoming* to sail to London to visit Carlyle, and to Paris to visit Lowell and

Holmes, and then to the Nile. Emerson felt rather oppressed by the famous ruins. He found the whole trip "a perpetual humiliation, satirizing and whipping our ignorance. . . . The sphinxes scorn dunces; the obelisks, the temple walls, defy us with their histories which we cannot spell."

George Bancroft, who was three years older than Emerson but somewhat spryer, had also left Berlin early in 1873 to visit warmer climates, so he took the sage of Concord under his protection. He escorted him to breakfast at the palace of the Khedive, who told his guests about some of his innovations and reforms. "Immense progress in female life," Bancroft duly noted in his diary. "Fifteen years ago, women could not read or write; now are educated, take an interest in public affairs, read a newspaper, converse on what they read. No authoritative interference to break up the Harem; but it is left open to influence of Europe. . . ."

The trip up the Nile was a long one, about three months, all within the confines of one of those lateen-rigged river boats known as *dahabeahs*. The Adamses inspected several before choosing a relatively small vessel named the *Isis*. "We have a dining room about twelve feet square," Clover wrote back to Boston, "three single cabins, a bathroom, and a double stateroom in the stern; the upper deck roomy, with a table and two sofas and well sheltered by awnings. The crew sleep on the lower deck, where all the cooking, washing, etc. is done." These collections of oarsmen, cooks, and errand boys—all headed by a dragoman—gossiped and competed against other crews while their Bostonian masters encountered and kept company with other Bostonians. The Emersons, for example, set out on the *Aurora* with a Mr. and Mrs. Whitwell and their daughters May and Bessie, and in due time they encountered Samuel Ward, the Boston banker and brother of Julia Ward Howe, and then the Roosevelts, a merchant family from New York, including a fourteen-year-old son named Theodore, who seemed interested mainly in bird-watching. Clover Adams, in turn, met many of the same people—she met Bancroft, "enthusiastic about everything he has seen and done"; and also Mrs. Ward as she was returning from her "fearful" climb to the top of the Great Pyramid, returning "radiant, propped up by four disgusting Arabs, vowing it was the most delightful thing she ever did."

Clover's first reaction to the poverty of Egypt was predictable. "By sober daylight," she wrote to her father, "this is the dirtiest and most hideous place I ever imagined. The worst suburbs of New York are beautiful in comparison." She was soon charmed, however, by the Nile. "On the river itself there is much life; the boats of the country filled with hay or loaded with poultry and vegetables are continually passing. . . . The climate is simply perfect, and air bracing and soft, the sunshine almost incessant." And again, ten days later, "Egypt is certainly a wonderful country and impresses one more and more. It is on such a grand scale that other places must seem commonplace after it. . . . The number of towns and villages that we pass every day is astonishing; many of them ugly and miserable but the greater part, seen at a respectful distance, look very attractive lying half hidden in a grove of palms with smiling green fields on every side. . . . We stopped at Sioot for a day to let the crew bake bread, and as it happened to be Christmas Day we had our boat dressed with palm branches in default of the orthodox hemlock. We met a New York family named Beekman who were on their way down the river. They insisted on our dining with them on Christmas Day and were friendly and pleasant. We explored the town on donkey-back. . . ." And finally the great monuments at Abu Simbel: "The rock temple is the most wonderful thing we have yet seen—an immense dome-shaped mountain rising sheer from the river's edge. A temple is cut into it. On each side of the entrance immense colossi are seated, between sixty and seventy feet high. The faces of several of them are quite perfect and the expression of power and sweetness is very striking. Henry has been working like a beaver at photographing."

One of the unstated rules of Clover's weekly letters to her father was that she must always try, like any good daughter, to be cheerful, to be high-spirited and full of enthusiasm. From time to time, though, there were hints that the idyll on the Nile was less than idyllic. "It is slow work when we have no breeze," she wrote, "the crew alternately pushing the boat with long poles or towing it from the shore. . . . I wish I had something entertaining to tell you, but . . . one day is so like another so far that we do not even remember the names of the days. . . . We breakfast about nine; sit on deck all day reading or studying or doing nothing, and get an hour's walk on the banks before sunset. We never sail at night and often lie to by some very dirty village." Sometimes, these stops had to be lengthened. "Today the river has been so rough that we tied up from noon till sunset as it was not comfortable. We have been printing photographs to pass the time." And two weeks later: "We have had a prolonged struggle with cold north winds. . . . too much wind to sit on deck with any comfort and the boat pitching and rolling in a most unpleasant manner. . . . We were wind-bound at Manfalut for a whole day and had a fearful dust storm to increase our discomfort."

Aside from these physical difficulties, Clover felt a strange sense of dissatisfaction with the great temples that she and Henry had come so far to see. "I must confess," she wrote from Thebes, "I hate the process of seeing things which I am hopelessly ignorant of, and am disgusted at my want of curiosity. I like to watch pyramids, etc., from the boat, but excursions for hours in dust and heat have drawbacks to people so painfully wanting in enthusiasm as I am. But I shall leave this open for a day or two and perhaps launch forth into glowing and poetical disquisitions on Karnak." A few days later, however, she was blaming herself for her failure to produce such disquisitions. "It is useless to try to tell you how it all looks," she wrote. "I never seem to get impressions that are worth anything, and I feel as if I were blind and deaf and dumb too. The fields are green and filled with sweet flowers and it is hard to imagine that you have snow and ice."

At about this point, perhaps at Karnak, something important seems to have happened. Clover apparently suffered an attack of profound depression, which may have brought her to the edge of a nervous breakdown. One chronicler of the Adams family, Francis Russell, speaks of Clover undergoing "a brief neurasthenic collapse," but there is no documentary evidence for such a clinical statement, and it is quite possible, as often happens with attacks of madness, that there was nothing sudden, no specific symptoms that a psychiatrist could identify with any confidence. Clover's letters reveal nothing, nor do Henry's, though Clover does mention having written "several dyspeptical and gloomy" letters to her usually equally gloomy mother-in-law, who presumably threw them away.

The origin of the story about Clover's breakdown on her honeymoon seems to lie in Harold Dean Cater's book, *Henry Adams and His Friends*, a collection of Adams letters published in 1947. Speaking of Clover's depression after her father's death in 1885, Cater wrote: "A kind of nervous collapse had set in accompanied by depression. Of this condition Henry had always been apprehensive, ever since there had been a severe strain from it on the Nile in 1872, caused by boredom from the sun, the flat landscape, and the unpredictable winds." In his footnotes, Cater attributed this mainly to a "confidential source," presumably some member of the family. A skilled researcher who looked through Cater's own papers could find no evidence to support his statement. Cater's footnote went on to say that there was a letter in Harvard's Houghton Library from Clover to Mrs. Samuel Ward "which may confirm" the report of Clover's breakdown. But the only such letter has only one sentence that might be so interpreted, and that sentence is ambiguous indeed. "From much we have lived through this winter," Clover wrote, "we feel as if we went home with a new lease on life and happiness."

Still, although we lack the basic details of Clover's breakdown, her letters home do seem to reverberate with a certain ill-defined unhappiness: "slow work . . . some very dirty village . . . the boat pitching and rolling, disgusted at my want of curiosity. . . ." In addition to all the physical discomforts of three months of confinement on a cramped river boat, there was something else that was bothering Clover, something about the awesome antiquity and grandiosity of those gigantic stone figures that stare blindly out from the temples of the upper Nile, and something, too, about the wrinkled scholarship of the bald little man with whom she shared her heaving river prison. It is unreasonable, perhaps, to try to analyze the possible causes of a breakdown about which we know so little, and yet it is also difficult not to be impressed by Clover's fear and dislike of the Nile temples. Or, more specifically, her reaction to other people's reactions to those temples.

Ralph Waldo Emerson, for example. The philosopher, whom Clover's mother had once saluted in sarcastic verse for "the victories / which thou on thought's broad, bloodless field hast won," now found the temples of the pharaohs to be "a perpetual humiliation." He abandoned his river boat at Thebes and returned to Cairo by train. Clover learned of this from a Mr. Smith, who lived in Luxor, and she was appalled by Emerson's forthright decision to do what she herself would have liked to do. At the same time, she blamed herself for her desire. "He [Mr. Smith] told me Mr. Emerson . . . was not interested in Egyptian antiquities, which for a philosopher is quite shocking," Clover wrote to her father. "I confess that temples do begin to pall—but that is an aside—so much the worse for me. How true it is that the mind sees what it has means of seeing. I get so little, while the others about me are so intelligent and cultivated that everything appeals to them."

It was in Cairo, at the end of the descent of the Nile, that Clover acquired the new bible that still lies in the attic in the country, mysteriously inscribed with the cipher: P. 16.8 E. 19. 18. Into the back of it she also pasted her photograph of Henry sitting with bowed head amid the palm fronds and the gilt mirrors and the overstuffed sofa and the heaps of books in the paneled stateroom of the *Isis*.

There are only six books of the Bible that begin with "P," and only two of them are long enough to contain a sixteenth chapter with an eighth verse. *Psalms*, 16–8: "I have set the Lord always before me: because he is at my right hand, I shall not be moved. *Proverbs*, 16.–8: "Better is a little righteousness than great revenues without right." Of the six books that begin with an "E" (including Esther), only one has a nineteenth chapter with an eighteenth verse. *Exodus*, 19–18, tells of the proclamation of the Ten Commandments: "And Mount Sinai was altogether on a smoke, because the Lord descended upon it in fire: and the smoke thereof ascended as the smoke of a furnace, and the whole mount quaked greatly."

The quotations may have some meaning that still eludes us, but they do not seem to provide any solution to the riddle of Clover. Near the chapter numbers, she drew a small tau cross.

Looking back from the deck of a Mediterranean steamer, where she was still reading *Middlemarch* ("and though it's dreary, I like it"), Clover pronounced "our winter in Egypt a great success . . . a great bath of sunshine and warmth and rest." But it was really Italy that revived her spirits. Naples revived her, and Pompeii and Amalfi. "We went on ponies, the path lying between stone walls covered with ferns and violets, with oranges and lemons hanging over our heads. Old women with distaffs in their hands, like Michael Angelo's Parcae, smiled and kissed their hands to us. . . . We picked huge bunches of wild flowers and were glad we had not died when we were babies."

And shopping revived her. "Our game in Naples was old Greek vases from the tombs, water colors and some Persian embroideries." And society revived her. She encountered once again her old friends Henry James and Lizzie Boott, and she went to visit James' friend, the celebrated sculptor, William Wetmore Story, whose studio was the social center for Americans in Rome. "And oh! how he does spoil nice blocks of white marble," Clover wrote. "Nothing but Sibyls on all sides, sitting, standing, legs crossed, legs uncrossed, and all with the same expression as if they smelt something wrong. . . . Mrs. Story is very stout and tells lies." Clover went to call on another artist named Elihu Vedder, whom she and Dr. Hooper had visited in Paris during her first trip to Europe, and she made a remarkably stern judgment of the painter's wife: "She is an ordinary little girl and won't push him up to anything great." Henry James, who was spending the season in Rome and absorbing the details that were to become the setting for *Roderick Hudson*, was amused by Clover's sharp tongue. He referred to the young couple as "the Clover Adamses," and later he was to declare that "Mrs. Adams . . . is a perfect Voltaire in petticoats."

But sickness once again struck them down. Clover called it "a Naples fever," and a doctor in Rome prescribed "rest, broth, quinine and wine." They stayed in their hotel for a fortnight, then proceeded to Paris, where they fell ill again. They received a visit there from Henry's irascible brother Charles, who already saw himself as an industrial prince, now on his way to Vienna with Henry Lee Higginson to serve as a U.S. commissioner at an international trade fair. Charles was engraged from the start because two sisters-in-law had failed to meet him, because he could speak no French, and because the Adamses were offering him a room "about the size of a kennel."

Charles wrote to his wife that he found Henry "sitting over a bowl of gruel . . . in a state of cold and general debility and very depressed and Clover in bed with 'grippe' and fever. . . . They talked in weak, watery voices, until I wanted to shake some strength into them, and then they offered to me—to me, a tired, disappointed traveller—a cup of Turkish coffee. Damn their Turkish coffee! . . . My brother has grown to be a damned, solemn, pompous little ass, and his wife is an infernal bore. They are the most married couple I have yet seen; and when I came into the room I found (oh, Lord, how I hate her!—she talks in a low voice, and prances along like a palfrey—bah! . . .)—well, I found them sitting together and she holding his hand, and then she makes cups of Turkish coffee and makes everyone drink them, even me. . . ."

In London, Clover revived again because Henry's friend Gaskell had insisted on lending them his house at 28 Norfolk Street, just off Park Lane. "Oh! the bliss of putting one's clothes in a bureau after nine months of hard travelling . . ." she wrote to Dr. Hooper. "This house is not large but bright and clean, and has new chintz and fresh curtains and books and pretty china and shiny mahogany inside. A study on the first floor and a large sunny dining-room looking over Hyde Park; over that, a large and handsome parlour with a piazza, which I shall fill with boxes of flowers, and we can sit and smoke there summer nights. . . . We meant to hire a one-horse brougham, but our fairy godfather has a new one to be finished in a few days which he insists our taking the new off of. If we smash it, we shall buy it."

The shopping resumed, for the house that still existed only in Clover's mind's eye. She bought a set of blue-and-white Danish china "for every day," and some "common" linen from Belfast to spare the fancy linen that she had acquired from Dresden. She bought a large Indian carpet, "the exact color of the Nubian desert," for the sum of £44, and three smaller Turkish carpets that showed "a good deal of yellow." Henry found and presented to her "a charming little sketch in red and black crayon by Watteau—a girl lying asleep on a couch, bare feet, etc." She inquired whether Ned would like her to buy him a Blake watercolor of the demented King Nebuchadnezzar eating grass. Henry's friend Palgrave had bought the picture, but "Mrs. Palgrave hates it." Since the Palgraves were "not opulent," they were willing to part with it for ten pounds. "We think it very striking," Clover wrote, "but quite ghastly."

And then the social rounds. "If I were a boy I should say that we are having a 'bully' time," Clover wrote. "Being a staid matron I can only say we are enjoying ourselves extremely." Henry, as usual, was a bit more malicious. "We have been prancing about town all afternoon in a brougham, leaving cards," he wrote to a friend, "—mostly on Americans, however, as Madame is proud and will call on no British female who doesn't intimate a wish to that effect." With her mixture of touchiness and belligerence, Clover delighted in playing that Jamesian role of the young republican in the decadent monarchy. Her English acquaintances were courteously inclined to indulge her. "There was a question of precedence at our dinner Friday as to which ought to take me in," Clover wrote her father, "so I told them they might fight it out among themselves, that their 'effete monarchical customs were a matter of no concern to me!'—and they enjoy such chaff."

Clover's pugnacity toward the British animated many of her individual encounters in London. When she first met Robert Browning at a dinner party, for example, she wrote that "the poet sat next to me and was not amusing—he is growing old and his Promethean spark is put out—he was nice enough but not thrilling —he said he should come and see me for afternoon tea." A fortnight later, she reported with some distaste that Browning "tapped me familiarly on the arm and said, 'I'm coming to see you,' in the tone of 'keep up your spirit.' . . . I don't hanker to see him again." The occasion for this latest confrontation was a party at Westminster Abbey, given by Dean Arthur Stanley. "The Dean looks like a hungry little gray rat," Clover observed, "and skipped about in small clothes and silk stockings with big paste shoe buckles and a broad crimson ribbon round his neck. The supper was at midnight —syrup and water, tea, bread and butter—and in a room high up, and some of the women crawled out of the window on to the roof to see the moonlight in among the buttresses and spires, which looked very imposing."

Like Henry, like all the Adamses, like most nineteenth-century Americans, Clover was fervently nationalistic, and on celebrating her first wedding anniversary in London, she yearned for nothing more than to go home. Of post-imperial Paris, she had nothing but bad memories. "Paris is only a vulgar shop now; everything in decadence . . . theatres nasty and stupid; cooking, bad; climate, worse. They are at the devil. . . ." London she found somewhat more congenial—"I like giving dinners in such a big society—one can get more variety of material than in Boston"—but she was sharply aware not only of the aristrocrats' condescension but of the workers' poverty. "England is charming for a few families but hopeless for most," she wrote, "and a large family is spoken of as a private and national calamity. Thank the Lord that the American eagle flaps and screams over us."

And so it came time to pack. China and glass, books and carpets, some blue-and-gold-colored cloth and fringe for a window seat, and green silk in a Chinese pattern for some new curtains in Dr. Hooper's back parlor. And Ned did want Blake's picture of the insane Nebuchadnezzar crouching in the field and eating grass. "Nebuchadnezzar is bought; it is fearful!" Clover wrote. So they returned as they had come, with a visit to the Gaskells' estate at Wenlock Abbey, and then on to the docks at Liverpool. "We have enjoyed much," Clover wrote in her last European letter, July 23, 1873, "but are quite ready to come home and buckle down to hard work."

10

THERE WILL BE SOME LIVELY
HISTORY TAUGHT

BOTH THE ADAMSES were, as before, miserably seasick on the voyage
home. "My wife, I think, suffered rather more than I, and was more
used up," Henry later wrote to Gaskell. Clover was further stricken
by a sudden toothache. It "inflicted on her the agonies of the next
world for about a week," Henry noted, "and obliged her to weep
night and day." As soon as the boat docked in drought-stricken
Boston, Clover fled to the arms of Dr. Hooper in Beverly Farms,
leaving Henry to proceed by himself to visit his own parents in
Quincy. His mother, Abigail, wrote to Charles, Jr., that they had
had a "nice quiet and comfortable talk," but she added that "it don't
seem natural for him to go off to Beverly to see his wife." Their only
occupation until winter, she said, would be to find and furnish a new
house. "But that," she added with the *hauteur* of an Adams mother-
in-law, "I think Clover likes, if he don't."

Within a month, the Adamses had acquired a small brick house
at 91 Marlborough Street, which just happened to be around the
corner from Dr. Hooper's house on Beacon Street. Both houses
stood in the half-built settlement that was generally referred to in
Howells' *Rise of Silas Lapham* as "the new land" but now is known as
Back Bay. Just a few years earlier, Marlborough Street had been a
swamp, infested by rats and irrigated by a common sewer that
poured out its wastes at what is now the corner of Beacon and
Arlington Streets. Even after the new project was well under way,
George Santayana recalled, there "rose now and then the stench
from mudflats and sewers."

Boston, in those days, was still a mere spit of land, connected to shore only by five bridges and a 1,000-foot-wide southern isthmus known as Boston Neck. But as the waves of European immigrants kept sweeping in—the city's population soared from 25,000 in 1800 to 58,000 in 1825 to 137,000 in 1850—the pressure to build kept increasing. The city's five hills were torn apart and dumped into the harbor. From eight different railroad stations, the steel rails stretched out in all directions. The prospering port demanded civic institutions that would trumpet its wealth and pride—the new Music Hall in 1852, the Boston Theatre in 1853, the Public Library in 1858, the new City Hall begun in 1861, the Free City Hospital opened in 1865.

Still, the largest area for building remained the mud flats of the Back Bay on the western side of the city, where the Charles River flowed toward Boston Harbor. For about two miles, from the Boston Common to Gravelly Point, now known as Kenmore Square, the only road across the wasteland was what had once been an Indian footpath. Here, the ingenious Bostonians began in 1814 to build a causeway named the Milldam to connect a series of dams that had been installed to harness the tidal waters. In 1849, however, the Boston Board of Health proclaimed the whole area to be "one of nuisance, offensive and injurious." In the 1850's, finally, the city authorities decided to turn the Milldam into an extension of Beacon Street and to fill in everything behind it, adding about 450 acres to the 780 of the original peninsula. There were no more hills to destroy, so they built a railroad spur along what is now Commonwealth Avenue and began digging out the gravel pits of Needham at a rate of 3,500 carloads a day.

This stupendous operation—has any American city been so physically altered over the years as Boston?—kept armies of incoming Irish laborers at work for more than thirty years. As early as 1860, the gravel had extended one block west of the Boston Garden to the corner of the newly named Clarendon Street, and all through the Civil War, speculative builders kept erecting brick and brownstone buildings, three and four stories high, with bay windows looking out over the first saplings budding in the wasteland. By 1870, when Henry Adams returned to Boston, they had moved another two blocks westward, to Exeter Street.

The inspiration was French—the grand boulevards that Baron Haussmann was carving through the center of Paris, and the grand office buildings and apartment houses with which the French bour-geoisie lined those boulevards—but Boston's version of the Second Empire style was inevitably more staid and domestic. It bestowed on its grid of new avenues a series of pleasantly old-fashioned English names—Marlborough and Newbury, Exeter, Dartmouth, and Gloucester. It built its houses on a smaller and pleasantly provincial scale, with porches and mansard roofs, bordered by brick sidewalks and rectangular gas streetlights. "It is all very rich and prosperous and monotonous. . . ." Henry James wrote in *The American Scene*, "but oh, so inexpressibly vacant. . . . A bourgeoisie without an aristocracy to worry it is, of course, a very different thing from a bourgeoisie struggling in that shade, and nothing could express more than those interminable prospects of security the condition of a community leading its life in the social sun." Or, as James put it on another occasion, after gazing down the length of Marlborough Street, "Do you feel that Marlborough Street—is, precisely—*passionate?*"

It was here, at the corner of Marlborough and Clarendon Streets, that the Adamses bought a four-year-old house, four stories high, their first home. Clover was "tolerably well satisfied with it," Henry wrote to Gaskell. "It is very small but quite pretty," he went on, "and the library especially, which holds about 2,000 books, is quite a gem." He then proceeded to draw a floor plan: The house was sixty feet long, twenty feet wide, a dining room and a drawing room and a center hall on the ground floor, with the master bedroom over the dining room and the library over the drawing room. "We are fashionable in situation," Henry rambled on, "and consider ourselves quite respectable people in many ways. When you come to stay with us, you shall have the second floor to yourself and shall ask all the young women you fancy to come in and flirt with you in the library alcove. For this small paradise we give about £10,000, including furniture. . . ."

But what a quantity of furniture! Not until the Adamses actually moved into the house, on October 20, did the ship finally arrive with the twenty-five boxes of goods that Clover had searched out and bought and packed and sent from Europe. She spent a week opening up the crates, finding, to her delight, that all the china and glass had survived the Atlantic. "Nothing was broken except one bottle of claret," Henry wrote, ". . . whereat I danced gleefully." They spent a whole afternoon unpacking the paintings and watercolors and showing them off to Ned and Nella. "The only thing that breaks my wife's heart," Henry wrote, "is that her yellow carpet is too large for any of her rooms."

Clover's heart did not remain broken for long. She decided to fold the corners of the rug underneath and to install it in the oval-ended dining room, where, Henry wrote a week later, "it matches the wall paper and produces an effect which can only be called grandiose. . . . Our water colors adorn the walls above it." But Henry kept apart the Blake portrait of the demented Nebuchadnezzar eating grass. He put that in the library, "where it stands in state and excites frantic applause." He jocularly suggested that he was thinking of opening the house to the public one day a week and "admitting people by tickets to view the Nebuchadnezzar. Children given to fits to be left on the doorstep."

Since Clover no longer needed to write every week to her father, who now lived just around the corner, we do not have her own account of this important move, this creation of her first household. We know nothing of the anxieties that generally accompany the decisions about where and how to arrange one's possessions, only that Clover worked very hard. "My wife . . . seems to thrive under a tremendous amount of work and care," Henry wrote to Gaskell, assuming, as he usually did, that Clover must find pleasure in any stress that didn't actually overwhelm her. In any case, he left her to solve her various domestic problems as best she could. "My wife reigns supreme at home," he wrote, "and I know of what is done only by seeing it in its completed state."

In this sanctuary that Clover created on Marlborough Street, Henry Adams resumed his role as the radical of the Harvard history department. It was, of course, a very elegant radicalism. Just as he had once gathered his protégés to his rooms in Wadsworth House, now he gathered them to his fireplace in Marlborough Street. He sipped sherry while questioning them on the intricacies of Anglo-Saxon law, and he puffed on expensive cigars while pondering their answers. Neither luxury was offered to the students. That would have been informal, demeaning. It would have betrayed the aristocratic style.

What was new and fashionable in 1873 is old and fashionable now. The brick sidewalks on Marlborough Street seem charmingly antiquated, as do the Victorian street lights that once were lit by gas. The ugly brick houses, with their stone stairways and their bay windows, all radiate security and comfort and middle-class complacency. Social historians have noted that the Burlington Railroad moved its headquarters from Boston to New York in 1875, an illustration of Boston's self-satisfied abdication of commercial leadership. Fifteen years later, William Dean Howells, having abandoned the editorship of *The Atlantic*, was to make the same move —describing Boston's intellectual climate as "death-in-life," and symbolically shifting the nation's intellectual capital from the Charles to the Hudson.

Ninety-one Marlborough Street still stands, as solid and stable as when Clover first filled it with her Indian carpets. It has not survived a century without change, however. The front door that Clover entered is a bay window now, for the house was combined with its neighbor at 273 Clarendon Street in 1890, and a new entrance onto Clarendon Street was built. Mrs. George P. Denny, of Milton, Massachusetts, grew up in the house at the turn of the century and remembers it as little changed from the days when Clover lived there. "On entering the front door, one climbed a few stairs to the first-floor hall," she recalls. "In the grate at the far end, a coal fire burned day and night. Old tapestries hung on the walls. . . . The front parlor, decorated in green, held the grand piano, from which the doleful sounds of children practicing filled the air. . . . The hallway led to the library, where my father held sway and no roughhousing was allowed. However, we were allowed to bounce on the velvet sofa. . . ."

The children grew up and moved on, and in the Depression Clover's house fell into the hands of the Episcopal City Mission, which sold it in 1973 to another charitable institution named Edward Everett Hale House, Inc. The name is appropriate, for Hale was a distant relative of Henry Adams, a nephew of that distinguished Edward Everett who married Henry's mother's sister and became president of Harvard, governor of Massachusetts, Secretary of State, and principal speaker at the commemoration of Gettysburg. Hale, who is known today mainly as the author of *The Man Without a Country*, was in his time a prominent Unitarian minister, chaplain to the U.S. Senate, biographer of Emerson and Lowell, and founder of the Lend-a-Hand Societies. The Hale House, Inc., acquired Clover's home for $250,000 as a residence for the aged. The place now has, the organization proudly states, "42 private bedrooms, most with washbasins."

It is pleasant enough, in its way. There is still a grand piano in the front parlor, and if Clover's dining room is now filled with more than a dozen spindly tables with white tablecloths, that is probably inevitable. So is the protective array of pipes and sprinkler systems that snake along the ceilings. So is the air-conditioning unit that hums noisily alongside the African violets in the bay window. The goal, says one of the brochures produced by Hale House, "is to provide a secure residence close to downtown religious and social activities which are meaningful to older persons."

The Adamses' Harvard of the early 1870's was in a state of crisis, as Harvard so often is. Indeed, the whole history of the university, extending now over nearly three and a half centuries, can be interpreted principally as a history of reforms and counterreforms, of conflicts between the rival principles of freedom and authority, sweeping to and fro like tidal waves over the same immutable rocks of youthful ignorance.

The very concept of grading students' work was originally considered a necessary reform, a curb on indulgence. It was promulgated in 1825 and soon degenerated into the disciplinary "Scale of Merit" that proved such a bane to the students of Henry Adams' generation. Conservatives nonetheless clung, as they still do, to the idea that the purpose of education was to instill in all students a certain corpus of knowledge. Thus all Freshmen entering the college in the fall of 1868, the last year of the pre-Eliot era, were required to study the same courses of Latin, Greek, Mathematics, French, Elocution, and Ethics. Yet a report by the General Court had complained as long ago as 1850 that such elitist requirements were irrelevant to modern life, that students should "seek specific learning for a specific purpose," and that a college should help them to become "better farmers, mechanics or merchants."

Harvard had endured six presidents during the twenty years before Eliot, all of them ministers, none of them very successful at his academic post. The last of these, Thomas Hill, resigned because of a personal bereavement in the fall of 1868, and the Board of Overseers dawdled for five months before approving even a search for a successor. "They . . . felt," as Charles Francis Adams,

Jr., later wrote, "that a classical education was the important distinction between a man who had been to college and a man who had not been to college, and that anything that diminished the importance of this distinction was essentially revolutionary and tended to anarchy . . . and that it was to be deferred, so far as possible, to the future, if it could not be postponed altogether."

Charles William Eliot was hardly a revolutionary, much less an anarchist. He was a descendant of that Andrew Eliot who came to America from East Coker, Somersetshire, where, as another of his descendants has written:

> *Houses rise and fall, crumble, are extended,*
> *Are removed, destroyed, restored. . . .*
> *In my beginning is my end.*

Four generations later, Samuel Eliot rose from impoverished gentility to make a fortune in trade and to leave his eight children an estate of $1,200,000. His son, also named Samuel, served briefly and decorously as mayor of Boston but he eventually found his vocation laboring in such semi-philanthropic roles as president of the Boston Academy of Music, treasurer of Harvard, and superintendent of the Prison Discipline Society. In his house at 31 Beacon Street, there was born, on March 20, 1834, his third child and only son, Charles William, cursed in his first moment of daylight with a huge, swollen, liver-colored birthmark that blotched most of the right side of his face. "You must realize," a cousin of Eliot's once said about his lifelong quality of reserve, "that when he was a boy he was hooted off the Boston Common because of his face."

Eliot was a diligent student, organized, efficient, rigorously self-disciplined. "Dear Mother," he wrote in a characteristically solemn letter in the spring of 1854, "I have chosen the profession of a student and teacher of science. . . . 'To do all to the glory of God' should be the ruling motive of a Christian's life. Man glorifies God, 1st by being *useful*. . . ." That fall, at the age of twenty, Eliot became a tutor in mathematics. To make the study of trigonometry more attractive, he took his students out of the classroom and began a survey of the college grounds, the first accurate map of the area ever made. To avoid the embarrassments of oral examination, which may have embarrassed him as much as his pupils, he persuaded a reluctant faculty to permit the novelty of written exams. Within a few years, when he began teaching freshman chemistry, his restless intelligence involved itself in all manner of college problems. He placed orders for the library for literary works from Germany, he supervised the construction of Appleton Chapel, he negotiated with the Cambridge Gas Company for the conversion of dormitories from whale-oil lamps to natural gas.

When the Rumford Professorship on the Application of Science to the Useful Arts became vacant in 1863, Eliot hoped to win it. Despite all his gifts as a teacher and an administrator, however, he suffered a fundamental handicap, noticeable even to one of his young pupils, William James, who observed in a letter: "I don't believe he is a very accomplished chemist." Professor Agassiz and several other members of the faculty argued strenuously that the appointment should go to the distinguished Wolcott Gibbs, and their arguments prevailed. Eliot, heartbroken, resigned and set out for Paris with his wife and two young children. He sought what Gibbs had—a European training—but he soon found himself less interested in European science than in European teaching. In France and then in Germany, he proceeded from classroom to classroom, interrogating teachers, observing their methods, noting, for example, that Marburg had five chemistry courses to Harvard's one, that every one of the new polytechnical institutes on the continent was subsidized by the government, and that "a man can learn many things in Germany which are not taught at all with us."

Eliot was not alone in his observations. On the contrary, national political and social forces were already creating the conditions that were destined to bring Eliot to power, and to keep him there for forty years, to make him the most influential educator of his time. In 1863, the very year of Eliot's humiliation and exile, Congress passed the Morrill Act, providing for a number of so-called land-grant colleges devoted to the new technologies that would be needed for the conquest of the West and the industrialization of America. As soon as the war ended, the Massachusetts Institute of Technology opened its doors, and President William B. Rogers offered "a general education founded upon the mathematical, physical and natural sciences, English and other modern languages, and mental and political science." One of Rogers' first moves was to write to Eliot in Germany and invite him to join the original faculty of ten. Eliot happily agreed. And when not enough students appeared to fill the new building on Boylston Street, M.I.T. advertised in the newspapers, offering to teach empirical laboratory techniques to schoolteachers who had previously used only textbooks. Eliot found his middle-aged pupils "eager to learn the novel method, but they had not the faintest idea how to learn it, how to work themselves with their own eyes and fingers, to make their own experiments and to draw their own inferences." Eliot and a colleague named F. H. Storer summed up their methods in a textbook of their own, A Compendious Manual of Qualitative Chemical Analysis, which rapidly became a standard work, even in Europe. For a more general audience, Eliot organized his views in two articles that appeared in The Atlantic Monthly in February and March of 1869. In his coolly organized way, Eliot insisted that America must begin "a system of education based chiefly upon the pure and applied sciences, the living European languages, and mathematics instead of upon Greek, Latin, and mathematics, as in the college system." As for the tradition-minded opponents of this view, Eliot declared that "the vulgar argument that the study of the classics is necessary to make a gentleman is beneath contempt."

Within six years of his repudiation by Harvard, then, Eliot had transformed himself from a man judged inadequate for a chair in applied science into a national authority on the process of scientific teaching. And he had accomplished this feat during a period of personal disaster. His philanthropic father had made a financial misjudgment, gone bankrupt, and soon died. Just a few months after the birth of Eliot's fourth child, his wife Ellen collapsed. She was found to have tuberculosis, and urged to go to Europe again, and so the whole family sailed for France. There the baby died. Ellen did not improve. Afflicted with all these anxieties, Eliot came to the edge of a nervous breakdown. At one point, he wandered off a train at the wrong station and lost contact with his family for several hours. Only by a fierce act of will did he manage to recover his self-control and move his establishment back to Cambridge.

The Harvard Corporation's first choice for the vacant presidency was Charles Francis Adams, newly returned from London. Adams declined, saying that he had "no especial fitness" for the office, and that it would "involve a necessity of breaking up all my arrangements." The corporation brooded further. For those opposed to a young scientist like Eliot—still only thirty-five years of age—the natural candidate was the Reverend Andrew Peabody, professor of Christian Morals, who was already acting as president pro tem. For those willing to compromise between the demands of science and religion, the favorite candidate was Ephraim Gurney, who had been a classicist before he turned to history.

When the corporation finally decided on Eliot on March 10, he himself had qualms. His cousin, Theodore Lyman, recorded in his diary that "Charlie" Eliot was very sad because "Ellen was very low, and her life was now measured by hours." Lyman urged him to prayer and hard work. Only then did Eliot disclose that he had been offered the presidency of Harvard, and that "he doubted of accepting, because 1. Some would oppose—Agassiz and others. 2. He was very young. 3. He now occupied a place in another institution and might not come in fittingly. 4. This was a public position and the mark on his face might take from its dignity. I debated each of these points." Eliot duly agreed to accept the post, and in fact said proudly, "It is a tremendous success!" Lyman was moved. "I put my arms around him," he recalled, "and kissed him." Ellen Eliot lived just long enough to hear of the tremendous success. When Charles told her of the corporation's decision, she whispered, "That is a big hole for my boy's boots to fill." The next day, she died.

On a raw, gray day the following October, Harvard gathered to witness its new president's inauguration, and to hear him outline its future. He insisted that there was really no conflict between science and religion, or between technology and humanism, and that Harvard must teach all of them at a much higher level than before. "A university must be indigenous; it must be rich; but, above all, it must be free," said Eliot. "The winnowing breeze of freedom must blow through all its chambers." One woman in the audience recorded that Ralph Waldo Emerson was there, right in front, "listening and smiling and assenting." And John Fiske, the young apostle of Herbert Spencer, and of that "Social Darwinism" that was to provide the creed for all the demands of postwar capitalism, found the whole speech "grand and impressive." He wrote to his wife: "We are going to have new times here at Harvard. No more old fogyism."

The fact that Emerson and Fiske were sitting in the First Parish Church was itself a sign of the new times at Harvard, for Eliot, having appointed Gurney as the college's first dean and put him in charge of all undergraduate disciplinary problems, determined to start his regime by reorganizing and reforming the graduate schools into some semblance of a European university. "The ignorance and general incompetence of the average graduate of American medical schools . . . is something horrible to contemplate," Eliot declared. He insisted, for the first time, and against the opposition of traditionalists like Oliver Wendell Holmes, on stiff entrance requirements and annual written exams. He imposed the same reforms on the law school, which then had only three professors and an army of students who had never finished college. Finally, Eliot inaugurated and established and embellished the idea of a graduate school of the arts and sciences. But his first and most fundamental reform was to seek out new teachers.

He summoned both Emerson and Fiske to give a series of lectures on philosophy. He summoned William Dean Howells, too, to lecture on modern Italian literature. Eliot appreciated famous names, but he was just as ready to gamble on the unknown, the young and the inexperienced. Many of his choices have inevitably disappeared into the mists, but the cumulative quality of his early appointments is impressive: Oliver Wendell Holmes, Jr., instructor in the Constitution; William James, instructor in psychology; Charles Eliot Norton, lecturer on the fine arts; Christopher Langdell, professor of law, and, of course, Henry Adams, assistant professor of history.

It is sometimes difficult to imagine, in the Cambridge now dominated by massive brick libraries and twisting steel science centers, how small and crude and primitive Harvard was when Adams appeared there a century ago. One of Eliot's first reforms outside the intellectual field was to demolish the cluster of outdoor privies that had stood behind University Hall for as long as anyone could remember, along with the thicket of evergreens that were supposed to disguise them. In place of this public arrangement, he ordered the first toilets built in the dormitories, which had not even had running water until a tap was installed in the cellar of Grays Hall in 1863.

The Harvard Square of a century ago was still little more than a village. A handsome elm stood at the center, which is now dedicated entirely to a subway station. Around the elm, there were no more than a dozen shops, and a pump with a watering trough for passing horses. Cows stood tethered, amiably chewing their cuds, in the fields beyond the Common. It was, of course, a very intellectual village. Every week or so, a dozen worthies like Howells and Norton met at Craigie House on Brattle Street to hear the white-bearded old Longfellow read aloud the latest canto of his translation of Dante—reading, as Howells later recalled, "with a mellow resonant murmur, like the note of some deep-throated horn." They analyzed each line, suggesting variations, elucidating obscurities, while Longfellow's terrier groaned and snuffled on the carpet.

Howells, the Ohio printer's son who had become editor of *The Atlantic*, was deeply impressed. He judged "the best society" of Cambridge to be "better even" than that of Boston—better because, although "family counted . . . family alone did not mean position," and because "one could be openly poor in Cambridge without open shame, or shame at all, for no one was very rich there." Not very rich, perhaps, but rich enough to maintain a library and to cultivate the Harvard spirit. Howells encountered Henry James the elder, the Swedenborgian philosopher of Quincy Street, and reported James' delight at an exchange with Oliver Wendell Holmes of the medical school.

"Holmes, you are intellectually the most alive man I ever knew," said James.

"I am, I am," said Holmes. "From the crown of my head to the sole of my foot, I'm alive! I'm alive!"

Professor Henry Adams was contemptuous. The literary figures of Cambridge were "the most sociable people in America," he declared, but they "united in Cambridge to make a social desert that would have starved a polar bear."

The Harvard curriculum was equally rudimentary. The history department consisted of three people. Ephraim Gurney taught the history of Greece and Rome, while Henry Torrey taught the history of modern Europe. Between them, as Adams later recalled, "lay a gap of a thousand years, which Adams was expected to fill." He immediately started teaching, to nearly one hundred juniors and seniors, a "general history of Europe from the 10th to 16th centuries." In his second year, he began a seminar in "mediaeval institutions" for seven juniors who were studying for honors—the first such seminar in the bleak history of American education. By his fifth year, he was teaching a graduate seminar in Anglo-Saxon law—again the first of its kind, the first experiment in the postgraduate study of history. In that same year, he also escaped from medieval history sufficiently to create a course that his ancestry required: History V: Colonial history of America to 1789. And the following year came History VI: History of the United States from 1789 to 1840. "The assistant professor had no time to waste on comforts or amusements," Adams later recalled in the *Education*. "He exhausted all his strength in trying to keep one day ahead of his duties. Often the stint ran on, till night and sleep ran short. He could not stop to think whether he were doing the work rightly. He could not get it done to please him. . . ."

Adams makes himself sound like a harried village schoolmaster, but he had very definite plans for what he wanted to do. "The devil is strong in me," he wrote to Jacob Dolson Cox, a civil service reformer who was then serving as Secretary of the Interior, "and my rage for reform is leading me into an open war with the whole system of teaching. Rebellion is in the blood, somehow or other. I can't get on without a fight." To his old friend Gaskell, he sounded equally fierce: "I thoroughly dislike and despise the ruling theories of education in the university," he wrote. "So I . . . shall quietly substitute my own notions for those of the College and teach in my own way. There will be some lively history taught, I can tell you. I hardly know how I am getting on with the students. . . . As a rule they are supernaturally lazy and ignorant. I pound at them in vain nine hours a week."

The accounts left by the victims of his pounding indicate that he was a brilliant innovator and a brilliant success. A small man, thin, frail, nearly bald in his middle thirties, Adams appeared before his students as rather a dandy. "Every feature, every line of his body, his clothes, his bearing, his speech," according to one student, Lindsay Swift, "were well-bred to a degree." He professed a "profound contempt" for all facts. "I rejoice," he said, "that I never remember a date." When a student asked him to explain the meaning of transubstantiation, he answered, "Good heavens! How should I know? Look it up." Such acerbity naturally had its effect. "There was no closing of eyes in slumber when Henry Adams was in command," according to Swift's account. "All was wholly unacademic, no formality, no rigidity, no professional pose."

If this seems banal today, it must be remembered that the Harvard students of Adams' day were expected to memorize long passages from their textbooks, and that they were graded on their ability to recite these texts from memory. Adams' technique, by contrast, was to assign a text and then to interrogate his students on its teaching, challenging both the accuracy and the logic of everything they had read. Henry Cabot Lodge, who previously had "never had my mind roused to any exertion," professed himself unable to explain exactly how Adams' methods "aroused my slumbering faculties," but he did record that Adams "awakened opposition to his own views, and that is one great secret of success in teaching." Actually, Adams often kept his own views secret throughout his interrogations—that is, after all, the Socratic method—and when it came to exams, he wrote to Gaskell, "my rule , . . is to ask questions which I can't answer myself. It astounds me to see how some of my students answer questions which would play the deuce with me."

In late spring of every year, even before Adams had finished grading what he called the "dreary waste of examination books," he abandoned Harvard and accompanied Clover to the seaside village of Beverly Farms. The Adamses bought their first horse, and a phaeton, in which Clover, in Henry's words, "meanders about the country." She also seems, however, to have helped him with some of his work, for he wrote to Gaskell that he had "deputed to my wife all that I could get her to do."

As soon as the exams were graded, the Adamses slipped into an almost stupefyingly peaceful existence. Aside from riding about in Clover's phaeton, Henry observed, one of his "favorite amusements" was "to weed flower beds and train nasturtiums and morning glories to grow up a cord." Another amusement was to go for long walks in the pine forests along the Atlantic Ocean. "I plunge wildly into the depths of the forest," Adams reported, "and on reaching a sheltered spot, I lie down on my back until dinner time. This soothes me. Just now it is strawberry season, and the strawberries also tend to soothe me. On the whole, I am a great deal soothed."

Adams was being, as usual, somewhat disingenuous. He was actually using this summer of 1874 to read for his new course on the American colonial era, the era in which his great-grandfather had first emerged from his barnyard in Quincy. And in the course of his reading, his eyes suddenly failed. It may be tempting to suggest psychological reasons for such a mysterious illness, perhaps an inability to survey one's own origins, but we do not even know the symptoms of Henry's difficulty. He refers quite nonchalantly to "the fact that my eyes suddenly broke down" and adds that "I have neither read nor written anything more than was absolutely necessary."

Clover read to him, and took charge of his correspondence. She also resumed the classical studies that had preoccupied her when she first met him. "My wife flourishes like the nasturtiums which are my peculiar joy," Henry wrote after he had recovered his health. "She studies Greek. All our young women study Greek. It has become the correct thing to do. As I am innocent of Greek and would have to go back twenty years to pick it up, I have to keep her in check with Mediaeval Latin." It all sounds quite Arcadian, and yet in another letter to the same friend in England, Sir Robert Cunliffe, Adams suddenly blurted out an angry indictment that can hardly be dissociated from Clover's Greek. "Our young women are haunted," Adams wrote, "by the idea that they ought to read, or to labor in some way, not for any such frivolous object as making themselves agreeable to society, nor for simple amusement, but 'to improve their minds.' They are utterly unconscious of the pathetic impossibility of improving those hard, thin, one-stringed instruments which they call their minds, and which haven't range enough to master one big emotion, much less to express it in words or figures."

Nor were the Adamses the only people haunted by half-hidden anger in this luxurious seaside resort. One of their neighbors, whom Henry described as being "very worthy," suffered some kind of crisis that Henry could only attribute to his "being out of spirits because he had too much of all he wanted in the world except content." Having made that diagnosis, Henry could quite tranquilly report that his neighbor "sat down in his . . . avenue and blew his brains out as calmly and as practically as if he were a Britisher and was bored with life. There was no flourish, no pathos, no moral, and, except for his poor children and his old father and mother, no tragedy about it. We are a practical people. . . ."

On this bucolic site, the Adamses decided to buy some 20 acres of land and to build a house, right next to that of Dr. Hooper, just as their house in Boston was around the corner from his. It was to be a modest place. Henry referred to it as "our log-hut in the woods," and he estimated the cost of both land and house as "not much more than £3,000." Once he started building, of course, things became somewhat more complicated. There had to be a balcony and dormer windows and pine paneling in the living room and stained-glass windows in the dining room. The price rose to nearly £5,000, but Henry took pride in the fact that he and Clover had "designed and superintended every detail," and that "life for the moment hinges on . . . the projection of a roof-beam."

When it was all done, according to one of Clover's five nieces, it was "rather an ugly house," but another one of the nieces recalled it as an enchanted place. "A footpath, strewn with fragrant pine-needles and bordered with ferns and lichened rocks, led to the Uncle's and Aunt's summer house . . ." Ned Hooper's daughter Mabel wrote. "The nieces remember him as he sat at his desk, in cool white summer clothes—his fine head and thoughtful forehead dominated a small frame; his movements were deliberate—only the scratch of his pen would break the silence of the room. . . . Often in the afternoon, the nieces would watch—almost enviously—the two figures on horseback vanishing into the flickering sunlight of the woods. An impression of oneness of life and mind, of perfect companionship, left an ideal never to be effaced."

The Rubaiyat of Omar Khayyam, as translated by Edward Fitzgerald, was once fresh and new. It appeared as an anonymous pamphlet in 1859, and then was discovered by Rossetti and Swinburne. Henry Adams bought a copy of the third edition, published in 1876, and presented it to Clover. It still lies among the relics of her childhood library, with various verses lightly marked in pencil, indicating that either Henry or Clover must have seen and treasured some message that the modern eye finds hard to discern in these honeyed Romantic verses. Thus:

> *Whether at Naishapur or Babylon,*
> *Whether the Cup with sweet or bitter run,*
> *The Wine of Life keeps oozing drop by drop,*
> *The Leaves of Life keep falling one by one.*
> *Each Morn a thousand roses brings, you say;*
> *Yes, but where leaves the Rose of Yesterday?*

And again:

> *Ah, make the most of what we yet may spend,*
> *Before we too into the Dust descend;*
> *Dust into Dust, and under Dust, to lie,*
> *Sans Wine, sans Song, sans Singer, and—sans End!*

Just three blocks to the south of the Adamses' new house on Marlborough Street, there arose, during these years, a vast construction of Milford granite that would remain forever after, somewhere at the edge of their memory, as a somber, hulking image of Christian faith. In an administrative sense, the new Trinity Church was probably the conception of Henry's second cousin, Phillips Brooks, the impressively handsome orator for the Union cause, who, on becoming rector of Trinity in 1869, at the age of thirty-one, undertook to move it from Summer Street out to Back Bay, to a site on the eastern side of Copley Square, which was described by Bishop William Lawrence as "a desert of dirt, dust, mud and wind."

But when the church building committee solicited competing designs, in the spring of 1872, for a monumental edifice to cost not more than $200,000, the winner was Henry Hobson Richardson, that Falstaffian figure whose heroic bulk testified not only to his robust appetites but also to the chronic disease that would kill him before he was fifty. Richardson, too, was a friend of the Adamses —"Adams made no acquaintance [as a Harvard student] that he valued in after life so much as Richardson," Henry wrote in the *Education*—and it is only reasonable to suppose that they made periodic visits to Copley Square to watch the builders at work.

The project was troubled from the start. The original Trinity Church had burned down in the great fire of 1872. The new site in the wilderness was a rectangle, but that changed into a peculiar polygon through the purchase of an adjoining triangle. Even after the first mighty piles were finally driven into the Back Bay mud in the closing months of 1873, changes kept being made—the parish house moved to one side, the apse enlarged, the central tower reduced. This central tower itself was apparently the object of some major improvisations. The painter John LaFarge, who had traveled widely abroad, sent Richardson a photograph of the Romanesque church at Salamanca, Spain, to show him how he thought the tower should look.

The photograph pleased Richardson and almost overwhelmed his friend Stanford White, who immediately sketched an adaptation that would fit Trinity Church. And so it was done, the "Salamanca Tower," rising to completion during the summer of 1874. Despite his fondness for solemn masses, though, Richardson conceived of Trinity as what he called a "color church," and to achieve this effect, he summoned LaFarge to design a series of stained-glass windows. And LaFarge, under instructions to complete the work within the few months that lay between the appropriation of funds and the deadline for the consecration in February of 1877, called in the young Saint-Gaudens to help with some of the angels. They were all young, these extraordinary talents who gathered under Richardson's aegis to construct this somber hymn of granite. (LaFarge was the oldest, at thirty-nine, when his idea of the Salamanca Tower arose in 1874; Stanford White, who sketched it, was a precocious twenty-one, Saint-Gaudens twenty-six, and Richardson himself just thirty-six.)

The best evidence that Henry and Clover Adams joined in the building, the surveying and inspecting and altering and polishing, is that Adams recreated a very similar scene as the setting for his second novel, *Esther*. It is the most literal of novels. Not only is the heroine based very closely on Clover, but there is very little difficulty in identifying LaFarge as the autocratic painter, Wharton; or Phillips Brooks as the charismatic minister, Hazard, whose first appearance at the consecration of the new church of St. John's sends "a ripple of excitement . . . across the field of bonnets [like] a murmur of rustling cornfields." The Church of St. John is still being decorated, and so it is that Esther is commissioned to help Wharton by painting a mural of St. Cecilia. "The great church was silent with the echoing silence which is audible," Adams wrote. "Except for a call from workmen below to those at work above, or for the murmur of the painters as they chattered in intervals of rest, or for occasional hammering, which echoed in hollow reverberations, no sound disturbed repose. Here one felt the meaning of retreat and self-absorption."

As the election of 1876 approached, Henry Adams could not stay away from politics. Just two years earlier, he had written to his friend Gaskell that "for once no member of my family is a candidate for any position, and it is very unlikely that the result will affect us at all." He also wrote in the same letter that he had lost all interest in politics. "I prefer to stick to my professorship for some years to come, if not for life. There, at any rate, I can make myself useful." A year later, however, he was writing to Gaskell of starting a new "party of the centre."

Such ambitions took him to Washington, inevitably, and there he planned to move in with Clover's Uncle Sam, the Congressman, from whose house she had once sallied forth to watch General Grant review the Army of the Potomac. Sam Hooper's family had sailed off to Europe in the early months of 1875, and so his house was nearly empty, and, as Henry put it, "very agreeable." On their arrival, however, the Adamses found that the Congressman was gravely ill with pneumonia. Clover promptly took charge of her uncle's household, just as she had always taken charge of her father, while Henry looked on with a certain amount of displeasure.

"We had to assume control of everything," he wrote to Gaskell, "and after growing steadily worse, he at last died yesterday morning and is to have a big state funeral from the Capitol tomorrow, at which I, who had by no means a high regard for him, must figure as one of three chief mourners in the face of all Congress. Verily, life is an eccentric article! . . . There would be a good reason for it if any of his millions came to me, but I am not profitted, I regret to say, by his demise."

Henry Adams, too, was undergoing what James Russell Lowell had called "a professor change." In his first year at Harvard, 1871, he had joined his brother Charles in publishing *Chapters of Erie and Other Essays*, which combined Charles' attacks on railroad corruption with the best of Henry's political reporting, including his brilliant account of Jay Gould's gold conspiracy. Five years later, in 1876, Adams financed and published his second book, this time a collaboration with Lodge and two other graduate students, entitled *Essays in Anglo-Saxon Law*.

From his original interest in the family as the basis of early society, Adams had now devised a sweeping theory that the very idea of representative government had come to England (and thus to America) from the primeval forests of Germany. "The long and patient labors of German scholars," he briskly began, "seem to have now established that the entire Germanic family, in its earliest known stage of development, placed the administration of law, as it placed the political administration, in the hands of popular assemblies composed of the free, able-bodied members of the commonwealth. This great principle is . . . the most important which historical investigation has of late years established."

It had not, of course, been established. The evolution of political institutions is far more complicated than that. But the "great principle" fitted well with Bancroft's view, a standard American view, of Bismarckian Germany as a force for progress and enlightenment, justly triumphant over the extravagant incompetence of Napoleonic France. The great principle also served to legitimize the rebellion of Adams' ancestors—a need less manifest now than in Adams' time—for if the principle of representative government could be traced back to Anglo-Saxon origins, then the claims of Britain's kings could be shown to represent, as Adams put it, "a mere historical blunder." The great principle served yet another purpose, and that was to demonstrate that the postwar talk about popular democracy should not obliterate the original creators of the very idea of democracy. From these roots it had come; here let it remain.

In our time, the prevailing wisdom is that the Germanic tribes were simply savages, that all they bequeathed to their successors was savagery, and that Adams' thesis is simply wrong. But the "professor change" lies not only in Adams' support of mistaken theory but in his retreat from political reform into academicism. From that opening sentence, which betrays a stylistic pomposity that rarely appeared in his Washington reports, Adams soon descended into fretful arguments with rival authorities and extended quotations from Anglo-Saxon legal documents (". . . *manna daeg for syxtigum mancesa claenes goldes aeghwelces* . . ."). Scholarly reviewers of the time were impressed. The *Law Magazine and Review* of London praised Adams' book as "so interesting," and the *American Law Review* called it "remarkable." A modern reader poring over the yellowed and crumbling pages in a library reading room is more likely to agree with Lodge's view that the whole subject is "inexpressibly dreary."

Yet in Adams' wanderings through the wilderness of medieval law, he kept mulling over a question that was older and more

fundamental than any law—the family, once again, and more particularly the creators of families, the women. And can we not hear,
in the background, Clover saying, just as Abigail had said of John
Adams' constitutional studies: "Remember the ladies"? In any case,
that was the subject on Henry's mind when he was selected in the
winter of 1876 for that splendid Boston institution, the Lowell
lectureship. John Lowell, dying on the Nile, had written a will
declaring that he was "gazing in awe" at the ruins of Thebes and
wanted to leave $250,000 to sponsor an annual series of free lectures
by various scholars who believed in "the divine revelation of the
Old and New Testaments."

Agassiz had been one of the first, and all manner of scholars
followed in his wake. Lowell's will had specified that the audience
be "neatly dressed and of orderly behavior," which meant in practice that it consisted mainly of the lecturer's friends and relatives.
To these, Henry Adams addressed himself on the topic of "Primitive Rights of Women."

It was then the popular view—to some extent, it still is—that
the women of ancient times were sold by their fathers to their
husbands as slaves, and that only the coming of Christianity had
modified their servitude. Adams disagreed strongly. Just as he had
found in the forests of Germany a birthplace for representative
government, so he now discovered in the same wilderness the free
woman. He began by suggesting that all people had once lived in
an "idealized golden age . . . when all were of one family, and all
products of the earth . . . were held in common." He conceded
that "such pure communism, if it ever existed in real life, ceased at
an early time," and that "no society in which communal marriage
was practiced has been found." Still, Adams evoked the evidence
that could be found in primitive societies—not a common practice
among academicians of the nineteenth century—to argue that
women had once enjoyed civil rights equal to those of men.

He started with the American Indians, whom he considered
approximately analogous to the Germanic tribes of Roman times.
The evidence that Indians bought their wives simply indicated an
exchange of gifts, he said—an argument that remained just as true
for Bostonian marriages of the nineteenth century. A bought or
captured bride "became neither a slave nor property," Adams
wrote, "but remained as before, in most cases, a member of her

own family and clan; her children followed her line of descent, and the husband belonged to her as much as she belonged to the husband. . . . In most cases she was the head of the family; her husband usually came to live with her, not she with him, and her children belonged to her clan, not to their father's."

From here, Adams turned back to the Egyptians: "The female line of descent was followed regularly if not invariably among Egyptians, as among American Indians. The queen sat on the throne with her husband; her statue rests in the tomb by his side. . . ." And the Greeks: "The wife . . . was always a free woman, with rights which her husband could not disregard. The whole story of both the Iliad and the Odyssey is little more than a running commentary on the Greek law of marriage." And finally the Norsemen who settled in Iceland and produced the *Njalsaga*, which, "like the poems of Homer, turns on the character of a woman."

Adams took an almost gleeful pleasure in recounting the various marriages of Hallgerda, who "was fair-haired, and had so much of it that she could hide herself in it." Hallgerda was sold and married by her father, without her approval, to a suitor named Thorwald. "She revenged herself upon her husband by her intolerable temper until . . . her husband was stung by an insult to such anger that he gave her a blow on the face that drew blood. That same day she caused him to be murdered, and then she rode home to her father." Hallgerda's father, by law, had to pay off the family of his murdered son-in-law, so he was more cautious in arranging her second marriage to another suitor with the splendid name of Glum. Hallgerda's property had "accumulated until it had reached a great sum," but Glum matched it, and both Hallgerda and Glum agreed that "they were to go shares, half and half." Adams is rather cryptic about Glum's fate, telling us only that "her want of heart was again the cause of her second husband's murder by the same hand which had slain the first."

Hallgerda once again returned to her father's house, once again recouped her fortunes and once again was married off, this time to Gunnar, "a wise and high-minded man." Hallgerda promptly "made his life miserable" by her efforts "to embroil him with his friends and neighbors in quarrels of every sort." He even caught her stealing from him, and so he slapped her, and so she called in the murderers. There seems to have been a rather large band of them, since Gunnar killed two and wounded eight before one of the attackers cut his bowstring. Gunnar begged Hallgerda to give him two locks of her hair to make a new bowstring. Hallgerda reminded him of his slap and then sat by to watch as his enemies slowly closed in on him and killed him. And she lived on, Adams concluded, "to enjoy the wealth acquired from her three murdered husbands, and to bring more misery and death on her friends." The lesson to be learned from this saga was clear. "Surely," Adams declared, "a woman of this stamp was no slave, no descendant of slaves, no possible connection of slaves. All the fierce and untamable instincts of infinite generations of free, wild animals were embodied in her."

Quite so. One imagines the enlightened ladies of Boston, assembled in the snow-covered lecture hall, nodding sagely at the little professor's account of Hallgerda's homicides. And the very following evening, Susan B. Anthony was to make a speech urging the women of Boston to fight for their right to vote. How, then, had it happened that the descendants of these "free, wild animals" had been deprived of the right to decide their own political fortunes? It was the Christian Church, Henry Adams told them, which, far from protecting and exalting women, as many clergymen of the day liked to preach, had stripped them of their ancestral rights. "The Church was a Roman church," he said. "It rose to power under the intense moral reaction against the corruptions of the Empire; and of all the corruptions of the Empire none had been more scandalous than the corruption of the women. . . . The Church felt with reason that society should be taught to obey; and of all classes of society, the women . . . were obliged to learn it most thoroughly. The Church established a new ideal of feminine character. Thenceforward not the proud, self-confident, vindictive woman of German tradition received the admiration and commanded the service of law and society. . . . In reprobation of these the Church raised up, with the willing cooperation of the men, the modern type of Griselda—the meek and patient, the silent and tender sufferer, the pale reflection of the Mater Dolorosa, submissive to every torture that her husband could invent. . . ."

How fascinating, to the enlightened ladies of Boston, to hear this diminutive professor preach that they had once been, and should again be, proud and self-confident and dominant even to the point of avenging an insult by assassination. And who, in that audience, could have listened with more intense fascination than Clover Adams?

Somewhere in the depths of his soul, Henry Adams knew that it was not his destiny to be a Harvard professor. His grandfather, John Quincy Adams, had been, for a time, the Boylston Professor of Rhetoric, but that had been only an interlude. His father, Charles Francis Adams, had declined the presidency of the university as an interruption of his editing of the family papers. How, then, could Henry content himself in lecturing to youths? "The instruction of boys," he noted, "is mean work."

"Since being married I do less than ever before," he wrote to Gaskell from Beverly Farms, with a curious mixture of dissatisfaction and complacency, of self-accusation and self-indulgence. "Here is another winter gone, and I am again nursing nasturtiums and feeding mosquitoes. I am going on to thirty-eight years old, the yawning gulf of middle age. Another, the fifth, year of professordom is expiring this week. I am balder, duller, more pedantic, and more lazy than ever. . . . My fits of wrath and rebellion against the weakness and shortcomings of mankind are less violent than they were, though grumbling has become my favorite occupation. I have ceased to grow rapidly either in public esteem or in mental development. One year resembles another and if it weren't for occasional disturbing dreams of decay, disaster or collapse, I should consider myself as having attained as much of Nirvana as a man of my race and temperament can expect to do. . . ."

There were, however, those occasional dreams of decay and disaster, which were also dreams of conquest and power. Unlike Charles Francis Adams, who had come to enjoy his exile in Quincy, Henry still could not accept the idea that the dynasty had ended. If the routines of a Harvard professor represented Nirvana, then Nirvana was not really Adams' goal. "Anything," he wrote bitterly to Lodge, "which takes a man morally out of Beacon St., Nahant, and Beverly Farms, Harvard College and the Boston press, must be in itself a good." It was not morality, of course, that attracted Adams to Washington, but rather a passionate sense that he belonged there, if not as a politician, then as an observer of politicians. "It is no end of fun to come back here," he had written to Gaskell during a visit to the capital in 1874. "And although our politics just now are very deep in the mud, and our politicians are a feeble kind of forcibles, still it is fun to see them wriggle and it gives one a lofty sense of one's own importance to be able to smile contemptuously on men in high places."

That, yes, was one of Adams' greatest delights—and Clover's too—but Henry had not yet given up the idea, nor had Clover, that he might himself become, somehow, one of those men in high places. Not a president of course, nor even a cabinet minister or a senator, but nonetheless a man of influence, a man who could make himself heard at the center of power.

11

WE ARE OF USE IN THE WORLD

"The president is detested by everyone," Henry Adams wrote to one of his English friends early in 1875 about Ulysses S. Grant. "All the most important men of both parties unite in denouncing him as a most objectionable person and a very dangerous one. Society talks about him as a great blackguard. . . ." In this situation, Henry apparently saw an opportunity for the last great assault on the White House by the Adams family. He decided to join in the creation of a new political party. "I am engaged single-handed in the slight task of organizing a new party to contest the next presidential election in '76," he wrote to Gaskell. "As yet I have only three allies, a broken down German politician, a newspaper correspondent, and a youth of twenty who is to do all the work. With these instruments, I propose to do no less than decide the election of 1876. You will see. . . ."

The pronouncement sounds absurd, but American politics had reached a point of absurdity. President Grant, no matter how debauched and discredited he might seem in Boston, yearned for the exoneration implied in a third term. The orthodox wing of the Republicans, known as the Stalwarts, could not decide whether to support their bungling president or a younger and more efficient pirate like House Speaker James G. Blaine or Senator Roscoe Conkling of New York. The Reform Republicans, led by Senator Carl Schurz of Missouri (that "broken down German politician"), hoped to steer the party toward some more respectable figure like Treasury Secretary Benjamin Bristow. The Democrats, still cursed with the stain of rebellion, saw their first real opportunity in a decade in the candidacy of the puritanical reformer from New York, Governor Samuel Tilden. In the midst of such confusion, Henry Adams really believed that a small band of reformers could play a pivotal role. "My scheme is to organize a party of the centre and to support the party which accepts our influence most completely," he wrote to Gaskell. He did his best to sound worldly, but he added a wistful postscript: "In no case can I come in for any part of the plunder. . . . My father and brothers block my path fatally, for all three stand far before me in the order of promotion."

Senator Schurz seems to have believed that the nation was finally ready for his friend Charles Francis Adams, who by now had served as a reluctant presidential candidate for almost thirty years. Adams was still reluctant, and his son, for one, knew it. "To make my father president next year [was] Schurz's most earnest wish and hope," Henry wrote to Gaskell, "but emphatically it was no part of my plan, and I am much afraid that we shall all shipwreck on that rock." Some two hundred of the self-styled Independents—among them such notable editors as William Cullen Bryant of the New York *Evening Post* and E. L. Godkin of *The Nation*—convened in New York that May to decide on their strategy. A resolution to nominate Adams attracted little support, and so the gathering decided to wait and see what happened at the Republican convention. When the Republicans decided to nominate the uninspiring but respectable Governor Rutherford B. Hayes of Ohio, the reform movement claimed credit for having checkmated the party's worst candidates, and then collapsed. Schurz rejoined the Republican regulars, and Charles Francis Adams was nominated, to his surprise, as the Democratic candidate for governor of Massachusetts. Following his customary strategy, Adams promptly left for Philadelphia to attend the centennial exposition. He stayed away from Massachusetts until the end of September, made no speeches, attended no rallies, and was soundly defeated.

Henry and Clover also went to the Philadelphia exposition. They both caught colds and disapproved of everything. "From my soul I hate and contemn these big shows . . ." Henry wrote. This one, he added, "is bigger, noisier, more crowded, and its contents more uniformly indifferent and vulgar, than any of its predecessors." Adams' own contribution to the national centennial was to devote the October issue of *The North American Review* to the subject. It was a rather bleak survey. Adams featured articles on the Whiskey Ring and the Tweed regime in New York, and he ended by urging all independent voters to cast their ballots for Tilden. The magazine's publishers, Osgood and Houghton, objected to such an affront to worthy Republicanism. Adams was happy to seize on what he called "a trifling disagreement" and resign from the burden of editing the financially ailing *North American*. The publishers could only insert a note in the October issue announcing that the editor had "retired . . . on account of a difference of opinion with the proprietors as to the political character of this number," and that the proprietors were not committed to "the opinions expressed therein."

Henry was enraged by the whole experience of that election year. He had devoted many hours to meetings and intrigues. He had entered into serious negotiations to buy either the Boston *Advertiser* or the Boston *Post* as the organ of the reform movement. And in the end, he had accomplished nothing whatsoever. "We organized our party, and as usual have been beaten," he wrote to Gaskell. "After our utmost efforts we have only succeeded in barring the road to our opponents and forcing them to nominate as candidate for the Presidency one Hayes of Ohio, a third-rate nonentity, whose only recommendation is that he is obnoxious to no one. I hope to enjoy the satisfaction of voting against him." And again, to Lodge: "Politics have ceased to interest me. I am satisfied that the machine can't be smashed. . . . We have ourselves saved it by a foolish attempt to run it, which we shall never succeed in." And again, to Lodge: "I cannot help laughing to think how, after all our labor and after we had by main force created a party for Schurz to lead, he himself, without a word or a single effort to keep his party together, kicked us over in his haste to jump back to the Republicans. . . . I am not angry with him, but of course his leadership is at an end. . . . I hope he will get his cabinet office, and I hope he will forget that we ever worked to make him our leader." And again, to Gaskell: "We dissolved, like a summer cloud. I am left smiling at the ruins." And yet again, to Lodge: "Presidential elections make me sick."

Despite Adams' anger, Hayes' victory in the disputed election of 1876 was, in a perverse way, a kind of victory for the reformers. After a century of investigation, it is still difficult to tell exactly what happened in that confusion of bribes and threats, of canvassing boards and electoral commissions and occupation troops. It seems almost certain that bribery combined with Republican party loyalties to produce fraudulent ballot counts in Louisiana and Florida. On the other hand, it seems equally certain that Democratic intimidation prevented many black voters from getting to the polls. If both parties had been honest, Tilden probably would have won the election, but when Hayes came to power, he did his best to placate the reformers and to install an honest administration. Carl Schurz was rewarded for his "loyalty" by being made Secretary of the Interior. William Evarts, who had served with Charles Francis Adams as U.S. counsel during the *Alabama* proceedings in Geneva, now became Secretary of State. "My political friends, or one wing of them, have come into power," Adams wrote to Gaskell early in 1877, but he could not refrain from adding that they had come to power "under circumstances which prevent me from giving them more than a silent and temporary sympathy. This is an illustration of the way politics work; always unsatisfactorily."

What brought Adams back to Washington actually had very little to do with the politics of the Gilded Age, but rather, as so often happened, with the politics of his grandfather and his great-grandfather. Albert Gallatin, dead for nearly thirty years, had come to America from Geneva and taught at Harvard and speculated in land and became a congressman and argued successfully against John Adams' efforts to build a navy to fight the French. He had become Jefferson's treasury secretary, and frugally reduced the national debt by more than $14 million—a type of man, obviously, to appeal to John Quincy Adams, who first came to know him when they were both commissioners assigned to negotiate the Treaty of Ghent, and who, on being elected President, appointed Gallatin to be minister to Britain. Now his son and literary executor, Albert Rolaz Gallatin, was looking around for someone to edit his father's papers. Perhaps through the good offices of George Bancroft, who had returned from Berlin to finish the tenth and last volume of his epic history of America, Gallatin entered into correspondence with Henry Adams.

The two men had known each other slightly for a decade, but it was only now that Adams had embarked on teaching his course on the colonial period that the outcome was obvious. Gallatin offered Adams the assignment of editing what Adams called the "great mass of papers" that the former treasury secretary had left behind, and Adams, who was already groping, in the depths of his mind, toward the great ancestral history that would occupy him for most of the next two decades, was delighted to accept. Besides, he was sick of Harvard. "I regard my university work as essentially done," he wrote to Gaskell early in 1877. "All the influence I can exercise has been exercised. The end of it is mere railing at the idiocies of a university education."

William Evarts, the new Secretary of State and an old friend of the family, offered Adams a desk in the State Department and free access to the diplomatic archives. Adams was delighted to resign from Harvard and to move south. "The fact is I gravitate to a capital by a primary law of nature," he wrote that November. "This is the only place in America where society amuses me, or where life offers variety. Here, too, I can fancy that we are of use in the world, for we distinctly occupy niches that ought to be filled. We have taken a large house in which we seem lost. Our watercolors and drawings go with us. . . ."

Aside from all political consideration, Adams had always felt a mysterious affection for Washington. On first visiting it as a boy from Boston, he had hated the confrontation with slavery ("Slavery struck him in the face," he recalled in the *Education*. "It was a nightmare; a horror; a crime; the sum of all wickedness!"), and yet he loved the indolence of Southern society: "The want of barriers, of pavements, of forms; the looseness, the laziness. . . . the pigs in the streets; the negro babies and their mothers with bandanas; the freedom, openness, swagger, of nature and man, soothed [him]."

Twenty years later, the Washington Monument which had been started in 1848 still stood uncompleted, and Mark Twain used it as a splendid metaphor for the capital of the age that he named in his novel *The Gilded Age* (written in collaboration with Charles Dudley Warner and published in 1873). "The Monument to the Father of his Country towers out of the mud—sacred soil is the customary term," Twain wrote. "It has the aspect of a factory chimney with the top broken off. The skeleton of a decaying scaffolding lingers about its summit, and tradition says that the spirit of Washington often comes down and sits on these rafters to enjoy this tribute of respect which the nation has reared as the symbol of its unappeasable gratitude. . . . You can see the cow-sheds about its base, and the contented sheep nibbling pebbles in the desert solitudes that surround it, and the tired pigs dozing in the holy calm of its protecting shadow."

All of Washington's city inspired Twain to varying degrees of contempt. Casting an eye from Capitol Hill along Pennsylvania Avenue, he observed that "the stores and hotels that wall in this broad avenue are mean, and cheap, and dingy." And at the far end, there was "a fine large white barn, with wide unhandsome grounds. The President lives there. It is ugly enough outside, but that is nothing to what it is inside. Dreariness, flimsiness, bad taste reduced to mathematical completeness is what the inside offers. . . ." In the streets around the White House there were so many lounging job seekers that Twain described the whole city as "the grand old benevolent National Asylum for the Helpless," and the unpaved streets themselves were in such condition that "you wonder at the short-sightedness of the city fathers . . . in that they did not dilute the mud a little more and use them for canals."

There had been a lot of paving of streets in those postwar years, however, and some 60,000 trees had been planted as markers in the dusty wilderness. The city was beginning—though still inhabited by only 150,000 people, about half the population of Boston—to indulge in the pretensions that were soon to become imperial. "Washington seems to be becoming more and more of a resort for people who want to amuse themselves in the winter in a mild climate, and is greatly changed in all respects . . ." E. L. Godkin of *The Nation* wrote to Charles Eliot Norton back in Cambridge. "A great many new houses have gone up, and a general air of smartness and enterprize has come over the place. There is something pathetic in the appearance of the crowds of 'plain people' from the country one sees going into the Capitol every morning in their best clothes, and crowding the gallery and looking down at the legislators with mingled awe and admiration. I think what strikes one most about members of the House is the cleanliness of their shirts."

To this primitive and provincial capital, hardly worthy of being a suburb of such newly invented capitals as Brasília or Rawalpindi, Henry Adams brought Clover. And with great good cheer and optimism. They were very rich, of course, and that tends to make life pleasant. Their joint income has been estimated at $25,000 a year, which, in those tax-free times, when factory workers earned less than a dollar a day, was quite comfortable. Besides, Dr. Hooper sent substantial checks every Christmas. Large houses could be bought and furnished, and servants hired. Still, at the ominous age of thirty-nine, Henry had just quit the only regular job he had ever had and embarked on the first full-scale historical work he had ever attempted.

A time for nervousness and anxiety, surely, but also an escape from the familial burdens of Boston, and Henry regarded his new headquarters with delight. "One of these days this will be a very great city . . ." he wrote to Gaskell. "Even now it is a beautiful one, and its situation is superb. As I belong to the class of people who have great faith in this country and who believe that in another century it will be saying in its turn the last word of civilization, I enjoy the expectation of the coming day, and try to imagine that I am myself [one of] the first faint rays of that great light which is to dazzle and set the world on fire hereafter."

Henry and Clover arrived in Washington on November 10, 1877, and moved into a house they had rented from William W. Corcoran, a place known as the "yellow house," at 1501 H Street. "We strut round as if we were millionaires," Clover wrote to her father. "Henry says for the first time in his life he feels like a gentleman." The new house was just a block from the park in front of the White House, then known as President's Square but soon to acquire its present name of Lafayette Square. It was an almost inevitable location. "As for the White House," Adams later wrote in the *Education*, "all the boy's family had lived there. . . . The boy half thought he owned it, and took for granted that he should some day live in it." But the stone figure on the prancing horse in Lafayette Square was that of John Quincy Adams' successor, Andrew Jackson, and now the occupant of the White House was a man whom nobody could easily imagine on any horse at all, the staid and stolid ex-Governor of Ohio, Rutherford B. Hayes. Lucy Hayes insisted that no liquor be served at the presidential table.

In our time, every President is so swathed in official admiration that it is hard to imagine a period when the chief executive of the nation, the commander in chief of the armed forces, was widely regarded with a mixture of amusement and contempt. This had been, nonetheless, the fate of Fillmore and Tyler and Buchanan, and now it was to be the fate of Rutherford B. Hayes, who had not even, after all, won the election. One of Clover's first letters from Washington back to Dr. Hooper in Boston reported a dinner-table encounter with the wife of Senator Stanley Matthews of Ohio. The

Senator, Clover wrote, "looks just like all Ohio members—light-haired, big, broad-faced, expressionless," but she thought better of his wife, "a simple motherly old soul with white curls—no non-sense about her except that she continually said 'no maam' and 'yes maam' to me! She likes 'Alice in Wonderland.' " Mrs. Matthews was the first woman Clover met in Washington who proved to be "very intimate with the Hayeses," and she was delighted to report that "they suffer much from rats in the White House, who run over their bed and nibble the president's toes! 'Uneasy lie the toes that wear a crown.' "

Two weeks later, toward the end of November of 1877, Clover and a group of her Washington friends condescended to visit the White House and pay their respects to the President's wife. "Mrs. Hayes received us very simply and graciously," Clover reported back to her father. "She is quite nice looking, dark with smooth black hair combed low over her ears and a high comb behind—her dress a plain untrimmed black silk, a broad white Smyrna lace tie round her neck—no jewelry. Miss Platt, her niece, was unaffected . . . tho' she does talk through her nose badly."

Clover engaged in conversation with the white-bearded old George Bancroft, her kinsman, the historian, and with General Sherman, the hero of the march to Atlanta, and then with a passing diplomat named Stoughton, the new minister to Russia, who "looks like a handsome unprincipled old buffalo," and then with the new Attorney General, Charles Devens. It was while she was talking to Devens that "a stout, common-looking man came in and came towards me and held out his hand." Clover did not recognize the common-looking man, and one can only imagine the chill with which she regarded his outstretched hand. The Attorney General, of course, was more deferential. "It didn't dawn on me that it was the master of the house," Clover continued, "till Devens said, 'The President,' upon which, of course, I got up and shook hands. He is the same Ohio type as Garfield and Stanley Matthews—stout, sandy hair, ordinary and very complacent. Mr. Hayes looks amiable and respectable—not a ray of force or intellect in forehead, eye or mouth."

Although Clover failed to recognize the master of the White House, she soon acquired a large number of friends in the more sophisticated circles of Washington society, particularly the diplomatic community. Clover delighted in the malicious wit of the

Turkish ambassador, Gregoire Aristarchi Bey, whom she taught to play the new card game Go Bang ("and he ungenerously beat me"). And in the exotic envoys from the newly opened empire of Japan. (When Mrs. Yoshida came to call, with an interpreter, Clover was surprised to see that "her dress was European and in quite good taste," whereas Clover herself wore a new blue gown that made her "look more Japanese than [Mrs. Yoshida] did.") She liked General Sherman ("We had a little talk about Indians") and she particularly liked Carl Schurz ("After the other guests had gone I persuaded Mr. Schurz to play on the piano, which he did deliciously—partly Chopin as I have never heard it played before, partly improvising. . . .") Then there were always visitors from academia, like William James ("pleasant as always but nervous and a wee bit hypochondriac") or Hermann von Holst, from Freiburg, whose *History of the United States* Henry had reviewed in the *North American*. Von Holst impressed Clover as "very nice—about forty-five—eyes like trout pools—clean as a Quaker, with such hands and nails as are an anachronism in a German professor."

The President and the wealthier members of the cabinet gave large state dinners, but the Adamses insisted on being fastidious. "I have instituted 5 o'clock tea every day, thereby escaping morning visitors and it's very easy," Clover wrote. And almost every night there was a dinner for a carefully selected half-dozen diplomats and Southern Congressmen and reforming journalists and pretty girls. "We have had all the society we wished and have found everyone friendly and ready to amuse us and to be amused," Henry wrote to Gaskell after the first Washington winter. "Our little dinners of six and eight were as pleasant as any I ever was at, even in London." Adams found this all very placid and amiable. "Such a quaint little society, you never saw or imagined," he wrote. "We do not even talk scandal. There is no scandal to talk about. Everybody is virtuous and the highest dissipation is to play whist at guinea points. I don't even indulge in this. We are all of the Darby and Joan type, and attached to our wives. It is the fashion. . . ."

Clover's letters are somewhat more barbed, and Henry observed that she habitually "takes malicious pleasure in shocking the prejudices of the wise and good." Clover refers to a visit from "old Governor Swan of Maryland" and adds casually, "I hear he lives mainly on opium." She encounters Gail Hamilton *née* Mary Abigail

Dodge, a frenetic journalist whose enthusiasms ranged from embroidering slippers for James Greenleaf Whittier to crusading for the rights of Colorado Indians, and offers this description: "Gail looks like a caricature of a scarecrow—both eyes squinting madly —mostly like a dying sculpin—hair like Medusa. . . ." And poor Kate Sprague, the daughter of Chief Justice Salmon P. Chase, married to the alcoholic Senator Sprague and infatuated with the rascally Senator Conkling. "She made a long call—told me *en passant* that she had no money and no carriage . . ." Clover wrote. "I pity her in a way. To marry a fool with 17 millions—to lose the latter and keep the former plus indefinite whiskey—is hard. However . . . I don't take to her and was glad to be engaged and so not go out to her spree."

Sometimes, in fact, Clover could be remarkably rude, not only in her descriptions of people she disliked but in her confrontations with them. On one occasion, for example, she was furious at "the lady who 'presides' over [Congressman] Fernando Wood's establishment" for having "forced on me the other day an introduction to a certain Miss Edes whose sole distinction I am told was a flirtation with Vice P. Wilson [Vice President Henry Wilson] of blessed memory. I made an arctic bow and immediately walked off." Clover thought her behavior would prohibit any further relationship but "my efforts were rewarded by a speedy call and an invitation to lunch written alternately in the 3rd and 2nd person." Clover refused to give way. She pleaded a previous engagement. "In this social vortex one has to steer gingerly," she observed, "tack reef and at times scuttle one's ship."

The confrontations kept occurring. The wife of Simon Newcomb, the astronomer at the Naval Observatory, was, according to Clover, "a dreadful female," who "clawed me one day last week" by saying that she wanted to bring to tea Mrs. Horatio King, the wife of the editor of the Chicago *Tribune*, a hostess who liked to stage what she called "literary reunions." Clover "muttered a temporary excuse" and then returned home to plan more drastic action. She and Henry forthwith collaborated on "a mutual epistle informing Mrs. N. that we 'particularly disliked literary entertainments and begged her to divert Mrs. King from calling on me'—a strong measure but a necessary one. It's a process of picking off burrs, which is not pleasant, but we are not official and have a right to choose our friends and associates."

Perhaps the most unpleasant of these encounters during Clover's first year in Washington involved a Mr. and Mrs. Theo Shellaber of San Francisco, who arrived with a letter of recommendation from William Wetmore Story, the celebrated sculptor, whose Roman studio figured in Hawthorne's *Marble Faun*. "I hear they are very rich and her diamonds are outrageous," Clover wrote, "but what I saw of her at a short call was very simple and pleasant." Clover invited them to dinner with George Bancroft, the historian, and John Chandler Bancroft Davis, the diplomat, and Mr. Shellaber was apparently a disaster. Clover described both him and his wife as "vulgar shoddy people" and blamed Story for having "thrust [them] on to us very coolly not to say impertinently." Her only description of what went wrong at dinner was that "Henry and Mr. Bancroft and Mr. Davis talked over his head and he said little—only once rose to the surface to tell a nasty story—of which no one took any notice."

The Shellabers seem not to have realized that they were in disgrace. Mr. Shellaber sent flowers to Clover and Mrs. Shellaber invited the Adamses to dinner. Clover declined with what she called "a very cool note." Mrs. Shellaber, not to be dissuaded, asked Clover to name any evening when she would be free. "And I, with a brazen courage which Casabianca might have envied if he had stayed on shore and lived to grow up, begged her to 'count us out—this week was quite full and I was expecting an invalid friend —and wished to make no engagements.' The effort made my knees shake and she looked much hurt but I think took the hint." And yet the contretemps was still not over. The unfortunate Mrs. Shellaber sent another basket of flowers, which Clover took to the kitchen and donated to one of the servants, Maria, who, in turn, took it to her church "to propitiate either the Lord or the poor old defunct Pope." Pope Pius IX, newly decreed to be theologically infallible but stripped of the Vatican's provincial lands, had died in sorrow and defeat just two weeks earlier, and the donation of Mrs. Shellaber's flowers inspired Clover to further frivolity. "How depressing for Pius IX to wake up in another world," she wrote, "and find himself 'sold,' the remains of an exploded fallacy, beginning life as a street sweeper in the New Jerusalem."

As for Mr. Shellaber, he seems to have exacerbated his disgrace by getting drunk at Wormley's Hotel. "It has been a lurid drama this week," Clover wrote, "Wormley has given him some very stiff talking to though and tells me he is now and since 'quiet as a lamb.' " Not quite. The following week, Clover reported that "there was another drunken row at Wormley's in the room of our friends and Wormley ordered the brute to leave his house at once —which he did." Mrs. Shellaber, however, refused to go quietly. The day after the expulsion from the hotel, she accosted Clover at a reception and announced that she was going to pay a farewell call. She intensified Clover's mistrust of Californians by explaining that another Western family named McAllester "represent the 'fashionable set in California,' " whereas the carousing Shellabers personified "the 'steady—somewhat *literary* side.' " Clover gave her butler "emphatic orders not to let her in and I hope that nauseous chapter is closed."

So the Shellabers of California failed to meet Clover's exacting social standards. Most of Washington's political notables were similarly inspected and found wanting. In contrast to the Washington hostesses of our time, who judge and are judged by the degree of their intimacy with the political powers, Clover was remarkably scornful in her view of the leaders of the Gilded Age. At the Bancrofts', for example, she had dinner with Chief Justice Harrison Waite and reported to her father that he was a man "whom I dislike the more I see him—he looks so unutterably vulgar and unjudicial." Even people whom she liked were harshly judged. General Richard Taylor, for example, the son of President Zachary Taylor and brother-in-law of Jefferson Davis, came almost daily to Clover's five o'clock teas and sent her baskets of roses, but although Clover found his "devotion . . . touching," she regarded him as "a light weight for a man who has commanded armies and led national councils." Even Carl Schurz, the old family friend who was now Secretary of the Interior, had to be rebuked. "We told him that he was not half so pleasant now that he is in the cabinet and muzzled," Clover wrote, "that his conversation was trivial and uninteresting to the last degree."

Almost no one of consequence escaped Clover's scrutiny and Clover's judgments. She reported that the Spanish Embassy ball in January of 1878 had been "a handsome show," with all the diplomats and military officers "in full toggery," and that she had "escaped" at eleven thirty, just before a fire broke out. "The draperies caught fire after we left and it made one shudder to think what danger there had been—a seething, struggling mass of inflammable women and only one door for entrance and exit—but as a holocaust would have included Blaines and Conkling and Butler and George

B. Loring and Fernando Wood the country might have bowed to the 'overruling of a wise Providence.' "

One of the aspects of Washington society that irritated Clover was the general assumption that the wives should enjoy remaining in a kind of purdah. It was an assumption that she encountered everywhere. At the home of the French ambassador, for example, she called on Mme. Maxime Outrey and "asked her little girl . . . how the puppy was whom she brought to see me. The infant turned on me with an expression of infinite disgust and said, 'Mrs. Adams, we have discovered that he is *a woman.*' "

That was a joke, presumably, but Clover was not amused by invitations to the Washington institution known as the ladies' lunch. "That is a form of amusement I hate," she wrote; "too many women, too much food." Artfully arranged dinners were fine, however, and she took particular pleasure when one of her guests appeared in an elaborate Worth gown ("The twenty wax candles in my chandelier lighted her up to great advantage"). What she most enjoyed, though, was an expedition to the frontiers of the new society. To Washington's Signal Bureau, for example, where she and Henry and Godkin of *The Nation* inspected the latest technology. "I talked through a telephone to an orderly in Virginia who stood at the other end of forty-three miles of wire," Clover gleefully reported to Boston. "After putting him several questions, I thanked him and he said, 'Very welcome, Ma'am.' I had always supposed there was an electric battery connected with it, but it's only wire and any fool might have done it in the last ten thousand years."

The tentacles of society inexorably dragged her back to what she herself considered a woman's duty. "After an hour [at the Signal Bureau], I had to go on to a large female lunch at Mrs. Judge Hunt's," she wrote. "I gnashed my teeth and rent my garments—but the hostess is very nice and I had no excuse. . . . To sit and see 25 women between fifty and seventy years of age eat for two hours is a discipline worthy of the Spanish Inquisition. I said to myself, 'This too shall pass away.' "

By modern standards of rudeness, of course, Clover's assertiveness was mild and elegant. Indeed, she herself sometimes had difficulty in convincing her victims that she did in fact mean to reject their invitations and their flowers and their hearty good wishes. Among the Adamses, however, every word was weighed with the precision and scrupulosity of the diplomatic corps. Dr. Hooper had been amused by Clover's remark that Henry's new house made him "feel like a gentleman for the first time in his life." He quoted it to someone, as he often quoted from her letters. "If you have one spark of paternal affection and honour," Clover pleaded, "burn my scrawls one and all—I would scorn to keep even a love letter from the Great Mogul." On this occasion, though, someone quoted her remark to someone else, and in due time it reached 57 Mt. Vernon Street.

Charles Francis Adams, who seems never to have been very fond of Clover in the first place, was displeased. When Charles Francis Adams was displeased, he communicated his displeasure to whoever had displeased him. "I want you to be very careful in quoting anything I say in my letters," Clover wrote unhappily to her father. "I try my best not to commit myself but this week a most amazing *pin* 300 miles long, twisted and sharpened, has come in a letter from Boston—I may have said to you that we found this house charming but as we are not used to such fine quarters Henry 'never felt like a gentleman before—' That, as I say, returns as a long sharp *pin* and one would suppose Henry was a fool from the new interpretation put on it. If we are fools we are—and too old to reform. . . . *Burn this.*"

There were other incidents, too, of an enigmatic sort. The previous winter, when Henry's mother was in New York for treatment of a painful and crippling rheumatism, she wrote indignantly in answer to some complaint from Charles Francis: "As to Henry and Clover, I am disgusted. I presume she did know you was there, as their room is on the same floor as his library, and besides the woman who cares for him would have told her. . . . I have no patience with such folly. She is always on the bed or sofa with that pillow. To let you go, so cold as it was and at your age, was too bad." The tone of hostility is unmistakable, but what on earth can have happened? One conjures up an image of the white-haired Charles Francis paying a call at 91 Marlborough Street and being told, through some misunderstanding among the servants, that Clover was not at home, and then discovering somehow that she really was at home, and writing his grievances to his wife, who cherished such things. In another letter, she described Clover simply as "a queer woman."

Since the documents are never entirely complete, we do not know how this contretemps was resolved, or how Henry later explained his remark about feeling like a gentleman. But perhaps we can infer some of the fearful weight of Charles Francis Adams' disapproval from the solemnity with which he lifted that weight. "With regard to the little matter touching accidental reports of words ascribed to you, which you disown," the statesman wrote to his son, "I was very glad to find that they had no foundation in fact —as such I dismiss it."

But he did not dismiss it. All of his sons, he continued—Charles, the hot-tempered railroad magnate; John, the perpetually unsuccessful politician; Henry, the fledgling historian; Brooks, the brilliant eccentric who had been slow to read, slow to learn any skill at all—all of them, said the puzzled father, "seem to me more or less given to a degree of severity upon others at times which they do not desire. . . . Do not let that habit grow upon you. That is all."

In the bleak January of 1879, Henry and Clover suddenly decided to escape from Washington and visit the frozen masses of Niagara Falls. Their friend Sir Edward Thornton, the British minister, had some business in Ottawa, and his two daughters begged to see the famous falls, and the Adamses joined in. They traveled in style. Congressman Hewitt sent a message to the Erie Railroad, and the railroad president's private Pullman was promptly made available to carry them through a blizzard. The falls were splendidly solidified ("imagine icicles one hundred fifty feet long," Clover wrote her father, "the smaller ones *blue* in colour—the roar shakes the house. . . .") They walked across the frozen cliff, "jumping the crevasses—it was most exciting with the morning sun making every icicle sparkle and glitter and the American fall thundering a few yards off." And went sleigh riding, and lunched on "mince pie and pickles and heaven knows what," and played whist and poker and twenty questions, and sang popular ballads of the day, of which the only one that Clover recorded was "Give My Chewing Gum to Sister, I Shall Never Want It More."

Clover was suffering from a sore throat, but her letters described it as an idyllic trip. Henry kept all the details in his mind as the setting for the figure who was to represent Clover in *Esther*.

It was not in Clover's nature to serve as Henry's amanuensis, but there are some indications that she accompanied him to the State Department from time to time and helped him with the Gallatin papers. "Henry and I have been working hard," she wrote on one occasion, "from one to four collating manuscripts at the State Department and have made much progress. I like the work and the new building is very comfortable." Another time, she described herself and Henry as looking like "Cruikshank's illustrations to *Old Curiosity Shop*, Sampson and Sally Brass on opposite stools."

Clover also accompanied Henry on a number of expeditions to visit historic sites and to interview people who had known Gallatin. To Brownsville, Pennsylvania, where Gallatin had overawed the riflemen of the Whiskey Rebellion, and to Mount Vernon, where Clover inspected "the bed in which 'George' died and no wonder —he must have been tough to live through one night in it." And to Baltimore, where Henry tried to interrogate the ninety-three-year-old Elizabeth Patterson, onetime wife of Joseph Bonaparte. She turned out to be a miser, Clover reported, "dressed in old calico duds [in] a squalid room high up in a boarding-house, no carpet on the floor, no anything anywhere. . . ."

In "six months of steady application," as Adams put it, he finished the editing of the Gallatin papers (he billed the financier's son only for his expenses, $237.80), and started in on the biography that was to accompany the three volumes of documents. Adams had a high admiration for his subject. "After a long study of the prominent figures in our history," he later wrote to the uninaugurated president, Samuel J. Tilden, "I am more than ever convinced that for combination of ability, integrity, knowledge, unselfishness and social fitness, Mr. Gallatin has no equal." Ability—integrity —knowledge—unselfishness—Henry was describing all the characteristics that seemed in his mind to define the Adamses. And as he pored over the archives in the State Department, he realized that the Gallatin papers represented the merest beginning, for what lay before him now, thanks to Secretary Evarts' benevolence, were the vast collections left by Gallatin's patrons, Jefferson and Madison. And as he studied these treasures, there rose before him the spirit of that cunning genius—"subtle" was to be his favorite adjective for Thomas Jefferson—who had subverted and driven from office his great-grandfather, John Adams. Even as Henry dutifully finished his biography of Gallatin, he began to see that this was only a preface to a much grander work, a portrait and redefinition of the Jeffersonian America that had rejected the Adamses.

It is hard to determine exactly when or how Adams first conceived the idea of his vast history. Like most grand ideas, it had been in his mind for some time, unrecognized. Perhaps he had imagined such a work when he first organized his Harvard lectures on American history. Perhaps the idea had originated in that Roman spring of 1860, almost two decades earlier, when he had gone to sit in that same church garden where Gibbon had first thought of writing of the fall of Rome. "The young man had no idea of what he was doing," Adams later wrote in the *Education*. "The thought of posing for a Gibbon never entered his mind. He was a tourist even to the depths of his subconsciousness . . . [but he] went on reposing to himself the eternal question:—Why! Why!! Why!!! . . . Substitute the word America for the word Rome, and the question became personal."

Gallatin was doomed from the start. The publication of a small edition by J. B. Lippincott in 1879 was apparently subsidized by the Gallatin family, with a payment of more than $5,000, and many of the reviews were unfavorable. *The New York Tribune*, for example, said that the book showed "no extraordinary skill or practice in the arts of literary composition"; *The North American Review* said it was "too voluminous, and has too much the character of a digest of material, to be attractive to the general reader"; *The Atlantic* objected that Gallatin himself was "questionably of the first importance." The most unkindest cut, though, came from Godkin, whom Adams had regarded as a friend. An anonymous two-part review in Godkin's *Nation* fiercely attacked the biography for "ponderosity" and "clumsiness" and even for its densely printed appearance, which the reviewer regarded as "little short of an outrage." In deluging the reader with the minutiae of Gallatin's public life, and with scores of documents that he had not deigned to translate from the French, Adams had "sinned knowingly and is accordingly entitled to no mercy."

Godkin managed with some difficulty to keep secret the fact that his censorious reviewer was Charles Francis Adams, Jr., engaged in the perpetual Adams practice of scolding younger relatives. Charles wrote to Godkin that his sole purpose was to administer "medicine," to persuade Henry "not to treat any audience at all as

a thing beneath an author's consideration." He had decided to administer his medicine anonymously, however, partly because of his
anxiety about Clover. "My good sister-in-law don't favor me much
now," he wrote, "and if she finds it is I who dared criticize her
adored Henry, my goose will be finally cooked." Godkin worried,
nonetheless, about what the Adamses might think of being attacked
in *The Nation.* Clover was cool. "If as you say a genial and suave
notice of the Life of Gallatin was intended to 'do Henry good,' "
she wrote, "I've no doubt it will." (Clover actually had little enthusiasm for Henry's work. The biography itself "may interest you in
places," she wrote to Dr. Hooper, "but why did you try the *Works?*
They are only for reference.") Henry was even more Olympian
about *The Nation's* anonymous attack. He "never dreamed of taking
offense" at the review, he said, since it was nothing but "the most
commonplace newspaper comment." But he did take the criticisms
to heart, referring, in a letter to Lowell, to "my poor ponderous
Life of Gallatin . . . my one ewe lamb or prize ox. No one has ever
read it, or ever will, but perhaps, some centuries hence, antiquaries
will use it."

Clover liked to go out on long walks through what was then a
kind of semitropical wilderness along the Potomac. "Henry and I
went off [with] Chas. for a walk in the woods behind Georgetown,"
she wrote to her father in the early spring of 1878, "and brought
home much blood root and other flowers—there are no end of
dogwood trees. . . ." But her true passion was horseback riding.
Henry acquired a horse named Prince and then bought Clover a
bay mare from Virginia named Daisy. Clover thought her "a little
beauty." She and Henry went out riding every morning in the
wilds of Rock Creek Park, then returned to H Street for an early
lunch so that Henry could repair to the State Department for a
solid day of archival research. He customarily worked from noon
to six P.M., and then it was time for another social dinner. The
household schedule seemed perfectly organized, and the household
too. "Now our establishment is set afloat à la Noah's Ark," Clover
wrote, "H and I—2—2 dogs . . . and 2 horses—2 women servants
and 2 men servants."

There was one missing element, of course, in the absence of two
children. Despite the modern view that most nineteenth-century

women spent their lives in varying states of pregnancy, Clover and her contemporaries were by no means all destined for motherhood, or for marriage, for that matter. Emily Dickinson, for example, was destined to write great poetry and Mary Baker Eddy to found a religion. The Adams family was philoprogenitive, however, like all great families, and President John Adams' five children gave birth to seventeen grandchildren. Even among the Adamses, though, there were odd gaps. Charles Francis Adams' first two sons had eleven children; his two daughters had three; his two younger sons had none.

Was this evolution accidental, or is it possible that there was some drying, some shriveling of the tribal passion for tribal repro-duction? Henry Adams publicly affected disdain for the whole topic. "I have myself never cared enough about children to be unhappy either at having them or not having them," he wrote to Gaskell, "and if it were not that half the world will never leave the other half at peace, I should never think about the subject." He was being somewhat disingenuous. No son of Adams could "never think" about the disintegration of the family line, and in old age he was to become passionately fond of his nieces. In another letter to Gaskell, he wrote a slightly more revealing account of his situation. "One consequence of having no children," he reported, "is that husband and wife become very dependent on each other and live very much together. This is my case. . . ."

Clover, too, came from a family of large families, a family in which it was taken for granted that the function of the women was to bear and rear children. Clover's mother, the poetess, dead at thirty-six, had borne only three, but she was herself one of six, and Dr. Hooper was the seventh of nine. There could be no question among the Hoopers, then, of anyone being indifferent to the matter of having children. Indeed, there is a family legend that Clover was by no means so dispassionate as Henry pretended to be. "If any woman ever says to you that she doesn't want children, it isn't true," Clover is said to have burst out once to her cousin, Anne Lothrop. "*All* women want children!"

After Clover's death, some of that longing re-emerged in the eulogy of her friend, Ellie Shattuck Whiteside, who observed that Clover had had "all she wanted, all this world could give, except perhaps children." If Clover really wanted children, was there then some physical disability that prevented her from having them? She seems to have been, like many women of her time and background, subject to mysterious coughs and aches and other illnesses. She remarked on one occasion, for example, that she had been "struggling with a vile sick headache," and Henry reported not long afterward that "my wife has been suffering from an abominable autumn catarh for six weeks which . . . has brought us both to fitness for any crime." Throughout her years as a Washington hostess, Clover often mentioned getting tired and needing to go to bed early. At one point, an ear infection filled her head with what she called "shrieking," and then there was a tooth that had to have the root killed with arsenic. But even a sore throat, Henry wrote, could reduce Clover to a state in which she "could neither speak, nor sleep, nor swallow, nor breathe, nor stand, nor sit, nor lie."

These are all perfectly commonplace complaints, of course, and there is no real way of connecting the childlessness of the Adamses to their physical condition. But the question does not go away. Childlessness in the nineteenth century was not ordinarily a sign of independence but of some obscure failure, some mystery that needed explanation. Ernest Samuels, for one, finds it significant that Henry acquired at some point a book by Dr. J. Marion Sims, entitled *Clinical Notes on Uterine Surgery—with special reference to the management of sterile conditions.* It was published in New York in 1873, the year after the Adamses' marriage. Significant, perhaps, but in what way? "How typical!" exclaims a woman who is writing a book on this period. "How typical to think that if there was something wrong, it had to be something wrong with the woman!"

But Clover too sensed something wrong, and not limited to herself, and not limited to the management of sterile conditions either. She was startled to hear in the spring of 1879 that one of Dr. Hooper's friends had voluntarily confined himself in the Sommerville insane asylum because of his dread of eternal damnation. The news touched off a burst of raillery, in which she remarked that "the goal of every good and conscientious Bostonian" seemed to be the insane asylum. "Babies and insanity the two leading topics of interest," she went on. "Mrs. So & So has a baby, she becomes insane and goes to Sommerville—baby grows up and promptly retires to Sommerville—it's all nonsense—"

Although we do not know what was wrong then, it seems increasingly likely that there really was something wrong.

12

THE OBJECT OF THE JOURNEY

As EARLY AS AUGUST of 1878, long before *Gallatin* was finished, Henry Adams had begun entertaining an interesting hypothesis about the origins of the nation. If the State Department vaults were filled with the secret chronicles sent from Europe by diplomatic pioneers like Thomas Jefferson—not to mention the Adamses' reports from Paris and St. Petersburg and London, some of these last arduously transcribed by Henry himself—then there must be gorgeous tapestries of gossip about the early days of the American republic buried in the diplomatic archives of Europe. Having divined the existence of these papers, like the existence of some star too remote for an ordinary telescope, Adams took a journalistic delight in the prospect of discovering them for himself.

The archives of the Jefferson era—in Europe, it was naturally regarded as the Napoleonic era—were still so new, the Corsican tiger being scarcely a half-century dead, that no outsider had ever been permitted to study them. Diplomacy was the Adamses' family sport, however, and Henry enjoyed playing it. "The whole object of my journey," he wrote to Gaskell, "is to study the diplomatic correspondence of the three governments [Britain, France, and Spain], in regard to America, during the time of Napoleon, from 1800 to 1812. . . . So I am straining every nerve to open in advance the doors of three Foreign Offices." He listed the various official introductions that he planned to accumulate, but he added that "if you ever see the Salisburys [Lord Salisbury was Disraeli's Foreign

Secretary], you might facilitate my movements by sounding for me there."

So they sailed for England, on the *Gallia*, on May 28, 1879, without any certainty that Henry's mission could be accomplished at all, and when Clover duly met Lady Salisbury at a reception at the Royal Academy—a reception at which the women's dresses impressed her as "fat fugues in pea-green, lean symphonies in chewing-gum colour, all in a rusty minor key"—she observed that the foreign secretary's wife "has the manners of a discouraged cook." Still, with his own diffident form of persistence, Henry finally managed to get the Foreign Office to open the doors to the archives.

July 13, 1879: "Henry began his labours in the Record Office yesterday, having gained his point. And if this weather lasts we shall make this our headquarters till September."

While Henry began his researches, Clover lived well. "London is pleasant to get back to," she wrote to her father, "and I agree with Dr. Johnson that 'he who is tired of London is tired of life.' " Having simply rented some furnished rooms on Half Moon Street, Clover was looking for a house somewhere in Mayfair. She also spent a lot of time at the art galleries. She went to the Grosvenor, "the refuge of the Pre-Raphaelites," where she observed that Whistler's new portrait of a dancer named Connie Gilchrist (now in the Metropolitan Museum in New York) was "all that Ruskin could ask to justify his charge that it was 'flinging a paint pot in the face of the public.' "* She herself considered the picture worthy of the Worcester Hospital for the Insane, one of Dr. Hooper's favorite charities, and she observed that "any patient at Worcester who perpetrated such a joke would be kept in a cage for life."

Clover inspected the novelties of the theater, too, and Emile Zola fared scarcely better than Whistler. "We went to see a fearful play, *Drink*, adapted from *L'Assomoir* . . . well acted and beautifully put on stage, but gruesome and terrible. For ten minutes at least, in a delirium tremens scene worked up in a London hospital, I could

---

* Whistler responded to this celebrated accusation by suing for libel, and after protracted litigation, he won a judgment of one farthing.

not look on, and was even driven to putting my fingers in my ears."

Roving around London, invited everywhere, Clover kept meeting what she called "many queer and pleasant folks"—at a Sunday tea at the Grosvenor Gallery, Gustave Doré and William Holman Hunt, and "poets good, bad and indifferent; fat duchesses, American beauties with diaphanous reputations; a social *olla-podrida.*" And then the next evening, after the opera at Covent Garden, Henry had "pipes and grog, to meet Spencer, Huxley, etc. at John Fiske's rooms." And then the next day, at tea with Mrs. Bryan Procter, Clover had "a chat with Anthony Trollope . . . a rosy-gilled John Bull." And the next day, at a garden party at Holland House, she found "royalty thick as huckleberries—one had to shuffle so as not to tread on a prince." And the following week, Lillie Langtry "in white, no flowers or jewels and really very handsome." And at the same party, "someone introduced Whistler to me, even more mad away from his paint pots than near them. His etchings are so charming, it is a pity he should leave that to woo a muse whom he can't win."

July 20, 1879: "Henry is pegging away hard at Record Office. . . ."

Clover was consistently critical of the English style. In contrast to a party at the Russell Sturgis estate, where she remarked on the "twenty-four Spaniards in costume who played on twenty-four guitars," she described an English dinner as "stiff and dull, as all English parties are." She then went on to explain her judgment in the most merciless terms. "The women mostly frights and now that 'high art' dressing has entered into them like demons, they are fearful and wonderful to behold. Harmonies in yellow—discords in pea-green—heads blooming with sunflowers and crowned with rag-bags. . . . The social *savoir faire* and ease is what one would expect in Pawtucket Centre—the suppers, barring the absence of pie and pickles, resembling those of a remote village in New Hampshire." One senses in these indictments that Clover often felt herself patronized, for she bristled in her description of British manners. "They are islanders, uncouth . . ." she wrote. "I doubt if they are conscious of their lapses in good breeding half the time.

Judicious snubbing is the only means of protection." At one particular dinner, she reported, she was "obliged to tomahawk an offensive baronet who took me down and made sneering remarks about
America. I laid him out stiff."

These criticisms represented a political judgment as well. England was in the last months of a Tory administration, and Clover,
in all her condemnations as a Boston Brahmin, condemned above
all the Tory ruling class. "At this Belshazzar's feast," she wrote to
Dr. Hooper, "not only do we see the handwriting on the wall, but
the givers of the feast do too—and they are scared and say it's
giving way. On all sides are wails of unlet farms, discontented
tenants, no money, good servants who won't wear livery. The
39,000,000 who get no cake and ale think it's about time for the
1,000,000 who do to treat. The signs of the times are clear to read
in many ways, small and large."

August, 10, 1879: "Henry found so much stuff of value to him in
the Record Office in London that if Paris and Madrid are opened
to him and have as much, it will be tight work to get through by
October 1880. As we both much prefer America to live in, we shall
go home then, even if we have to sit up nights in order to finish."

"Harry James is standing on the hearthrug, with his hands under
his coat-tails, talking with my wife exactly as though we were in
Marlborough Street," Henry Adams wrote to Lodge. And Clover's
letters of this same period reflect a hostess' irritation that James
kept inviting himself to dinner, and staying late, but they also
reflect an interest in the fact that the elusive novelist kept returning
to her hearth. James was, in fact, interested in something other
than Adams' erudition. "The Henry Adamses are here," he wrote
to Elizabeth Boott in that summer of 1879, "very pleasant, friendly,
conversational, critical, ironical. . . . Clover chatters rather less,
and has more repose, but she is very nice, and I sat up with them
till one o'clock this morning abusing the Britons. The dear Britons
are invaluable for that. . . ."

James seems to have thought that he was responsible for spon-
soring the Adamses in London society. He wrote to his mother
that he had taken them to a series of receptions and introduced

them to a number of distinguished people. "They seemed to enjoy it greatly . . ." he went on, "and they appear indeed to be launched very happily in London life. They are extremely friendly, pleasant and colloquial, and it is agreeable to have in London a couple of good American *confidents.*"

Clover was somewhat more critical of London, and of James' role there. "It is high time Harry James was ordered home by his family," she wrote to her father. "He is too good a fellow to be spoiled by injudicious old ladies in London—and in the long run they would like him all the better for knowing and loving his own country. He had better go to Cheyenne and run a hog ranch."

August 31, 1879: "If Henry can get hold of Mr. Waddington, he wants to get to work in Paris. Time is an object to us now that we have come for work."

Clover was writing from Dieppe, which was then regarded as "this French Newport," and she considered it "a very picturesque town, many quaint costumes and houses [but] so far no fashion or display." The Mr. Waddington to whom she referred was William Henry Waddington, son of a British businessman, educated at Rugby and Cambridge, a professional archaeologist, and now, by the oddities of politics, Premier of France. He happened to be vacationing with his American wife at Deauville, so the Adamses went calling on him to get his help in opening the diplomatic archives. "Mr. Waddington . . . thinks Henry will be able to see such papers as he wants, but here, as in London, vacation puts a stopper to work until October 1st, which is aggravating. . . ." The Adamses thought of spending the intervening fortnight in a leisurely tour of Brittany, but "it blew a gale and the rain came in gusts," so they decided to turn toward Paris and wait there.

There Clover celebrated her thirty-sixth birthday, and Henry gave her "a nice vase," and Harry James turned up, and Jack and Isabelle Gardner from Boston, and all five of them went out to dinner at an open-air restaurant. "And then to the *Cirque*," Clover wrote, "where Mademoiselle Jutan, an angelic blonde, filled our hearts with wonder and joy—then ices on the boulevard in front of a cafe and home at midnight. We have quiet mornings to study in, noon breakfasts and Bohemian dinners." And she went with Mrs. Gardner on her first visit to "the great Mr. Worth" and ordered a copy of a gown he had designed for the Grand Duchess of Württemberg. It was dark green merino trimmed with dark blue. While Clover was trying it on, she was delighted to watch "a compatriot, I should imagine a prosperous grocer from Iowa, with a fat wife for whom he wanted a smart dress. To see him in his smart spruce broadcloth frock-coat and awe-struck expression, 'hefting' the silks to be sure he was getting his money's worth . . . was an inspiring spectacle." Clover joked about Henry's insistence on her going to Worth, but the results gave her immense satisfaction. "My Worth gown . . . not only fills my small soul but seals it hermetically. . . . What doesn't show is as good as what does, so that when the right side is quite worn out I shall simply wear the wrong side out."

The Adamses went often to the theater and found it, just as Abigail had a century earlier, scandalous but funny. At a play called *Voyage en Suisse*, Clover reported, "in defiance of all sense of decorum we laughed to a shocking extent." Another play at the Gymnase she described only as "very indecent and charmingly acted," adding that "if huissiers had come in and borne actors and audience to the nearest station house, I should have conceded that they had a strong case." And then there were rides in the Bois "in the loveliest of September days," and explorations of the Louvre, where "every time one comes back to the good pictures they seem better," and shopping expeditions for watercolors and etchings and Japanese bric-a-brac. And when Ned sent her the local news in a copy of the Boston *Herald*, she noted that their stake in the Calumet mines, which Alex Agassiz had discovered and reorganized and recommended to all his Boston friends at five dollars per share, had just passed 200.

Clover seems to have been truly happy in Paris in that autumn of 1879, though she would admit to her father nothing more than that "we are very content here." But she must have glowed. Henry James kept writing about her with a rare admiration. "I have seen no one here, to speak of, but the Henry Adamses . . . with whom I fraternise freely," he wrote to his mother. "I have become very fond of them—they are very excellent people." And again: "The Henry Adamses, who are very good company, I frequently—almost daily—see; and we usually dine together at a restaurant.

Henry is very sensible, though a trifle dry, and Clover has a touch of genius. . . ."

October 12, 1879: "Here we are still dangling on the Boulevards, the knots in French red tape being so hard and numerous that Henry's fingers are blistered with trying to pick them. You get a polite answer that when so and so returns you may by applying to this one or that get what you want, but the 'Open Sesame' is not yet in any dictionary and it's an endless 'Open Barley' and 'Open Corn.' So on Wednesday next we shall turn to pastures new and try our luck in Spain."

Adams' chief hope in Spain was the fact that the American ambassador was his old friend James Russell Lowell, with whom he and Clover had crossed the Atlantic on their honeymoon. It had taken Lowell only two years to realize that the life of an expatriate poet was not for him. Eliot lured him back to Harvard, and then he became active in politics, anxious to fight against the reports

> . . . *of public scandal, private fraud,*
> *Crime flaunting scot-free while the mob applaud.*

Lowell served as a reform delegate from Massachusetts to the Republican convention in Cincinnati in 1876, took part in the shift to Hayes, and later let it be known that he would welcome a diplomatic assignment. President Hayes, who admired Lowell's *Bigelow Papers,* agreed to his being offered either Russia or Austria. Lowell mysteriously declined that proposal but hinted to his friend Howells, whose wife was a cousin of the new President, that he would welcome an assignment to Spain because he would like to see the plays of Calderón. To even this, the admiring administration agreed.

Once Lowell had established himself in Madrid, his second wife, Frances, a genteel but impoverished woman who had served as governess to his children during his widowhood, fell desperately ill. It seemed at first to be an attack of typhus. She suffered a high fever and twice slipped to the edge of death, her face livid, her nose cold, her lips black. No sooner had she recovered from this than she went, as Lowell wrote to Adams, "perfectly mad." She thought that she was living under the Inquisition, that the authorities wanted to torture her on the rack, that strange figures emerged from secret passageways behind her walls to torment her. She refused to take any food or medicine, saying she would live on ice water. Doctors finally forced a pump into her stomach to feed her. She slapped her nurses and accused her husband of persecuting her. One time, she chattered and gesticulated for twenty-two hours; another time, she slept for thirty-six hours. Her legs mysteriously swelled—she accused the doctors of breaking them—and then they were put in plaster molds.

In the middle of all this arrived the Adamses, seeking archives. "Mrs. Lowell is still in a most suffering and critical condition," Clover wrote her father, "with both knees swollen and utterly helpless. He has nursed her night and day for more than four months, since June 15, for three months not leaving his house. And yet he keeps up bravely and is as kind and cheerful as possible to us. We can, I fear, do nothing for them. It is terrible, but there is no escape."

The Duke of Tetuan, Spain's foreign minister, promised that Henry could have access to the diplomatic archives of the Napoleonic era, but there seemed to be some difficulty in finding them. "No one knows where they are," as Clover tartly put it. "It may be Simancas, near Valladolid, a nasty hole—perhaps Alcalá, near here —maybe Seville! *Quien sabe?* 'Tomorrow' we shall know. *Tomorrow* is the time for Spain and a driving Yankee must forget *today* and smoke and possess his soul in patience." So they waited. They had pleasant rooms and a cheerful fire, and they liked Madrid.

They weren't quite sure why. "I never saw an uglier city," Clover wrote, "not one handsome building, no grass in its parks, a few scrubby little locust trees, and a swarming, ill-dressed dirty populace who order one off the sidewalk at every step." Still, the mountain climate was—as it still is—astonishing. Henry described "a sky so blue that one can scoop it out with a spoon; a sun so glorious that the shadows are palpably black; a dry crisp air that tightens all one's muscles." And then there was the Prado. "Day after day," Clover wrote, "we stroll into the gallery and gorge ourselves with Titian, Tintoretto, Veronese and Velasquez." Of one large Titian, she wrote that "nothing can describe the colour—it looks as if it were painted with powdered jewels soaked in sunshine." Henry would not attempt such a metaphor. He said of the museum only that "it knocks all my expectations flat."

Lowell did not think that Clover should visit his wife because "he fears my seeing her would excite her and suggest home, for which she longs unspeakably when she is herself." Instead, the Adamses went and sat with Lowell himself, often twice a day, "to try and change the current a little for him," as Clover put it. They seem to have helped. Lowell told his secretary that they were "a godsend." He then changed his mind and urged Clover to visit his stricken wife after all. "I saw her for the first time on Monday, I think," Clover wrote, "and she was quite natural and quiet and glad to see me, looking much less worn than I feared. Wednesday in a very weak, unhappy, crying mood, saying she should go home that night—she could bear it no longer. Friday and yesterday in a deep lethargic sleep. . . . Mrs. Lowell has gleams of reason when she says most pathetically, 'You can't patch me up. I can never again be good for anything.' "

November 2, 1879: "Poor Henry has had a great blow. Duke of Tetuan, after promising him any papers which might turn up, wrote on Monday to Mr. Lowell that his Chief of Archives reported he had found the papers but that they were of 'too reserved a character to be shown,' was very sorry, etc. etc.—so that our object in this long journey is utterly defeated."

Clover, who already knew French, German, Latin, and Greek, had been studying Spanish for months. Even while staying at an abbey in Lancashire that summer of 1879, she wrote that "O' nights we have a blazing fire and read Spanish aloud—a thrilling romance with 25 murders in the first five chapters." By the time the Adamses reached France, Clover was well into *Don Quixote*. When the rains descended on Madrid to such an extent that "we thought that death would be to us a welcome alternative to Madrid," the Adamses boarded a train southward to Cordoba and Granada, and so they happened to encounter a family that occupied the rest of the railroad compartment, and, as Clover put it, "we soon fell to prattling."

The head of the family turned out to be a rich merchant returning to Málaga from a trip to Italy. Clover, having nothing better to talk about, urged Henry to ask the merchant if by any chance he knew the chief of archives in Seville. "Henry, true to the characteristics of his first ancestor, wished me to 'bite first.' So, with an assumed air of casual curiosity, I bit deep into the core, and asked if by any chance he was acquainted etc. etc." The merchant did not know the chief of archives but he knew a lawyer and professor of Arabic in Granada who did know the archivist, and so he recommended them to Don Leopoldo Equilaz, who took the Adamses on a tour of the Alhambra and read them the Arabic inscriptions and told them stories and promised to see what could be done.

While waiting, the Adamses decided on a quick visit to Gibraltar and then to Morocco, which must, in those days, have been something like the lands of the anthropophagi. After crossing the strait to Ceuta, they set off in a caravan of donkeys—the Adamses, a white-bearded rabbi, a postman, and two guides—for a nine-hour ride over a palmetto-lined mountain path to Tetuan. "Once my beast took fright at an imaginary snake," Clover wrote, "gave a big jump, and fled with me into the bushes, bringing me into abrupt contact with the soil of Africa. . . ." As they approached Tetuan, the town looked "white and beautiful in its frame of violet mountains," but when they reached it, they found "a howling mob of Moors, Jews, and Spaniards, half-smothered in garbage." That night, Clover had a nightmare. She dreamed that a black man who had waited on table at the inn "came into our room and [clutched] my throat." The next morning, when the landlady asked her how she had slept, she recounted the dream and was surprised to see the landlady burst into laughter. The waiter, the landlady reported, was a pardoned galley slave who had been sent to the galleys for cutting his wife's throat.

Clover was told that she was the first American woman ever to appear in Tetuan, and the Moroccans seem to have found her as exotic as she found them. Merchants came streaming to her inn and sold her what Henry later described as "a mule-load of rugs and embroideries." She was even tempted to buy a "grinning, red-turbaned, bare-legged Timbuctoo negress," who was a servant in the house of a local notable and who "begged me to take her to America" for a payment of only twenty dollars to her owner.

Back in Seville, Henry renewed his assault on the archives. He called on a friend of Don Leopoldo, a professor at the university, and found that all public institutions were closed because of the festivities surrounding the marriage of King Alfonso XII to the Archduchess Maria Christina. "Henry came back vanquished," Clover wrote, "said it was all up, luck had turned etc." But Henry was out when the professor returned the call, and Clover found him "young, good-looking and sympathetic." She mustered "all my diplomacy and Spanish" and inquired whether it might not be possible "to give a present to some sub-official who might let us in for the sake of a new gown for his señora."

Possible? The professor had a friend who knew the celebrated head archivist himself, and the very next day, the doors finally opened. This archivist, whom Clover never named, had worked among the documents for sixty-five years. He could remember Washington Irving coming to Seville in the 1820's to do research for his biography of Christopher Columbus. He could remember William H. Prescott coming to Seville in the 1830's to do research for his biography of Ferdinand and Isabella. Clover discovered all this because she had to entertain the old gentleman while Henry explored "what he was in search of . . . among millions of bundles." Clover did her share valiantly. "It's no joke," she reported to her father, "to talk for three hours to an old man whose speech is paralysed and whose face contains one lonely tooth, but the interest I took in his son's house in the country, his granddaughter's progress on the piano, and the treatment he pursued when he became paralysed, was under the circumstances genuine. And I had to admire the original bull given by the pope to Columbus, allowing him to go in search of America. . . . In short I feel as if I had personally ploughed an acre of land. But anyhow we've carried our point and it's a great satisfaction."

December 14, 1879: "Henry got permission on Thursday to work on papers in the [French Ministry of the] Marine and this week will probably get at his other archives—is up to his eyes all day in fascinating work and very happy."

Shortly after the Adamses reached Paris, unfortunately, Premier Waddington was forced to resign, and for several weeks the politicians engaged in the traditional quadrille known as forming a new government. "The confusion is not to our advantage," Clover wrote. As in England, however, she watched with great interest the checking of President MacMahon's imperial ambitions and the increasing authority of the Republican leader, Leon Gambetta. She also watched with a certain prejudice. "My sympathies," she wrote, "always go with the radicals."

The Paris to which Clover returned in December was not the Paris she had left in September. Perhaps the city had become a bit too familiar, or perhaps she missed the idle chatter of Harry James, or perhaps she was simply weary of traveling. She enjoyed returning to the House of Worth for another dress. "It would amuse you to see the profound interest which the elderly gentleman and his lovely black spaniel have taken in constructing it—he gives a pull here—a long rip with impatient disapproval there—and his dog curled up in front of the glass drinks it all in." But the Parisian theater no longer amused or interested her. She visited the classical company at the Theatre Français and decided never to return. "Each time it bores me unutterably . . ." she wrote to Dr. Hooper. "Judging by the yawns of one's neighbors I can't help suspecting that a large number go because they think it's the thing." As for the company's star, Sarah Bernhardt, Clover acknowledged that she was "chic and the rage," but she added, "We detest her—voice, posing, looks and all."

Henry did soon get permission to study the French archives— Waddington apparently signed the necessary papers on his last day in office—and so the Adamses slipped into a routine that Clover called "an existence of Trappist monks." Henry scrutinized documents, and Clover, having nothing much to do, grumbled. She seems to have been, like many temperamental people, unusually susceptible to the influences of the climate. In Paris, in December, the skies are leaden and the trees bare and the streets glisten in the endless drizzle. This can be, depending on one's circumstances, very romantic or very bleak. Clover found it imprisoning. She complained of "the atmosphere like gray pea soup—no sunlight for eight days now and often hard to read even at high noon though our windows command the whole Tuileries Garden."

Though she once had devoted herself wholeheartedly to Henry's search for diplomatic documents, Clover now found that her devotion was succumbing to her need to escape. She began pressing Henry to finish his researches and move on.

January 25, 1880: "Henry worked till late on Wednesday and has finished all that was needed though he could have occupied himself for many more months at his beloved archives. We started at dawn on Thursday. . . ."

Clover was not excessively fond of the English, either, but she had learned to love the possibilities of a season in a house of one's own in the heart of London. The very day after her arrival, an agent showed her a place on Bird Cage Walk, at the edge of St. James' Park, near the pond where Charles II used to feed the ducks. London, like Paris, was shrouded in fog, but after having "plunged through the darkness of high noon to see the house," Clover found herself delighted. "It is fascinating—and just what we want—all newly done over with charming Morris papers and rugs—tiled fireplaces . . . and the back bowing onto the great oaks of St. James' Park and open to the afternoon sun which is due in May."

If the house was, as Clover put it, "a perfect gem from top to bottom," the circumstances of her taking possession were hardly less engaging. The owner had left behind only "a pretty little house maid," but Mrs. Harry Sturgis, one of Clover's London cousins, sent over her own cook-housekeeper to take charge. Clover was surprised to find that this newcomer "feeds us very well, keeps all the books and receives a weekly cheque for the total. . . . I buy nothing and never ask what we are to have." At the same time, Henry James provided a butler, "who, if his letters and certificates speak the truth is too good for this world of sin and sorrow." The butler endeared himself to Clover by warning her that "the laundry should be cautioned about your table linen—I never saw any so beautiful before." And when she rented "a nice little coupé" for twenty guineas a month, the carriage master offered to " 'put your monogram and harms on the doors for nothing hextra but hif you 'ave your harms on the buttons you will furnish those.' " She jocularly told him that she was thinking of decorating the carriage doors only with a large American flag.

Thus established and outfitted, Clover set forth once more to inspect the imperial capital of the western world. She found it a whirlpool of contradictions and absurdities, but just as she had felt called to attend the triumphant return of the Army of the Potomac, she felt called now to survey the institutions of Victorian England. The first of these, of course, was Victoria herself, and so Clover went to watch the Queen open Parliament. "In the last coach, all glass and gold, came Victoria, in white, an ermine cloak and white cap and veil. . . . She was drawn by eight cream-colored horses nearly smothered in brass trappings and blue tassels and fringe. . . . She was fat and red-faced and ducked her old head incessantly from side to side."

A week later, Clover went to see Parliament itself. She found herself not only segregated but almost hidden from sight. "As if in a harem," she wrote to Dr. Hooper, "we looked down through a lattice screen from the ladies' gallery." Clover was happy to observe all the rituals, the functionary bearing a brass mace, the speaker in what she called "a hornet's nest wig," but she was even more delighted by the attitudes of the parliamentarians toward their own formalities. Prayers, for example, had become an object of partisan histrionics, and Clover cruelly observed Sir Charles Dilke, "who cremated his wife as a sign of wide views, chewing a sheaf of papers and scratching his bald young head while the royal family were prayed for." When the opening round of speeches had been finished, Clover added, she and a friend went to have tea and bread and butter "in a little room set apart for ladies."

Clover observed these wonders only from a certain distance. The people she met and knew and liked and talked to were, as she put it, "the same set" as the Adamses had known in Washington, people who were "respectable, mildly literary and political, who have no affiliation with court or camp." Some were old friends, like Henry James, who made himself quite at home in Bird Cage Walk. "He comes in every day at dusk and sits chatting by our fire," Clover wrote, "but is a frivolous being, dining out nightly—tomorrow being an off night, he has invited himself to dine with us." Nor would he go home. Clover complained of guests who had the "bad notion of staying on till midnight," and she added, "Harry James, who comes in of his own accord, often is ruthless in that respect." Others were new discoveries, like Matthew Arnold, whom Clover kept encountering at dinner parties. She found him "facile and gay and full of talk and curiosity about America and its people, which he wishes much to see. If the trustees of the Lowell

Institute made him a tempting offer to deliver a course of lectures next autumn I should think it might please him and them."

One evening in April, the Adamses went to dinner at the home of William Lecky, the Irish scholar who was then in the midst of writing his celebrated *History of England in the 18th Century*, and whose Dutch wife struck Clover as "a pleasant-mannered Holbein-faced little woman." The guest of honor, on Clover's left, was Ernest Renan, author of the *Life of Jesus*, who was in London to give a series of lectures. Clover found him "charming, most sympathetic. . . . as big as a whale, no neck and a jolly round face rising direct from his shoulders. You can think of nothing but a full harvest moon rising above the mountains and a curious survival of the Jesuit in his expression—I fancy only death can wipe out that." On Clover's right sat John Tyndall, the investigator of the opacity of gasses and of the blueness of the sky, who turned out to be "very agreeable, full of talk and liveliness [and] looks like a typical Yankee storekeeper, just the keen, lantern-jawed, brush-bearded face which Punch is always giving to Brother Jonathan." They talked of Dr. Holmes back in Boston—Tyndall had toured the U.S. as a lecturer—and Clover showed him one of Holmes' new poems, and Tyndall pronounced it "like the man, graceful, musical, tender."

Sandwiched between Renan and Tyndall, Clover was able to remain at a distance from some of the other guests who pleased her less. Robert Browning, for one, whom she kept meeting and kept avoiding. "He is not attractive to me and less so the oftener I meet him," she observed. "His voice is like steel—loud and harsh and incessant. None but a poetess could have written the 'Portuguese Sonnets' to such a husband." Or, just a bit farther down the Leckys' dinner table, Herbert Spencer. "Herbert Spencer," Clover wrote, "looks like a complacent crimson owl, in spectacles, with an assumption of omniscience in his manner which is reassuring in this age of disbelief. You are led to imagine that his very first principle of all is belief in himself."

Clover's letters are sprinkled with references to "good talk," but the discourses of Renan and James and Browning were hardly representative of the London dinner party. Gossip was the standard fare, and the most startling bit of literary gossip that spring was the news that George Eliot had married a young American stockbroker named John Cross. The news "burst like a bombshell in an evening party at which we were," Clover reported. Thomas

Hughes, the author of *Tom Brown's School Days,* was another one of the guests and idly remarked that he "never could read one of her books," a judgment that Clover thought "seems to subtract from his powers rather than hers." Most of the gossip was about the lovers' respective ages. "She is about 55—J. Cross 38, they say— the comments are likely to be many and hard," Clover reported, but she proudly added the Adamses' own view of the situation: "We declare that a woman of genius is above criticism."

From gossip, it was only another step to parlor games. At the Regent's Park mansion of Laurens Alma-Tadema, the Belgian painter gave Clover a tour of the ceilings made of beaten gold leaf and the windows filled with panes of jasper and then began telling jokes. "We even fell into lower depths, into conundrums," Clover reported, "which to his simple Belgian mind seemed immensely funny, such as 'Why is an African woman like a prophet?' Of course I gave it up so that he could have the pleasure of telling me, 'Because she has little on her in her own country.'"

And who should arrive in the midst of this social whirl but James Russell Lowell, who, as a result of further intrigues by Howells and Norton, had just been appointed ambassador to London. No sooner had the appointment been made than his convalescent wife suffered a relapse, but Lowell set off to London without her. Clover drove to Victoria Station to welcome him and found him "looking well and handsome." Henry hastened to offer Lowell a place in Bird Cage Walk, saying, with some awkwardness, *"Mi casa sta à la disposicion de usted."* But Lowell had come to London only to present his credentials to Queen Victoria, who asked after Mrs. Lowell with what the poet called "a *human* tone," and then he returned to Madrid to deal with his prostrate wife. He had her borne over the Pyrenees to a house that had been offered him in Biarritz, and then to the home of some friends in Hampshire. The poet seemed relieved at his own release from the sickroom in Madrid. Clover saw him one evening that spring all dressed up in knee breeches for a ball at Marlborough House, while Mrs. Lowell remained home, barely able to "shuffle across the room with a nurse on each side to support her."

Another kind of mental breakdown affected the Adamses more directly. From Quincy, Charles Francis, Jr., wrote to Henry that their father was steadily deteriorating. His memory was fading. He could no longer organize his thoughts in any systematic way. The deterioration "became painfully clear the other day," Charles wrote, when the old man, now seventy-three, tried to compose a centennial address to the Academy of Arts and Sciences. As he worked on it, he found that he had mistakenly copied some passages in such a way that the whole speech had become confused. He became so agitated about his incapacity that Abigail and Charles persuaded him to give up the whole project. He agreed not only to cancel the speech but to make no more public appearances. In fact, he even decided to abandon the voluminous journal that he had kept for more than half a century. "He is the mere wreck of his former self mentally and aging rapidly physically," Charles wrote to Henry. "It is not painful at all, for it seems to take merely the form of loss of memory and incapacity for sustained mental effort." From now on, the old man's only destiny was to wait stoically, with his crippled wife, for the death that did not come.

England, like France, was feeling the tremors of reform, and most of the Adamses' friends were Liberals, Gladstone Liberals, who believed in at least some modest extension of the franchise and some limits on Disraeli's imperial belligerence in Egypt, Afghanistan, and South Africa. Clover was presiding over "a very impromptu dinner" on a Monday evening in early March when Gaskell came "bringing the news of the sudden dissolution of Parliament announced an hour before." Clover originally saw the election purely in terms of her social calendar. "All politicians and aspirants fly to their boroughs," she reported, "and dinner engagements go to the wall." She also took a characteristically pessimistic view of her friends' predictions. "The Liberals pretend to hope," she said, "but it strikes one that they are whistling to keep their courage up."

Throughout the campaign, Clover's letters reflect the same skepticism toward any political commitment. She notes only that one dinner host "has to fly the next day at dawn for a remote little borough in the North which he hopes to capture." And that another lady, busily furnishing her South Kensington house with Morris papers, is "all alone while her husband is electioneering in Edinbro'." She was amused to see that the Tories put up posters decrying the celebrated Sir Charles Dilke as "the man who fried his own wife." But when she heard the editor of the *Spectator* predict a Liberal majority of 70, she said that his prophecy was treated as "harmless but undoubted madness."

Little wonder then that the Adamses were, as Clover put it, "amused, surprised and interested in the huge spring tide of liberalism which has risen over the land this week. . . . Few people whom we see weep over the Tory corpses which are floating out of sight." The tide swept in such friends as Gaskell and Sir Robert Cunliffe and even James Bryce, the future author of *The American Commonwealth*, who had campaigned in a traditionally conservative borough. In all of this, Clover saw portents, and she gloated over them, for she really never liked the gilded ceremonies of Victorian England. On going to Whitehall to watch the Dean of Windsor hand out used shoes and stockings to the poor, she observed that "the amount of anthems and prayers and self-glorifications which accompanied the giving away seems to a dissenting mind unnecessary." And on watching an assembly of robes and wigs beneath the dome of St. Paul's, she wrote that "these old pageants and mummeries seem like a joke and I rejoice that I am an alien and belong to a race who kicked out of this old harness so long ago." So the downfall of the Tories in the spring of 1880 seemed to herald great changes. "There are ominous creakings and snappings of rotten old timbers," she wrote, "and the house of lords and bishops (I began to spell bishop with a big B but better not) are beginning to think of packing up."

Clover also saw corruption, charging that £10 million had changed hands "in what they decline to call bribing—it's very disgusting." She was far less critical, however, of the process by which James A. Garfield won the Republican presidential nomination that same summer. He had, after all, been poor, born in a log cabin, largely self-educated, a schoolteacher, a carpenter, and a farmer. He had worked with Charles Francis Adams, Jr., to reform the railroads and with Henry to expose the Jay Gould gold conspiracy, and he had praised Henry as "a clear and powerful thinker." Besides, he was blue-eyed and charming and eloquent, and so, since President Hayes refused to run for a second term, and since the bosses' efforts to bring back General Grant were encountering passionate opposition, and since the Republican convention therefore remained deadlocked through more than thirty ballots, what better compromise than the former House speaker and newly elected Senator James A. Garfield?

"He will continue the regime of clean government," Clover wrote her father on hearing of the nomination. In offering that judgment, she lightly overlooked the fact that the Republicans had also nominated for vice-president Chester A. Arthur, a representative of New York's corrupt Conkling machine. She could hardly overlook the revelations that soon followed, that Garfield had been one of the congressmen who received Credit Mobilier stocks as part of the grand scheme to defraud the government in the building of the Union Pacific Railroad. Just a week after praising the new Republican nominee, Clover wondered whether he was "fit to be president." Henry, however, remained loyal. "Garfield seems to me a very strong candidate . . ." he wrote. "I shall vote for Garfield."

The object of the journey, as Henry had written to Gaskell, had been to unearth and analyze the European diplomatic reports on the troubled regimes of Jefferson and Madison. After more than a year of wandering and inquiring, of diligence and drudgery, he considered that object fulfilled. "My work is done, at least so far as it ever will be done," he wrote to Lodge in July of 1880. "My material is enormous, and I now fear that the task of compression will be painful. Burr alone is good for a volume . . . and Napoleon is vast. I have got to contemplate six volumes for the sixteen years as inevitable. If it proves a dull story, I will condense, but it's wildly interesting, at least to me."

There are occasional indications in Clover's letters that she helped him in these researches. In describing their daily schedule in that spring, for example, she reports that they have taken to delaying breakfast until 11:30, "so before breakfast we get time for writing notes, reading papers, etc. and after that we both go to the British Museum and work till it closes." And again, offhand, a few weeks later: "Friday after our work was over. . . ." Despite these hints, however, Clover never gives any indication of what her share in the work might have been. Indeed, she never makes any comment about the substance of Henry's researches, about Ambassador Yrujo's efforts to subvert the Jefferson administration, for example, or the outrage that Britain's Ambassador Merry felt at being received by the President in worn slippers. She may, of course, simply have thought that the gossip of 1805 would not have interested Dr. Hooper.

From what she did tell Dr. Hooper, however, it is clear that neither research nor gossip nor fashion nor anything else could reconcile her to another year in Europe. "The six months in London wound up most happily . . . a pleasure to look back to," she wrote, "but we know no regret or longing for more." And again: "The more I see of England the less I care to live in it, charming as it is for a temporary halt." And finally: "I'd rather winter in a first-class American *coffin* than in any house on this side. My cheerful heroism of last winter would not stand a protracted strain." Henry James came around to read her with morbid relish the hostile reviews of his *Hawthorne*, in which he had enumerated some of the riches that America lacked: "No State, in the European sense of the word . . . no aristocracy, no church, no clergy, no army, no diplomatic service, no country gentlemen, no palaces, no castles . . . nor thatched cottages nor ivied ruins. . . ." Clover was unimpressed. "The savage notices of his *Hawthorne* . . . are silly and overshoot the mark in their bitterness," she wrote, "but for all that he had better not hang around Europe very much longer if he wants to make a lasting literary reputation."

In returning home, in search once again of the mythical home that still did not exist, not on H Street nor on Marlborough Street nor even at Beverly Farms, Clover once again brought along a boatload of accumulated treasures. From Spain alone, her acquisitions included a sixteenth-century writing cabinet, five feet high, ornamented with carved screens and gilded metalwork backed with red velvet, and, for her amusement, a series of secret drawers. And a hanging of Salamanca embroidery on linen, eight feet by six, and, in the words of Don Leopoldo, "pure Renaissance." By the time the Adamses reached London, they were interested mainly in pictures, and their prize acquisition there was a Turner landscape— "a castle on a hill, a river, sheep, and two women." Clover excused the expense by explaining that it was an investment transferred from "some dead and buried and forgotten R.R. bonds." Then, after a brief swing through Scotland, the Adamses paid a last visit to Paris, where Henry had some more research to complete and Clover could not stay away from the House of Worth. She was delighted at the couturier's special attentions, at the way he "soothed my nerves and flattered my vanity and the cavalier manner in which he set aside Mrs. Vanderbilt and Mrs. Astor." Henry wrote to a friend with some bemusement that "15,361 gowns and other articles of dress have been delivered and there remain only 29,743 to come."

Two days later, with eight Worth gowns fitted and finished and packed, Clover once again celebrated her birthday in Paris. It was her thirty-seventh. The only present that Clover recorded was the one from Betsy Wade, the devoted servant back in Beverly Farms, who sent to her former charge a six-leaf clover. And then it was time to go home. The Adamses had booked passage at the end of the month on the *Gallia*, the same boat on which they had sailed to Europe more than a year before, and they had even booked the same cabin they had used then. The ship sailed from Edinborough, with Moorish writing desk and Worth gowns and packets of Foreign Office documents, and, as Clover boarded it, she seemed to know that a part of her life was over. So did Henry. "I have little doubt," he wrote, "that we are now bidding goodbye to Europe forever."

BOOK FOUR

The Knot
of Existence

After great pain a formal feeling comes—
The nerves sit ceremonious like tombs . . .
This is the hour of lead
Remembered if outlived
As freezing persons recollect
The snow—
First chill, then stupor, then
The letting go.

EMILY DICKINSON

Poor Mrs. Adams found, the other day, the solution of
the knottiness of existence.

HENRY JAMES

13

THE FIVE OF HEARTS

WHEN THE ADAMSES moved back to Washington in October of 1880, to a large old house at 1607 H Street, they were pleased to find that the town was still gossiping about the authorship of the anonymous novel entitled *Democracy*. Henry had delivered the manuscript, dashed off in a few months after the completion of *Gallatin*, just before his departure to Europe, and Henry Holt had published it as part of his Leisure Hour Series in the spring of 1880. "It is intimated," *The New York Tribune* intimated, "that many readers will see portraits in this book."

The portraits of Washington in the Gilded Age were vivid, and merciless. At the White House, for example, *Democracy*'s widowed heroine, Madeleine Lee, encountered "two seemingly mechanical figures, which might be wood or wax, for any signs they showed of life." These two figures were the President and his wife, not specifically identified as Rutherford and Lucy Hayes, who happened to have been occupying the White House, but remarkably similar. "They stood stiff and awkward by the door," the anonymous novelist continued, "both their faces stripped of every sign of intelligence, while the right hands of both extended themselves to the column of visitors with the mechanical action of toy dolls."

And then the corrupt Senator Silas P. Ratcliffe, whom nobody could fail to identify as Senator James G. Blaine, the "plumed knight" and perennial presidential candidate. Mrs. Lee first described him as "a great, ponderous man, over six feet high, very senatorial and dignified, with a large head and rather good features." Another character soon corrected Mrs. Lee's description by calling attention to the senator's eyes, "cold eyes, steel gray, rather small, not unpleasant in good-humour, diabolic in a passion, but worst when a little suspicious; then they watch you as though you were a young rattle-snake, to be killed when convenient."

Harpooned, gushing blood, Senator Blaine dove into the depths, then gathered his strength and eventually emerged at a dinner party in New York, where he declared, according to E. L. Godkin of *The Nation*, that these libels were the work of a malicious female, expressing all the venomous bitterness of a Brahmin family in exile—that *Democracy*, in short, was the secret work of Clover Adams. Henry was delighted. "I understand . . ." he wrote, "that Hon. J. G. Blaine at a dinner party in New York said that Mrs. H. A. 'acknowledges' to have written *Democracy*. You know how I have always admired Mr. Blaine's powers of invention!" Clover was even more delighted to hear of Blaine's charge that she had written what she called "that mistresspiece," and to hear that another expert attributed "Mrs. Adams' bitterness [to the fact] that there are refined circles in Washington into which she cannot gain admittance."

Clover did, in fact, sometimes jokingly "acknowledge" having written the scandalous work. "Emily Beale declared at dinner Sunday that the novel called *Democracy* was 'a horrid, nasty, vulgar book, written by a newspaperman not in good society . . .' " Clover reported to Dr. Hooper. "Harriet Loring says 'Clover your aunt Tappan says you wrote it. . . .' I said, 'Yes, I did, and *you*, Harriet, are the Dare girl. I hope you don't mind.' " Clover added mysteriously that "Aunt Tappan is *Minerva* in the novel I am writing now," but when Dr. Hooper actually seemed to believe the gossip about Clover's involvement in *Democracy*, she categorically denied it. "I am much amused but not surprised at your having suspected me of having written *Democracy*," she said, "as I find myself on the 'black list' here with Miss Loring, Arthur Sedgwick, Manton Marble, Clarence King and John Hay. . . . All I *know* is that *I* did not write it. Deny it from me if anyone defames me absent, and say to them, as Pickering Dodge of his parrot: 'If she couldn't *write* better than that I'd cut her———head off.' "

If Washington gossip could not solve the riddle of the authorship of *Democracy* (the first correct guesses began appearing in England about a decade later but were not publicly confirmed until after Henry's death), it was at least suspected that the culprit was a member of what the Adamses liked to call their "set." Someone who came regularly to the white house on H Street for Clover's five o'clock tea, someone fascinated by the workings of politics and yet aloof from the routine of the capital, someone who displayed an aristocratic elegance without necessarily being an aristocrat.

Someone, perhaps, like Clarence King, one of that little group known to its members as The Five of Hearts. Almost forgotten today, though there is a mountainous tooth in the Sierra Nevada named after him, King once shone among his contemporaries like a kind of Apollo. John Hay, the future Secretary of State, described him as "the best and brightest man of his generation." Even the white-bearded old John Ruskin was so charmed on meeting King that he offered the visiting American the choice between his two best paintings by Turner, and King was the kind of man who could buy both of them, remarking as he did so, "One good Turner deserves another." Henry Adams was equally bewitched. "His wit and humor," he wrote in the *Education*, "his bubbling energy which swept everyone into the current of his interest; his personal charm of youth and manners; his faculty of giving and taking, profusely, lavishly . . . marked him almost alone among Americans. He had in him something of the Greek—a touch of Alcibiades or Alexander. One Clarence King only existed in the world."

A short, stocky man with a closely cropped beard, King had grown up in Newport, in rather clouded circumstances. His mother, Florence Little King, claimed ancestors aboard the *Mayflower*, but the Littles were by no means wealthy. At sixteen, Florence married the third son of Samuel King, a slightly older contemporary of Captain Sturgis and principal partner in the East India trading company of King and Talbot. But while Captain Sturgis retired to Church Green and accumulated riches, the Kings kept returning to the storms and fevers of China. James King fell ill and died on Amoy, leaving Florence a widow at twenty-three, with a six-year-old son.

Clarence King went to Yale, became fascinated with the study of geology, and persuaded a newly expansive postwar government in Washington to subsidize him in a monumental adventure, the first thorough survey of all the minerals that might actually be found between the Mississippi and California. One night in the summer of 1871, while King was exploring Estes Park in northern Colorado, he heard a rustling outside the door of his cabin. Two or three friends who were sharing the cabin went out to investigate, and in the light from the cabin door they saw a weary mule, and on top of the mule, hopelessly lost, Professor Henry B. Adams of Harvard. "Adams," as Henry later wrote, "fell into [King's] arms. . . . They shared the room and the bed, and talked till far towards dawn. King had everything to interest and delight Adams. He knew more than Adams did of art and poetry; he knew America, especially west of the 100th meridian, better than anyone; he knew the professor by heart, and he knew the Congressman better than he did the professor. He knew even women; even the American woman; even the New York woman, which is saying much."

He knew them, perhaps, but only through the odd prisms that the New England mothers of the nineteenth century used for the education of their sons. "I have never known a more perfect human tie than that which bound my son and myself," Florence Little King was to say shortly after Clarence's death. "We were one in heart and mind and soul." King might well have agreed, but some of his writings imply a deep hostility toward all women of the type that his mother had taught him to respect. "Think of the stunted and petty women and their incredible meanness," he once observed, "of the primeval monkey scale of their average intelligence; remember how few wholesome, sweet, strong women are found in that army of distorted, diseased creatures who march between the covers of English fiction. . . . Or, to come nearer home, recall the pretty, brightish, smug little people who are made with inimitable skill to illustrate the sawdust stuffing of middle-class democratic society."

Despite such outbursts of misogyny, King seems to have been very fond of Clover, and she of him. "No one is as good company," she once wrote to her father, and when Henry came to portray her in *Esther*, he depicted an affection just short of love between Esther and the skeptical scientist, George Strong. Clover and King spoke to one another as New Englanders, and yet when he offered her presents, they were always exotic things from the wilds, such as, at New Year's, the head of an antelope that he had recently shot. Indeed, the wandering scientist "never comes empty-handed," Clover reported, and she never failed to be charmed. In February of 1878, for example, King turned up with "a blanket made by the sister of a Pi-ute Indian chief who was buried in Mr. King's dress coat by particular request. The coat was an object of envy to the tribe—who poisoned him on that account—he was buried in it— afterwards dug up and robbed of it by a subsequent Pi-ute who wore it in Mr. King's presence."

King had too many different kinds of talent. Not only was he a brilliant geologist, but his youthful book *Mountaineering in the Sierra Nevada* (1871), remains, like Parkman's *Oregon Trail* and Dana's *Two Years Before the Mast*, a classic account of the New England will pitted against the wilds. Yet neither science nor literature satisfied King's hunger. He yearned, with the characteristic yearning of his time, not for something more but for something less—to be rich. Had not Alex Agassiz said that it was impossible to be a scientist in America without first making enough money to pay for indepen- dent research? And had not Agassiz then gone out and become rich, and made his friends rich as well? King's goal was much the same: To use his geological knowledge to discover buried treasure in the Sierra Nevada, to use his enthusiasm and his friendships to raise capital back in Boston, to become lord of a vast mining con- glomerate and then to devote his wealth to scholarship, and also to the acquisition of Renaissance paintings and Chinese carvings and every manner of silks and jewels and porcelains and tapestries. "Whatever prize he wanted lay ready for him," Henry Adams later recalled, "scientific, social, literary, political—and he knew how to take them in turn. With ordinary luck he would die at eighty the richest and most many-sided genius of his day."

King almost succeeded. He recruited scouts and agents all over the Southwest, and the treasure was undoubtedly there to be taken from the mountains of Mexico. There was a lode of gold and silver at Prietas, in Sonora Province, which priests had mined until the Indians rebelled against them, and now it was flooded and aban- doned. King went to his friends, Alex Agassiz and Agassiz's two brothers-in-law, Henry Lee Higginson and Quincy Shaw, all of whom were still reaping profits from Agassiz's discovery of the Calumet and Hecla copper mines. They put up more than $500,000 to buy the Prietas mine. Then one of King's agents dis- covered another flooded mine at Yedras, in Sinaloa. The three Bostonians bought it for $200,000. And finally there was Sombrer- ete, at the foot of a mountain in Zacatecas, which had been mined by the Spaniards and then by the English and the Mexicans, yielding some $150 million before it had been abandoned. But the thirty-nine shafts extended down only about 1,000 feet, where they had been flooded, and King was sure that they could be deepened by another 1,000 feet. The Comstock Mines in Nevada, after all, extended more than 3,000 feet. The Bostonians organized a new company capitalized at $5 million.

But King could not escape the shadow of his father, that vague dreamer who had died of fever in the China trade. With all his charm and all his expert knowledge, King also needed vast amounts of both capital and labor. Heavy equipment had to be brought up into the mountains by mule. The Yaqui Indians were in a state of rebellion, and the Apaches were not the best of neighbors. King tried hiring Italian immigrants, then Chinese coolies. New problems kept arising, new demands for more capital before the profits would begin flowing in. Back in Boston, however, the Agassiz' and Higginsons and Shaws demanded respectable returns on their investments so that they could proceed with their favorite charities, such as the creation of the Boston Symphony Orchestra. They began to regard King as a visionary, impractical, unsound.

King fled to London in May of 1882, seeking new financing. He was optimistically convinced that he could arrange everything within a few months. But he was so charmed with London society, with the Prince of Wales and Baron Ferdinand de Rothschild and, inevitably, Henry James, that he dallied from dinner parties to country weekends for a full two years. In this evasion of his difficulties, he was becoming coolly irrational, and Henry Adams was one of the few to see it. "Is King insane or not?" he wrote to Hay. "Agassiz seems seriously to think he is and I myself sometimes suspect it." When Hay objected, Adams became more emphatic: "Be not mad at my calling King mad, for mad he certainly is."

King did finally manage to launch the Anglo-Mexican Mining Company, capitalized in 1883 at £350,000, but when it came time to pay the Boston owners $1 million for the Yedras mines, King couldn't raise the money among his new friends in London. And when he finally sailed back to New York with crates and crates of bric-a-brac, having let his underfinanced mines bumble along while he spent most of his time in art galleries and noble estates, he found his imaginary empire in ruins. It would take him some years more to recognize the ruin, to realize that the Mexican mines would swallow up all the money he could raise, and that not even his best

friends were prepared to finance indefinitely his fantasies of riches.
"Waste and frittering," said Quincy Shaw.

In all of King's efforts to raise fortunes by means of his charm,
there is no indication that he ever tried to use that charm on the
dowagers and heiresses who might have saved him. On the contrary, there are jocular references throughout the literature on King
to his fondness for more primitive types, Mexicans, Indians, all
women of color. Historians of a psychoanalytic turn would emphasize that King had been cared for by a black nursemaid in his
orphaned childhood. Friends simply noted, as Henry Adams
wrote, that "if he had a choice among women, it was in favor of
Indians and negroes." Or, more generally, that he was not interested in "the modern woman" but rather in "the archaic woman,
with instincts and without intellect." In his roving bachelorhood,
King presumably satisfied himself in a series of paid encounters,
but in 1887, when he was forty-five, he finally fell in love. His
discovery was a black girl named Ada Todd, scarcely twenty-one,
who worked as a nursemaid in the home of one of King's friends in
New York.

"No one ever loved a woman as I do you," King wrote to Ada.
But he didn't tell her his real name. He used his father's first name,
James, and when he appeared with Ada, he took her last name and
called himself James Todd. Ada was determined to get married,
and so a little ceremony was staged in September of 1888 at the
home of Ada's aunt, on West 24th Street in New York, at the edge
of the Tenderloin district. A black Methodist minister proclaimed
the couple man and wife, and King, in a dress suit, put a ring on
Ada's finger. But there was no legal marriage certificate. King insisted on that. He and Ada were to have five children, and he
supported them all, but he never acknowledged that the Todd
family that he visited secretly in Brooklyn was in any way related
to the Kings of Newport. If his aged mother ever learned of the
situation, he believed, the knowledge would kill her.

The difficulties of King's illicit marriage—"it will not do to have
too many people see me," he once wrote to Ada after failing to visit
the Brooklyn ménage—only added to the pressures of his mining
failures, his ventures into banking and railroads, all virtually destroyed in the panic of 1893, and to the general sense that the youth
who had once been regarded as "the best and brightest man of his
generation" was now a graying wreck of fifty who had never really

accomplished much of anything. And his health was ruined. He was suffering from a painful polyp on the spine. After a month-long exploration of some mines in British Columbia, he returned to New York looking gaunt and unkempt and complaining of memory lapses. On October 29, in that dark year of 1893, King got into some mysterious kind of conflict at the lion house in the Central Park Zoo. King later claimed that other people had "jostled" him against a black butler from one of the nearby mansions. Two detectives arrested him for "acting in a disorderly manner in the presence of a large crowd." When the case came to court, on Halloween, two doctors testified that King was mentally disturbed, suffering from acute depression, and should be confined. King consented to being so confined—for only two months, as it turned out—in the Bloomington Asylum. "Most of us would have liked to do" the same, Henry Adams observed. "That all one's acquaintance should retreat into asylums seemed at one time the only way to escape hopeless ruin and collapse."

No, Clarence King had the talent to write *Democracy*, but he dissipated that talent in a lifetime of wandering and collecting and speculating on future empires. Besides, the novel was a Washington novel, written by someone who knew all the back stairways of the State Department, all the cracks in the ceilings of the White House. Someone, perhaps, like John Hay, the future Secretary of State and another founding member of the Five of Hearts. "My dear heart," Henry Adams addressed Hay on the special stationery that Clover acquired in the early 1880's, stationery with a letterhead that resembled the playing card of the five of hearts. And again, "Sweet heart" and *"Cher coeur."* The founders of this exclusive club were to remain its only members: Clover and Henry Adams, Clarence King, John and Clara Hay. And of these, Clover was always to be, according to King, "first heart."

Like Clarence King, John Hay was a man of great charm, great talent, and great uncertainty about what to do with his life. Unlike King, however, Hay was a man blessed by luck. Indeed, "luck" was his answer, on a young lady's questionnaire of the type that was known in those days as a "Mental Photograph Album," to the question: "What trait of character do you most admire in a man?" The other questions also serve, in a way, to produce a shadowy photograph of a good-humored young man of the 70's: "Your favorite . . . tree? Industry. Object in nature? School girls. . . . Character in Romance? George Washington. Character in History? Susan B. Anthony. . . . What epoch would you choose to have lived in? The Twentieth Century. Where would you like to live? Everywhere. . . . If not yourself, who would you rather be? Her second husband. What is your idea of happiness? A bad character and a good digestion."

. Hay was born in 1838 in what was then regarded as the West, in Salem, Indiana. His father was a country doctor who soon moved his family still farther westward to the Mississippi river town of Warsaw, Illinois. When Hay came east to study at Brown, he came, like Howells, as a kind of pilgrim, awed by the complacent wealth and sophistication of the East. He dreaded going back to Illinois to read law in the office of his uncle Milton Hay, but that was where his luck awaited him, for one of the firm's partners was an aspiring politician named Abraham Lincoln. When Lincoln was elected President the following year, he took Hay to Washington with him as a personal secretary. In Washington, Hay encountered for the first time another ambitious political secretary, Henry Adams. They were both the same age, twenty-two.

Hay served Lincoln faithfully until the end, then spent five years abroad as a secretary at the United States legations in Paris, Vienna, and Madrid, but diplomacy did not fulfill his ambitions. He wanted to write. He returned to New York and found a job composing editorials for Horace Greeley's *New York Tribune*. But all this time, he was writing poetry, and in 1881, he published a collection entitled *Pike County Ballads*, as well as a collection of sketches, *Castilian Days*. Hay's verses seem little better than doggerel in an age that has been taught to struggle with the complexities of Wallace Stevens, but in the 80's, when Melville was forgotten and James regarded as unpatriotic, American connoisseurs of literature delighted in the finale to Hay's "Ballad of Jim Bludso":

> *He seen his duty, a dead-sure thing, —*
> *And went for it thar and then;*
> *And Christ ain't a going to be too hard*
> *On a man that died for men.*

247

Unlike Clarence King, who floundered about in his yearning to find riches, John Hay emulated the more successful of the Adamses by marrying well. His discovery was Clara Stone, a stately girl, something less than a beauty and perhaps just a bit dull. Clover never really regarded her as worthy of being the fifth heart—she "never speaks," she observed—and even Hay, in announcing his engagement to his friend John Nicolay, could only describe her as "a very estimable young person—large, handsome and good." Still, she was the daughter of Amasa Stone of Cleveland, bridge-builder, railroad financier, patron of Western Reserve University, and self-made millionaire. Luck—once again—in the West. Stone liked young Hay, urged him to move to Cleveland, paid him a handsome allowance, established him as a manager of the Stone investments. Hay complied.

Writing editorials for the *Tribune* was not, after all, a very exalted vocation. Hay knew, at least as early as his marriage in 1874, and perhaps a decade earlier, that he had a far grander literary mission —to join with Nicolay, Lincoln's other secretary, now marshal of the Supreme Court, in writing the first full biography of the murdered President. The mission would eventually require ten volumes, and fifteen years of their lives. But there were distractions, and the view from Cleveland was inevitably different from the conventional perceptions of the East. In 1877, for example, the very year in which Clover and Henry abandoned Boston and moved to Washington so that they could observe at first hand the machinery of American society, that same machinery appeared, in Cleveland, to be breaking down.

The four major eastern trunk railroads, having expanded too much and too quickly, announced to their underpaid employees a general wage cut of 10 percent, the second since the panic of 1873. This at a time when the average pay for a fireman on the New York Central was $41.08 per month. On July 18, the day after the wage cut took effect, workmen on the Baltimore & Ohio seized a number of stations and refused to let any freight trains leave. The governor of Maryland called out the state militia. President Hayes ordered federal troops to restore order. The strikers were supported by crowds of tramps and idlers (there were between two and three million unemployed throughout the nation), and the crowds started stoning the troops. The soldiers opened fire. On the first day of fighting in Baltimore, nine people were killed, more than twenty wounded.

And the unorganized strike kept spreading. In Pittsburgh, the soldiers killed about twenty-five people, then retreated into a railroad roundhouse. The strikers set it on fire. As the soldiers retreated, crowds broke into long lines of freight cars and began pillaging. Women appeared and made off with crates of silk and laces. Liquor stores were plundered. And still the strike spread, to Chicago (ten killed), to St. Louis and San Francisco. For about a week in that July of 1877, all major railroad traffic, which meant virtually all long-distance transportation, shut down. It was the first nationwide strike the United States had ever seen—though the textile workers of New England and the anthracite miners of Pennsylvania had rebelled and been crushed two years earlier—the first proof that this land of farmers and traders now had acquired an industrial working class ready to fight for survival.

In Cleveland, where John Hay had been left in charge of Amasa Stone's empire while the financier went off to Europe, the railroad strike appeared almost a portent of revolution. "Since last week," Hay wrote to his father-in-law, "the country has been at the mercy of the mob. The shameful truth is now clear, that the government is utterly helpless and powerless in the face of an unarmed rebellion of foreign workingmen, mostly Irish. . . . I was advised to send my wife and children out of town to some place of safety, but concluded we would risk it. The town is full of thieves and tramps waiting and hoping for a riot but not daring to begin it themselves. If there were any attempt to enforce the law, I believe the town would be in ashes in six hours. . . . There is a mob in every city ready to join with the strikers, and get their pay in robbery, and there is no means of enforcing the law in case of a sudden attack on private property. . . ."

The strike was suppressed, of course, and there was no concerted attack on private property, at least not on the handsome estates that lined Euclid Avenue. But John Hay, kindly, courtly, amiable John Hay, the diplomat and poet, had experienced a shaming moment of panic, and he determined to write a novel explaining why the workers should be satisfied with their work and why the wealthy were entitled to their wealth. He even interrupted his researches on Lincoln during the winter of 1882–1883 in order to produce his defense of frontier capitalism. It was called *The Bread-Winners*, and though it appeared anonymously, it was immensely successful. *The Century* printed it in six installments and Harper & Brothers sold an astonishing total of 25,000 hardcover copies. It was quickly translated into French, German, Swedish.

The "Bread-Winners" were a group of workmen, in the easily recognizable midwestern city of Buffland, who had banded together to seek higher wages and better working conditions. They had to meet in secret, in those pre–A.F. of L. days, and the anonymous author of *The Bread-Winners* regarded them as nothing but agitators and ruffians. That is clear enough in his physical description of the group's principal organizer, Andrew Jackson Offitt. The man had "a face whose whole expression was oleaginous. It was surmounted by a low and shining forehead covered by reeking black hair, worn rather long. . . . The moustache was long and drooping, dyed black and profusely oiled. . . . The parted lips, which were coarse and thin, displayed an imperfect set of teeth, much discolored with tobacco. The eyes were light green. . . ."

Offitt is scarcely a romantic figure, and yet Hay makes him not only the organizer of the Bread-Winners but the suitor of Maud Matchin, the modern girl, who, having graduated from one of the new high schools, is no longer content to be a servant and wants to work in a library. Hay later claimed, in fact, that Maud was his original inspiration. He had been talking with a carpenter in Detroit who told him that "there is hardly a carpenter's daughter in this town who will marry a carpenter." Maud Matchin, a carpenter's daughter, has the upstart ambition to marry the distinguished Captain Farnham, who lives in one of the estates on Algonquin Avenue and "has the gentleness of one delicately bred." Farnham, in turn, is considering marriage to Alice Belding, who inhabits one of the neighboring estates and blushes whenever Farnham addresses her. But Maud is aggressive. She pursues Captain Farnham into his study and tells him that she loves him. Captain Farnham frowns, but not for long. "He looked down on her, and the frown passed from his brow as he surveyed her flushed cheeks, her red full lips parted in breathless eagerness." Captain Farnham so far forgets himself as to bend and kiss her. "You do love me, do you not?" gasps Maud. "I certainly do not," says Captain Farnham.

Romance was clearly not Hay's forte. His main purpose in writing *The Bread-Winners* was to denounce and exorcise the strikers of

1877. They were, he said, "the laziest and most incapable workmen in the town—men whose weekly wages were habitually docked for drunkenness, late hours and botchy work." When the strike began, they naturally turned to looting, and they could just as naturally be stopped by a few resolute men. "Use your clubs as much as you see fit, if you come to close quarters," Farnham tells the squad of private bodyguards whom he has assembled outside his house, and with those instructions, the guards easily disperse the mob.

The wicked Offitt, avoiding honest combat, has already gone next door and broken into Alice Belding's house. She runs upstairs and locks herself in a bedroom, and the excitement provokes her into a shameful indiscretion. "She ran to her open window . . . and sent the voice of her love and her trouble together into the clear night in one loud cry, 'Arthur!' She blushed crimson as the word involuntarily broke from her lips, and cried again as loudly as she could, 'Help!' " Captain Farnham is already leaping across the lawn, then pummeling the intruders downstairs. A few moments later, he knocks on her door. "Alice stood by the door a moment before she could open it. Her heart was still thumping, her voice failed her, she turned white and red in a moment. The strongest emotion of which she was conscious was the hope that Arthur had not heard her call him by his [first] name. She opened the door. . . . 'Good evening, Captain Farnham' was all she could find to say. . . ."

Though *The Bread-Winners* was to be an immense success, Hay's luck repeatedly pulled him back toward politics. In Cleveland, as a prospectively rich young man, not yet fully embarked on his biography of Lincoln and not overworked in helping to manage his father-in-law's fortune, he began to think of himself as a Congressman. So did the local Republican leaders, who made it clear that the only necessary qualification was a payment of $20,000. Hay didn't have the money. His father-in-law did, but angrily declined to pay. There were others, however, who wanted Hay back in the government on more reputable terms. President Hayes' Secretary of State, William Evarts, asked him to become assistant secretary. Hay at first declined, saying it was "an honor as far beyond my ambition as it is beyond my merits." Evarts insisted, and Hay once again complied.

He moved back to Washington in 1879 while the Adamses were in Europe, and thus was at the scene of the crime at about the time when *Democracy* was written. Henry Adams liked to amuse himself by pretending to believe that Hay really had done the deed. "I was always confident that you wrote that book," he wrote to Hay in June of 1882. Carrie Tappan, however, apparently remained convinced that Clover was responsible. "I have reason to think that our aunt Tappan has numerous acquaintances in England," Henry continued to Hay, "for I receive no end of messages and letters from there asking whether my wife wrote this work of the Devil. Hitherto I have replied with indignation that my wife never wrote for publication in her life and could not write if she tried."

When the book was publicly attributed to yet another suspect, Arthur Sedgewick, Adams wrote to Hay a more serious observation: "Now . . . I can say what I did not care to say to you so long as you were the author, that the book is one of the least sufficient, for its subject, I ever read. Since it came out we have had half a dozen dramas here that might reasonably convulse the world. . . . Therefore, I repeat that your novel, if it was yours, is a failure because it undertook to describe the workings of power in this city, and spoiled a great tragic subject such as Aeschylus might have made what it should be."

There is no reason to doubt Clover's denials on the authorship of *Democracy*, but that does not mean that she had no part in it whatsoever. On the contrary, there are numerous descriptions of the Washington landscape that sound remarkably like Clover's letters, descriptions of riding through wooded hillsides, descriptions of the spring thaw and the flowering of the laurel. Even more idiosyncratic is the detailed account of how the great M. Worth designed the gown that Mrs. Lee's younger sister Sybil wore to a ball: "An imperious order brought to his private room every silk, satin, and gauze within the range of pale pink, pale crocus, pale green, silver and azure. . . ."

It is hard to imagine Clover actually writing parts of *Democracy*, but it is not at all hard to imagine Henry showing her the manuscript as it progressed, and paying considerable attention to her many comments and suggestions. "I make it a rule," he once wrote to Hay, "to strike out ruthlessly in my writings whatever my wife criticises, on the theory that she is the average reader, and that her decisions are, in fact if not in reason, absolute." In later years,

Henry adopted the luxurious practice of privately publishing a few copies of each of his books and then circulating them among his closest friends. Henry designed these preliminary copies with very wide margins so that his friends could write down their observations, and he took those observations into consideration in his final revisions before the formal publication.

Whatever role Clover may have had in the composition of *Democracy*, there can be little doubt that she inspired it. Scholars of the Adams canon suggest that the portrait of Madeleine Lee was based on Mrs. Bigelow Lawrence, who rented the Adamses' house at Beverly Farms during their voyage to Europe, and who was such a good friend of Senator Blaine that Clover once remarked, "If Blaine were a widower, she would not long be a widow." But when Adams tried to describe his thirty-year-old heroine, he started by saying that she was "indescribable." Then he tried again. "Madeleine was of medium height with a graceful figure, a well-set head, and enough golden-brown hair to frame a face of varying expression. Her eyes were never for two consecutive hours of the same shade, but were more often blue than gray. People who envied her smile said that she had cultivated a sense of humor in order to show off her teeth. Perhaps they were right."

Henry may have been describing Mrs. Lawrence, but the portrait clearly included several touches of his view of Clover. And when he went on to describe Mrs. Lee's intellectual inclinations, the object became unmistakable. "She had read philosophy in the original German," he reported, "and the more she read, the more she was disheartened that so much culture should lead to nothing." And again: "She had read voraciously and promiscuously one subject after another. Ruskin and Taine had danced merrily through her mind, hand in hand with Darwin and Stuart Mill. . . ." And yet again: "Though not brighter than her neighbors, the world persisted in classing her among clever women." This was not really Clover, to be sure, but it came remarkably close to the image that Henry seems to have had of her, a woman who read widely but lacked a man's mastery of her reading, a woman of charming volatility who nonetheless yearned to dominate the world around her.

Even before Henry married Clover, he remarked somewhat maliciously that she was "desperately ambitious and wants to be daughter-in-law to a President more than I want to be a President's son." In trying to explain why the widowed Madeleine Lee should want to come to Washington, he attributed to her an abstractly intellectual version of what he conceived to be Clover's ambition. After establishing a metaphor of a steamship passenger searching for the secrets of the engine room, he elaborated on that search. "She wanted to see with her own eyes the action of primary forces; to touch with her own hand the massive machinery of society; to measure with her own mind the capacity of the motive power. She was bent on getting to the heart of the great American mystery of democracy and government. . . . What she wished to see, she thought, was the clash of interests, the interests of forty millions of people and a whole continent. . . . What she wanted was POWER."

The image of the engine room as "the massive machinery of society" anticipated the image of the dynamo before which the white-bearded Henry Adams of a later era bowed down in prayer, and so, just as Flaubert said that he was Madame Bovary, Henry might have confessed that Madeleine Lee was to some extent a self-portrait, a disguised self-portrait all in pastels, the face half-hidden behind veils, but recognizable nonetheless. It was Henry, after all, who had come to Washington to "get to the heart of the great American mystery." And Henry still believed, just as much as Clover, that the great American mystery was a kind of morality play, in which each political leader must be torn between the conflicting demands of the reigning plutocracy and the Puritan conscience. But if Madeleine Lee finally emerges as a composite of both Henry and Clover (plus a bit of Mrs. Bigelow Lawrence), she then illustrates how strongly the Adamses had grasped that quality that can be found in the most intense of marriages, the synthesis of two identities into one.

Madeleine Lee moves to Washington and rents a house on Lafayette Square and devotes much energy to redecorating it in the cluttered Clover style. "The wealth of Syria and Persia was poured out upon the melancholy Wilton carpets; embroidered comets and woven gold from Japan and Teheran depended from and covered over every sad stuff-curtain; a strange medley of sketches, paintings, fans, embroideries, and porcelain was hung, nailed, pinned, or stuck against the wall; finally the domestic altar-piece, the mystical Corot landscape, was hoisted to its place over the parlor fire, and then all was over."

Once Mrs. Lee has decorated her salon, she begins inviting in the diplomatic corps, together with a few genteel Congressmen. "Her parlor was a favorite haunt of certain men and women who had the art of finding its mistress at home; an art which seemed to be not within the powers of everybody." There we find the aged Baron Jacobi, the Bulgarian minister, "a witty, cynical, broken-down Parisian *roué*," who considers Washington "more corrupt than Rome under Caligula." And Popoff, "an intelligent, vivacious Russian, with very Calmuck features, susceptible as a girl, and passionately fond of music." And Congressman C. C. French of Connecticut, who "aspired . . . to purify the public tone." He was —Adams could not resist being malicious about reformers— "rather wealthy, rather clever, rather well-educated, rather honest, and rather vulgar." And Nathan Gore, quite recognizable as the historian John Lothrop Motley, "abominably selfish, colossally egotistic, and not a little vain; but he was shrewd; he knew how to hold his tongue; he could flatter dexterously. . . ."

Among all these Washington figures—these "fame-hunters, heiress-hunters, gold-hunters," as Melville described the characters in *The Confidence-Man*, "happiness-hunters, truth-hunters, and still keener hunters after all these hunters"—the giant puppet-master is Senator Ratcliffe of Illinois. He nearly won the last presidential nomination, only to see it slip into the hands of an obscure Midwestern governor, but he is still the master of Congress, and thus of the Washington establishment. Mrs. Lee is interested. She appeals to what Adams calls the "one general characteristic of all Senators, a boundless and guileless thirst for flattery." She wonders whether there is a risk in being fulsome. "Was I right," she asks Ratcliffe, "in thinking that you have a strong resemblance to Daniel Webster in your way of speaking?" The Senator, Adams reports, "rose to this gaudy fly like a huge, two-hundred-pound salmon; his white waistcoat gave out a mild silver reflection as he slowly came to the surface and gorged the hook."

Despite his raillery, Adams means to present Ratcliffe as a serious character. If Mrs. Lee wants to understand the workings of Washington politics, Ratcliffe is the man who can explain them, for Ratcliffe himself embodies them. He "told her frankly that the pleasure of politics lay in the possession of power . . . and he meant to be president." A widower, flattered and fascinated by the interest of a beautiful woman twenty years younger than he, Ratcliffe soon involves Mrs. Lee in the ambiguities of his career. The hostile President hopes to entrap Ratcliffe by offering him a cabinet post, where he can be isolated from his Senate colleagues and ultimately discarded.

"And now, Mrs. Lee, I want your advice," says the Senator. "What shall I do?"

"I say again, Mr. Ratcliffe, what I said once before," she answers. "Do whatever is most for the public good."

"And what *is* most for the public good?"

Far from Mrs. Lee's salon, meanwhile, Ratcliffe and his legions have been maneuvering to enmesh and paralyze the new President from Indiana. "Every device known to politicians was now in full play. . . . State delegations with contradictory requests were poured in upon [the President]. Difficulties were invented to embarrass and worry him. False leads were suggested, and false information carefully mingled with true. A wild dance was kept up under his eyes from daylight to midnight, until his brain reeled with the effort to follow it." Once Ratcliffe agrees to accept the post of Secretary of the Treasury, as he lures Mrs. Lee into recommending, he becomes not the isolated ex-Senator but the principal power in the cabinet. "He knew everybody and everything. He took most of the President's visitors at once into his own hands and dismissed them with great rapidity. He knew what they wanted; he knew what recommendations were strong and what were weak. . . ."

After much social maneuvering, many dinners and dances and even an excursion to Mount Vernon, Ratcliffe duly proposes to Mrs. Lee a political marriage. "You are kind, thoughtful, conscientious, high-minded, cultivated, fitted better than any woman I ever saw, for public duties. Your place is there. You belong among those who exercise an influence beyond their time." Mrs. Lee is tempted. She is not in love with Ratcliffe, but she is much impressed by him, and, as Adams puts it, "a woman must be more than a heroine who can listen to flattery so evidently sincere, from a man who is pre-eminent among men, without being affected by it." But Ratcliffe is vulnerable, for Ratcliffe is corrupt. "Only fools or theorists," he says at one point "imagine that society can be handled with gloves or long poles. One must make oneself a part of it. If virtue won't answer our purpose, we must use vice, or our opponents will put us out of office." This is not just a matter of theory. In the turmoil of a recent election campaign, Ratcliffe raised money by accepting a $100,000 bribe to change his vote on a steamship subsidy. Another one of Mrs. Lee's suitors, a mournful Virginia lawyer named John Carrington, has learned about the bribery, though he cannot prove it. When Mrs. Lee seems on the verge of marrying Ratcliffe, Carrington tells her. She is horrified. If she came to Washington to learn about the workings of democratic politics, and if Ratcliffe took bribes and even justifies the taking of bribes—as he does when she confronts him with Carrington's accusation—then the machinery of society is nothing but the buying and selling of people.

"I have learned enough to prove that I could do nothing sillier than to suppose myself competent to reform anything," Mrs. Lee tells Ratcliffe when he persists in his marriage proposal, but "I will not share the profits of vice; I am not willing to be made a receiver of stolen goods, or to be put in a position where I am perpetually obliged to maintain that immorality is a virtue." Ratcliffe has no answer except that of his own passion: "Mrs. Lee! Madeleine! I cannot live without you. . . . For God's sake, do not throw me over!" When she once again rejects him, he accuses her of being a coquette, and then she really becomes indignant. "For one long hour," she says, "I have degraded myself by discussing with you the question of whether I should marry a man who by his own confession has betrayed the highest trusts that could be placed in him, who has taken money for his votes as a Senator, and who is now in public office by means of a successful fraud of his own, when in justice he should be in a State's prison."

For those who are primarily concerned with the mind of Henry Adams, *Democracy* is interesting for its political insights, for its judgments on the democratic process and the corruption of the Gilded Age. But there is another aspect of *Democracy* that is no less interesting, and that is Adams' portrait of Madeleine Lee as a self-destructive and implicitly suicidal personality. Adams attributes this partly to Mrs. Lee's history. About five years before her arrival in Washington (it is also one of the reasons for her restless wandering), she had suddenly lost her husband, and then, just a week later, her only child. "She was wild with despair . . . almost insane," Sybil tells Carrington. "Indeed, I have always thought she was quite insane for a time. I know she was excessively violent and wanted to kill herself, and I never heard anyone rave as she did about religion and resignation and God. After a few weeks she became quiet and stupid and went about like a machine; and at last she got over it, but has never been what she was before."

Adams also attributes this quality in Mrs. Lee partly to what he considers to be the feminine temperament, a temperament willingly dedicated to self-sacrifice. "She had a woman's natural tendency toward asceticism, self-extinction, self-abnegation," Adams observes at one point, and when he describes Mrs. Lee's efforts to decide whether to marry Ratcliffe, whom she admires but does not love, he poses a curious rhetorical question: "What was there in her aimless and useless life which made it so precious that she could not afford to fling it into the gutter, if need be, on the bare chance of enriching some fuller existence?" A bit later, when Carrington ventures to declare his love and to call her "perfect," she suffers a similar urge toward self-abasement. "She! perfect! In her contrition she was half ready to go down at his feet and confess her sins; her hysterical dread of sorrow and suffering, her narrow sympathies, her feeble faith, her miserable selfishness, her abject cowardice. . . ."

One can only speculate on whether Henry derived these views of "woman's natural tendency" from his family background, from his observations of contemporary men and women, or from his knowledge of Clover herself—or whether she, in reading his novel, imagined this aspect of it to represent his opinion of her and of the role he expected her to play. In any case, Mrs. Lee, like so many women of her time, is publicly exalted as a lady of great beauty and wit and yet shown to be deeply conscious of her own unworthiness. Even in her view of politics, which Ratcliffe attempts to demonstrate as a series of complex maneuvers and exchanges, Mrs. Lee tends to see visions of nothingness. When she looks at the robotlike figures of the President and his wife stiffly shaking hands at the White House door, she suddenly bursts out to a friend: "Yes! At last I have reached the end! We shall grow to be wax images, and our talk will be like the squeaking of toy dolls. We shall all wander round and round the earth and shake hands. No one will have any object in this world, and there will be no other." And when she learns at the end of Ratcliffe's corruption and deception, she can only cry out: "Oh, what a vile thing life is! Oh, how I wish I were dead! How I wish the universe were annihilated!" The universe inevitably goes on, and so does Mrs. Lee. Instead of being annihilated—the realization of that image still lay ahead—Mrs. Lee ends by sailing off to Egypt, a land of which both Clover and Henry must have held rather enigmatic memories.

Democracy is certainly not a great book. It is too thin, too brittle, too artificial. At the same time, it is gracefully written and has considerable charm. It has always been popular. There were more than a dozen editions in Adams' lifetime, and the novel has finally passed the ultimate test that Stendhal once proposed—to be still read a century after publication. Originally, it benefited from notoriety, not only for its thinly disguised portraits of famous men but for its derision of what democracy had become, a subject on which many Americans were acutely sensitive. *The Atlantic* complained that it "misrepresented and misunderstood the people." The *New York Tribune* observed that "the book contains enough truth to be a wholesome rebuke, and also it contains enough falsehood to be a cruel libel." In Britain, this aspect made it even more popular. The *Edinburgh Review* called it a "most damaging impeachment," the Prince of Wales praised it as "the first American book . . . which seems true all round," and Prime Minister Gladstone was said to be recommending it to his circle. "Written in such a *handy* style, you know," one of Henry James' friends quoted Gladstone as saying. A number of English reviewers compared it favorably with the works of Disraeli and Trollope, though one more expert reader was less impressed. "Who is it by, or attributed to?" Henry James wrote to a friend in America. "A man or a woman? It is good enough to make it a pity it isn't better."

One man who thought he had partly solved the riddle was Charles Francis Adams, Jr. When John Hay's *Bread-Winners* appeared anonymously in 1883, Charles wrote to E. L. Godkin, who knew the secret of *Democracy* but not of *The Bread-Winners*, with a remarkable suggestion. "Who the author is . . . I am sure I do not know," he declared, "but one thing is to me very plain. It is written by the same hand that wrote the novel 'Democracy' some years ago. . . . It has the same coarse, half-educated touch; and the Nast-like style of its portrait and painting is unmistakable. . . . Could you have a short paragraph . . . suggesting this idea?" Godkin promptly forwarded the letter to Henry, with a note at the bottom, asking, "What shall I say to this?" Henry was delirious. "I want to roll on the floor," he wrote to Hay, "to howl, kick and sneeze; to weep silent tears of thankfulness to a beneficent providence which has permitted me to see this day. I want to drown my joy in oceans of Champagne and lemonade. Never, No, never, since Cain wrote his last newspaper letter about Abel was there anything so droll." He concluded by signing himself "Ever your poor, coarse and half-educated friend, Henry Adams," adding, "My coarse and half-educated wife has had a fit over her brother-in-law's Nast-like touch."

At Henry's suggestion, Godkin urged Charles to write his theory himself, and he duly printed it in *The Nation* over the signature, "A." Charles compared the two novels and found them both "crude," lacking in "fine" touches. "We are conscious of the same keen, observant eye, working through a hand which is quite lacking in training, and which . . . is unequal to a sustained effort. I fancy it would be safe to guess that the author had worked on a newspaper. He certainly has seen a good deal of politics, and was never a man of business. That he was once in the army is plain." This is so close to the mark, and so barbed in its categorization of both Henry and Hay, that some of Adams' biographers suspect that Charles really knew quite well what he was doing. This theory is particularly plausible since *Democracy* and *The Bread-Winners* are not really similar at all, except that both are anonymous novels dealing with political issues. Adams' work is light and tart, Hay's is polemical and sentimental, and only a rather inept critic would attribute both works to one author. Charles was malicious enough to indulge in such a trick, but he was also unsophisticated enough to misjudge his subject and to pride himself on his misjudgments. He prided himself, too, on being the most mercilessly candid of all the Adamses, so it seems unlikely that, if he really had guessed the riddle, he would have ended his little piece by declaring: "Who [the author] is I have not the remotest idea."

14

IN THE MIDST OF LIFE

EVEN BEFORE the Adamses' return from Europe in the fall of 1880, they had negotiated with William Wilson Corcoran, the financier, to lease for six years his three-story brick house and garden at 1607 H Street, just across the park from the White House. It was a good place in which to settle, "a solid old pile," Clover reported. Above its ground-floor dining and living rooms, the second floor contained six bedrooms and two bathrooms and a new staircase to the servants' rooms on the top floor. Though the rent was only $200 per month, Corcoran agreed to build a five-room servants' establishment over the nearby stables. Besides that, the Adamses wanted the interiors redone. They had to find a cabinetmaker to build bookcases for Henry's books, and other artisans to install new wallpaper and new lights.

"It will be at least another month before I shall be able to settle again to my work . . ." Henry wrote to Lodge. "I am . . . watching carpenters, plumbers, painters, paperers, and gas-fitters." Apparently he did more than watch. He fussed and corrected. He criticized a German painter so sharply that, according to Clover, the painter "lost his temper with Henry, saying he 'couldn't please him.' Henry tried to soothe him and I went in and mollified him in such execrable German that he came round and was very polite." The painter's quiet was deceptive, for he was already on the edge of madness. After leaving the Adamses' house, he went to his employer's paint shop and stole a putty knife, then went home and cut his wife's throat. Clover must have been shaken, though she observed only that "if he had chosen to stick his putty knife into us a few hours earlier, it would have been uncomfortable all round." The murder represented an ominous sacrifice in the rites of building, but the building did finally get finished, and Clover professed herself content. "Henry pegs away at his work," she wrote, "and thinks his house charming."

Although Rutherford B. Hayes had abdicated the presidency, he still occupied the White House, and so, while President-elect Garfield struggled with his cabinet nominations, Lucy Hayes sent an offering of cut flowers across Lafayette Square to H Street, "a nice little attention," as Clover put it, "from our new opposite neighbor." Despite the Adamses' disapproval of the Hayeses' plodding Ohio ways, they went to pay a last call, " our annual call," as Clover said, and "sat in big Hadley rocking chairs in front of a wood fire" and staunchly defended Henry James' new work, *Daisy Miller*, against the patriotic criticisms of a stout Mrs. Smith from Chicago. Two months later, as the Hayeses were preparing to leave, the Adamses even condescended to go to the White House for dinner. Clover was pleased to find herself escorted to the dinner table by an old friend, President Daniel Coit Gilman of the newly founded Johns Hopkins University, but she was startled by the china plates set before her. "The new dinner set, which is said to have cost fifteen thousand dollars, is fearful," she wrote to her father. "To eat one's soup calmly with a coyote springing at you from a pine tree is intimidating, and ice cream plates disguised as Indian snowshoes would be esthetic, but make one yearn for Mongolian simplicity."

Henry Adams had enjoyed reasonably cordial relations with the incoming President Garfield, but the change of administrations confronted him with a practical problem. In Garfield's effort to conciliate the rival Republican factions led by Senators Blaine and Conkling, he decided to make Blaine the Secretary of State. "It's a gross insult to the moral sense of the community," Clover declared. The practical problem, though, was that the State Department archives, to which Henry had had privileged access throughout the Hayes administration, were now falling under the control of a man whom the Adamses despised, both politically and socially. "For us it will be most awkward," Clover wrote. "Never having called on them before, it will simply be impossible to make up to them now.

. . . Henry will hurry up his work . . . so as to finish by March 4th, not wishing to be a protégé of a man he does not recognize socially." It is possible that Blaine was not fully aware that the Adamses did not recognize him, but Henry took the matter very seriously. "I assure you," he wrote to Gaskell with grand hauteur, "that to stand alone in a small society like this, and to cut the Secretary of State for Foreign Affairs, without doing it offensively or with ill-breeding, requires not only some courage but some skill."

The change of administrations brought other losses as well. Interior Secretary Schurz, who needed more money to support his family, went to New York as editor-in-chief and part-proprietor of the *Evening Post* (Adams supported the new ownership with $20,000). John Hay, too, was glad to leave the State Department. President Garfield tried hard to keep him as his private secretary, but Hay was tired of politics. "The constant contact with envy, meanness, ignorance, and the swinish selfishness which ignorance breeds, needs a stronger heart and a more obedient nervous system than I can boast," he wrote to Garfield. "I am not fit for public office." Instead, he went to New York and edited the *Herald* for six months while Whitelaw Reid got married and took an extended honeymoon in Europe. Hay then returned to Cleveland to work seriously on his biography of Lincoln.

The Adamses did not bother to attend Garfield's inauguration. "We sat by our firesides on March 4th," Clover wrote, without any specific explanation, "and heard distant drums and fifes." The social season was nearly over, she added, and "the chances are ten to one that we shall see nothing of the new administration." She started to read Gibbon's *Decline and Fall*, "a bone which will take months to gnaw." Within a week, however, the departing John Hay came by and urged the Adamses to join him in a visit to the White House. "As we wanted to have it over," the Adamses reluctantly agreed. There was a large crowd, and they exchanged only a few words with the new First Lady, but Clover liked her. "She made a very pleasant impression on us," she reported, "quiet, ladylike, dignified and far more at her ease than Mrs. Hayes." Clover predicted that the Adamses would never again have "the same intimate cosy set that we did," but she added that "in this ever-shifting panorama of course we shall find new combinations."

Among those who came to Washington for Garfield's inauguration was a frail, bearded fanatic named Charles Julius Guiteau. His
father, Luther Guiteau, had been a harsh-tempered bank cashier in
Freeport, Illinois, and a passionate convert to the "Bible Communism" of John Humphrey Noyes, founder of the Oneida Community in upstate New York. After the birth of Luther Guiteau's
fourth child, Charles, on September 8, 1841, his wife Jane had her
head shaved and stayed in her room for months, suffering from
what was described as "brain fever." She died three weeks after
Charles' seventh birthday. The boy was slow in learning to speak
and appeared extremely nervous. After struggling through school,
he transferred to the Oneida Community and spent the Civil War
years there. He disliked the menial work, however, and even
though the community endorsed the idea of "free love," Guiteau
couldn't find a girl who would have him.

He decided, suddenly, that God had chosen him to start a newspaper, the *Daily Theocrat*, to convert the nation. He moved to New
York, wrote a prospectus, tried in vain to sell subscriptions, then
retreated to Oneida. This time he stayed only three months. He
moved back to the Midwest, begged money from various relatives,
started to study law, returned to New York, tried unsuccessfully
to find an editorial job on Henry Ward Beecher's *Independent*, then
turned against the Oneida Community and filed suit for wages he
claimed were owed him for working four years in the community
kitchen and craft shops. "I regard him as insane," the Oneida Community's John Humphrey Noyes wrote to Guiteau's worried father, "and I prayed for him last night as sincerely as I ever prayed
for my own son, that is now in a Lunatic Asylum."

Unsuccessful in his suit, Guiteau returned once more to Chicago
in 1868 and did manage to pass the lenient standards of the bar.
Unable to win any cases, he eked out a living as a bill collector
while he continued his studies at the Y.M.C.A. library. He became
friendly with the librarian, Annie Bunn, and married her in 1869,
then began beating her and locking her in a closet. "I am your
master," he once shouted, "you are to submit yourself to me." The
marriage ended in 1874. By then, Guiteau was deeply involved in
a theology of his own devising. He wrote a tract entitled *The Truth:
A Companion to the Bible*, which he cajoled a gullible printer into

publishing on credit. He wandered from town to town, renting halls and offering lectures on such questions as "Is there a hell?" His disjointed orations sometimes lasted no more than ten or fifteen minutes, and then Guiteau would flee the hall, with his creditors in pursuit. "To my mind he is a fit subject for a lunatic asylum," the elder Guiteau wrote to his daughter, "and if I had the means to keep him would send him to one for a while."

In 1880, Guiteau's father died, and that liberated him, in a way, to turn from mere preaching to active politics. He began loitering about at Republican Party headquarters at the Fifth Avenue Hotel in New York. He wrote a disordered campaign speech for Garfield and sent it out to various newspapers. Since no one was willing to publish it, he recited it himself to a gathering of about a dozen blacks. When Garfield won, Guiteau was immensely pleased with his success. "We have cleaned them out," he wrote to the new President. He went to Washington and began applying for various diplomatic posts—minister to Austria, consul-general in Paris, consul in Liverpool. "I think I have a right to claim your help," he wrote to James G. Blaine, the new Secretary of State. When Guiteau finally managed to accost Blaine, the Secretary rebuffed him. "Never bother me again about the Paris consulship as long as you live," said Blaine.

That convinced Guiteau that Garfield was mistaken in his efforts to reconcile the Blaine faction with Conkling's "Stalwarts." He wrote to Garfield that Blaine was "a wicked man," and that Garfield "ought to demand his immediate resignation." When Garfield did not answer, Guiteau suddenly realized, while lying in bed one night, that the President had to be killed for the good of the country. "The Deity inspired me," he later testified, "to remove the president."

Guiteau bought a .45-caliber revolver and spent three weeks practicing with it on the banks of the Potomac. He also spent three weeks following Garfield around, even pursuing him into church to see where he might be vulnerable. He wrote an "Address to the American People," in which he proclaimed the President insane. "In the President's madness he has wrecked the once grand old Republican party; and for this he dies. . . . I had no ill-will to the President. This is not murder. It is a political necessity."

On July 2, 1881, Garfield was to leave Washington to attend the graduation ceremony at his alma mater, Williams College, and then to take a vacation. As he walked through the Baltimore & Potomac Railroad Station, accompanied by Blaine and a retinue of aides, Guiteau darted forward, fired two bullets into his back, then strode hurriedly toward the exit. He was arrested before he got out of the station. A doctor gave Garfield some brandy and spirits of ammonia and told him that the wound was not serious. "I thank you, doctor," said Garfield, "but I am a dead man."

In this same season, just a week before Garfield's inauguration, death came suddenly to Fanny Hooper, Ned's wife, the good-hearted young music student who had been so surprised when Ned came home from the war and proposed to her. For nearly ten years, they tried unsuccessfully to have a child, the first of Dr. Hooper's grandchildren, and then one day in 1872 Fanny joyously wrote to an aunt: "Next November the only cloud which rested over our happiness is to be removed, if all goes well, and we shall have a darling of our own." The baby was named Ellen Sturgis Hooper after her aunt and next-door neighbor, Ellen Gurney, and also after her grandmother, the poet. Two years later, in 1874, came Louisa; then, in 1875, Mabel; in 1877, Fanny, and in 1879, Mary. The very next year, Fanny developed a cough so serious that doctors had to be consulted, and the doctors decided, just as they had decided about the dying Ellen Hooper forty years earlier, that the best treatment for lung trouble was a trip to the South. As before, nothing worked, and in February of 1881, Clover received word that her sister-in-law was deathly ill.

"Your Sunday letter makes us feel very sad with its account of Fanny's increased suffering," she answered. "Write or telegraph me if we can be of any earthly use either to Fanny, Ned, or the children, or to help lighten Ellen's care. I will be nurse or read story books all day long or play games or anything to fill any gaps. . . . I can leave at two hours' notice. If I were in trouble Ned would find fifty ways of helping us and we feel like two brutes to keep five hundred miles off and do nothing." Four days later, she heard that Fanny was dead. "We knew from your last Sunday letter that the end was near," she wrote. "That it was so peaceful after the long struggle is some comfort. How strange it seems that those whose life is full to the very brim should have to give it up and those who long to throw it away, like Aunt Anne, must stay on and on. . . . I want to go on and see all of you, but after turning it over have decided to wait at least a few days. Henry flatly refuses to let me go alone and I am not willing to pull him up from his work. . . ."

There is something odd in this, in Clover's coolness about Fanny's death, in her obviously half-hearted offers to go to Cambridge and help out, her claim that Henry's work could not be disturbed and that Henry forbade her to leave without him. Clover seems never to have been very close to Fanny, but she was strongly attached to Ned—her letters to Dr. Hooper are full of messages to her brother, who had by now become the treasurer of Harvard, a distinguished art collector, and very much a Cambridge institution. Ward Thoron, who was to marry the second of Clover's nieces and to act as editor of a volume of Clover's letters, sensed the reserve in her reaction to Fanny's death and tried to explain it in a footnote: "A stoical custom, inherited from their grandfather William Sturgis and followed by several of his children and grandchildren, discouraged conventional outward signs of mourning."

That hardly seems an adequate explanation. What is odd about Clover's reaction is not the absence of "conventional outward signs of mourning" but the absence of any real compassion toward her brother and his children. She acknowledges that "if I were in trouble Ned would find fifty ways of helping," and yet although she realizes that the whole family has been wounded by Fanny's death, she remains remarkably cold. In her letters responding to the news, she changes the subject as quickly as she possibly can. Since Clover was not by any means a cold or unfeeling woman, one can only suspect that it was death itself that she turned away from, refused to accept. "My silent prayer," she once wrote her father, "is for heart disease or lightning when my time comes." It is worth recalling Henry's remark about Madeleine Lee, that she had a "hysterical dread of sorrow and suffering." He attributed that to her own suffering on the death of her husband and her son. Clover, however, had never felt such pain, except possibly on the death of her mother long ago. If she dreaded sorrow and suffering, it was perhaps a sorrow yet to come, a sorrow whose footfalls she could barely hear. And if Henry refused to let her go to Cambridge by herself, it seems only reasonable to suppose that he understood her vulnerability and was trying to protect her from all the grief that awaited her there.

Approaching forty, Clover was becoming set in her ways, and she truly enjoyed the routines that she and Henry had created for themselves in Washington. Her letters of the early 1880's are full of satisfaction. "Weather enchanting and we've ridden nearly every day, finding our old haunts very glad to see us. . . . We peacefully reading and writing and reading under the bluest of skies and the greenest of trees. . . . Mr. John Hay, Clarence King and the new secretary of war, Robert Lincoln, to dine; a good deal of good talk. . . . I shall be surprised, if I ever get to heaven, to find a better day than this. . . ." She went to see the new Gilbert and Sullivan operetta *Patience*, which she liked, and Sarah Bernhardt's touring production of *Camille*, which she didn't. She was already adopting a pose of staid middle age, sitting to one side during the legation dances, chaperoning young friends to the theater, and admiring their high spirits.

One of these was Emily Beale, daughter of General Edward F. Beale, a friend of Grant's, who occupied a house on the adjacent side of Lafayette Square. Henry used Emily as the model for the madcap Victoria Dare in *Democracy*—she was also one of those suspected of writing the book—and Clover took equal delight in her impish frivolity. Once, for example, when she was returning from Philadelphia with the very worldly Congressman George Robeson, he asked conversationally whether she knew of any permanent place for him in the government, and she gigglingly told Clover that "without forethought or afterthought she answered, 'Why you know the penitentiary has been yawning for you for years.' "

One wintry day in 1881, Emily came to Clover's house with another young woman, and the two of them rapped on Henry's window with their umbrellas. When asked why she didn't simply ring the doorbell, Emily explained that "it's better than ringing because you can't say [you're] engaged." "They were very jolly," Clover went on, "and begged for some good tea as they'd been to a house where the tea was too bad and the sugar impossible." The second visitor was Elizabeth Cameron, and a week later, Clover was writing to Dr. Hooper that the two of them had once again come to tea and "are great fun." Mrs. Cameron, she went on, "is very pretty, not more than twenty-four, is staying with the fair

Emily while she gets her big new house in order. They are deep in politics and 'Stalwart' to the fingertips."

That was rather an understatement. The founder of the family dynasty was Simon Cameron, an orphan who had accumulated a fortune in banking and railroads, then became a senator from Pennsylvania, then Secretary of War in Lincoln's first cabinet. Cameron distributed War Department contracts with such knavery that even in an age of epidemic corruption, he was forced to resign in 1862 and formally censured by the House of Representatives. Cameron was unrepentant. His Pennsylvania political machine, which returned him to the Senate in 1867, was the envy of his rivals. He was credited with the classic definition of an honest politician as a man who "when he is bought will stay bought."

Cameron's son, James Donald, went to Princeton and learned the family business. He served for a year as Secretary of War under Grant, then as chairman of the Republican National Committee during the Hayes campaign, then inherited, as if by legal bequest, his father's seat in the Senate. By then he was a widower. His wife had died in 1874, leaving him with six children. When he remarried, in 1878, he was forty-five and Elizabeth Sherman was twenty-one. She thus married into a family that represented everything the Adamses despised. The Camerons, father and son, were corrupt entrepreneurs and power brokers, and among their closest allies were men like James G. Blaine. Yet because of young Lizzie Cameron's beauty and charm, both Henry and Clover set aside all the standards they ordinarily applied with such fierce rigor.

The Senator could simply be patronized. "She's drawn a blank in Don, I fear," Clover wrote, "for all his money and fine houses." But Henry became quite captivated. "We were asked to a charming dinner [at the Camerons'] the other evening," he wrote to Hay, "and I am now tame cat around the house—Don and I stroll round with our arms round each other's necks. I should prefer to accompany Mrs. Don in that attitude, but he insists on my loving him for his own sake." Henry kept trying, nonetheless, to treat the Camerons separately. "I adore her," he told Hay, "and respect the way she has kept herself out of scandal and mud." When the Camerons sailed on a visit to England, however, Henry wanted to give her some letters of introduction but decided that he could not "saddle my friends with Don." To Gaskell, he wrote about "my dear little friend Mrs. Don Cameron," adding a warning that the Senator was "not my ideal companion."

Henry wrote yearningly to Lizzie that Washington "is deserted without you," and Clover joined freely in the correspondence. To one of Henry's letters she added a long postscript, urging Lizzie to search out a specific Van Dyke in the Louvre, providing the address of an antique store on the Rue Halévy, passing on a message from Henry James, promising new photographs of her dogs, and telling about a moonlit sail up the Hudson to inspect H. H. Richardson's new capitol building in Albany ("nothing in that played out old hemisphere in which you are wasting your young life can hold a candle to it"). As for Henry, who had not given a very full account of his activities, Clover provided the details. "My husband is working like a belated beaver—from 9 to 5 every day—in garbling the history of his native land as run by antediluvian bosses called Thomas Jefferson, James Madison and James Monroe. At 12 we feed—we do not *dine*—today, as the Queen says in *Alice in Wonderland*, 'We have no gingerbread today—we have it yesterday and tomorrow.' Then at 5 we ride. . . ."

Charles J. Guiteau's only defense was insanity. He was, of course, insane, but that is a difficult defense to use when a whole nation demands an execution. It was difficult, too, because of the state of psychiatric knowledge in 1881. According to the established experts, Guiteau's lifelong history of grandiose schemes, public pronouncements, frauds, deceptions, and lawsuits demonstrated nothing more than a depraved character, eminently deserving of punishment. Among the few progressive doctors who hoped to save him, on the other hand, the prevailing theory was that insanity was an inherited physical condition, demonstrable principally by a history of family eccentricity and a pattern of physical deformity in the head.

Guiteau insisted on taking part in his own defense, which enabled him to interrupt and argue with everyone else involved in the trial. His impassioned interjections struck contemporary witnesses as an attempt to feign insanity and thus to deceive the jury, but they impress a modern observer less for their insanity than for their wild braggadocio. Guiteau spent much of his time in court ostentatiously reading a newspaper or signing autographs, but whenever he was criticized, he was apt to burst into invective. "You are a consummate jackass, Cornhill," he shouted at the district attorney, "and if you had any self-respect you would go out West and go out digging." To one of the district attorney's associates, he declared: "You are altogether too talky this morning. You are worse than a bear with diarrhea." And when another prosecutor referred to him as a vulgar criminal, Guiteau interrupted to say, "There is nothing vulgar about this case. It is all high-toned."

The trial, which lasted from November until January of 1882, was naturally the main attraction in Washington that season. Everyone went to see the monster engage in combat with his prosecutors, and when an official on the National Board of Health offered special passes to the Adamses, they too made their way to the crowded court. "It was intensely interesting," Clover wrote to Dr. Hooper. "The assassin was in front of me, so I could only get his profile—a large strong nose, a high straight forehead. . . . He bullied and badgered everyone, banged his fist on the table. . . . As to the court being unruly or disorderly, it's all nonsense. How Judge Cox keeps his gravity is a marvel. The beast's sallies are more than unjudicial muscles can stand. . . . Every word Guiteau says tightens his noose now."

The National Health Board official, Dr. Charles Folsom, needed to go to the jail to give Guiteau an eye examination. He invited the Adamses to accompany him, and they, after some hesitation, agreed. When they entered the jail, Clover must have been flustered by the unusual surroundings, for she did not recognize the man sitting in a rocking chair with a group of four or five other men in a corner. "He got up," she wrote, "and came forward very courteously, saying, 'How do you do, Doctor?' and shook his hand. Dr. Folsom introduced Henry and me and supposing it must be the jailer I met his offered hand. I felt rather overwhelmed when it broke upon me who the man was . . . the accursed beast."

After a trial of two months, it took the jury just one hour to return a verdict of guilty. "My blood be on the head of the jury!" cried Guiteau, and when he was later asked whether he had anything to say before being sentenced, he declared: "It was God's act, not mine, and God will take care of it." Guiteau carried that faith to the gallows. On the morning of his execution, June 30, 1882, he wrote a kind of hymn that he recited in a high-pitched voice on the scaffold:

I am going to the Lordy, I am so glad,
I am going to the Lordy, I am so glad,
I am going to the Lordy,
Glory hallelujah! Glory hallelujah!
I am going to the Lordy. . . .

As soon as Henry James had finished *The Portrait of a Lady*, which was running as a serial in *The Atlantic*, he decided that it was time to return to America, to bask in the praises that he anticipated and to revisit his family—*"les miens,"* as he referred to them in a letter. No sooner had he reached Quincy Street in early November of 1881 than he wrote to Clover, rather giddily inviting himself to Washington, a city he had never seen before. "I cannot longer delay to let you know of my arrival," he declared, "conscious as I am that it is fraught with happy consequences for you." He recalled her "last charming words" when they had parted in Europe, that only on being reunited in America would they "really meet *familiarly!*" James was full of anticipation. "I must tell you," he went on, "that I am prepared to be intensely familiar!" He told her about the continuing bafflement over the authorship of "that charming little anonymous novel *Equality*," and then begged her to send him an invitation. "I should be so glad," he concluded with a flourish, "to have a word from you letting me know that you count on me as I do you! Love to Henry. Ever dear Mrs. Adams, impatiently and irrepressibly yours."

On hearing of James' impending arrival, Henry reserved two sunny rooms for him at Number 720 Fifteenth Street, with access to the nearby Metropolitan Club. Both the Adamses had grown very fond of James, and Clover, unlike Henry, read and liked his work. She had some misgivings, however, about *The Portrait of a Lady*, which James had hopefully sent her. "It's very nice and charming things in it," she wrote to her father, "but I'm ageing fast and prefer what Sir Walter [Scott] called the 'big bow-wow style. . . .' It's not that he 'bites off more than he can chaw,' as T. G. Appleton said of [his brother] Nathan, but he chaws more than he bites off." It is true that James' early masterpiece was among the first to display that ruminative style, that endless probing and poking at moral subtleties, that was to become his hallmark, but Clover may well have been influenced by her passionate disapproval of James' increasingly permanent expatriation. "That young emigrant

272

has much to learn here," she wrote to Dr. Hooper. "He is surprised to find that he can go to the Capitol and listen to debates without taking out a license, as in London. He may in time get into the 'swim' here, but I doubt it. I think the real, live, vulgar, quick-paced world in America will fret him and that he prefers a quiet corner with a pen where he can create men and women who say neat things and have refined tastes and are not nasal or eccentric."

But the young emigrant was indeed learning, as he always did. Like the young Count Otto von Vogelstein, whom he later used as his narrative observer in the story entitled "Pandora," James went strolling along Pennsylvania Avenue, which he found to be "a long vista of saloons and tobacco shops." He found the Capitol itself "a splendid building but it was rather wanting in tone." He even encountered, at a tea party, the President, who "looked eminent but . . . relaxed." This was an approximation of the newly in-stalled Chester A. Arthur, onetime New York Port collector for the corrupt Conkling machine and now the nation's third President within less than a year. In his private letters to Boston, James elaborated a bit. He had met Arthur at Blaine's house and judged him to have "a well-made coat and well-cut whiskers." To his mother, James added with marvelous disdain that the President "pleased, if he didn't fascinate, me. He is an agreeable 'personable' man, with an evident desire to please, and aspirations to culture."

James was no less watchful toward his friends Clover and Henry, whom he customarily referred to in his letters as "the little Ad-amses." When he came to portray Clover as Mrs. Bonnycastle in "Pandora," he wrote that her house was "the pleasantest in Wash-ington," but he also recorded "the complaint sometimes made that it was too limited, that it left out, on the whole, more people than it took in." While Clover might have considered that a compliment, James was more malicious in private. "I notice that they [the Ad-amses] are eagerly anxious to hear what I have seen and heard at places which they decline to frequent," he wrote to Godkin. "After I had been to Mrs. Robeson's they mobbed me for revelations; and after I had dined with Blaine, to meet the president, they fairly hung on my lips." James saw, however, that this apparent hypoc-risy was simply the consequence of a split between the Adamses' social life and their political interests. Socially, as James wrote of Mrs. Bonnycastle, "it struck him that for Washington their society was really a little too good." But the best political gossip inevitably involved the scoundrels whom the Adamses didn't want at their dinner table. When it seemed for a time that Blaine was about to be disgraced for his financial involvement in the Chile–Peruvian war, James observed that "the little Adamses, who are (especially Mrs. A) tremendously political, are beside themselves with excitement."

James took note, too, of the Adamses' outspoken preference for American rather than European society, and when he came to translate his Washington experiences into fiction, he used Clover as the model not only for Mrs. Bonnycastle but also for Marcellus Cockerel, the pugnacious traveler who despises everything foreign. "Though we've an immense deal of pie-eating plainness," Cockerel argues, in *The Point of View*, "we've little misery, little squalor, little degradation. There's no regular wife-beating class, and there are none of the stultified peasants of whom it takes so many to make a European noble." Clover was not at all offended. "Some of [Cockerel's] remarks . . . I plead guilty to," she told her father, "but that [they] should be spotted as . . . mine I can't imagine."

Clover willingly pleaded guilty, furthermore, to a hostility toward another visitor from Europe that season. The success of Gilbert and Sullivan's *Patience* had aroused American interst in the man who was thought to be the model for the foppish esthete, Bunthorne. Although Bunthorne was probably based on Swinburne or Rossetti, a lecture agent promptly proposed an American tour to Oscar Wilde. Wilde was already making a career out of being Wildean. He really did tell the customs officer that he had "nothing to declare but my genius." And when sixty Harvard students paraded into his lecture carrying sunflowers and lilies, he really did say that "caricature is the tribute that mediocrity pays to genius."

It is hard to determine exactly what Americans thought of Wilde's behavior, for homosexuality was not generally a subject of public discussion. In fact, Thomas Wentworth Higginson and Julia Ward Howe managed to debate how Wilde should be treated without ever quite mentioning why they were debating in the first place. Higginson was a kind-hearted ex-clergyman who had commanded the first Civil War regiment of Southern blacks and who later encouraged and edited the poetry of Emily Dickinson, but he publicly objected to Wilde's being received by the ladies of Boston in their private homes. Mrs. Howe, who had received him herself, answered that women were not just "the guardians of the public purity" but also "the proper representatives of tender hope." Their treatment of Wilde was therefore to be considered therapeutic. "If, as alleged, the poison found in the ancient classics is seen to linger too deeply in his veins," Mrs. Howe wrote, "I should not prescribe for his case the coarse, jeering, and intemperate scolding so easily administered through the public prints but a cordial and kindly intercourse with that which is soundest and purest in our society."

By the time Wilde reached Washington, reporters were asking him about his private life, and Wilde turned them away by saying, "I wish I had one." He paid his respects not only to Mrs. Howe but also to Henry Ward Beecher, Jefferson Davis, and General Grant, and Clover seems to have feared that his tour would inevitably lead to her door. "I have asked Henry James *not* to bring his friend Oscar Wilde," she wrote. "I must keep out thieves and noodles or else take down my sign and go West." James agreed. He had told Godkin that Wilde was an "unclean beast," and he described him to Clover as a "fatuous cad." But he said that only after having gone to pay Wilde a call. "When Henry James told him he was very homesick for London," Clover reported, "he said, 'Really! You care for *places?* The *world* is my home.' "

At eleven o'clock on Sunday night, January 29, Henry James suddenly appeared on Clover's doorstep. Pale, confused, he said that he had just received a telegram from Cambridge telling him that his mother had suffered a severe attack of bronchial asthma. The telegram from his sister-in-law Alice urged him to come home immediately. James had tried, but there was no train until morning. It took him until five o'clock the next day to reach New York, and there he learned that Mary James had died the night before. It took him another whole day to reach Boston and to trudge home to Quincy Street through a driving snowstorm. "It will be a heavy blow to him," Clover wrote as soon as she heard the news, "the more so perhaps that he has been away for six years from her and it's the first time death has struck that family."

Historians have been rather kinder to Chester A. Arthur—when they have noticed him at all—than the Adamses were. Once considered a creature of the Conkling cabal, Arthur soon made himself fairly independent, and though he was never quite adequate to the presidency, he did try, in his indolent and unremarkable way, to do his best. To Washington society, he was chiefly notable for the changes he brought to the atmosphere of the White House. A widower, tall and commanding, generally attired in a braid-bound black Prince Albert coat, with a black silk scarf fixed by an onyx pin, he was much admired by the ladies of the capital. His married sister, Mary McElroy, served as White House hostess and held "afternoons" at which the Marine Band played. Arthur also installed a French chef in the White House kitchen and had red wine served at dinner. It was a pleasant change after the aridity of Lucy Hayes, but nobody could take Arthur very seriously, even as a host. Mrs. Blaine, for instance, was impressed by "the damask, the silver, the attendants, all showing the latest style and an abandon in expense," but she felt that the President seemed to care only for "flowers and wine and food, and slow pacing with a lady on his arm, and a quotation from Thackeray or Dickens, or an old Joe Miller told with uninterfered-with particularity."

Clover could scarcely let herself be outdone by Mrs. Blaine in withering comments on the new occupant on the opposite side of Lafayette Square, and it was undeniable that Arthur continued, like most Presidents, to apply the levers of patronage. When he appointed a man of questionable merit as the revenue collector of Boston, Clover described it as "a brutal slap in the face to all decent men in the party." Civil-service reform finally seemed to be a possibility—indeed, the Pendleton bill, or "your Boston bill," as one leading Congressman angrily described it to Clover, was to pass in the next session of Congress—but Arthur's support of reform was open to skepticism, and skepticism was one of Clover's specialties. "His highfalutin phrases as to civil service reform were mere buncombe," she wrote. "He is a ward politician, neither more nor less, and the daily widening breach in the Republican Party may give the Democrats a clean walk-over in 1885." Henry felt much the same. "The new administration will be the centre for every element of corruption, north and south," he wrote to Lodge. "The outlook is very discouraging."

Clover's friend Lucy Frelinghuysen, whose father was the new Secretary of State, invited the Adamses to go with her to a reception at the White House, but the Adamses demurred. Officially, they still didn't know the President. "Henry hasn't left a card yet," Clover wrote in April of 1882, more than six months after Arthur had been sworn in, "which is not over-civil to a new opposite neighbor who likes social attention." The following month, when Arthur himself invited the Adamses to another White House reception, Clover stayed home, but Henry "went for a *mauvais quart d'heure* just to bow the knee to Baal and brought away a violent influenza which had laid him low since."

Eventually, of course, they did both encounter the President, from time to time, and they regarded him as rather frivolous. "Our good King Arthur was there—" Clover wrote of a diplomatic dinner that same season at the home of Sallie Frelinghuysen Davis, "all the pretty girls taken up to him and presented—it was all more like royalty than anything I have ever seen. Not being a pretty girl, I did not compete in the ceremony." Henry was a bit more specific in referring to rumors that the President was infatuated with Mrs. Davis, appointing not only her father as Secretary of State but her husband as assistant secretary. A newspaper had brought out "the whole scandal," he wrote to Hay, but he insisted that he didn't read the story and didn't want to hear about it. "I have stopped everyone who has mentioned the subject to me, and have never opened my lips outside my own circle of two. . . . I do not go to the White House because I see and hear things I don't like, but I am quite alone, and in a few years more I shall either have to go there or go to prison."

And it was galling, in a way, that President Arthur, the ruddy epicure, servant of Mammon, should betake himself every Sunday morning to the Church of St. John, almost next door to Clover's house, and there engage in public worship. The ceremony often happened at the very hour that Clover, who had been unable to bring herself to attend church in many years, consecrated to writing to her father. "There goes our chuckle-headed sovereign on his way from church!" she burst out one Sunday early in 1883. "He doesn't look as if he fed only on spiritual food."

John Hay's father-in-law, Amasa Stone, the Cleveland financier, took great pride in his skills as an engineer, and when he built a factory or a bridge, he liked to review the plans himself, and to change them in any way he saw fit. So it was that he arbitrarily changed the designer's plans for a new iron bridge near Ashtabula, Ohio, and when the bridge collapsed, eighty-four people were killed. Stone was severely criticized. And so, while the Hays were en route home from their visit to England in May of 1883, Amasa Stone took a gun and shot himself.

"Poor Mrs. John Hay will get the sad news of her father's death on landing next Saturday," Clover wrote. "—Amasa Stone of Cleveland, who leaves six million dollars and only two daughters. John Hay [had written] to ask if we could meet them in New York and have a little fun together. It will come hard to them." Henry was more sanguine. He sounded almost jovial as he wrote to Gaskell: "John Hay's father-in-law, who had fifteen millions, blew his brains out the day the Hays left Queenstown, and we all opened our eyes at hearing that the estate was valued at only three millions and a half, so that John will get only a beggarly hundred thousand pounds. He'll not care!"

Scarcely six months after Henry James returned to London, he received news that his father was sick and immediately sailed once again for America. He arrived in Boston only in time to learn that his father had been buried that very morning, and that his sister Alice was prostrate with grief. He himself began suffering from a headache so painful that he took to his bed for three days. On the last day of 1882, he trudged through the snow to the Cambridge cemetery, where his father now lay buried beside his mother, and read aloud in the cold, clear air a letter that had just been received from William James in London. "Darling old father," James read over the silent grave, "We have been so long accustomed to the hypothesis of your being taken away from us that the thought that this may be your last illness conveys no very sudden shock. You are old enough, you've given your message to the world in many ways and will not be forgotten. . . . If you go, it will not be an inharmonious thing. . . ."

James wrote to Clover not long afterward, inviting himself once again to Washington but warning that he was tied to Boston by the settling of his father's estate and by anxiety over his sister's collapse. He added that he was having lunch almost every Sunday with Clover's sister Ellen, whom he was later to describe as "the exquisite Mrs. Gurney, of the infallible taste, the beautiful hands, and the tragic fate." James went only briefly to Washington, however, and never saw much of Clover. One reason may have been that he had discovered in Boston something that fascinated him, something that was to become the subject of one of his most interesting novels.

"I wished to write a very *American* tale, a tale very characteristic of our social conditions," he wrote in his notebook that April 8 as he tried to analyze the beginnings of the idea, "and I asked myself what was the most salient and peculiar point in our social life. The answer was: the situation of women, the decline of the sentiment of sex, the agitation on their behalf." This was, of course, one of the noisy public issues of the day—less than a year later, Susan B. Anthony was to lead 100 women into the White House and to ask President Arthur whether women "ought not . . . to have full equality and political rights," and to hear the President answer that "we should probably differ on the details of that question"—but James was particularly interested in the private feelings that animated the women of Boston. Specifically, he was struck by the intense friendship between his semi-invalid sister, Alice, and her companion, Katherine Loring, a woman Alice described as having "all the mere brute superiority which distinguishes man from woman, combined with all the distinctly feminine virtues."

"The characters," James wrote to his publisher, J. R. Osgood, ". . . are for the most part persons of the radical reforming type, who are especially interested in the emancipation of women, giving them the suffrage, co-educating them with men, etc. . . . The heroine is a very clever and 'gifted' young woman, associated by birth and circumstances with a circle immersed in these views and in every sort of new agitation, daughter of old abolitionists, spiritualists, transcendentalists etc. . . . She has a dear and intimate friend, another young woman, who, issuing from a totally different social circle (a rich conservative exclusive family), has thrown herself into those questions with intense ardour and has conceived a passionate admiration for our young girl." There we have, more than a year before the first chapter was begun, the basic plan for *The Bostonians*.

The fierce Olive Chancellor and her protégé Verena Tarrant were really quite different from Alice James and Miss Loring—and James had no conscious intention of satirizing the late Swedenborgian of Quincy Street—but it was splendidly observant of him to attribute Verena's oratorical "gift" to a childhood spent among threadbare soothsayers, and to combine with one hurried "etc." the high-minded abolitionists with the quacks of mesmerism, table-rapping, and Mrs. Eddy's new Christian Science. Having stated this eminently Bostonian social framework, however, James did little to develop it, for he was really more interested in the psychological drama of Olive's struggle for possession of Verena.

Olive's passion for Verena seems somewhat exaggerated, as passions often do, but James has no fear of sounding a reverberating tone. "Will you be my friend, my friend of friends, beyond everyone, everything, forever and forever?" Olive begs Verena, and when Verena agrees to come and live with her on Charles Street, Olive simply pays off Verena's father, the itinerant faith-healer, to let her go. It was observant of James, too, to pit against Olive not a charming and wealthy suitor but a rather arrogant and self-indulgent lawyer from war-ruined Mississippi, a man who responds to one of Verena's public performances by asking: "Do you really believe all that pretty moonshine you talked last night?"

Olive is almost a reincarnation of Elsie Venner. Her eyes have "the glitter of green ice," the hand she offers to Basil Ransom is "cold and limp," and she is perpetually "filled with silent rage." To her, then, the women's rights movement represents an opportunity for an omnivorous revenge on men. "All the bullied wives, the stricken mothers, the dishonored, deserted maidens who have lived on earth and longed to leave it, passed and repassed before her eyes. . . . Men must pay!" To Basil Ransom, on the other hand, the ladies who gather to hear Verena's speeches are less the oppressed than the oppressors. "The whole generation is womanized," he declares to Verena, "the masculine tone is passing out of the world; it's a feminine, a nervous, hysterical, chattering, canting age, an age of hollow phrases and false delicacy and exaggerated solicitudes and coddled sensibilities, which, if we don't soon look out, will usher in the reign of mediocrity, of the feeblest and flattest and most pretentious that has ever been."

It is hard not to suspect that James shares in Ransom's exaggerations more than in those of Olive Chancellor, but as a novelist, he declines to commit himself. The point he wants to emphasize is that both of them regard Verena as an object to be possessed, and that Verena, like the traditional nineteenth-century girl, ultimately accepted this role because "it was in her nature to be easily submissive, to like being overborne." In recent years, when all manner of things have been beclouded by sexual interpretations, it has become common to regard Olive's relationship to Verena as essentially lesbian, but there is no evidence that James thought of either of them that way (any more than he did of Alice and Miss Loring). On the contrary, he seems to have regarded their attachment as a product of their region and caste. "The relation of the two girls," he wrote in his original outline to Osgood, "should be a study of one of those friendships between women which are so common in New England." In making such a study, James was quite aware that such friendships often ended in a marriage to someone else, even to some patronizing figure like Basil Ransom. When James chose that ending for his novel, however, he was not simply bowing to the conveniences of fiction, for this was not to be a happy ending. After breaking with Olive and the women's movement, Verena burst into tears. "It is to be feared," James relentlessly added in his last sentence, "that with the union, so far from brilliant, into which she was about to enter, these were not the last she was destined to shed."

There was one highly beneficial result of Chester Arthur's arrival in the White House, and that was the departure of James Blaine from the State Department. "The new regime is a great relief to us," Clover wrote. "Henry resumed work at the State Department the day Blaine went out." Blaine's successor, Frederick Frelinghuysen, had the odd idea that Henry might like to be sent abroad and the even odder idea that he might like an appointment as minister to five Central American republics. "Think of us in Guatemala City!" Clover wrote. "I wish we wanted it, it would be so new and fresh." Henry did not want it, however. Henry wanted only to work on his *History*. "I . . . have felt for a long time a sort of nervous fear of losing time," he wrote to Lodge. "My conscience reproves me for neglecting not only my friends but family; yet life is slipping away so fast that I grudge every day which does not show progress in my work. I have but one offspring, and am nearly forty-four while it is nothing but an embryo." And to Parkman: "I am struggling with my own little historical mud pie, and doing my best to give it shape and cohesion. The task is a slow one and sadly discouraging to one who would like to do more than he knows how to do. Nevertheless it amuses me, if not my readers."

Almost every morning, from nine to eleven, as Clover often

reported, she and Henry went riding through the woods or along the river. Almost every night, as Clover also reported, there was a dinner with Senator Lamar or Congressman Hewitt or the diplomatic corps, the De Struves of Russia, the Outreys of France, the Eisendeckers of Germany. What Clover wrote about very little—would Dr. Hooper have cared?—was that every day between noon and five in the afternoon, Henry immersed himself in his archives. To that, Clover made only occasional references, like "History goes on quietly" or "Henry pegs away at his work." But as Henry pegged away, filling page after page of ruled legal paper with his round, impeccable script, he felt an immense satisfaction. He seems to have had no sense at all that his future might not roll onward in much the same way. "If I felt a perfect confidence that my history would be what I would like to make it," he wrote to Gaskell, "this part of life—from forty to fifty—would be all I want. There is a summer-like repose about it."

It was Henry Adams' private conceit that he was writing an American counterpart to Gibbon, that he would somehow equal the grandest historical work in the language. As a young man, he had sat, like Gibbon, on the steps of Santa Maria di Ara Coeli, and now, at the height of his powers, he had embarked on a monumental account not of imperial decline and fall but of republican growth and triumph. Yet there was a major difference of tone evident in the very first sentence. "In the second century of the Christian Era," Gibbon had begun with characteristic sweep, "the empire of Rome comprehended the fairest part of the earth, and the most civilized portion of mankind." Adams began, by contrast, with an almost defiant bluntness: "According to the census of 1800, the United States of America contained 5,308,483 persons."

He thus announced his intention to write a history that would be, first and foremost, scientific. He later tried to explain his purpose, in the *Education*, by proclaiming that he had "no other purpose than to satisfy himself whether, by the severest process of stating, with the least possible comment, such facts as seemed sure, in such order as seemed rigorously consequent, he could fix for a familiar moment a necessary sequence of human movement." That was part of it, that effort to find the necessity in a sequence of events, but necessity alone was not sufficient. It must be the goal of the scientific historian to find the direction and the purpose of that necessity. This was, to be sure, an ancient goal. The chroniclers of the Middle Ages made it their purpose to demonstrate in the necessities of history the workings of God's will and God's benevolence. But the nineteenth century was an age that believed, more passionately than ours, in the certainties of science, certainties which, if not yet known, must nonetheless be knowable.

To the scientists themselves, each chemical or biological revelation was a new justification of science itself. The scientific method —experimentation and verification—was henceforth to be the only method, and scientific facts were to be the only facts, not to be doubted. Every other approach could be dismissed as romantic, mystical, superstitious. Enlightened theologians tried to avoid such accusations. Instead of denying such challenging theories as the evolution of man, they began trying to interpret these new mysteries as fresh evidence of upward progress in God's plan. The merchants and soldiers of the period found their own ways to make use of scientific teachings, as justification for the rich to become richer and for the strong to prey on the weak.

The most eminent advocate of applying scientific thought to the processes of society was Herbert Spencer, who contributed the phrase "survival of the fittest," and who taught that both natural and human development progressed inexorably from the homogeneous to the heterogeneous, from the simple to the complex. (Clover, we may recall, observed that he "looks like a complacent crimson owl.") Spencer's principal disciple in the United States was John Fiske, another one of President Eliot's bright young teachers at Harvard, who believed that the development of mankind was preordained. "As surely as the astronomer can predict the future state of the heavens," he wrote, "the sociologist can foresee that the process of adaptation must go on until in a remote future it comes to an end in proximate equilibrium." Henry Adams had acquired a rather similar view as early as his days in the London legation, where he wrote to his brother Charles that "the laws which govern animate things will be ultimately found to be at bottom the same with those which rule inanimate nature, and . . . I am quite ready to receive with pleasure any basis for a systematic conception of it all."

Almost thirty years later, long after Clover's death, Adams was to write his concluding chapter of the *History* as though he had fulfilled his goal. "The scientific interest of American history centred in national character," he declared, "and in the workings of a society destined to become vast, in which individuals were important chiefly as types. . . . In American history the scientific interest was greater than the human. . . . Nowhere could [one] study so well the evolution of a race." At the very start, then, Adams wrote as though scientific pursuit were his chief object. He began by describing the primitive physical conditions of the United States in 1800, the number of houses in Utica, New York (50), the number óf miles of post roads between Maine and Georgia (20,000), the size of the cotton crop of 1801 (20 million pounds). Unfortunately for Adams' theory, however, history is not a science, and his ponderous accumulations of statistical data illustrated no thesis and proved no conclusion.

Yet even if history is only a chronicle—as had been so richly demonstrated by the "Romantic" Boston historians whom Adams scorned, Parkman and Prescott and Motley—Adams showed a rather peculiar sense of what constitutes a narrative chronicle. After his opening chapters, he paid very little attention to either commerce or culture but devoted vast numbers of pages to relatively minor diplomatic skirmishes. Partly, this was the Adams family bias, the inherited view that delicate international negotiations were richly important and richly interesting. Partly, too, Adams became, like many historians, a prisoner of his materials. Once he had ransacked the archives of Europe for the unpublished reports sent home by the envoys of Britain, France, and Spain, he could hardly resist bringing on their superiors as well. "Canning and Perceval are figures that can't be put in a nutshell," he wrote to Gaskell in 1880, "and Napoleon is vast."

The central figure, though, the figure who animated and unified the whole first half of the book, was inevitably that same figure who had fascinated and tormented Adams ever since he had begun the study of his forefathers. Thomas Jefferson had dominated the background in Adams' *Gallatin*, and in the brief biography of John Randolph that Adams carved out of his unfinished *History* in 1882; but only in the opening volumes of the *History* itself does Jefferson burst into life. Adams admired him, in many ways, and he knew that Jefferson was a type who represented, far more than all the Adamses did, the America of the future—not only represented it, in fact, but created it. And so it was with a pretense of praising the vanished hero that Adams began his infinitely malicious portrait. "According to the admitted standards of greatness," he wrote, "Jefferson was a great man. After all deductions on which his enemies might choose to insist, his character could not be denied elevation, versatility, breadth, insight, and delicacy; but neither as a politician nor as a political philosopher did he seem at ease in the atmosphere which surrounded him. . . . The rawness of political life was an incessant torture to him, and personal attacks made him keenly unhappy. . . . His yearning for sympathy was almost feminine."

Having sketched Jefferson as a frail and somewhat disingenuous idealist, Adams goes on to describe him as a ruler who indulges in all the autocratic excesses with which he had charged his predecessor,* a man so ambitious that he does not hesitate to violate the constitution for the sake of greater power. The Louisiana Purchase is Adams' first major instance, and there is no doubt that Jefferson seized his opportunity without worrying about the niceties involved. Adams makes it sound like a dark crime: "Within three years of his inauguration Jefferson bought a foreign colony without its consent and against its will, annexed it to the United States . . . and then he who found his predecessors too monarchical . . . made himself monarch of the new territory."

Adams is not usually so polemical, however. For the most part, he is suave and aristocratic, generously quoting from Jefferson's own proclamations and preachings but relentlessly pointing out Jefferson's innumerable contradictions and evasions and changes of course. With the benefit of hindsight, Adams found the political squirmings of the early 1800's rather funny. Nothing delighted him more than Jefferson's social confusions. Upon his inauguration, the President insisted that the White House would be democratically open to everyone and that all visitors would be treated with absolute equality. He democratically welcomed them in worn slippers and faded corduroy overalls, his hair often uncombed and his beard unshaven. At dinner, he democratically insisted on a system known as *pele-mele,* by which the guests seated themselves more or less at random. The diplomats of Europe, to whom Adams attached great significance, were appalled. The British minister, in uniform and sword, considered it an insult to be received in slippers. The Spanish minister's wife refused to go to the White House at all, and when her absence was inquired about, the minister pointedly in-

---

* For some mysterious reason, Henry almost never speaks of John Adams by name. He is generally referred to only as Jefferson's predecessor or the second President.

formed everyone that her health was excellent. "There was probably not a white man [in all Virginia], or even a Negro slave, but would have resented the charge that he was capable of asking a stranger, a woman, under his roof, with the knowledge that he was about to inflict what the guest would feel as a humiliation," Adams wrote with all the disdain of Clover's salon at 1607 H Street. "Reasons of state sometimes gave occasion for such practices. . . . Napoleon in the height of his power insulted queens, browbeat ambassadors. . . . Jefferson could not afford to adopt Napoleonic habits. His soldiers were three thousand in number."

As Henry plunged on, volume after volume, the future stretched out ahead of him—it was indeed to take him longer to describe the administrations of Jefferson and Madison than it took the two presidents to live through them. "I foresee a good history if I have health and leisure the next five years," he wrote Gaskell early in his labors. "But as time passes, I get into a habit of working only for the work's sake and disliking the idea of completing and publishing. . . . I don't think I care much even to be read. . . . On the other hand I enjoy immensely the investigation, and making little memoranda of passages here and there. Aridity grows on me. I always felt myself like Casaubon in Middlemarch, and now I see the tendency steadily creeping over me."

15

NO LAND IN SIGHT

"WE ARE GOING TO BUILD!" Clover wrote excitedly just before Christmas of 1883. It was time—the last time—to move again, and after having lived in a variety of other people's houses, the Adamses were planning to create something new and unusual. Henry jokingly described it as "quite unutterably utter." Though the lease on the Corcoran house still had nearly three years to run, the Adamses were being somewhat pressed. The large empty lot just to the east of them, at the corner of H Street and 16th Street, had been sold by Corcoran earlier that year to a young builder named Fred Paine, who planned to erect a seven-story apartment house. The sale, Clover wrote, made the Adamses feel "very uneasy about our future life." She heard that three of her favorite trees would be cut down, and she had visions of being driven out "by darkness and smoky chimneys."

John Hay had inherited enough money to buy out any prospective builder, and so, with Henry acting as broker for his silent partner, there followed what Clover called "ten days of haggling and negotiation." Paine was offered a handsome deal: a full refund of his $64,000 investment, plus a year's interest, plus a $5,000 profit—a total of $73,500. "Well, I'll take it," Paine finally said. Adams and Hay had already agreed on their own division of the property. "Hay is the capitalist and takes the corner," Adams wrote to Gaskell. For almost two-thirds of the purchase price, Hay would get slightly more than half the land, the corner and the whole 16th Street side. Henry, for $25,000, would get a lot with a 44-foot front on H Street and extending 131 feet back to an alley that led into 16th Street. To pay for this, he planned to sell, for a $30,000 profit, the Hecla and Calumet copper shares that Alex Agassiz had sold to his friends so many years ago.

The house that the Adamses planned to build here, for another $30,000 that was soon to be Henry's share of the estate of his grandfather Peter Chardon Brooks, was already clear in their minds. So was the tradition of Victorian ornamentation that they wanted to avoid. "We shall build a square brick box," Clover wrote to her father, "with flat roof, pine finish, no stained glass, no carving—kitchen, laundry and hall 9 feet high on level with the street —library, study and dining room above—*no* parlor—for extra furniture we shall need only two new corn brooms and a nice ice cream freezer. . . . We drew our plans before we got the land and know just what we want." In a letter to Mrs. Cameron, who was then touring Europe, Clover added: "I who have always been utterly opposed to building am the one who jumped first—I like to change my mind all of a sudden."

The new house would give her further opportunity for that, for the Adamses' plans still needed to be translated into the reality of building. Within a week, Clover was observing that the Washington newspapers "tell us. Richardson is to be our architect." The Adamses themselves had not made any such decision, but it was almost inevitable. Not only was Henry Hobson Richardson the most gifted architect of his generation, not only had Adams long known and admired him, first as a Harvard classmate and later as the builder of Trinity Church, but Richardson was now the favorite designer of expensive homes for some of the people the Adamses knew best. They admired his imperial tastes and his yellow waistcoats and his expert knowledge of champagnes. The Gurneys, for instance, had commissioned Richardson to build them a handsome stone summer house at Pride's Crossing, just west of Beverly Farms. Richardson's first Washington house, just three blocks from the Adamses', at 16th and K Streets, had been newly created for General Nicholas Longworth Anderson, another Harvard classmate who had shared in Henry's German *Wanderjahr.* Henry thought it "just a gem." The Anderson house "does Richardson great credit," Clover commented," [and] if we had thirty thousand a year it would suit us to a T." She blamed the soaring costs on Anderson's inability to deny Richardson his love for carved mahogany and silk wall hangings. Anderson, who liked to grumble about Richardson's lavishness but declined Hay's offer of $100,000 for the house, was "not educated as to what is ultimate," Clover wrote. More sophisticated clients, she added, would find it "possible to curb [Richardson's] extravagance."

Richardson himself had not yet even been consulted. He still had to meet Hay, and he was phenomenally busy. He had spent much of the autumn designing a huge cathedral for Albany (the competition called for a Gothic church, but Richardson preferred to design a Romanesque one, and his plans were rejected). At the same time, he was in the midst of his successful plans for the Allegheny County Courthouse, which still stands like a hulking stone dungeon in the center of Pittsburgh. He was also seriously ill. In fact, he was to outlive Clover by only a few months. He had been stricken several years earlier with Bright's Disease, or nephritis, which not only bloated his body but gave him a craving for food and drink. His doctors insisted on diets, forbidding wines and spirits, milks and cheeses, but Richardson defied them, wolfing down food until he swelled to a gargantuan weight of 345 pounds, unable to go anywhere except by carriage. Adams and Hay, perhaps unaware of the reasons for Richardson's cravings, joked mercilessly about his corpulence in their correspondence. Henry called him "the man-mountain Richardson," adding that he was "an ogre [who] devours men crude and shows the effect of inevitable indigestion in his size."

In January of 1884, Richardson finally came to Washington, met Hay, listened to the Adamses' wishes—Henry had even made scale drawings of the whole interior—and agreed to design them a house. Clover seems to have thought the plans could be finished in a few days, but Richardson simply went back to work on his other projects and left the Adamses to wait.

Winter broke early that last full year in Clover's life. In February, she was already writing of a turn in the weather. "There's a promise of spring in the air which makes one's heart dance. We are too busy and life is too full to care much about what the weather is but when it does turn to spring it's so much gained." Another month passed, and the forsythia burst into yellow, before Richardson telegraphed that the plans were being sent. Even before they arrived, Clover was worrying about Richardson's penchant for extravagance. "We think that as we know just what we want and don't want in the new house that Richardson will consider our wishes," she wrote. "Our present furniture and fittings pitch the key note beforehand. We cannot have a mahogany dining room with our present black walnut and cherry furniture nor can we go in for carving without making what we have seem *mesquin.*"

The following week, there came an omen. A two-by-five-foot section of the Adamses' parlor ceiling fell in with a loud crash just before nine o'clock on a Wednesday morning. "If we had been early risers we should have been corpses inevitably," Clover observed, "as we take our tea in that spot." The accident made the prospect of a new house all the more attractive, and Richardson's plans, when they finally arrived for approval, struck both Adamses and Hays as admirable. "Richardson has worked up something very satisfactory to all of us," Clover wrote. "The problem of windows and general scale we gave him was a difficult one and he has dealt with it like a master. . . . We shall have the best stock—plumbing etc.—but resist extras—carving and so on. . . . We do not wish a fine house—only an unusual one and that we certainly shall have."

What Richarson had designed was yet another of his Medieval fortresses, in what Clover called his "neo-Agnostic style." It was comparatively simple and boxlike, as Clover had wished, but only by comparison to the gables and turrets that sprouted from Hay's adjoining château. Both houses were to be four stories high, rising from two flattened arches for the Adamses' entry on H Street to a row of Romanesque windows for the servants' quarters just beneath the slightly slanted roof. Richardson did, however, give up his desire for sandstone when the Adamses insisted on brick. And inside, he followed their wishes exactly—kitchen and laundry on the ground floor, a large hall with a baronial fireplace leading to the long library with three French windows on the second floor. Still there were arguments, as can be inferred from Clover's observation, after all her rejections of carvings, that "he can do a bit of carving, as the devout do in their churches." It was typical of Adams to complain to Richardson that the design for Hay's larger and more grandiloquent house seemed more of a success than the one for his. "Your liking Hay's house better than your own," Richardson retorted, "is accounted for easily I think by the fact that in designing the former I was left entirely untramelled by restrictions wise or otherwise."

There were several further steps needed before anything could be built at all. Richardson's preliminary designs had to be turned into a working plan, and builders had to be consulted for their estimates of actual construction costs. Hay sailed off to London, leaving Henry a power of attorney to handle all details. Weeks passed. Clover noted that she had found apple blossoms to put on her table, and still there was no sign of the building plans. The daffodils faded and the lilies of the valley bloomed, and then came Clover's roses, dozens and dozens of the rich red hybrid known as General Jacqueminot, and not until the end of May did Richardson's plans finally arrive. "Very promising," Clover called them, but by then it was time to retreat once again to the cool seashore at Beverly Farms.

Clover had long been familiar with the new vogue for photography—the archive in the country contains eighteen of Brady's grim war scenes, corpses sprawling in trenches and blasted meadows, that Clover bought and inscribed on her trip to Washington when she was eighteen—but it was not until 1882 that she acquired a camera, "my new machine," and began recording the circumstances of her life.

This was more than an idle hobby. She wrote often of the people she had persuaded to pose for her. She drove to Arlington, for example, with "little Mme. Eisendecker," the twenty-year-old wife of the German minister, who delighted Clover by her guileless enthusiasm for such American novelties as mashed potatoes, and there "photographed the old house and Mme. Von E—and some graves under the trees—the latter I think fairly good but the first two by some crass idiocy I took on the same plate and so both are spoiled." And George Bancroft, by now eighty-three and a neighbor in Washington, "sitting at his library table writing history, a profile view, his hair and beard come out silvery and soft in the print." She drove to Senator Lamar's rooms on C Street and was dismayed to find that he had "brushed his long hair to the regulation smoothness and then I refused to take his likeness until he had rumpled it all up." And young Jerome Bonaparte, who lived near the Adamses in gilded exile. Though he was only "a pretty little brown-eyed Italian-looking boy of six," Clover evoked his imperial connections by posing him "astride of a chair, blowing a trumpet." As word inevitably spread around Washington of Clover's new preoccupation, a letter duly came from an editor who wanted to publish some of her work. Richard Watson Gilder, of *The Century*, asked specifically about her portrait of Bancroft and wondered if Henry would write a few words to go with it. Clover scorned the idea. "I've just written to decline," she told her father, "and telling him 'Mr. Adams does not fancy the prevailing literary vivisection.' The way in which Howells butters up Harry James and Harry James Daudet and Daudet someone else is not pleasant. . . ." She was not interested, in other words, in becoming a professional, or in turning her activities into a commercial career.

It is difficult, now that every suburban father can take Polaroid snapshots of his children sprawling under the Christmas tree, to recall how complex and exotic the craft of photography once was. Over and over, during Clover's last two years, her letters refer to entire mornings spent in her new darkroom just for the production of two or three pictures. From the late 1850's until the late 1880's, when George Eastman began persuading Americans to send the films from his new Kodaks back to his factory for processing, the basic procedure required each photographer to maintain a rather complicated laboratory of his own. The first step was to cover a newly washed glass plate with collodion, a glutinous mixture of guncotton in alcohol and ether, and then to soak it in a bath of light-sensitive silver nitrate, which would record the photographic image, but also blackened the fingers and ate into the photographer's clothes. The sticky plate then had to be placed, still wet, in a light-tight shield and inserted into the camera to await the moment when the subject was posed and prepared. Somewhat more than a moment, in fact. "One, two, three, four, five, six, slowly and deliberately pronounced in as many seconds, either aloud or in spirit," one contemporary instruction manual directed. As soon as possible after the picture was taken, the photographer had to return to the darkroom, develop the plate in a bath of pyrogallic acid or photosulphate of iron, then in hypo (potassium cyanide), then in running water—often to see the emerging image appear blurred or fuzzy or whitened by the sun.

Clover kept records of all this, in a small red notebook that still survives inside a cardboard box at the Massachusetts Historical Society. She listed not only every picture she had taken but usually the exposure and sometimes the results. Thus: "Francis Parkman in front of rocks at Beverly Farms, large stop, 2 seconds." And again: "Jan. 18,1884. H. H. Richardson in Henry Adams' study, large stop 10 seconds—good." She also devoted herself to the chemistry of the art, copying down, for example, a formula for printing from Sir William Abney's *Treatise on Photography:*

". . . Float sheet of paper eight minutes as for sensitizing— When dry is ready for exposure which is somewhat long. To get a brown picture float the printed surface on

Potassium ferricyanide	1 gramme
Nitric acid	2 drops
Water	250 cc.

In about five minutes the whole of the detail will be visible. . . ."

The difficulties of photography seemed only to attract people. The chemical problems made the mere creation of a print, an exact reproduction of reality, seem so miraculous that it overwhelmed artistic problems of tone and composition. Edgar Degas became fascinated with the new phenomenon of photography, and so did the astronomer Sir John Herschel. Oliver Wendell Holmes took pictures of the human leg so that he could improve the artificial legs being constructed for wounded war veterans. Emile Zola made photographic studies from the top of the Eiffel Tower, and Lewis Carroll focused on the seraphic profile of Alice Liddell. "Every sanguine little couple who set up a glass-house at the commencement of summer," wrote Lady Eastlake, wife of the first president of the Photographic Society of London, "call their friends about them, and toil alternately in broiling light and stifling gloom, have said before long, in their hearts, 'Photography, thy name is disappointment!' But the photographic back is fitted to the burden."

Women seem to have been particularly attracted to the fad. Observers with a Freudian turn of mind might find significance in this, for it has been argued that photography itself is a psychologically significant occupation. The photographer, according to this line of argument, enjoys a fantasy of "seeing" other people while he himself remains invisible, and thus of dominating other people while he remains invulnerable. But Freud, at this point, was still an obscure clinician who had just received his doctorate, and perhaps the popularity of photography among Victorian women may be attributed to nothing more complicated than the fact that Victoria herself was amused by it. She served as patroness of the first exhibition at the Photographic Society and even had a darkroom built at Windsor Castle. In her wake came Lady Hawarden, who persistently photographed her children, sometimes with Christmas tree ornaments attached to their foreheads, and Lady Filmer, who made collages out of portraits framed with watercolor drawings of birds and flowers. Photography thus became one of those arts in which ladies were not only permitted but even encouraged to amuse themselves. Slightly more advanced than embroidery or the playing of waltzes, it was considered an appropriate pastime for the more adventurous women of the 80's.

Regardless of its debatable quality as an art, or as a psychological mechanism, photography retains a valuable function as a documentary record. So just as Thomas Eakins was filming the precise movements of a man jumping, and Eadweard Muybridge the gallop of Leland Stanford's horses, Clover was creating a photographic portrait of upper-class America in the leisurely seasons of the Gilded Age. Senator Lamar, with his hair newly rumpled, seems to have been lost, and so has the six-year-old Jerome Bonaparte blowing his trumpet, but here is Henry Adams, sitting on the wooden steps that lead to Clover's garden. He is wearing an impeccable double-breasted tweed suit, impeccably buttoned up to the neck, and an impeccable white hat. With one outstretched hand, and with a look of grave authority, he is holding up the shaggy front end of an adoring Skye terrier. This is Marquis, who, with Possum and Boojum ("For the Snark *was* a Boojum, you see"), was constantly being played with and petted. And here Clover has laboriously posed all three dogs on chairs surrounding a tea table with a teapot on the piazza at Beverly Farms. And here is Dr. Hooper, with his white mustache and a derby hat and a bow tie, sitting easily in his buckboard behind his mare, Kitty. And here, in Quincy, sit the older Adamses, Charles Francis with his legs tightly crossed and his left hand clenched on the arm of his chair, and Abigail with her lace-trimmed hat and her cane, both of them looking impenetrable and immutable. But the Adamses by now were totally prisoners of their infirmities, Abigail constantly tormented by pain and Charles Francis suffering the gradual disintegration of his mind, until he could remember almost nothing except that he must rise to his feet whenever his wife entered the room. And Dr. Hooper, so jaunty in his bow tie—his days, too, were numbered.

Clover was almost obsessively busy during these last years. Apart from the new house and the photography and the horses and the dogs, she ran what she often called a hotel. Even with her six servants, whom she characteristically spoke of as a burden, she often went marketing herself ("loaded up with May flowers—nasturtiums—Potomac shad, fresh rhubarb, asparagus from Norfolk etc.") And although she may never have washed a dish in her life, she kept a close eye on her kitchen ("I've invented some new dishes which I will teach you. . . . Tell your cook to stew some oysters and maccaroni together a little—then to chop them in equal quantities—to season properly and roll in beaten egg . . . and fry lightly in a wire fry basket").

But while her constant entertaining had once been a series of challenges and discoveries, repeatedly described by the phrase "much good talk," the social pressures of Washington now often struck her as oppressive. Her salon was too famous, and too many ambitious people besieged it. "As to the society rabble at this season," she wrote to Dr. Hooper in February of 1884, "it is nauseating and the only way of existing at all is to keep out of it. Hardly a day passes that someone doesn't bring a letter of recommendation. . . ." And again: "The winter watering place part of this life is getting intolerable and the pushing people who almost force their way into your house have to be adroitly met. No one is admitted now by my majestic Cerberus if they ask if I 'receive' and so only those who walk in without asking come at all."

One of the distinguished visitors who most irritated Clover was Matthew Arnold. When she had first met him in London, she had rather liked him, finding him "facile and gay and full of talk," but after encountering him at a few dinners there, she decided that he lacked "weight." She herself had suggested that Arnold should be invited to Boston to give the Lowell Lectures; when he arrived for a series of talks in 1883, she found him vain and pretentious. He offended her, at the start, by indulgently observing that "In Boston, there is no fashionable society, is there?" When Clover replied that there was indeed, he showed "extreme incredulity," and so, she added, "I had to suggest gently that 'fashionable people never go to lectures.'"

Arnold's lectures—on Emerson, on "Literature and Science,"

and on the political dangers of "Numbers"—were troubled from the start. At his first one, at Chickering Hall in New York, he sounded so indistinct that the audience began vainly calling for him to speak louder. General Grant left early. Andrew Carnegie urged the visitor from Oxford to take lessons in elocution. In smaller centers of culture, there were other problems. Arnold's address at the Jersey City Aesthetic Club, for example, was preceded by the Meigs Sisters singing "God Save the Queen" and Henrietta Markstein performing piano variations on "Old Black Joe." Arnold was not overly sympathetic to the more idiosyncratic aspects of American culture. It is not true, as was often reported, that he gestured toward a plate of pancakes and told his wife, "Do try one, my dear, they are not nearly so nasty as they look." He did, however, refer to Mark Twain as *"that* sort of thing." Walt Whitman, in turn, described the touring poet as "one of the dudes of literature."

For Clover, part of the game was to collect and pass on reports of Arnold's wanderings among the unworthy, and of the "lectures which seem to be better in quantity than in quality in the opinion of correspondents." John Hay wrote from Cleveland that Arnold was staying "as the guest of our richest and most ungrammatical self-made men," and when he heard that the tickets for Arnold's lecture were going unsold, he secretly bought them up and distributed them free among students. In Bridgeport, Connecticut, Arnold accepted an invitation to stay with P. T. Barnum, who told him, "You, Mr. Arnold, are a celebrity, while I am a notoriety." Clover observed that she fully expected Barnum to "induce Lord Tennyson to come over and ride the white elephant in his hippodrome."

When Arnold reached Washington, he stayed in the Blaine house, now being rented for $10,000 a year by a newly wealthy Chicago merchant named Levi Leiter, co-founder of the Marshall Field empire and father of the future Mary Curzon, another friend of Henry's old age.*

Clover met Arnold in the street, and they went walking together. Arnold "had a bad cold and confided to me that they had neither open fires nor dressing rooms in that big house. I wanted to say,

---

* The mention of Arnold's new circumstances inspired Clover to tell of an encounter between Mrs. Leiter and Emily Beale, who said, *à propos* heaven knows what, "Our cook gets drunk." Mrs. Leiter: "So does ours—what do you do with yours?" Miss Beale: "Father swears at her." Mrs. Leiter: "We pray with ours."

'Serves you right for staying with folks you don't know merely to save hotel bills.' "

By the time it came Christmas, Arnold was indeed in a hotel, unhappily, and Clover took pity on him by inviting him and his wife and daughter to eat turkey and plum pudding on H Street. The Christmas dinner seems not to have reconciled Clover to her guest, however. "Matthew Arnold cannot see anything larger than his lectures in this big country," she wrote her father, "and brings vividly home to one the deep saying of R. W. Emerson that 'every Englishman is an island.' . . . We have an acute indigestion for every Britisher just now." Clover was never very fond of visiting foreigners—"How I do hate a Frenchman!" she wrote after being taken in to dinner by a French royalist who "thinks republics vulgar"—but what gave her the most acute indigestion was the literary celebrity. "I never wish to know again an author whose work I like, nor to see a cook after eating his soup," she wrote. "I cannot read anything of Arnold's until I forget him. I've never enjoyed Browning since knowing him. By and by Herodotus will be all that is left."

Having brought the first two volumes of his *History* to a resounding conclusion with an account of William Eaton's march across the Libyan desert to attack the Pasha of Tripoli, Henry Adams decided, in the spring of 1883, that it was time for a little relaxation. In fact, he was growing a little bored with the Founding Fathers. His idea of relaxation was to indulge himself in writing another novel, devoted this time not to the corruptions of American politics but to the controversies between religious faith and the new theories of Darwinism—and to a portrait of some of the people he knew best. Like a true Adams, he would spare neither himself nor the subjects of his ironies. He seems to have finished the whole book during that summer of 1883, at the seaside house in Beverly Farms, for he was already correcting proofs by the following November.

As a kind of experiment, Adams persuaded the publisher, Henry Holt, to test the American public by issuing *Esther* without any announcements or advertising of any kind, without even sending out copies to reviewers. As a pseudonym, Henry selected the lugubrious name of Frances Snow Compton. The results of these mystifications were sufficiently bleak to satisfy his most misanthropic expectations. There was only one wary review in *Publishers Weekly* ("Quite unconventional in plot, characters and denouement . . ."), and of the 1,000 copies printed, only about 500 were somehow sold. Henry bought back the rest himself and had them destroyed.

It is possible to speculate that Henry had secret reasons for secrecy, that he wanted not only to disguise the authorship of his story but also to limit the number of people who might hear of it. (Thus did King Midas' barber whisper the secret of the king's donkey ears to a hole in the ground.) Henry posed, however, as a man interested only in testing the public taste. "As you know, I care very little for readers and dread notoriety more than dyspepsia," he wrote to Holt. And after it was over, he concluded somewhat bitterly: "My experiment has failed. . . . So far as I know, not a man, woman or child has ever read or heard of *Esther*. . . . My inference is that America reads nothing—advertised or not— except magazines."

As a novel, *Esther* probably deserved its fate, which it could have achieved even without Henry's experiment in taciturnity. Its characters are pale, its plot thin. It is an exemplar of that moss-hung species known as the Novel of Ideas, which, ever since the stately dialogues of Voltaire and Hume, has produced little of value either as novels or as ideas. Still, precisely because Henry's gifts as a novelist were so fragile, he turned to writing about friends and relatives and thus filled his work with elements of biographical interest. The whole book, in fact, can be read as a terrible confession and a terrible prophecy.

As in *Democracy*, no character represented Adams himself, though there are elements of a self-portrait, combined with a sketch of Clarence King, in the figure of George Strong, a geologist, a professor, but alone in the world and rich enough to do as he pleased. "His forehead was so bald," Henry wrote after a figurative glance in the mirror, "as to give his face a look of strong character, which a dark beard rather helped to increase. He was a popular fellow. . . ." Strong's friend Stephen Hazard, a "tall, slender, large-eyed, thin-nosed, dark-haired figure," had studied with him in Germany, then wandered through the Orient, now come to be pastor at the newly built Fifth Avenue Church of St. John's. He is easily recognizable as Henry's cousin, Phillips Brooks, the rector of Boston's Trinity Church, official preacher at Harvard, and ultimately bishop of Massachusetts (and author of "O Little Town of Bethlehem"). And from that band of artists who had helped Richardson to build and decorate Trinity, Adams now re-created the painter LaFarge as Wharton, a man with a sensual mouth and a ragged yellowish beard, given to long silences "until his shyness wore off, when he became a rapid, nervous talker, full of theories and schemes, which he changed from day to day."

The central character, of course, is Clover—renamed, for some mysterious reason, after the Esther Dudley who appears in one of Hawthorne's *Twice Told Tales*. The hypercritical young man who had once written that Clover Hooper was "certainly not handsome" was scarcely more complimentary a decade later. "In the first place she has a bad figure . . ." says Wharton. "She is too slight, too thin; she looks fragile, willowy, as the cheap novels call it, as though you could break her in halves like a switch. . . . Her features are imperfect. Except her ears, her voice, and her eyes, which have a sort of brown depth like a trout brook, she has no very good points." Having criticized her appearance, Wharton goes on, in words again similar to those that Henry had once used about Clover, to deride her talent and her intelligence. "She tries to paint, but she is only a second-rate amateur and will never be anything more. . . . She picks up all she knows without an effort and knows nothing well. . . . Her mind is as irregular as her face." Yet in this irregularity, Wharton manages to find a certain charm. "She is interesting," he concedes. "She has a style of her own. . . . She gives one the idea of a lightly sparred yacht in mid-ocean; unexpected; you ask yourself what the devil she is doing there. She sails gayly along, though there is no land in sight and plenty of rough weather coming."

If there was any ambiguity about Esther's identity, Adams hammered it flat in his description of her father, and of the relations between them. Like Dr. Hooper, Mr. Dudley is an amiable and humorous man, deeply skeptical about religion and science alike. He was trained as a lawyer but inherited enough money "to make him indifferent to his profession." He too was a widower, and since Esther was an only child, he "amused the rest of his life by spoiling this girl." Since the age of ten, Esther had been "absolute mistress of her father's house." Dudley acquired various unspecified injuries in the war, and now he is a semi-invalid, under death sentence from his doctors. He wants to get Esther safely married, and he confesses that his prospective and still undiscovered son-in-law—i.e., Henry Adams in Henry's own view of his position—is an enemy. "I have hated the fellow all his life," Dudley remarks to his sister-in-law, Mrs. Murray. "About twice a year I have treacherously stabbed him in the back as he was going out of my front door. I knew that he would interfere with my comfort if I let him get a footing." Mrs. Murray, commissioned to find Esther a husband, responds with a burst of liberated epigrams: "Marriage makes no difference in [women's] lot. All the contented women are fools, and the discontented ones want to be men. . . . If Esther is sensible she will never marry; but no woman is sensible, so she will marry without consulting us."

Since Henry had no narrative idea that would bring his puppets together, he recreated that Boston season in which he and Clover watched Richardson and his friends building Trinity Church just a few blocks from 91 Marlborough Street. The novel opens with Esther and her cousin George Strong sitting in the new church of St. John's to hear Strong's friend Hazard preach his first sermon. It does not take long for them to meet Wharton, who is still engaged in painting the church murals, and for Esther to join in the painting. Since the plot requires another woman, Adams introduces a young visitor from Colorado who is staying with Mrs. Murray. She is Catherine Brooke, who may take her last name from Henry's mother, or possibly from the heroine of *Middlemarch*, and on whom he lavishes all the feelings of infatuation that had been inspired by Elizabeth Cameron. At twenty, Catherine is "fresh as a summer morning" and "pretty as a fawn," and "no one could resist her hazel eyes." Her complexion resembled "the petals of a sweetbriar rose" and "the transparency of a Colorado sunrise."

Esther begins painting a mural portrait of Catherine as St. Cecilia, and Wharton soon falls in love with the young model (until his disreputable wife appears from Paris and has to be driven off with threats and annuities). Hazard, a more serious character, begins paying court to Esther, but she is diffident, feeling unworthy. There is much talk about translating Petrarch sonnets, and about the nature of portrait painting, and Esther herself unhappily accepts her own failure.

" 'I wish I earned my living,' she said. 'You don't know what it is to work without an object.'

" 'Much of the best work in the world,' said [Wharton], 'has been done with no motive of gain.'

" 'Men can do so many things that women can't,' said she, '. . . I am fit only for trifles. . . . What I could do nicely would be to paint squirrels and monkeys playing on vines around the choir, or daisies and buttercups in a row, with one tall daisy in each group of five. That is the way for a woman to make herself useful.' "

One day, Esther wakes up in the morning to learn that her father has suffered a paroxysm. The doctors tell her that he has only a short time to live. She abandons everything else to take charge of the sickroom, to watch by the bedside day and night. Mr. Dudley is stoical. " 'It's not so bad, Esther, when you come to it,' " he whispers. Esther sits in silent misery, holding his hand. "Although he soon dozed again, she did not alter her position, but sat hour after hour. . . . She meant her father to know, as long as he knew anything, that her hand was in his."

Mr. Dudley's death plunges Esther into a profound depression, a profound sense of loneliness and emptiness. "To be alone, with no one to interpose as much as a shadow across her path, was a strange sensation; it made her dizzy . . ." Adams writes. "Esther felt languid, weary, listless. She could not sleep. A voice, a bar of music, the sight of anything unusual, affected her deeply." In these circumstances, Esther sees a good deal of Stephen Hazard, and they talk at length about those questions that are his vocation and now her obsession, the invulnerability of the spirit and the triumph of life over death. In these circumstances, furthermore, it is almost inevitable for Hazard to declare his love, and for Esther, despite her feeling of unworthiness, to accept him.

No sooner has she accepted, however, than his religion becomes a point of conflict. She goes again to his new church and dislikes every aspect of the ceremonies. "By the time the creed was read," Adams writes, "she could not honestly feel that she believed a word of it, or could force herself to say that she ever should believe it." Her more worldly friends cannot understand her scruples. Catherine Brooke observes that a lawyer's wife need not concern herself about his cases. Esther insists on her unworthiness. "I'm not fit for him," she says. "Where do you expect the poor man to get a wife," Catherine retorts, "if all of us say we are not fit for him?"

This argument dominates the last third of the novel. Esther believes she can become worthy of Hazard only if she can master his philosophy, a view that puzzles her friends. "Yesterday, when I took her to drive, she was in tears about the atonement," says Mrs. Murray, "and today I suppose she will have gone to bed with a sick headache on account of the Athanasian creed." Unable to find faith in books of theology, she turns to her cousin, the scientist, and asks him: "Is religion true?" Strong first equivocates ("Ask me something easier! Ask me whether science is true. . . . There is no science which does not begin by requiring you to believe the incredible") and then argues on Hazard's own grounds: "If you have faith enough in Hazard to believe in him, you have faith enough to accept his church. Faith means submission. Submit!" "I want to submit," cries Esther, in what Adams calls "accents of real distress and passion," but she has to add, "Why can't some of you make me?"

The whole issue of faith may seem chimerical in our secular age, but it was timely enough in Adams' day, not only as a question of philosophy but also as one of social behavior. Adams informs us that Hazard's fashionable parishioners are "scandalized" by the prospect of his marrying "a woman whose opinions were believed to be radical." Mrs. Murray, specifically, tells Esther that "you must make him choose between you and his profession," or else "you will ruin him, and yourself too." Esther is unable to resolve these conflicts, so she renounces Hazard and flees with the Murrays and her friends to that spectacular shrine where Henry had taken Clover a few years earlier, where generation after generation of newly married Americans had gone on pilgrimages of discovery: Niagara Falls. There, staring into the thunderous mists, Esther experiences a strange kind of vision. Adams does not try to analyze it, reporting only that "she felt tears roll down her face as she listened to the voice of the waters and knew they were telling her a different secret from any that Hazard could ever hear." This leads her once again to an interrogation of George Strong:

"Do you believe in God?"

"Not in a personal one."

"Or in future rewards and punishments?"

"Old women's nursery tales!"

"Do you believe in nothing?"

"There is evidence amounting to strong probability, of the existence of two things . . . mind and matter."

302

"You believe in nothing else?"

"No."

"Isn't it horrible, your doctrine?"

"What of that, if it's true? I never said it was pleasant."

In the midst of this arrives the Reverend Stephen Hazard, eager to defend once more the doctrines of Victorian Anglicanism with sword and epithet. Esther remains unconvinced. "I never saw you conduct a service," she says, "without feeling as though you were a priest in a Pagan temple. . . . I half expected to see you bring out a goat or ram and sacrifice it on the high altar." Esther's rejection inspires Hazard to the lowest form of counterattack: "Can you . . . think of a future existence where you will not meet once more your father or mother, husband or children? Surely the natural instincts of your sex must save you from such a creed!" Esther responds with indignation: "Why must the church always appeal to my weakness and never to my strength! I ask for spiritual life and you send me back to my flesh and blood as though I were a tigress you were sending back to my cubs." The theology is largely a metaphor. What Hazard really demands is that Esther submit to his will and his view of life, and that is the one thing that Esther, try though she may, cannot do. For the last time, she rejects him and sends him away. "You have fought your battle like a heroine," Strong says after Hazard's departure. "If you will marry me, I will admire and love you more than ever a woman was loved since the world began." Esther can offer only a mournful conclusion: "But George, I don't love you, I love him."

If Esther is rather pallid as a novel of ideas, it is rich in personal implications. Indeed, once it is read as a roman à clef, it suddenly becomes a strange kind of attack on Clover, an exasperated, middle-aged, long-suppressed outburst against her at almost every point on which she was vulnerable. After more than ten years of marriage, things do change, but the Adamses were reluctant to admit any such change in their own lives. All they could admit was that the condition itself was a difficult one. "Marriage as 'egoisme à deux' is very well but à un not so gay," Clover remarked about an unhappy couple to Mrs. Cameron, who had already experienced the difficulties of marriage. "Henry and I often wonder how any man or woman dares to take the plunge—Capt. Webb trying the Niagara whirlpool is nothing to it." Even her studies of classical Greece began to take on a new color. "The result of a month's wrestling with Agamemnon," she wrote jocularly to a friend, "has brought me to feel a great sympathy with Clytemnestra. Put yourself in her place—Suppose your husband undertook to go after a pre-historic Mrs. Langtry, roping in all the nicest men in town, and then . . . for some days making mince meat of them. . . ."

The causes of a rift can sometimes be found far from the site of the crack, and in Henry's case, they probably came from a series of his own dissatisfactions. He was at the worst of ages, the late forties, an age at which his great-grandfather had already guided the Continental Congress to the Declaration of Independence, and now, having abandoned journalism for teaching, and teaching for the writing of history, he regarded his masterwork with dismay. "My poor history does not get on at all," he confessed to a friend in England, Sir Robert Cunliffe. "I have finished and actually printed for my private use two large volumes, 600 pages each; but two more will be needed to complete the work, and I am tired of it. For a month, I have hardly touched it, and my interest in it has gone. This is rather hard, as the result of ten years' work, with the prospect of five more. One shrinks from throwing one's life away like a third-rate novel; but, on the other hand, the bore of such a task without the stimulus of any interest but one's own is crushing."

Without the stimulus of anyone's interest but one's own, Henry cast about for someone to blame, and even in that same letter to Cunliffe, he abruptly turned against many of the activities that he and Clover had hitherto described as pleasures. "The life one leads here is too social for hard work," he complained. "One gives up the whole day after five o'clock to society. From two to five one must ride or walk or something. . . ." Once one begins to feel a general dissatisfaction, and begins searching for reasons, then nothing is immune. *Esther* provides evidence that Henry's search had already gone far, much farther, perhaps, than Clover had realized. At the most basic level, Adams relentlessly repeated his criticisms of Esther's appearance, her figure, her features, her style of dress. Not only does Wharton condemn her looks, but Strong, in attempting a heavy compliment, says, "Why Esther! Take care, or one of these days you will be handsome." And just as Clover had begun to experiment with photography, Henry now portrayed her as an untalented and unsuccessful painter, "a second-rate amateur."

The contrast with Catherine Brooke, so young, so beautiful, so lovingly modeled on Elizabeth Cameron, could scarcely be more extreme. Catherine's friends, like Mrs. Cameron's, reacted accordingly. "Catherine's innocent eagerness to submit was charming," Adams writes, "and the tyrants gloated over the fresh and radiant victim who was eager to be their slave." It is customary for novelists to insist that their characters are purely imaginary, bearing no resemblance to anyone living or dead, and Henry may well have made some such claim to Clover, but the characters in *Esther* are so recognizable that it would have been difficult indeed for Clover not to wonder, in the dark of the night, what Henry really felt about young Mrs. Cameron. It would have been even more difficult for her not to wonder, in the dark of the night, if his cruel portrait of Esther did not represent what he really thought of her.

The most remarkable aspect of *Esther* as a coded accusation, however, is its prophecy about Clover and her father. When Henry wrote his novel at Beverly Farms in the summer of 1883, Dr. Hooper was still pottering around nearby, in the best of health. Not until the following year would he suddenly be stricken by angina. Not until the following year would Clover rush to his bedside and nurse him day and night until his death. Not until the following year would she fall into a suicidal depression. Thus when Henry attributed to old Mr. Dudley a homicidal hostility to a prospective son-in-law who had not yet been identified, he was justifying in advance the homicidal fantasy that he himself was about to write down, describing with exquisite attention the old man's last hours. "In his extreme weakness, unable to lift a hand, his mind evidently beginning to wander, perhaps he . . . dreaded solitude and death. . . ."

One of the many mysteries about *Esther* is why Henry wrote it at all—that is, not only why he interrupted his grand history for such an essentially grim tale but why he devoted an entire novel to a woman's failure to achieve religious faith. Religion was not, so far as one can tell from his books and his letters up to that time, a matter of overwhelming importance to him. Nor do Clover's letters to her father ever deal with the subject except in terms of banter and ridicule. When one remembers the strong religious views of Clover's mother, though, it is possible to speculate that a childhood faith survived in her—suppressed or at least silenced by the skepticism of her father and her husband, but not dead. It even seems reasonable to suppose that there occasionally were arguments on the subject in the library on H Street. Not arguments, really, for there is no sign that Clover and Henry ever argued—but sharp interrogations and sharp answers, scenes much like those between Esther and Strong. If so, then *Esther* represents not only a personal attack on Clover, an attack not only on her appearance and her abilities and her family, but even an attack on her religion. Nothing was to be spared.

Esther also contains, strangely enough, the ultimate prophecy about Clover—unwritten. There were clues in the way the unhappy Esther spoke of herself: "I despise and loathe myself." And again: "Don't make me feel any more degraded than I am." Clarence King, for one, recognized such clues. He wrote to Adams that the resolution of the novel was basically false. He said that Esther's creator should have made her "jump into the Niagara as that was what she would have done." Adams agreed. "Certainly she would," he answered King, "but I could not suggest it." And then he wondered—this was the year after Clover had killed herself—whether he should ever have admitted anyone into his confidence, for if no one had known the identity of Frances Snow Compton, no one could connect Esther to Clover. "Perhaps I made a mistake even to tell King about it . . ." he wrote to Hay. "Now let it die! To admit the public would be almost unendurable to me."

Henry seems never to have realized what he had done—the Adamses traditionally thought that their stern judgments on one another were simply a matter of Bostonian principle—and Clover seems never to have told him. He acknowledged that Clover had served as a model for Esther, but he spoke of the portrait as though it showed only beauty and had been created only with love. "I will not pretend that the book is not precious to me," he wrote to Hay, still fretting over the absence of public acclaim, "but its value has nothing to do with the public, who could never understand that such a book might be written in one's heart's blood." And again, five years later, after the *History* had begun to appear, he wrote: "I care more for one chapter, or any dozen pages of *Esther* than for the whole history, including maps and indexes; so much more, indeed, that I would not let anyone read the story for fear the reader should profane it." By now a widower in his early fifties, he wrote that to the girl he regarded as fresh as a summer morning, Elizabeth Cameron.

In the spring and summer of 1884, the Republican oligarchy that had ruled the nation for more than two decades headed toward its ruin, to the spirited applause of reformers like the Adamses. President Arthur, whom they scorned as a mediocrity, had proved too independent for the party barons, and so the barons began organizing the nomination of Senator Blaine. The Adamses had voted Republican ever since the war, and they were hard-money conservatives in their economic ideas, but the prospect of Blaine—"a man tattooed with corruption," as Clover called him—was intolerable. "Blaine is gaining furiously," Clover wrote to her father after one of her political dinners, "so it's bound to be a bitter campaign fight all summer [with] all Blaine's crooked ways dished up ad nauseam. There is no alternative then for independents and Republicans who have any decency but to bolt and announce to the Democrats that if they put up a fit candidate like Gov. Cleveland or Bayard they can have all the reformers. . . . This rotten old soulless party may be laid in its grave."

The Adamses planned to go and watch the Republican convention in Chicago that June, but Henry finally decided that "the prospect was too black," so they stayed in Washington, watching only from a distance. One reformer who did attend the convention, however, was Frances P. Willard, a professor at Northwestern and president of the Women's Christian Temperance Union. It is customary nowadays to deride the temperance movement as a band of deluded zealots in bonnets, but the WCTU, with 200,000 members at its height, was once the largest women's organization in the country, and Miss Willard campaigned not only for sobriety but also for female suffrage, child-labor laws and compulsory education. And in an era when workmen were often tempted to spend the rent money on cheap whiskey and to beat their wives for protesting, the campaign against alcohol may have been as important to working-class women as the right to vote. The two were connected, of course, and so Frances Willard brought to the Republican platform committee a petition signed by 20,000 women, asking the party to support temperance. She was politely ushered in and out, then followed by a delegation of distillers and brewers. When shown the women's petition, one of the alcohol lobbyists urged the platform committee to "kick it under the table." After the meeting ended, the petition was found on the floor, streaked with dirt and tobacco juice. Miss Willard angrily urged her followers to campaign for Kansas Governor John P. St. John as the Prohibitionist candidate for President.

"The struggle of the majority of the Republicans to put Juggernaut Blaine in their car has succeeded," Clover wrote after the convention. "Now let's see if they get crushed under the idol's chariot wheels. It's a nice fight—every hungry restless blatherskite nestles under Blaine's wings and we know now just what we are fighting." Henry professed to be amused. "The public is angry and abusive," he wrote to Gaskell. "Everyone takes part. We are all doing our best, and swearing at each other like demons. But . . . no one talks about real interests. . . . Instead of this, the press is engaged in a most amusing dispute whether Mr. Cleveland had an illegitimate child . . . whether Mr. Blaine got paid in railway bonds for services as speaker." "Excuse so much politics," Clover wrote at the end of one of her letters, "but it absorbs our minds."

The campaign was undoubtedly much affected by trivia—they usually are—but since the basic issue was Blaine's lack of financial ethics, it was understandable for the Republicans to emphasize Cleveland's illegitimate baby (of uncertain parentage, actually, but supported by Cleveland in an orphanage, where he was now a boy of ten). Unlike tariff regulation and civil-service reform, these were "moral issues" that appealed to crowds at torchlight parades. "Blaine, Blaine, James G. Blaine, the continental liar from the state of Maine." The Democratic chant aroused an even more celebrated Republican chorus: "Ma! Ma! Where's my pa? Gone to the White House, Ha! Ha! Ha!" And when an obscure Presbyterian minister named S. D. Burchard saluted Blaine as the opponent of "Rum, Romanism and Rebellion," thousands of New York Irish were thought to switch their votes to Cleveland. In fact, some 25,000 New York followers of Frances Willard and Governor St. John also cast their Prohibitionist votes for Cleveland. No one faction is ever responsible for a presidential victory, of course, but Cleveland won by less than 25,000 votes out of 10 million. He captured 219 electoral votes to Blaine's 182.

"President Cleveland is a very honest, hard-working man, with plenty of courage and common-sense," Henry declared, "but he has little experience and is sure to make mistakes." As it turned out, the President soon filled his cabinet with such familiar H

Street figures as Senator Bayard in the State Department and Senator Lamar at Interior and Judge Endicott of Boston at the War Department. "My personal friends are more than ever in power," Adams wrote. "The government is wholly in their hands, and either the cabinet or their chief secretaries are all of our associates." It was only many years later, after Hay had become Secretary of State, that Henry reached the cynical conclusion that "a friend in office is a friend lost." Now, with the despised Blaine returned to private life, Henry looked forward to continuing his historical researches "as quietly under Mr. Cleveland as under Mr. Arthur."

And so, on a balmy day in March, when all of Washington looked like a gigantic tulip bed, the Adamses set out on horseback, Henry on Prince, Clover on Daisy, to see the great inaugural parade. Down to the State Department they rode, and then boldly up Pennsylvania Avenue to the main grandstand—"the dense crowd opening for us," Clover noted—and then to a vantage point near the Capitol, where they could observe the thousands of soldiers beginning to march past, the Philadelphia Guardsmen in Continental buff and blue, and a black regiment in tall bearskin hats, and the Virginians in rebel gray, singing "Dixie." Everyone, as she observed, looked gay and happy, as if they thought it was a big country and they owned it, which, in a sense, they did. They thought they had won, as did Clover and Henry, and what could seem more promising than a victory parade on a warm spring day? "When one is forty and on the home stretch," Clover wrote not long afterward, "it's consoling to find it suits one better to look ahead than behind." That conventional thought immediately led, by one of Clover's unconventional twists, to a mischievous Biblical metaphor that might or might not suggest that she had been thinking about *Esther*. "If Lot's wife hadn't been a morbid conservative she would have had a sweeter old age and been a pillar of strength to her reprehensible husband—but I suppose she looked back because with such a mate she had nothing to look forward to."

16

DISASTER

IT WAS MID-MARCH of 1885, a blustering season, windy and raw, when the inevitable news came. Dr. Hooper, at the age of seventy-four, had been stricken with angina. The prognosis was poor. Clover must come to Cambridge at once. She was to spend the next month at Ned's house in Fayerweather Street, sharing with him and the Gurneys the duties of the sickroom. There was very little to be done, the sheets and pillows to be freshened, broth and tea to be spooned out, and then waiting, endless waiting. It must have been much the way Henry had foretold the scene in *Esther:* "She knew that there was no hope and that her father himself was only anxious for the end, yet to see him suffer and slowly fade out was terrible. . . . Esther had been told that she must not give way to agitation, under the risk of killing her father, who lay dozing, half-conscious, with his face turned towards her. Whenever his eyes opened they rested on hers."

Henry had scarcely ever been separated from Clover before, and now, for the first time, he could talk to her only by letter. He wrote to her almost every day. Yet these letters to Clover on her death watch begin on a tone of excruciating self-consciousness. "Madam," he addresses her. "As it is now thirteen years since my last letter to you, you may have forgotten my name. If so, try to recall it. For a time we were somewhat intimate." The touch of nostalgia is not entirely ironic, nor is the irony entirely amused. Thirteen years of marriage have wrought their changes. But in concluding, Henry offers a halting yet obviously heartfelt gesture of affection. "There remains at the bottom of the page," he writes, veering off into the margin, "just a little crumb of love for you, but you must not eat it all at once. The dogs need so much."

Henry usually begins each letter by describing the weather ("gales of piercing wind; clouds of dust; and bitter cold"), then tells of his visits to the dentist ("I came home low in mind, and tried to work, but only felt helpless"). Visitors appear, as usual, Hay and Richardson, and Alex Agassiz, "brown and burned in Sandwich Island suns and swearing energetically at the arctic weather here." But much of the gossip is of difficulty and disease. Mrs. Beale has been "very ill of pneumonia," and Senator Lamar has a bronchial inflammation. "Lucy Frelinghuysen . . . told me that her father had been taken—in bed—to New Jersey and had remained in bed since. . . ." The Bancrofts were "deeply disgusted" that the retiring President Arthur, "the great booby," had gone to stay at the Frelinghuysens, ignoring the Secretary of State's illness in order to be near the secretary's beautiful daughter. Then there was more. "Nick [Anderson's] gossip included a tale that the ex-president Arthur is going to die, and that within a short time his complete collapse must occur."

Senator Don Cameron, too, was stricken with tuberculosis, and his doctors insisted that he move to California for an indefinite period, and Lizzy Cameron did not feel like accompanying him there, at least not for the present. Henry went to call, he wrote to Clover, and found the Senator sitting with his young wife on a sofa. "I greeted him with affection and said I was very glad to see him before he went off. His reply was characteristic. 'Are you truly?' he asked. 'Yes,' said I, 'truly.' The poor fellow seemed really pleased at this, and for the first time became open and companionable. . . . 'I am hit here,' said he, putting his hand on his lungs, 'harder than I supposed; I am badly hit; I'm not the least frightened but I am going to cure it if I can.' He thought himself not frightened, but he is scared to pieces. . . ."

As he wrote on, Henry's letters become more relaxed and conversational. He addressed Clover as "Dear Mistress," as "Dear Clo," "Dear Mugwump," "Dear Lady," and even "Dear Angel." He created little scenarios with the terriers. "The dogs and I have just come from picking some violets for you, which we have put in your . . . tea-pot on your desk. The new violets are only now in flower." He reported that Sally Loring had sent "a conundrum for you—'What is a little pig doing when he eats?' When you give it up, I will send you the answer." (The answer, disclosed by surprise toward the end of that letter: "Why of course little pigs when they eat make hogs of themselves.")

And there was always the house to write about. Henry reported that he had searched throughout the Smithsonian for various kinds of porphyry that might look well in the living-room fireplace, but he had found that most of them suggested the furnishings of a hotel. The one exception was a small slab of Mexican onyx, "of a sea-green translucency so exquisite as to make your soul yearn." He urged her to agree to it, and even to discuss it with Richardson, just as though her preoccupations were necessarily the same as his own. "Please have a sea-green onyx fire-place . . ." he wrote. "Strike for green!" But no matter what she did, the work proceeded. "The carpenters, gas men and pipe-fitters are swarming in our [house] and at this rate will soon give way for the lathers." He wrote her about "the great bell question"—exactly where to put the various bells to ring for the servants—and then he wrote that "all your bells are in, fifteen in all." And her bathroom was being altered. "If I cannot get a good yellow [plaster] should you mind having a red?" And a lift was being installed. And a safe and a burglar alarm system. "The plumbers are hard at work. The stairs are going in. The copper spout is on."

It was only at Clover's request, he wrote, that he had accepted another invitation to the White House, where he went with Richardson, one evening at nine, and sent in his card. The President's daughter Rose had them shown in. "Miss Cleveland received us," Henry wrote, "and took us into the red room where we found the president seated in a melancholy way, with four or five ladies round the middle of the parlor. . . . We must admit that, like Abraham Lincoln, the Lord made a mighty common-looking man in him. I expected it, and I was satisfied. He was very quiet. . . ." The President's daughter was more solicitous. "Miss Cleveland . . ." Henry wrote, "carries an atmosphere of female college about her, thicker than the snow storm outside my window. She listens seriously and asks serious questions. . . . We talked chiefly of George Eliot's biography, which she takes in an earnest spirit. I have seldom been more amused than in thus meeting a sister professor in 'the first lady of the land.' I liked her. . . . I explained why you were not with me, and she cordially asked me to bring you over in the evening."

Clover occasionally responded with messages asking Henry to join her in Cambridge, but he was not eager to go. "I dread trouble in my teeth," he explained, "and have much to do here." And when he did visit Cambridge, he did not stay long. "I bolt forward and back like a brown monkey," he wrote to one of Clover's friends. "Nobody wants me in either place. They won't take me for a nurse, and I can't live all alone in a big solitary house when it rains and I can't ride. Even the goldfish are bored, and the dogs fight to pass the time. . . ." Back in Washington, he wrote to Clover of a more tranquil domesticity. "Please imagine me seated by the library fire, writing this on my knee while Boojum snores at my feet. After the scrawl I sent you last night, I eat my little supper, read a play of Labiche, and went to bed. . . ." But he did manage to tell her that he was "uneasy . . . about you." He even managed to tell her, finally, that he sorely missed her. "How," as he put it, "did I ever manage to hit on the only woman in the world who fits my cravings and never sounds hollow anywhere?" He knew no higher compliments. He expected, however, to be reunited with Clover only when she summoned him on the occasion of Dr. Hooper's death, and he wrote, with the coldest of hearts, "I think your report indicates that I shall not wait long."

He was right. Three days later, on April 13, Dr. Hooper quietly died. "His humor and courage lasted till unconsciousness came . . ." Clover later wrote to Mrs. Hay, "and he went to sleep like a tired traveller."* Henry did finally go to Cambridge for the funeral, and to inter Dr. Hooper next to the long-dead Ellen Hooper in the Sturgis plot in Mt. Auburn cemetery. He was "touched," he wrote to Gaskell, "by the quiet and general respect which the society of Boston and Cambridge showed." (Among the mourners was Oliver Wendell Holmes, by now seventy-six, who later wrote to a friend that the funeral was "as if an autumn wind were tearing away the last leaves all around me. . . .") And he was "pleased," Henry added, to learn that he and Ned and Gurney were trustees

* Even in that sorrowful letter, Clover couldn't resist enclosing a gossipy clipping from the *Transcript*, reporting that the newest Henry James, William's son, then aged three, had been told to button his own shoes for the first time. After a series of audible grunts from his room, he was heard to cry out: "Oh God, why couldn't you have made me with my shoes on?" "Vive le roi déjà," Clover added.

and executors of a considerable estate. "His death alters our situation only as it severs one more tie," he concluded.

In Dr. Hooper's desk, after his death, Clover discovered and saved a quotation that her father had copied from somewhere, a memorable statement of the stoicism of the *ancien régime*, in Boston as in Paris:

"*C'est qu'on savait vivre et mourir dans ce temps là; on n'avait pas d'infirmités importuns. Si on avait la goutte, on marchait quand-même et sans faire la grimace; on se cachait de souffrir par bonne education.*"

Henry seems not to have realized that the end of Clover's tie to her father meant the end of her tie to much of life. "No one fills any part of his place to me but Henry," she wrote to a friend, Anne Palmer, "so that my connection to New England is fairly severed. . . ." In fact, she never recovered from that month by the sickbed and from the death that ended it. She was, in a way that she herself could not understand, utterly crushed. Nothing in her life seemed any longer to have any meaning.

Henry appeared to think only that Clover was physically tired, and he reported to Hay the following week that she was "in better condition than I feared." Clover refused, however, to return to Beverly Farms for the usual summer. Henry began casting about for other places to go. He made inquiries about the new Yellowstone National Park. He planned a six-week camping tour of the Rockies, and was dismayed to hear that early summer was the season for swarms of flies. He finally decided to start out in the traditional resorts in the Alleghenies, and on June 11, the Adamses set off with their two horses for White Sulphur Springs, Va. The hotel was one of those vast establishments that could house 800 vacationers, but the Adamses arrived on its opening day and found that they had the place practically to themselves.

Almost too much so, for a woman in the depths of melancholy. "A country less known to Bostonians could not be found," Henry wrote cheerily to Gaskell. "Imagine a sloping valley, half a mile or more in width, shut in by moderate mountains densely wooded. . . . On our first ride we nearly fell off our horses at seeing hillsides sprinkled with flaming yellow, orange and red azaleas, all mixed together, and masses of white and pink laurel. . . . On our second ride, we got a long way into the mountains by a rough path; and the groves of huge rhododendrons were so gloomy and shook their dark fingers so threateningly over our heads, that we turned about and fled for fear night should catch us, and we should never be seen any more by our dear enemies. . . ."

The Adamses had picked out a small wooden cabin for themselves, near the bathing pool, shaded by an oak tree fifteen feet in diameter. "Here we live, quite alone," Henry chattered on, "going for meals to the hotel, swimming, reading, writing, and riding. . . . Here we shall stay till we are bored; then try another spring. I am told there are about sixty." By the first of August, he had heard, the flies disappeared from the Rockies, and so he planned to head West on about July 25. He even ordered what he called "a regular eastern caravan," twelve pack animals, tents, a professional cook. But from the silenced Clover, whose moods could no longer be read in the Sunday morning letters that now had ended, there may have been some kind of rebellion, for by the middle of July the Adamses were back in Beverly Farms. "Various domestic necessities have forced us to return home," Henry wrote to Hay, "and to abandon our Yellowstone adventure." To Gaskell, he was a little more explicit, saying that the Yellowstone trip had to be canceled because 'we broke down." "My wife has been out of sorts for some time past," he added, "and until she gets quite well again, can do nothing."

Beverly Farms was perhaps the worst of all places for Clover to go. Every silent pine, every gentle pathway through the woods, every foaming inlet along the beach must have reminded her of her father, of their walks together, their laughter and easy confidences. Instead of escaping from her sorrow, she clung to it. New activities might have provided her with new ideas, but the diagnosis of physical exhaustion condemned her to a life of idleness. "My wife and I have had nothing to do since the middle of July," Henry wrote to his friend James T. Field, the publisher. "The days roll round without changing anything. . . . We vegetate." Henry tried to resume work on his history, "which is now a mere mechanical fitting together of quotations," and when that faltered, he amused himself with the construction of genealogical tables tracing Adamses and Hoopers back eight generations into the past.

In earlier summers, this indolent existence might have been as idyllic as Henry tried to make it appear, but Clover's numbness was that of a wanderer lost in darkness and snow. She once had told her sister, Ellen, of a dream in which she felt herself surrounded by a wall of ice, and now that had become a nightmare from which she was unable to awaken. At the same time that she suffered from this coldness of the spirit, she also began to experience agonies of guilt about every action that was now past recall. Ellen Gurney saw Clover often during that last summer at Beverly Farms, and tried in vain to help her. "She held Whitman and me to her heart as never before," Ellen later wrote to a friend. "She was so tender and humble—and appealing when no human help could do anything—sorry for every reckless word or act, wholly forgotten by all save her. Her constant cry was 'Ellen I'm not real—oh make me real—You are all of you real!' "

At about this time, there occurred the strange episode of the Assyrian lion. Richardson installed a large stone carving of the lion, backed by a cross, right between the two arches that sheltered the front entrance to the new house. Henry was horrified. "If you see the workmen carving a Christian emblem, remonstrate with them," he wrote to Theodore Dwight, the State Department librarian who was keeping watch on the house. "As yet I am myself uninformed as to their intentions."

Hay wrote to say that the winged lion "is magnificently *réussie.*" Henry wrote back that he had begun to "turn red, blue, and green of nights thinking about it and hiding my head under my pillow." In other words, he was not at all "uninformed" about the appearance of the emblem but strongly opposed to it. "I wish the Assyrian animal would walk off and carry the cross back to the British Museum," he wrote to Hay. After he had returned to Washington that fall, he was still angry about the mysterious figure "whose nose I hope to see broken off every time I look at him." He pleaded with Richardson to remove the lion, but Richardson declined, and Adams lapsed into sulking. "I can neither revolt nor complain, though the whole thing seems to me bad art and bad taste," he wrote to Dwight. "I have protested in vain and must henceforth hold my tongue. Don't quote me or repeat my grumblings. Our dear Washingtonians chatter so much. . . ."

One of the scholars of the Adams papers in Boston, Marc Friedlander, has raised the interesting question of why Adams could not persuade his own architect to remove from his own house a carving that he disliked so intensely, and why, moreover, he had to be so emphatic about the need for silence about his objections. "The conclusion seems unavoidable," Friendlander wrote, "that Adams was constrained to suffer silently . . . because Richardson, in carrying out the application of the cross and carving to the facade, was following the wishes of Mrs. Adams." Here too, then, Clover and Henry must have experienced, in twisted form, the controversies that had animated *Esther*, and Esther Dudley, whether a skeptic or a convert, was accustomed to having her way.

Now that the house was nearing completion, Henry could talk of little else. Even the previous fall, he had written to Hay that he was inspecting every detail of construction. "Ten times a day I drop my work and rush out to see the men lay bricks or stone." In Clover's last month, Henry equated her depression with his own autumnal mood, writing to Hay that "we are still in poor state and unfit for worldly vanities," but he kept prattling about the house. "We took in some coal yesterday to start the furnaces. . . . I am curious that you should see the library fireplace. Of all living fireplaces, this is certainly the most astonishing." A week later, he addressed Hay as "Dear Lord of Bath-tubs" and promised to move in by New Year's Day. "My house is really finished except for the papering. . . . The library is complete except the floor. . . . Both our furnaces are running. . . . Mrs. Don [Cameron] has come back, terribly used up; and takes a house on 19th Street. We are about as usual. . . ."

Clover could not share his enthusiasm. One of her friends, Rebecca Dodge Rae, used to visit her daily, bringing gossip and trying to cheer her up, but nothing could free Clover from the darkness. In the midst of a conversation, Mrs. Rae later recalled, Clover would lapse into silence, then rub her hand back and forth across her forehead as though trying to remember, or to forget, or to understand, something beyond her control. After one of Mrs. Rae's visits, Henry escorted her to the door and thanked her for her efforts.

"I shall never forget what you've done," he said.

"Done? What have I done?" Mrs. Rae asked.

"You made Clover smile," Henry said.

Other visitors had still more somber experiences, for Clover's thoughts had turned, perhaps inevitably, toward death. Henry's brother Charles, who once had impulsively warned Henry not to marry Clover because her family were "all crazy as coots," recalled his last meeting with Clover that fall as "painful in the last degree." He tried, in his brusque way, to make conversation, but Clover hardly even listened. "Her mind dwelt on nothing but self-destruction," he recalled later. "She was engaged the whole time in introspection and self-accusation."

The same two qualities inspired her last letter to Ellen, a letter that she never sent. She tried to explain how she felt, and what she was about to do. "If I had one single point of character or goodness I would stand on that and grow back to life," she wrote. And she tried, finally, to absolve Henry of any responsibility that might be attributed to him. "Henry is more patient and loving than words can express," she wrote, "God might envy him—he bears and hopes and despairs hour after hour. . . . Henry is beyond all words tenderer and better than all of you even. . . ."

That first week in December, Clover seemed better. She slept more. Richardson thought she seemed better. Alex Agassiz thought she seemed better. On December 6, another one of those Sunday mornings when Clover always used to write to her father, she and Henry had a late breakfast, about noon. Henry asked her how she felt. She said she felt better.

After breakfast, she went back to her room, alone. Henry prepared to go out for a walk by himself. At the front door, he encountered a lady who had come to visit Clover. He went back upstairs to ask her if she wanted to receive a visitor.

He found her lying on the rug before the fire.

Clover?

She must have fainted. Henry knelt down.

There was a strange smell. One of the chemicals that she used for her photography. Potassium cyanide. From the bottle lying there.

Henry picked up the body, still warm, soft, heavy, and dragged it over to the sofa. Clover did not open her eyes. Did not answer him. Did not explain. Did not move.

Henry suddenly turned and ran out of the room, ran out the door, ran down the street. He found a doctor whom he knew, Dr. Charles E. Hagner. He brought the doctor back to the house, back to the room where the fire burned in the fireplace, back to the room where Clover lay on the sofa. Silent. Still. That strange smell of the potassium cyanide. Dr. Hagner bent over the body.

Dead, said Dr. Hagner. Probably paralysis of the heart. Poison. She probably died almost instantly, said Dr. Hagner. Almost instantly.

"I can imagine nothing more ghastly than that lonely vigil in the house with his dead wife," General Anderson wrote to his son at Harvard. Anderson, who lived just three blocks away, had gone to call on Henry as soon as he heard the news, but Henry refused to see anyone. He had sent a servant out with telegrams notifying Ned Hooper and the Gurneys and his brother Charles, and then he just sat and waited. "God only knows how he kept his reason those hours," Ellen later recalled, "but when we got to him he was as steady and sweet and thoughtful of all of us as possible."

He resisted mourning. That Monday night, when he joined Charles and Ned and the Gurneys at dinner, he wore a bright red necktie, and he tore the mourning crepe off his arm and threw it under the table. Beyond that, he clung to simple things. He moved books around. He went for walks. He read Shakespeare. When John Hay, en route to Cleveland, telegraphed his desire to help, Henry insisted on continuing his routines. "Nothing you can do," he answered, "will affect the fact that I am left alone in the world at a time of life when too young to die and too old to take up existence afresh; but after the first feeling of desperation is over, there will be much that you can do to make my struggle easier. I am going to keep straight on. . . . Never fear me, I shall come out all right from this—what shall I call it—Hell!" Henry's letter is remarkable in making no mention whatever of Clover, speaking only of his own anguish. It was left to Hay, therefore, to write the only eulogy of the Number One Heart. "Is it any consolation to remember her as she was? That bright intrepid spirit, that keen fine intellect, that lofty scorn of all that was mean, that social charm which made your house such a one as Washington never knew before, and made hundreds of people love her as much as they admired her. No, that makes it all so much harder to bear."

The funeral was small and quiet, and then the body was taken to Rock Creek Cemetery. "She is laid on a sunny slope in a most peaceful church yard . . ." Ellen Gurney reported, "a place which they often went to together and where the spring comes early." And Henry took all their possessions (Clover left him an estate of more than $40,000) and moved into the new house, just as he had planned, and made it into a kind of mausoleum where he lived and worked for more than thirty years. "For the present," he wrote to Godkin, "I try to think of nothing but how to make the days pass till my nerves get steady again. . . . Never fear for me. I have had happiness enough to carry me over some years of misery; and even in my worst prostration I have found myself strengthened by two thoughts. One was that life could have no other experience so crushing. The other was that at least I had got out of life all the pleasure it had to give. I admit that fate at last has smashed the life out of me; but for twelve years I had everything I most wanted on earth. . . ."

That Christmas, three weeks after Clover's death, Henry gave away a piece of her jewelry. He gave it to Mrs. Cameron. She had been sick, and Henry was solicitous. "The little trinket which I send you with this," he wrote, "was a favorite of my wife's. Will you keep it and sometimes wear it to remind you of her?"

Why did she do it? Why does anyone do it? "No one ever lacks a good reason for suicide," said Cesare Pavese, the novelist, himself a suicide.

If we look back through the official records, we find many official reasons. During the five years between 1882 and 1887, the average number of suicides in the United States was 1,645 per year, the total 8,226. The most common method was shooting (2,668), with poisoning second (1,734), and the list extends downward to occasional cases of starvation (7), scalding (1) and falling on a pitchfork (1). Among all the suicides, the most common ethnic origin was German and the most common occupation farming (though "courtesans" ranked fourth and saloonkeepers fifth). The most common reason was simply "insanity . . . including religious delusions," which was listed as the cause of 1,765 suicides. Then came family trouble (1,044), business trouble (659), love trouble (585), "dissipation" (571), sickness (362), and destitution (270). Further down in the list, the statisticians included four cases of "election disappointment," two of "fear of assassination," and one each of fear of smallpox, denial of pension, and pimple on nose.

We may smile at the simplicity of anyone who would attribute a suicide to a pimple on the nose, and yet there is something equally simple in the attribution of so many cases to the term "insanity." Somehow the statisticians have managed to differentiate insanity from "love trouble," or, for that matter, "fear of assassination," but they have made no effort to differentiate one form of madness from another, or even to separate "religious delusions" from the secular kind. Nowadays, of course, many of these conditions have acquired impressive new names like "paranoid schizophrenia." Whatever terms doctors use, however, they continue to provide official diagnoses for what is essentially a mystery. One contemporary textbook still cites as authoritative the statement of Gregory Zilboorg in 1936: "The problem of suicide from the scientific point of view remains unsolved. Neither common sense nor clinical psychopathology has found a causal or even a strictly empirical solution."

In Henry Adams' view, perhaps in Clover's view, certainly in the view of her friends and family, her suicide was quite simply the result of her profound depression over the death of her father. This was undeniably a contributing element, perhaps the most important single element. Clover had been unusually close to her father all her life, and her marriage by no means ended her dependence upon him. They were bound together as Adam Verver and Maggie were bound in *The Golden Bowl*, by what Henry James called "an intense and exceptional degree of attachment, he peculiarly paternal, she passionately filial." Clover's Sunday morning letters to Boston were more than reports of dinner parties and collections of *obiter dicta;* they were almost a form of communion, in which Clover could hear and speak to her father as though they were, once every week, reunited. Even in middle age, she wrote once of hearing "your warning voice telling me to go to bed and not 'lose your roses.'" She was perfectly delighted to hear that a Miss Dulaney had compared her to her father and had found it "ridiculous that any man and woman should be so like one another." "Which of us," Clover wondered, "does she flatter most?" When she finally had to acknowledge that the warning voice from Beacon Street was still forever, the silence surrounding her in her new isolation was literally maddening. It has sometimes been said that the one common element in almost all suicides is a ravaging sense of loneliness.

If we wish to accept the death of Dr. Hooper as the cause of Clover's suicide, we can find ample explanations and justifications in the theories of Sigmund Freud, who argued that the impulse toward suicide derived from mixed feelings of love and hatred toward somebody else, somebody who could be destroyed, even after his own death, only by the destruction of one's own self. Grief is commonplace enough, but sometimes the victim is unable to understand his loss, or, as Freud put it in *Mourning and Melancholia* (1917), he "knows whom he has lost but not *what* it is he has lost in them." Then comes the devastating sense of worthlessness. "In grief the world becomes poor and empty; in melancholia it is the ego itself," Freud wrote. "The patient represents his ego to us as worthless, incapable of any effort and morally despicable; he reproaches himself, vilifies himself and expects to be cast out and chastised. He abases himself before everyone and commiserates his own relatives for being connected with someone so unworthy." There follows, quite naturally, the inability to eat, to sleep, to forgive oneself. Against every instinct of life and self-preservation, there arises what Freud called the *Todestrieb* or "death drive."

If we wish to understand Clover's sense of loss, however, we must go back beyond the death of Dr. Hooper, for everything that he represented to his daughter, that quality of protection and nurturing, he represented because he had been, for almost forty years, both father and mother to her. Clover had been just five years old when her mother, coughing and choking, had been taken away to Georgia, and wrote home: "Kisses for Clover on her eyes and ears and lips and the tip of her little nose." And wrote: "My precious silver gray, you know I love you as much as ever. I see your little stems of legs trotting up and down stairs. . . ." And wrote in one of her poems:

> *I give thee all, my darling, darling child,*
> *All I can give—the record of good things,*
> *All maxims, truths in memory's storehouse filed,*
> *And point thee to a rest 'neath angel wings. . . .*

When a child is five, the mind blacks out much of what it has seen—destroys, perhaps, all memory of a stately procession to a cavernous pit dug into a hillside of a Cambridge cemetery, and the rich smell of overturned earth, and the droning incantations of a minister reciting the litany of dust unto dust. The five-year-old mind does not consciously decide what it destroys, or tries to destroy. It remembers, as though at random, a parade of troops marching to war or the rustle of an elm branch against the shutter in the moment before the lightning—and nothing in between. But what it does not remember, it does not forget either. At the center of Clover's existence, almost all her life, was the vacuum that her father tried to fill, the vacuum caused by the death of her mother, and so when her father died, she lost her mother all over again, and in one old man's last gasp for breath, lost both parents at once.

Twelve years after Clover's death, Emile Durkheim published his classic study, *Le Suicide*, in which he tried to separate the act from the impassioned moral judgments upon it. Suicide had been widely tolerated under the Roman Empire, after all, and even courted by the early Christian martyrs. St. Augustine was among the first to condemn self-destruction as "a detestable and damnable wickedness," and by the time of Dante, all suicides could be consigned to the seventh circle of the Inferno, where they were turned into gnarled and stunted trees, with Harpies nesting in their dead branches. With the decay of Christian belief, in the nineteenth century, however, suicide seemed to be increasing once again, not only in its frequency but in its acceptability. Young Werther became a Romantic hero, and Goethe himself took a dagger to bed for many nights to practice his own death.

Durkheim argued that suicide, whatever the personal reasons might be, was a social act, and that it increased in relation to the incoherence, or *"anomie"* of society. He tried to distinguish among three basic types of self-destruction: "egoistic suicide," which derived from an individual's social isolation; "altruistic suicide," in which an individual died to fulfill society's demands (as in Japanese hara-kiri); and "anomic suicide," when death was a direct result of social breakdown (the bankrupt stockbroker on the window ledge). Durkheim's efforts to find social reasons for suicide, and to remove the moral stigma from the act, were admirable. It was also admirable to demonstrate that a society that destroyed family relationships and cultural coherence in the name of capitalist progress was a society that drove people to kill themselves. Unfortunately, though, the statistics proved unwieldy. If an unhappy farm boy runs away to the city, can't find work, takes to drink, suffers an unhappy love affair, and shoots himself, which of these various causes is to be considered a consequence of *anomie?* And when all of European society collapsed in the moral anarchy of World War I, it was inevitably noted, among the savants who now called themselves sociologists, that the suicide rate precipitously dropped.

Still, man lives in his environment. So does a woman. And in the sense that suicide is a passionate judgment on one's own life, it is a judgment on all the circumstances of that life, circumstances that may, in themselves, seem of little importance.

Consider, for example, the last days of Friedrich List, the German economist, a refugee to America, successful speculator in coal and railroads, U.S. envoy to Paris and consul in Leipzig. Afflicted by failing health and business reverses, he wrote a letter to a friend in November of 1846 trying to explain his imminent suicide: "My headaches and distress grow stronger every day, in addition, the horrible weather. . . ." Is it not surprising that an eminent man writing down the reasons for his suicide should pause to complain about the weather? Not necessarily. One researcher, C. A. Mills, investigated the fluctuations in suicide rates in nine Midwestern cities over a five-year period and concluded that they coincided remarkably with periods of sharply falling barometric pressure. "The data presented here," he wrote in *The American Journal of Psychiatry*, "indicate that probably the weather is a factor of major importance in this question of mental instability."

Clover was acutely conscious of bad weather. It was as though she suffered from some kind of rheumatism, or a bullet wound from some forgotten war, and the coming of rain made her ache. Many of her letters begin with accounts of clouds and storms. Her unhappiness in Europe was punctuated with reports of "heavy yellow fog . . . gray pea soup . . . fearful cold." Back in Washington, she regularly followed the weather maps in the newspapers to check the forecasts for both H Street and Beacon Street. And Washington winters are bleak, without any of the drama or the sense of survival that improves a New England blizzard. It just rains, and the dust turns to mud. "Nothing like the ferocity of this winter and spring has ever been known," Henry wrote to an English friend early in 1885. "Even here where the flowers should be opening, the sternest sort of weather still hangs on. We are weary and worn out with a long succession of violent changes, and a struggle with winds that wither us with colds. Something has gone wrong with the equator. . . . All my friends here have mortal diseases."

By the following November, the prospect of another gray winter must have been thoroughly depressing. The only festivity that lay ahead was Christmas, and that could only revive memories of Christmases past. "For the unhappy, Christmas is always a bad time," A. Alvarez has written in *The Savage God, A Study of Suicide.* "The terrible false jollity that comes at you from every side, braying about peace and good will and family fun, makes loneliness and depression particularly hard to bear."

Dr. Hooper had generally sent $1,000 every year, and Clover sometimes had difficulty in finding something special on which to spend it. In 1882, she could remember, she had bought a beautiful turquoise, and then sent the rest of the money off to an agent in Russia, to buy ten silver tumbler holders and silver spoons for the Russian tea with lemon that she drank with Henry every night. It had taken all that year to find just the right set, so when the tumblers finally arrived, it was almost Christmas again, and there was another check, and Clover warned her father that his extravagance would impoverish the whole family, and they could be saved only if Henry would sign a contract with D'Oyly Carte to write comic history. Now that the house was under way, though, the new Christmas check would be spent on some special element in the building. "Now I want no more jewelry or bric-a-brac," she wrote. "Our minds are set on drains, plumbing and bricks. [I shall] put it into one definite part of the new house—perhaps Spanish iron wrought grilles for the entresol windows. . . ."

The house that had been started with such gaiety may well have become another element in Clover's melancholy. A new house is, far more than one realizes, a commitment of one's identity. This can be a challenge—a threat—even when one is simply buying a finished house that already stands as an expression of someone else's plans. When one builds a new house for oneself, every decision from the location of a stairway to the color of the walls to the design of the roof represents a series of alternatives. Each alterna-

325

tive requires a new choice, and the possibility of irremediable error. Particularly for a nineteenth-century woman, then, a woman who had been taught to think of her home as the center of her existence and the expression of her identity, the acquisition of a new house was, even if all went well, a major crisis.

But Clover's house was not really her house. Even when she first wrote to Dr. Hooper about her plans for a simple pine box, it was basically Henry's plan that she was describing. It was Henry who drew the detailed sketch of the whole interior, placing his study at the center of the second floor, just as Charles Francis Adams' library had occupied the one sunny room of the wintry house on Mt. Vernon Street. It was Henry's friend Hay who had provided most of the money to buy the plot of land, and Henry's friend Richardson who had then designed the kind of house that he himself thought would be appropriate for the Adamses. If there were differences of opinion, it was Henry who clamored to have his way, who watched over the workmen and bombarded both Richardson and Hay with accounts of their progress. When Clover went to Cambridge to nurse Dr. Hooper through his last days, Henry's letters pursued her with details of the house, and when she returned to Washington after her father's death, it was noted among her friends that she seemed to have lost interest in the house. General Anderson, who understood nothing, wrote to his son that November: "I am afraid I am bitterly revenged on the Adamses for the fun they had with my architect troubles, for their house is not nearly finished, and Mrs. Adams is suffering from nervous prostration. . . ."

By then, death was all around her, or, as Henry had written, "all my friends have mortal diseases." Clover was forty-two years old, and that is what it means to be forty-two, to be aware, more and more every day, that death is at hand, waiting. *Memento mori*. Once remote, once an abstraction, death could now strike suddenly and almost at random, as when James A. Garfield, who had barely reached fifty, encountered Guiteau. "As for the poor President, let us consider it as a fever, like his wife's," Henry had said at the time, "or let us suppose that a brick fell on him from a house-top. . . . Practically this is what has happened. He has been hit by one of the disregarded chances of life."

But the disregarded chances of life keep striking closer. One encounters a friend whose face is ashen, like Henry James, having

heard that he must return to Cambridge as soon as possible. One
receives a letter announcing that a sister-in-law has suddenly succumbed, leaving five young daughters orphaned. Then one knows,
as one did not know it before, that sickness is not simply something
from which one recovers but often something from which one does
not recover. And sickness, at forty-two, is everywhere. The flesh
is weak, its failings mysterious. Henry Hobson Richardson suddenly begins bleeding from the nose. Young Emily Beale has to
have an operation, and old Mrs. Bancroft hasn't left her room for
six months, and even the mighty James G. Blaine looks, as Clover
reported, "very white and strangely." And the old Adamses grew
steadily worse. "My father and mother drag on at Boston," Henry
wrote to Gaskell early in 1885, "my father broken to pieces but
placid and not unhappy; my mother almost worse off than he in
physical condition and neither happy nor placid." That November,
in reporting briefly that "my wife is unwell," he added that his
father was still deteriorating. "Nothing is left of him but the form,"
he wrote, "and the quiet and dignity of his manner. He rarely
leaves his room or his chair."

Sickness is not only a portent of death, however. Sickness is a
declaration of limits. Sickness is a closing of possibilities. At forty-
two, one has probably seen and known more—particularly more of
the good—than one will ever see or know again. Toward the future, one can look only with a certain fear. Henry was deeply afraid
of the mental deterioration that he had to watch in his father. He
dreaded every new signal of weakened concentration and failing
memory. Clover must have suffered from similar fears, though in
her case, the evidence lay in Grandmother Sturgis and Aunt Susan
Bigelow, and perhaps in memories of the honeymoon on the Nile.
To fear madness is in some ways a symptom of sanity; in other
ways, it is the first symptom of madness itself.

"One consequence of having no children," as Henry had written
almost a decade earlier, "is that husband and wife become very
dependent on each other and live very much together. This is my
case. . . ." Since Henry and Clover did depend very much on each
other, and did live very much together, the question of Clover's
suicide must inevitably come back to her life with Henry. While it
is important that she wrote to her father every Sunday morning, it

is hardly less important that she was with Henry every day of the week. If she became isolated from the society around her, it was because Henry himself was her society. If the conditions and circumstances of her life came to grate on her spirit, the conditions and circumstances were those that Henry had created for her. The apparent mystery of Clover's suicide has always derived from the suddenness of the stroke, the shattering of such a pleasant existence, the rejection of a life in which, as Eleanor Shattuck wrote, she "had all she wanted, all this world could give." But perhaps the mystery is based on false assumptions. According to one expert, no happily married woman ever commits suicide, and according to another, no suicide, for whatever reason, is ever sudden.

Few figures in all of American history are so enigmatic as Henry Adams. He might have been thinking of a self-portrait when he said of Jefferson that all other Presidents could be painted in a few broad strokes but that the squire of Monticello "could be painted only touch by touch, with a fine pencil, and the perfection of the likeness depended upon the shifting and uncertain flicker of its semi-transparent shadows." A writer of genius, a thinker of sharp perception, a political reformer of high ambition, Adams devoted much of his life to an almost willful cultivation of failure. It was he, he insisted, who had rejected the family professions of politics and law, who kept repeating that his journalism was worthless and his teaching meaningless. Some of this was a pose, of course, yet nonetheless sincere, for we eventually become, as has been said more than once, what we pretend to be. As a writer, finally, Henry produced several works of impenetrable scholarship, and two novels that he never publicly acknowledged, and then he spent nearly a decade getting mired down in a vast history that came to bore him. "My dreary American history," he called it.

According to the testimony of his many friends, and of the Hooper nieces who doted on him in his old age, Henry was a man of immense charm, of immense kindness, thoughtfulness, delicacy, sensibility, and wit. They preserved as scripture the hundreds and hundreds of his letters—one of the richest collections in American literature—in which he ranged from sweeping historical analysis to the affectionate celebration of a neighbor's newborn child. Yet there is another element that threads through these letters, an element that is usually called wit but is actually something else. Henry liked the form of American humor that uses a pose of mocking irony in order to sting and wound. He rarely finished a letter to one of his aristocratic English acquaintances without a gibe at English manners, or even a letter of condolence without some citation of his own losses. He made jokes about wars and the bankruptcies of friends and the assassinations of Presidents. There was a fundamental coldness about Henry Adams, coldness and hardness and selfishness. And destructiveness. "Hating vindictively, as I do, our whole fabric and conception of society . . ." he once wrote to Mrs. Cameron, "I shall be glad to see the whole thing destroyed and wiped away."

But he loved Clover. And Clover loved him. And though they both seem at times to have been equally crustacean, it was just another illustration of God's mysterious purposes that these two strange creatures, each swimming alone in the frozen oceans, should have managed to find each other, and recognize each other for what they were, and love each other. They hardly ever wrote to one another of their love, and so we have no idea of their secret words and secret gestures, but we get one brief, vivid, startling glimpse of their intimacy in a crude and envious description of them by Henry's brother Charles: "I cheered a little as I thought that I was at last leaving my much married brother and his doting spouse. At 7 [A.M.] I knocked the mature Henry out of the arms of his Clover, for he's always in clover now (joke! ha! ha!) and the wretched, long-faced little ass sat on the sofa yawning with a shawl wrapped around his wretched legs while I painfully worked down the shadow of a breakfast. . . ."

They were young then—still on their honeymoon—and still so new to each other that every discovery was a revelation. But it is one of the elements of marriage, for better or for worse, that every discovery is eventually made, even those that remain unspoken. Clover was not a beautiful woman, and she knew it. Occasionally, very occasionally, she joked about it, as when she wrote to her father a parody of a Washington society report: ". . . Mrs. Adams has a most queenly presence, an aquiline nose rendered less prominent by full cheeks and wealth of chin. . . . Jewels flashed from her raven tresses and she had a winning Beacon Street welcome for all." As a woman gets older, such humor becomes less and less amusing, and Henry showed no sign of being amused at all. On the occasion of George Eliot's marriage to the young John Cross, he remarked that it was "not easy to explain" why Cross should marry an older woman, "for most men of thirty or forty prefer youth, beauty, children and such things, to intellect in gray hairs."

There was gossip around Lafayette Square that Henry was not simply infatuated with the beautiful Mrs. Cameron, who was still in her twenties, and without a trace of gray hairs, but in love with her. There was even gossip that Henry was the father of Mrs. Cameron's baby daughter, Martha, who was born the following June. Jonathan Daniels, for one, has recorded in his memoir *The End of Innocence* that the affair was a "legend which lingered long after Adams was gone," and that Clover "understood" that Henry was in love with her neighbor. Daniels implies that this knowledge was a major element in the mysterious suicide. Henry later contributed his share to this legend by guardedly describing himself in the *Education* as a "wrinkled Tannhäuser," fully aware that his readers knew the Wagnerian hero to be a knight who had abandoned his faithful Elisabeth in order to pay court to Venus.

Such hints invite scholarly investigation, and Ernest Samuels has pursued the question of Martha Cameron's parentage with an almost Medieval scrupulosity. He determined, in an essay entitled "Henry Adams and the Gossip Mills," that since the baby was born on June 25, 1886, and since there was no sign of her being premature, she must have been conceived between September 26 and October 21, 1885. Henry Adams was at Beverly Farms until October 17, and since Congress didn't open until December, the Camerons were probably at their home in Donegal, Pennsylvania, until mid-November. Though Henry doted on the child, the evidence indicates that he was not her father. "The more I struggle for a reputation of vice," he remarked to Mrs. Cameron some years later, "the more I am conspicuous as a pattern of sexagenarian respectability."

But what good did such respectability do Clover? She would have taken it for granted. It would have been beneath her to ask Henry about whatever rumors might be circulating. It would have been beneath her even to suspect him of any wrong. But at the same time, she knew—if only from the evidence of *Esther*—that he was too interested in Mrs. Cameron, cared too much about her, for anyone to believe the denials that were never requested and never made. That knowledge, to a woman as proud as Clover, was almost as bad as the knowledge of an actual affair. Nothing had happened, nothing would happen, but the golden bowl had a crack in it, and nothing could ever make it whole again.

Clover was to be trapped, then, just as Henry was trapped, in the prison of their own creation, the prison designed by the most distinguished of architects and furnished with all the treasures they had brought from Europe, the Moorish leather, the Japanese screens, the Turners and the Reynolds and Blake's demented Nebuchadnezzar eating grass. They would be trapped for ever and ever on the very edge of Lafayette Square, in full view of the White House, that citadel first inhabited by John and Abigail Adams, which Henry and Clover would never enter except as reluctant visitors, self-conscious, ever critical of the deplorable furnishings and the vulgarity of the inhabitants. In their own beautiful house, the chairs were specially selected for their small size, so that the "little Adamses," as James affectionately called them, would always feel comfortable and at ease, and their visitors would always feel clumsy and awkward, larger than life.

The logic of Clover's suicide may inexorably bring us back to her life with Henry, but suicides sometimes have a logic all their own. Or rather, they may derive, like madness itself, less from logic than from biology.

In the spring following Clover's death, a year after Dr. Hooper's death, Whitman Gurney suddenly fell ill and had to give up all his academic work. "Mr. Gurney is as serene under all these mysterious examinations and 'thumpings' as possible . . ." Ellen Gurney wrote to a friend, "and doesn't allow me even any illusions in his unflinching love of the truth and wishes to have day light, electric light and other light thrown if there is anything to be inspected in any corner." The doctors diagnosed pernicious anemia. Gurney quietly wasted away, and by autumn he was dead. Ellen shuddered and then took hold. "Well, all is right—as he would always say— and 'the past secure'—and I now would not dare to wish, if I could, to have anything other than it is," she wrote. "A look back—19 years—all seems as if it must be part of some great plan—and very wonderfully do things fit—and I mean to try and be patient and not . . . ask solutions to questions that can't be answered."

The great plan was indeed remarkable. Ellen and Clover, having grown up together and gone to school together, both married Harvard professors who were older than they. Both were childless. Both joined together in nursing Dr. Hooper on his deathbed. Both were stricken by his loss. Ellen, "the exquisite Mrs. Gurney," as James called her, seems always to have been the more balanced of the two, the more practical and sensible. Her letters, the few that we have, express a gentle stoicism, a willingness to accept her fate. But the fate was too hard. Not only her father's death but her sister's suicide and then her husband's fatal illness. The following November, on a Saturday evening, she went out of her house and wandered down along the tracks of the Fitchburg Railroad, near the West Cambridge depot. Perhaps she was confused in the darkness—"Her mind was seriously affected by reason of her husband's death," the *Boston Evening Transcript* later reported—more likely not. A passenger train came rumbling past. Ellen stood in front of it.

When searchers came looking for her, they found her lying beside the track, badly injured. She murmured to them that it had been an accident, that she had not meant to do it, that nobody was to blame. They quieted her and took her to Massachusetts General Hospital, and there she lay all that night, dying. The next day, Sunday, it was over. "Witnessing the final extinction of that delightful home was one of the saddest experiences I have ever had," Godkin wrote to William James after attending Ellen's funeral. "What made it worse was my belief that if someone sufficiently near to be entitled to do it, could have taken hold of her last November when I last saw her, and removed her from the scene of her sorrow and saved her from her lonely brooding, in those two empty houses, she might have been saved. But as Omar Khayyám says—

> ". . . *He that tossed you down into the field*
> He *knows about it all*—HE *knows*—*HE knows!*"

And then Ned, amiable, affectionate Ned, perhaps a little solemn, but good-hearted, he too cracked. The accumulation of losses was unbearable—his mother and father, his wife, both his sisters. He simply took to his bed and lay there numbly for two months, suffering from what Henry called a "long and trying nervous illness." Somehow, though, Ned managed to hold himself together. Perhaps it was simply his destiny to raise his five daughters, Dr. Hooper's only grandchildren. Perhaps it was his destiny to manage

Harvard's vast treasures (estimated even then at $10 million). So for a quarter of a century, Ned Hooper raised funds and invested funds and harvested the funds that he had invested, and even became, on his own, something of a connoisseur and patron of the arts, a collector of Post-Impressionist paintings, a pillar of Cambridge. But the demons were always there, the shadows under the rafters, the rustling behind the cellar doors, the dark powers that Cambridge has never admitted into its cathedral, and finally, in the spring of 1901, Ned Hooper plunged from the third-floor window of his house at 49 Beacon Street.

"His groans attracted the attention of members of the Puritan Club . . ." the *Evening Transcript* reported. "One of the attachés of the club . . . found him conscious but very weak, and bleeding freely about the head. This man and others carried him into the house." The *Transcript* said that Ned might have been killed instantly if the ground where he fell had not been softened by the rainfall of the previous day. It added that he had been confined to his room under a nurse's care for the past ten days. "Mr. Hooper's illness," it said, "was brought on by overwork, and practically amounted to nervous prostration." The newspaper went on to speculate that he might have "jumped from the window with suicidal intent" during a "temporary mental derangement," but it hastily added that "this theory was scouted by members of the family and the doctors." The doctors, particularly, "said that there was no evidence of any such thing." As evidence to the contrary, the newspaper said that if Ned had really jumped from the window with suicidal intent, he "would have been impaled on the spikes of the fence which runs along the Spruce Street side of the building. This fence is only about five feet away from the side of the structure [but] he was found directly below the window." Nobody suggested another alternative—that Ned Hooper might have aimed himself at the spikes and then succumbed, in the last moment, to fear.

The next day, Ned could remember nothing. The newspapers helpfully suggested that he had simply opened the window for some fresh air, and become dizzy, and fallen. It was only a temporary reprieve. Two months later, at the McLean Hospital in Belmont, which was and still is the main institution for the treatment of mental illness in the Cambridge area, he was pronounced dead of pneumonia, after what was officially described as "a short illness." "It is another part of myself that I lose," Henry wrote to

Mabel Hooper LaFarge, "and I know quite well that I must go on without it. But it long since ceased to matter much."

So if it was the circumstances of Clover's life that drove her to suicide, what was it that drove Ellen Gurney under the railroad train, and drove Ned Hooper, almost two decades later, out the window?

There have been many attempts over the years to create a whole theology of suicide. Thus Kirillov in Dostoevsky's *The Possessed:* "Every one who wants the supreme freedom must dare to kill himself. . . . He who dares to kill himself is God." And Wittgenstein: "If suicide is allowed then everything is allowed. If anything is not allowed then suicide is not allowed."

To the women of Boston of a century ago, however, God did not express himself in syllogisms. "What a pity to hide it," Alice James said of a hushed-up suicide of a friend. "Every educated person who kills himself does something toward lessening the superstition. It's bad that it's so untidy. There's no denying that, for one bespatters one's friends morally as well as physically, taking them so much more into one's secret than they want to be taken. But how heroic to be able to suppress one's vanity to the extent of confessing that the game is too hard."

That suppression of vanity, in turn, was another self-deception, for the game was not too hard. For Alice James, as for Clover, wealthy, intelligent, gifted, loved, the game should have been easy. Yet the missing element in all analyses of the causes of suicide is that they become causes mainly because of a lack of will to resist. Neither the death of Dr. Hooper nor the dark Sturgis heritage nor yet the circumstances of Clover's life provide in themselves an explanation for Clover's suicide. They were injuries and failures. They contributed to the lifelong erosion of her spirit, but the death of that spirit came from its inability to fight back. Like so many other women of her time and place and caste, Clover had been educated to think and believe and experience but not to fight. The only weapon given to her, apart from the powerful sense of superiority, was that of laughter, and laughter does not always provide protection. Laughter can become an evasion. Laughter can even become an expression of pain.

Otherwise, there is only silence. In the silent attic where Clover's

books are stored, there lies a copy of the New Testament in Greek
and Latin. It is inscribed by Henry and dated January 4, 1877, the
year the Adamses moved from Boston to Washington. Then or at
some time in the later years of her life, Clover wrote in the back of
the book a cruelly brief series of commandments on how to survive:

Fuge—late—tace

Meaning, "Flee—endure—be silent."
Underneath that, she wrote a similar warning against all conflict:

Aux coeurs blessés
l'ombre et le silence

A bit precious, perhaps, but elegant. To fight would have been
coarse, unworthy of a lady. Clover was born and raised to be a
lady, and she died a lady. And alone.

Alice James, with a rather similar background, had dreamed first
of murdering her father and then of committing suicide, and when
her father gave her permission for suicide, she had to think of some
other form of self-destruction, so she became an invalid. She suffered from various illnesses variously diagnosed: "rheumatic gout,"
"spinal neurosis," "cardiac complications," and "nervous hyperes-
thesia." Her brother Henry diagnosed her illnesses as "the only
solution for her of the practical problem of life." So it was almost
with relief that she finally learned that she was dying of cancer,
that the game, as she insisted, was too hard. She died a virgin, at
the age of forty-four, "a flaccid virgin," as she described herself in
her diary, but she was dearly loved in her last years by her companion, Katherine Loring, and Katherine Loring showed her, too,
late, some of her life's mistakes. "One day," Alice James wrote in
her diary, "when my shawls were falling off to the left, my cush-
ions falling out to the right and the duvet off my knees, one of those
crises of misery in short, which are all in the day's work for an
invalid, Kath. exclaimed, 'What an awful pity it is that you can't
say *damn*.' I agreed with her from my heart. . . ."

17

EPILOGUE

THE VIRGIN OF CHARTRES

The proper study of mankind is woman. . . .

HENRY ADAMS

THE GREAT OAKEN DOOR opens into darkness. A sound of shuffling feet, the blinded moving slowly forward. A smell of dust and mold, of old things in perpetual storage. Then suddenly a stabbing shaft of organ music, not a stately chorale, not Bach, but wild improvisations, foaming, spilling light through the musty darkness. Impassioned harmonies in extravagant keys like B major and B flat minor. Diminished sevenths. Then a violent pause, then a still more violent cadenza. The feet shuffle forward toward the rows of guttering candles in the chapel dedicated to Our Lady, and overhead, as blindness begins to fade, the great rose windows shine like mountain skies.

Make a joyful noise unto the Lord. The organist is simply one among many young musicians who have come to Chartres for a *concours internationale.* On Sunday, they will all perform their selections of Handel, Liszt, Widor, but now they are just practicing on the invisible throne, testing the sounds that seem to come from everywhere. The tourists with cameras accept them as part of Chartres, the kneeling pilgrims in black shawls accept the tourists, and Chartres, nearing the end of the twentieth century, accepts all things.

To say that Chartres is the glory of the twelfth century, and that the twelfth century is the glory of European civilization, is simply to emphasize the modern history of the church. The great cathedral that now stands there is the fifth Christian church to stand on the same site. Before that, there was a Roman temple, where the pious worshipped a wooden figure of the mother-goddess, and before that, before the Virgin Mary was even born, Chartres served as the principal meeting place of the Druids. Before that, nobody knows. The excavations of the vast crypt under the cathedral were abandoned in 1901, and what lies there remains, in the words of the guide, *terre inexplorée.*

The excavators did find, however, the *puits des Saints-Forts,* a pit more than 100 feet deep, into which the early Christian martyrs of Chartres were thrown. There it is, a dark hole that once echoed with cries of terror, silent now. Tradition tells, too, of a wooden figure of the Roman mother-goddess, which was transformed into Our Lady Under the Earth. It was venerated in this subterranean shrine until the French Revolution, when mobs stormed in here and smashed the stone faces of the saints and seized Our Lady Under the Earth and burnt her. A nineteenth-century copy of the figure stands here now, and women kneel before her.

It was Henry Adams' passionate conviction that the Virgin Mary built the Cathedral of Chartres. The modern eye sees violation everywhere. The *Place de la Cathedrale* is filled with Renaults and Citroëns. Busloads of tourists arrive from beyond the Rhine, and signs in their own language instruct them where to go. *Treffpunkt-hier.* A traveler who pauses to rest on one of the benches set among the beds of orange zinnias notices that the wooden planks are getting worn, and so the civic authorities have covered them with brown plastic sheaths that have been painted to resemble wood.

The blackened walls of stone are being cleaned. Ladders poke up into the eaves of the south porch and two workmen in blue uniforms reach upward to scrape at the eroded faces of the angels. High above the restorations, beyond the reach of the workmen, the wildness of the twelfth century survives in the form of little yellow flowers known as *giroflées sauvages,* which sprout recklessly in the crevices between the giant stones, sprout, flower, and die, all untended.

At night, when the moon shines on the dark cathedral and the heavy oaken doors are locked, the organists can still be faintly heard inside, practicing their scales.

Chartres accepts all things.

Guilt was what had ravaged Henry Adams ever since that day when he found Clover lying by the fireplace. Every self-exculpating voice of reason tried to blame the disaster on some kind of impersonal and unjudging destiny. "Fate," as Henry had written to Godkin, "has at last smashed the life out of me. . . ." But there were other voices that could not be stilled, voices whispering that no woman kills herself for nothing, that not even the maddest act of self-destruction is without cause.

In past centuries, it was the custom to defile and mutilate the bodies of those who had committed suicide, to cut off their hands, to set them adrift in rivers, to bury them at crossroads, with stones over their faces, all these procedures having been devised to prevent them from returning to haunt the living. In more enlightened times, the living feel they must accept their responsibilities to the ghosts that they deny. No accusation can be so cruel as self-accusation, no indictment so punishing as an indictment without hope of trial, and thus without hope of ultimate acquittal. Henry Adams destroyed all the journals that he had been keeping, as his father and forefathers required, since his boyhood. "I am horrified," he wrote in a new and more cursory journal, "to have left such a record so long in existence." And again: "I mean to leave no record that can be obliterated.

Flight is the only answer, unthinking, unseeing flight, and Henry Adams, like another Orestes, another Don Alvaro in the *Forza del Destino*, fled. Taking along John LaFarge as someone to talk to, he fled all the way to Japan, where he was much impressed by the imperial tombs at Nikko, and particularly by the statue of the merciful goddess Kwannon. "I have been and am living with not a thought," he wrote to Hay, "but from minute to minute. . . ."

On his return to America that fall, Henry once again encountered death. Gurney died, and then Richardson, and then it came

338

time for poor old Charles Francis Adams, seventy-nine years of age, and weary of everything. "Political preferment I do not want," he had written in his diary, when he was still able to keep a diary, "power and patronage have no charms for me,—social distinction and excitement I am not adapted to getting, nor in the past has it afforded me anything I now look back upon with satisfaction." On November 16, 1886, with his four sons dutifully assembled around his bedside, Charles Francis Adams quietly died.

His widow, Abigail, was miserable, an invalid, and ever subject to fits of temperamental depression, and so Henry stayed home for a time, working numbly to complete his *History*. "I write history as though it were serious, five hours a day," he observed to Hay, "and when my hand and head get tired, I step out into the rose beds and watch my favorite roses."

And so, finally, it was done. On September 16, 1888, he noted that the basic narrative had been finished, and just as he had once sat in Gibbon's place on the steps of Santa Maria di Ara Coeli in Rome, now he could scarcely help recalling Gibbon's solemn description of having written his closing lines just before midnight in the summer house in his garden: "After laying down my pen, I took several turns in a *berceau*, or covered walk of acacias. . . . The air was temperate, the sky was serene, the silver orb of the moon was reflected from the waters, and all nature was silent." Adams inescapably felt, as he had before, that the phantom of his predecessor was cruelly difficult to evoke in Quincy. "In imitation of Gibbon," he wrote in his new journal, "I walked in the garden among the yellow and red autumn flowers, blazing in sunshine, and meditated. My meditations were too painful to last. The contrast between my beginning and end is something Gibbon never conceived. . . . In the midst of gloom and depression I have come to the last page of my history. I wish I cared but I do not care a straw. . . ."

The following spring, just as Henry was completing a few final touches on the *History*, Abigail Adams, aged eighty-one, finally went mad, had to be quieted with drugs, and soon lapsed into a coma. "She died at half past ten o'clock, Thursday evening, June 6," the historian noncommittally noted. "I was present. We buried her yesterday afternoon by my father's side at Mt. Wollaston."

339

So the inescapable sense of guilt for the parents' death had to be
added to the sense of guilt for Clover's death, and in his desperation, Henry turned, more openly than before, to the beautiful
young Lizzie Cameron. They had always flirted, of course, but
they had done their best to make it all seem harmless. Even Clover
had had to accept that. They were all friends. Even Senator Don
Cameron.

Henry was devoted to the Camerons' infant daughter. "I have
made love to Martha Cameron," he wrote one spring day in 1888.
"And by dint of incessant bribery and attention have quite won her
attachment." He was hardly less attentive to the two-year-old's
beguiling mother. Almost every day, he appeared at her salon on
the far side of Lafayette Square to indulge in a slow mint julep. He
serenaded her with Swinburnian verses that trembled on the edge
of confession:

> . . . *and even this soft air of the terrace throbs*
> *With some low moan—sigh of a heart that sobs.*

They seem, however, to have been people of principle. They
decided to stop seeing each other, at least for a time. "I am not old
enough to be a tame cat," he subsequently wrote to her. "You are
too old to accept me in any other character."

Once again, he fled. To Hawaii, this time, and then to the South
Seas. His regular letters to Mrs. Cameron, and to Hay, came from
increasingly remote and exotic outposts, from Apia, in Samoa;
from Vaiale, Falealili, Papeete, Papara, Opunohu, Hitiaa. . . .

After more than a year of wandering, he returned to Europe,
where Mrs. Cameron had betaken herself, and found that he was
still a victim of his infatuation. He may have made some kind of an
advance to her; if so, she turned him away. Or perhaps the encounter involved nothing more than a series of possibilities. Some years
later, he wrote to her that he had heard "a story" about the two of
them and added: "I am so damn respectable that the story would
improve the social position of both of us, and I wanted no better
than to figure in that immoral role. Unfortunately no one will ever
believe it." And again: "I am much the older and presumably the
one of us two who is responsible for whatever mischief can happen.

. . . No matter how much I may efface myself or how little I may ask, I must always make more demands on you than you can gratify, and you must always have the consciousness that whatever I may profess, I want more than I can have. Sooner or later the end of such a situation is estrangement, with more or less disappointment and bitterness."

Mrs. Cameron told her admirer, finally, that he should find himself a good woman and marry her. "In my whole life," Henry answered, "I met only one woman whom I wanted to marry, and I married her."

He started wandering again, to Scotland, to Mexico, to the Swiss Alps. The Hays invited him to accompany them on a trip up the Nile. With some trepidations about revisiting the site of his honeymoon with Clover a quarter century ago, he agreed. As he had feared, the old wound tore open. "I knew it would be a risky thing," he wrote to Mrs. Cameron, "but it came so suddenly that before I could catch myself, I was unconsciously wringing my hands and the tears rolled down in the old way, and I had to get off by myself for a few minutes to prevent Helen [Hay] from thinking me more mad than usual. . . . A few hours wore off the nervous effect, and now I can stand anything, although of course there is hardly a moment when some memory of twenty-five years ago is not brought to my mind. The Nile does not change. . . ."

Throughout all these wanderings, Henry could not rid himself of a kind of self-hatred. He had, he wrote, "a little of the sense of being a sort of ugly, bloated, purplish blue and highly venomous hairy tarantula which catches and devours Presidents, senators, diplomats, congressmen and cabinet-officers, and knows the flavor of every generation and every country in the civilized world." Out of that feeling of loathing, combined with too much knowledge, Adams developed an almost supernatural dread. He sensed that he and all the world were spinning toward the abyss. "I apprehend for the next hundred years," he wrote to Brooks, "an ultimate, colossal, cosmic collapse; but not on any of our old lines. My belief is that science is to wreck us, and that we are like monkeys monkeying with a loaded shell; we don't in the least know or care where our practically infinite energies come from or will bring us to."

And again: "It's a queer sensation, this secret belief that one stands on the brink of the world's greatest catastrophe. . . . I have to get over it as I can, and hide, for fear of being sent to an asylum. . . ."

Adams had just finished complaining to Mrs. Cameron of "this dreary, eternal sense of my own moral death," when, as he later wrote in the *Education*, he "was rescued, as often before, by a woman." Mrs. Henry Cabot Lodge, a small and beautiful creature with large, violet eyes, invited him in the summer of 1895 to join the senator and their two sons on a tour through the northern cathedral towns of France, from Amiens to Chartres, by way of Rouen and Caen, Bayeux, St. Lo, Coutances—Coutances, that strange, slender creation that still towers over the cluttered market-place that was wrecked by the bombardments of World War II. Its unique clusters of spires are, as Adams was to write in *Mont Saint Michel and Chartres*, "as simple and severe as the spear of a man-at-arms," and its central "lantern" tower richly merits Adams' description: "so firm, so fixed, so serious, so defiant."

Adams was startled, almost shocked, by the towers of Coutances. "The Norman cathedral there was something quite new to me, and humbled my proud spirit a good bit . . ." he wrote to Clover's niece, Mabel Hooper. "I thought I knew Gothic. Caen, Bayeux, and Coutances were a chapter I never opened before, and which pleased my jaded appetite. They are austere. . . . They are worked with a feeling and a devotion that turns even Amiens green with jealousy. I knew before pretty well all that my own life and time was worth, but I never before felt quite so utterly stood on as I did in the Cathedral at Coutances. . . . The squirming devils under the feet of the stone Apostles looked uncommonly like me and my generation."

In subsequently writing to Hay of the same experience, Adams imagined himself in the role of his own Norman ancestors. He himself had built the cathedral of Coutances, "and my soul is still built into it. I can almost remember the faith that gave me energy, and the scared boldness that made my towers seem to me so daring. . . . Nearly eight hundred years have passed since I made the fatal mistake of going to England, and since then I have never done anything in the world that can begin to compare in the perfection of its spirit and art with my cathedral of Coutances. I am as sure of it as I am of death."

In February of 1901, when Adams returned from Paris to Washington,—"to my happy home at Rock Creek where I can take off my flesh and sit on my stone bench in the sun, to eternity"—he wrote to Mrs. Cameron that he had written a long poem, a prayer to the Virgin of Chartres. "It is not poetry," he hastily added, "and it is not very like verse, and it will not amuse you to read; but it occupies me to write; which is something—at sixty-three. . . ."

He was perhaps justified in his valuation of his offering, but it is interesting to see how he had already adopted the tone of prayer that was to become the tone of the most impassioned pages in *Mont Saint Michel and Chartres*. It is interesting, too, that he had already worked out quite fully the antithesis between the virgin and the dynamo, which was to provide the central argument of the *Education* and the connection between the last two works. Adams opens his poem by imagining himself a survivor of the twelfth century, a man who has debated with Abelard and prayed with Saint Bernard, "And when Saint Louis made his penitence, / I followed barefoot where the King had been." He confesses that he and all mankind have wandered off course, abandoned the medieval faith, followed the lures of reason and ended as worshippers of the machine. There follows a strange "prayer to the dynamo," which ends with a kind of shriek of destructive fury:

> *Seize, then the Atom! rack his joints!*
> *Tear out of him his secret spring. . . !*

Cutting short these metallic profanities, Adams turns again to the Virgin and begs for a restoration of the lost faith:

> *Help me to see! not with my mimic sight—*
> *With yours! which carried radiance like the sun. . . .*
> *Help me to know! not with my mocking art—*
> *With you who knew yourself unbound by laws. . . .*
> *Help me to feel! not with my insect sense, —*
> *With yours that felt all life alive in you;*
> *Infinite heart beating at your expense;*
> *Infinite passion breathing the breath you drew. . . !*

343

Adams sent one copy of the poem to Mrs. Cameron, "to put in your fire," and then he hid the manuscript in a wallet.

Now there was work to be done. Ever since the autumn of 1898, he had been writing and rewriting a book that he referred to as *The Miracles of the Virgin*, and in about a year he had finished enough to enable him to tell Martha Cameron, to whom he had read many pages, that "St. Thomas and the Virgin have got married." But early in 1901, he put the draft aside and spent much of the year in a renewed study of science, "working up to date," he said, "after twenty years of neglect." He pored over the reports of the Geological Survey; he interrogated eminent scientists about new developments in aeronautics. Not until the spring of 1902 could he report on his new labors on Chartres that he was "perfectly square with the Virgin Mary, having finished and wholly rewritten the whole volume." He was still not finished. That summer, he went on with his revisions in Scotland, where Senator Cameron had acquired a castle, and the following year he complained that the manuscript had "swelled and swelled to the size of an ox." Not until January of 1904 did he finally send it to the printer, whom he paid $1,000 for a private edition of 100 copies.

He adopted the rather arch pose of pretending that his searching study of medieval art was simply a guidebook for his nieces. He began *Mont Saint Michel and Chartres* by playfully citing an Elizabethan poet who declared that any future reader would become "my son in wishes," then adding that such a relationship would be too close in modern times. "The utmost that any writer could hope of his readers now is that they should consent to regard themselves as nephews, and even then he would expect only a more or less civil refusal from most of them." Nieces are more agreeable. "The relationship, too, is convenient and easy, capable of being anything or nothing. . . . The following pages, then, are written for nieces. . . ."

Adams was hardly exaggerating. He was surrounded by nieces, the five daughters of his two older brothers and the five daughters of Ned Hooper, with all of whom he maintained a spirited correspondence. At the time of his epiphany in Coutances, the Hooper girls ranged in age from twenty-three to sixteen, and the former Harvard professor found that it delighted him to lecture them and take them on tours, to teach them whatever he could. In 1897, Ned brought all five of his daughters to spend the summer in a house that Henry had rented outside Paris. "One memorable summer for the nieces," as Mabel Hooper later recalled, "the Uncle set up a household with them at St.-Germain, and taught them French history under the venerable cedars of the Pavillon d'Angouleme, and rode about the green forest-alleys of St.-Germain and Marly." Adams doted on the nieces. "The girls have been very happy," he wrote to a friend, "which is equivalent to saying that I have been very happy, for I find that my happiness is wholly dependent on those around me." And again: "My castle here is a scene of constant orgy of young girls, all the girl's-schools of Boston being let loose, I should say; and here and there a young man; but from these I gather little."

The device of a guide for nieces permitted Adams to deal with the most solemn subjects in a less than solemn way, to turn aside with a smile or a shrug whenever he approached too close to the awesome. Indeed, it had taken him several years to arrive at the form he wanted. He originally described the book to Mrs. Cameron as "my *Travels in France with Nothing to Say.*" At one point, he even thought of transforming his ideas into some kind of theatrical work, perhaps "a drama of the Second Crusade, with Queen Eleanor of Guienne for heroine and myself to act Saint Bernard and reprove her morals."

"What I do want," he wrote to Gaskell, "is to write a five-act drama, of the twelfth century, to beat Macbeth." What he did not want—"not technical knowledge; not accurate information; not correct views on history, art, or religion; not anything that can possibly be useful or instructive; but only a sense of what those centuries had to say"—what he did not want was an academic history of the kind that his academic critics periodically scolded him for having failed to write. The nieces thus served as a kind of check on Adams' characteristic tendency toward scholarly abstractions. When he finished his chapter on Thomas Aquinas, he sent it to one of his honorary nieces, Martha Cameron, adding: "I want [her to] tell me what she doesn't understand, so I can correct it." The girl was then fourteen.

The nieces are appropriate listeners, finally, because *Mont Saint*

Michel is, among other things, a book about women. It is Adams' thesis that medieval civilization evolved along a kind of arc, emerging from the warrior-priest societies of the eleventh century, represented by the *Song of Roland* and the massive fortress-church of Mont Saint Michel, to the gentler beauties of Chartres, "the finest thing in the world," and the scholastic constructions of St. Thomas Aquinas. By the end of the thirteenth century, the arc was curving downward toward the rationalism and commercialism that conventional observers regard as the glories of the Renaissance. Henry originally adapted this theory from the studies of his cranky and difficult younger brother Brooks, whom he once described as "a kind of exaggerated me." The two argued endlessly—Henry sometimes literally fled to avoid Brooks' persistent questioning—about Brooks' basic theory that all human history fluctuates between societies dominated by warriors, priests, and artists (and inspired by fear) and those dominated by merchants (and inspired by greed). When Brooks finally worked out his theory, brilliantly, in *The Law of Civilization and Decay* (1896), Henry graciously wrote him: "If I wanted to write any book, it would be the one you have written."*

At the apex of the medieval arc was that magic century from about 1150 to 1250, when the builders of Europe erected scores of cathedrals in honor of Our Lady, and built them in the style that Adams celebrated for "flinging its passion against the sky." He concentrated on the Gothic churches partly because he believed in the idea that "architecture [is] an expression of energy," but in searching for the direction of that energy, he decided that "the art leads always to the woman."

As a general principle, Adams restated his belief that "Nature regards the female as the essential, the male as the superfluity of her world." He suggested that "the best starting-point for study of the Virgin would be a practical acquaintance with bees, and especially with queen bees." Apart from natural principles, however, Adams found that women had acquired a position of unusual preeminence in twelfth-century society. "The superiority of the

---

* Poor Brooks, who had been tormented unmercifully by Charles and John when they were boys, was deeply grateful to Henry. "But for you, I never should have printed it," he wrote. "Most of what has attracted attention has been the result of your criticism. The form is, I think, wholly yours. . . . From the old days in England when I was a boy, you have been my good genius."

woman was not a fancy but a fact," he wrote. "Man's business was to fight or hunt or feast. . . .[He was] often absent from home for months together. The woman ruled the household and the workshop; cared for the economy; supplied the intelligence and dictated the taste. Her ascendancy was secured by her alliance with the Church, into which she sent her most intelligent children. . . . Both physically and mentally the woman was robust, as the men often complained, and she did not greatly resent being treated as a man."

If the art led always to the woman, the study of women led Adams always to Our Lady of Chartres. "The Virgin of Chartres was the greatest of all queens, but the most womanly of women . . ." he wrote. And again: "The Queen Mother was as majestic as you like; she was absolute; she could be stern; she was not above being angry; but she was still a woman, who loved grace, beauty, ornament—her toilette, robes, jewels;—who considered the arrangements of her palace with attention, and liked both light and colour. . . . She was the greatest artist, as she was the greatest philosopher and musician and theologist, that ever lived on earth, except her Son, Who, at Chartres, is still an Infant under her guardianship."

Adams freely acknowledges that this view of the Virgin violates orthodox Christianity. He adds, however, that "the worship of the Virgin never was strictly orthodox; but Chartres was hers before it ever belonged to the Church." Having proclaimed the supremacy of faith over reason and art over logic, Adams proceeds to argue that the Virgin herself designed and built the cathedral of Chartres for herself. "Every day, as the work went on," he writes, "the Virgin was present, directing the architects." And so, when the work is finally done, Adams imagines himself (and his nieces) among the congregation of worshippers. "There is heaven! And Mary looks down from it, into her church, where she sees us on our knees, and knows each one of us by name. There she actually is—not in symbol or in fancy, but in person, descending on her errands of mercy." The imagined scene was too awesome for Adams to maintain his attitude of avuncular irony. In a rare outburst of emotion, he tried to escape from almost two decades of what he had called his "posthumous" life. "People who suffer beyond the formulas of expression—who are crushed into silence, and beyond pain—want no display of emotion—no bleeding heart —no weeping at the foot of the Cross—no hysterics—no phrases! They want to see God, and to know that He is watching over His own."

Henry was not concerned with Christian orthodoxy, of course, any more than he was concerned with historic details (". . . not accurate information, not correct views . . ."). What he was trying to express was a vision, radiant in the jeweled colors of Chartres, and at the center of that vision was a woman, whom he called the Virgin, the greatest of all queens, ruling over the greatest of courts. To observe that this Virgin was not the true Virgin of Chartres but simply an invention of Henry Adams' is to argue the obvious. He himself was trying to say as much when he wrote a rather strange letter to Mrs. Cameron, declaring that he could be contented in a cloister "if only I still knew a God to pray to, or better yet a Goddess." He added: "As I grow older I see that all the human interest and power that religion ever had was in the mother and child and I would have nothing to do with a church that did not offer both. There you are again! You see how the thought always turns back to you."

That was very gallant, and a number of biographers have been tempted into portraying the Virgin of Chartres as a kind of idealization of Elizabeth Cameron, but she does not fit the role. She was pretty and flirtatious and sympathetic but hardly the regal figure that Adams saw in the shadows of the apse. More important, he had no reason to regard his friend as a figure sitting in judgment, and that is an essential aspect of his view of the Virgin. God—even in the redeeming form of Christ—must carry out the law, Adams argued. "In that law, no human error or weakness could exist; by its essence it was infinite, eternal, immutable. There was no crack and no cranny in the system, through which human frailty could hope for escape. . . ."

There was no escape, in other words, by appeal to the logic of God's justice. There was no escape at all except by prayer to the Virgin. "Mary concentrated in herself the whole rebellion of man against fate; the whole protest against divine law . . . the whole unutterable fury of human nature beating itself against the walls of its prison-house." To those who had been condemned by reason and justice, only the Virgin offered salvation. "She was above law; she took feminine pleasure in turning hell into an ornament. . . .

This was the reason, beyond all other excellent reasons, why men loved and adored her with a passion such as no other deity has ever inspired: and why we, although utter strangers to her, are not far from getting down on our knees and praying to her still."

That passion for exoneration, for absolution, was far beyond anything that could be fulfilled by Elizabeth Cameron, or perhaps even by the Virgin of Chartres. Perhaps nobody could grant Henry Adams that absolution. But the woman of whom he was asking it could hardly have been anyone other than the woman he had found lying before the fireplace—Clover, dead these fifteen years, Clover uncomplaining, unreproachful, unaccusing, and now no more than a shriveled skeleton in Rock Creek Cemetery.

"Life becomes at last a mere piece of acting," Henry wrote to his brother Brooks. "One goes on by habit, playing more or less clumsily that one is still alive. . . . We are *ancien régime;* we learn to smile while gout racks us. . . . We get out of bed in the morning all broken up, without nerves, color or temper, and by noon we are joking with young women about the play. One lives in constant company with diseased hearts, livers, kidneys and lungs; one shakes hands with certain death at closer embrace. . . ."

There was still work to be done yet, a kind of sequel to *Mont Saint Michel*, which would contrast the spiritual unity of the thirteenth century with the chaos of the twentieth, and which he would call, with a wonderful pretense of modest objectivity, *The Education of Henry Adams*. Remembering everything, the lilacs and peaches and sea-marsh smells of Quincy, the unforgiving scowl of President Grant, the austere towers of Coutances, he continued his doomed search for enlightenment up until the death of his oldest friend. "One warm evening in early July, as Adams was strolling down to dine under the trees at Armenonville, he learned that Hay was dead. He expected it; on Hay's account he was even satisfied to have his friend die, as we would all die if we could, in full fame. . . ." His only conclusion was to wonder if they might meet somehow on the centenary of their births, 1938, and "find a world that sensitive and timid natures could regard without a shudder." It is hard to imagine what Adams and Hay might have said to one another in 1938, the year of the *Anschluss* and the confrontation between Hitler and Chamberlain at Munich.

But Henry believed in prophecy, and in the application of scientific principles to human history. Having published his *Education* in 1907, in another private edition of 100 copies, he struggled on with his search for formulas that would reinterpret the past and predict the future in terms of the flow of energy (*The Rule of Phase Applied to History*) until something suddenly snapped. Broke. As when John Quincy Adams had slumped to the floor of the House and had to be carried out into the Rotunda and could only bring himself to say, "I am composed." One theory is that Henry suffered a strange sort of aftershock to the sinking of the *Titanic*. Henry had been booked to sail on its first return journey from New York to Southampton. Nine days after the sinking, booked now on the *Olympic*, he was dining alone in his fortress when his butler William heard the sound of a fall. He hurried in and found the tiny figure of Henry Adams lying on the floor.

"I can't get up," Henry managed to say. "You will have to help me."

The physical paralysis from the stroke was not severe, but after a week of apparent recovery, his mind faltered. He began muttering incomprehensibly. Occasionally, he lapsed into delirium. He asked to send a message to a friend who had long been dead. He thought that his mother had died on the *Titanic*. In lucid moments, he expressed dread of the mental senility that had overtaken both his father and his mother. He even tried, just like Ned Hooper, to throw himself out the window. But Henry was small and frail at seventy-four, easily rescued and put back in bed. And then he began to recover. Mrs. Cameron, still his close friend after all these years, came to take care of him. Henry James wrote solicitous letters praising "your great resource of contemplation, speculation, resignation. . . ." And soon Henry was out riding among the flowering dogwoods that he loved. He survived another five years of comfortable resignation, a tiny, white-bearded figure, his active life and work both finished. He had become, as he once described himself, "only a fluttering and venerable white moth [flickering] from perch to perch."

One day, March 27, 1918, when Henry did not come downstairs for breakfast, his housekeeper went upstairs to rouse him. "They found him asleep forever," as Mabel Hooper LaFarge later wrote, "with a look of thoughtful interest—almost of curiosity upon his face, as if this new journey was of more import to him than any other he had taken."

Only after Adams' death did someone open his wallet and find there, hidden for almost two decades, his prayer to the Virgin of Chartres: "Help me to see. . . . Help me to know. . . . Help me to feel. . . .

> Help me to bear! not my own baby load,
> But yours; who bore the failure of the light,
> The strength, the knowledge and the thought of God,—
> The futile folly of the Infinite!

It was Holy Week when Henry Adams died, and on the afternoon of Easter Sunday, after a simple service at the house on Lafayette Square, his body was taken to Rock Creek Cemetery. There he was buried next to Clover under the figure of the woman in bronze.

A NOTE ON SOURCES

The standard sources for a work of history are usually letters and memoirs and other documents, amplified by the works of previous historians, but sometimes the word "source" may have a completely different meaning. I have been asked a number of times how I ever happened to think of writing a biography of Clover Adams, a woman who never did anything, in the conventional sense, worthy of commemoration. I can only answer that in the spring of 1974, I went to Chartres to look once again at the magnificent rose windows, and then proceeded to the châteaux of the Loire and southward to Poitiers and on to Languedoc and the terrible scenes of the Albigensian crusade. I had no particular purpose in mind, but I took along a copy of Henry James' *A Little Tour in France*, thinking that it would be amusing to see what the master had said about some of these same provincial towns a century ago, and when I came back to New York, I began writing an article comparing James' tour and my own. What haunted me, though, was Chartres, about which the profoundly secular James had written very superficially, almost frivolously, and so I turned back to Henry Adams.

I once spent more than a decade trying to write a vast reevaluation of American literature. It was entitled *The Dark Tradition*, and it was to run from Jonathan Edwards through Melville and James to Nathanael West and Faulkner. After writing nearly a thousand pages, and vainly petitioning more than a score of publishers to publish it, I began to feel that my masterpiece was weighing on me as heavily as any albatross, and so I finally abandoned it, a one-towered windowless cathedral destined to remain forever unfinished. But one long chapter that was finished, though never published, was the chapter on Henry Adams, and as I began poking around to re-examine his observations on Chartres, I opened, for the first time in more than twenty years, the Modern Library edition of *The Edu-cation of Henry Adams*. An inscription inside the front cover reminded me that it had originally belonged to a Harvard classmate, and that I had stolen it from him, for some forgotten reason, in Paris in the spring of 1953. Inside the back cover, where I had scribbled some of my ideas for the Adams chapter in *The Dark Tradition*, there was a note that now struck me as prophetic: "Nothing on his wife—why not?"

For twenty years, then, the question of Henry Adams' silence about his marriage to Clover had been lying somewhere in the back of my head, and it was only when I re-encountered that question, while searching for the meaning of Chartres, that I finally recognized the book that I wanted to write.

The life of Clover Adams can be deciphered mainly from the letters that she herself wrote every Sunday morning to her father, Dr. Robert William Hooper. A large collection of these letters was published by Little, Brown in 1936, under the straightforward title, *The Letters of Mrs. Henry Adams, 1865–1883*. The letters were edited by Ward Thoron, the husband of Ned Hooper's second daughter, Louisa, who helped a great deal in collecting and editing these papers. The published letters cover the Adamses' first trip to Europe, from July of 1872 to July of 1873; their second trip, from June to September of 1879; and three years of their Washington life, from October of 1880 to May of 1881, from October of 1881 to June of 1882, and from October of 1882 to May of 1883.

Thoron wrote in his preface that the rest of the letters that Clover wrote to her father were "missing," but a large number of them were subse-quently found in the Adams Papers preserved at the Massachusetts His-torical Society. These unpublished letters, about 150 in all, cover most of the "missing" years—i.e., the Washington winter seasons of 1876 through 1879, the rest of the European trip from September of 1879 to September of 1880, and the Washington season of 1883–84. Almost all of these letters are to her father, but there are a few to Charles Gaskell, John Hay, and other family friends.

Like the rest of the Adams Papers, Clover's unpublished letters have all been microfilmed, and they can be found, along with other miscellaneous family papers of the same years, on Reels 595 through 599, out of 608 reels in all. Through a wonderful combination of archival technology, foundation money, and the public library system, these Adams Papers microfilms were produced in 1954 and then distributed to university li-braries throughout the United States, and I found a set of them at the Stony Brook campus of the New York State University. I then had the reels transferred one by one to the small public library in Locust Valley,

New York, where I regularly went to read them on my way home from work. Quotations from the Adams Papers are from this microfilm edition, by permission of the Massachusetts Historical Society.

Since 1976, the Massachusetts Historical Society has been assembling a valuable new set of microfilms of letters and other documents dealing with Henry Adams. These still-unfinished microfilms—33 reels as of mid–1978—contain not only what is already on the Adams Papers microfilms but also letters from many other collections, notably those of Henry Cabot Lodge, James Russell Lowell, George Bancroft, Francis Parkman, Abigail Adams Homan, who saved the twenty letters that Henry wrote to Clover while she was nursing Dr. Hooper during the spring of 1885, and Theodore Frelinghuysen Dwight, who, as Henry's private secretary, preserved many letters from such friends as Hay, King, James, Holmes, and others. Apart from the letters to and from Henry, this collection also contains about ten letters by Clover, mostly to Dwight, and nearly fifty to her. One reel at the end of the M.H.S. collection contains the Hay-Adams correspondence on file at the John Hay Library at Brown University. More papers will eventually be added from the various collections in the Harvard University library system. For permission to quote excerpts, I am again indebted to the Massachusetts Historical Society.

For permission to quote from unpublished family papers, I am indebted to two of the granddaughters of Clover's brother, Ned, Mrs. Robert Knapp and Mrs. John Swann.

A large part of Clover's life is to be found, of course, in the life and works of Henry Adams. Considering his fame and importance, these works are strangely difficult to find. There is no standard edition, no collected works. For official bibliographic purposes, his books may be listed in the following sequence:

Chapters of Erie and Other Essays, by Charles F. Adams and Henry Adams, Boston, 1871. (Includes Henry's articles "The New York Gold Conspiracy," "Captain John Smith," "The Bank of England Restriction," "British Finance in 1816," and "The Legal Tender Act.")

Essays in Anglo-Saxon Law, ed. Henry Adams, Boston, 1876.

Documents Related to New England Federalism, 1800–1815, ed. Henry Adams, Boston, 1877.

The Life of Albert Gallatin, by Henry Adams, Philadelphia, 1879.

The Writings of Albert Gallatin, ed. Henry Adams, 3 volumes, Philadelphia, 1879.

Democracy, An American Novel, Anonymous, New York, 1880.

John Randolph, by Henry Adams, Boston, 1882.

Esther, A Novel, by Frances Snow Compton, New York, 1884.

History of the United States During the First Administration of Thomas Jefferson, by Henry Adams, 2 volumes, printed privately in Cambridge, 1884; printed publicly in New York, 1889.

History of the United States During the Second Administration of Thomas Jefferson, by Henry Adams, 2 volumes, printed privately in Cambridge, 1885; printed publicly in New York, 1890.

History of the United States During the First Administration of James Madison, by Henry Adams, 2 volumes, printed privately in Cambridge, 1888; printed publicly in New York, 1890.

History of the United States During the Second Administration of James Madison, by Henry Adams, 3 volumes, New York, 1891.

Historical Essays, by Henry Adams, New York, 1891. (Includes "Primitive Rights of Women," "The Declaration of Paris," "Harvard College, 1786–1787," "The Session, 1869–70," "Napoleon at St. Domingo," and four essays reprinted from *Chapters of Erie.*)

Memoirs of Marau Taaroa Last Queen of Tahiti, by Queen Marau, privately printed in Washington, 1893.

Mont-Saint-Michel and Chartres, by Henry Adams, printed privately in Washington, 1904, printed publicly in Boston, 1913.

The Education of Henry Adams, by Henry Adams, printed privately in Washington, 1907; printed publicly in Boston, 1918.

The Life of George Cabot Lodge, by Henry Adams, Boston, 1911.

The Degradation of the Democratic Dogma, by Henry Adams, ed. Brooks Adams, New York, 1919. This is Brooks Adams' posthumous collection of three of Henry's late essays on history: "The Tendency of History" (1894), "The Rule of Phase Applied to History" (1909), and "A Letter to American Teachers of History" (1910).

Some of these works, such as *Essays in Anglo-Saxon Law* and the *Memoirs of Marau Taaroa*, can be found only in major libraries. I myself read them in the Caracallan reading room of the New York Public Library, taking my place, during lunch hours, among the grizzled alcoholics who come there to sleep. Some of Adams' other works have been reprinted and occasionally appear in secondhand bookstores. *Democracy*, for example, was republished by Farrar, Straus and Young in the 1950's (the printed copy gives no exact date) and enjoyed a certain vogue because President Kennedy considered it an exemplar of what he regarded as political sophistication. It was reprinted again in 1961, combined with *Esther*, in a paperback edition by Anchor Books, with an introduction by Ernest Samuels. This is now also out of print, but it survives in many libraries and is the standard version of *Esther*. (Some of these works, however, are listed in *Books in Print* as available in reprints from small publishers like Peter Smith, Queens House, Adler, and Regency.)

The *History* is very difficult to find in its original version. (Of the private edition, of which only six copies were made for Henry's friends, there are no known specimens at all.) I happened to discover in my parents' house a rather obscure edition reprinted in four volumes in 1930 by the now-defunct publisher Albert & Charles Boni, with an introduction by Henry Steele Commager. The most easily available version is a two-volume condensation, edited by Herbert Agar and published by Houghton Mifflin in 1947, under the title *The Formative Years*. Reprinted by the University of Chicago Press in 1974.

Adams' best historical essays were republished in a 1958 collection entitled *The Great Secession Winter of 1860–61 and Other Essays*, edited by George Hochfield. This includes "The New York Gold Conspiracy," "Primitive Rights of Women," and the two accounts of "The Session." A notable selection of essays and excerpts can also be found in "A Henry Adams Reader," ed. Elizabeth Stevenson, 1958. Adams' biography of George Cabot Lodge appears in the Edmund Wilson anthology entitled *The Shock of Recognition* (1943).

The only two books that are widely available are, of course, *Mont-Saint-Michel* and the *Education*. For the former, I have used Houghton Mifflin's paperback Sentry edition, originally published in 1963. For the latter, as noted above, I have gone back to my stolen Modern Library edition, originally published in 1931.

Henry Adams was one of the great letter writers in American literary history, and the process of accumulating and editing these letters, which by now total more than 4,000, has been going on throughout most of this century.

Worthington Chauncey Ford was the first to cull something from this treasure, a two-volume work entitled *A Cycle of Adams Letters, 1861–1865*, published in 1920, in which Henry joined the two Charles Francises and other prolific Adamses in a collective portrait of the Civil War years. Ford went on to compile the first collection of Henry's letters, a handsome two-volume work that is still fairly available: *Letters of Henry Adams (1858–1891)*, published in 1930, and *Letters of Henry Adams (1892–1918)*, published in 1938. Ford edited discreetly, according to the traditions of his time, and on comparing the published letters to the microfilmed originals in the Adams Papers, one discovers that Ford regularly deleted not only Adams' harshest commentaries on his contemporaries but also the mundane details of domestic life that sometimes most interest a biographer.

A small but interesting addition to the Ford collection appeared in 1920 under the title *Letters to a Niece*, edited by Mabel LaFarge. She was one of the Hooper girls whom Henry regarded as his protégées and pupils, and although his letters to her are scarcely of major significance, her book included the important and previously unpublished poem, "Prayer to the Virgin of Chartres."

In the 1940's, a young scholar named Harold Dean Cater appeared on the Boston scene and discovered that there were still many more Adams letters, which, for one reason or another, had not appeared in the Ford collection, Cater was a bit undiscriminating in assembling new letters, but the result of his labor was a densely printed (797 pages) and fascinating new collection entitled *Henry Adams and His Friends* (1947). It also included a long (107 pages) and excellent biographical introduction. For a sort of anthology of all these collections, see *The Selected Letters of Henry Adams*, edited by Newton Arvin (1951), one of a series of such selections.

Now, finally, a number of scholars have begun a major project to publish all of the Henry Adams letters in a set of six volumes. This project is under the general supervision of Ernest Samuels, the prize-winning biographer of Adams and a professor emeritus at Northwestern, with the assistance of two younger Adams experts at the University of Virginia, Charles Vandersee and J. C. Levenson. The National Endowment for the Humanities is subsidizing it, and the Harvard University Press will publish it shortly, perhaps beginning in 1979.

The authoritative biography of Henry Adams is the three-volume work by Ernest Samuels: *The Young Henry Adams* (1948); *Henry Adams: The Middle Years* (1958); *Henry Adams: The Major Phase* (1964), all published by the Harvard University Press. Samuels was already prying open the Adams Papers in the 1940's, and he was among the first to benefit from the general opening up of the papers in the 1950's. His work, winner of the Pulitzer, Parkman, and Bancroft prizes, is a traditional intellectual biography, in which Clover plays a rather small part.

Among the other biographies most worth noting are: *Henry Adams, a Biography*, by Elizabeth Stevenson (1956); *Henry Adams, Scientific Historian*, by William H. Jordy (1952), and *The Mind and Art of Henry Adams*, by J. C. Levenson (1957). Edward Chalfant, who has been described by Louis Auchincloss as "the scholar closest to the secrets of Adams' personality," wrote his doctoral thesis on *Henry Adams and History* at the University of Pennsylvania in 1954 and has been at work for many years on an unpublished three-volume biography of Adams. Auchincloss, in turn, wrote a 1971 study of Adams in the University of Minnesota series on American writers, as well as several shorter essays on Adams' life and work.

Henry Adams has long been an object of wonder in academia, and now that the lists of doctoral thesis have been computerized in a reference work entitled *Comprehensive Dissertation Index, 1861–1972*, published in Ann Arbor, Michigan, we find a total of nearly 50 such efforts, ranging from *Henry Adams' Concept of the American Character*, by Jeanette Ehrhardt Ingrusci, to *A Study of Henry Adams' Periphrastic Technique in the History of the United States*, by Richard Vitzthum, to *A Study of Non-Rational Elements in the Works of Henry Adams as Centralized in His Attitude Toward Woman*, by M. Aquinas Sister Healy. Computerized reprints are available for about $15 each to anyone who wants them.

CHAPTER 1. Much of this opening chapter is based, obviously, on my own observations. On Saint-Gaudens, see *The Reminiscences of Augustus Saint-Gaudens*, edited by Homer St. Gaudens (1913). Also *Saint-Gaudens and the Gilded Era*, by Louise Hall Tharp (1969). John LaFarge's account of Adams telling Saint-Gaudens what he wanted is from an interview in the *Washington Evening Star*, cited in Cater.

Mrs. Whiteside's observation on Clover's death is quoted in a long article by Katherine Simonds, "The Tragedy of Mrs. Henry Adams," published in *The New England Quarterly* in December of 1936, and the quotation from Samuel Eliot Morison, then one of the quarterly's editors, is from his commentary on that article. The comments by Thomas Boylston Adams are from an interview in *The New York Times*, March 11, 1975.

CHAPTER 2. Much of this chapter is based on the Hooper family papers in private collections. The official Sturgis genealogy is *Edward Sturgis of Yarmouth, Massachusetts, 1613–1695, and His Descendants*, by Roger Faxton Sturgis (1914). The only biography of William Sturgis is a 64-page sketch entitled *Memoir of the Honorable William Sturgis, Prepared Agreeably to a Resolution of the Massachusetts Historical Society*, by Charles G. Loring (1864). Captain Sturgis makes a brief appearance in *The Maritime History of Massachusetts, 1783–1860*, by Samuel Eliot Morison (1921).

The Hooper genealogy can be found in a privately printed work entitled *The Hooper Family*, by Charles Henry Pope and Thomas Hooper (1908). Ellen Sturgis Hooper's poems were privately printed by Edward Hooper in 1872 in an untitled collection of 119 pages. It is at the Houghton Library at Harvard.

On the life of Oliver Wendell Holmes, and for personal guidance and encouragement, I am indebted to Eleanor M. Tilton, professor of English at Barnard, author of *Amiable Autocrat, A Biography of Dr. Oliver Wendell*

Holmes, and now at work on the letters of Ralph Waldo Emerson. See also *Life and Letters of Oliver Wendell Holmes,* by John T. Morse (1896), as well as, of course, the good doctor's own works.

On Margaret Fuller, who has been much re-examined in recent years see *Margaret Fuller Ossoli,* by Thomas Wentworth Higginson (1884). Also *Margaret Fuller,* by Arthur W. Brown (1964), and *In Quest of Love, The Life and Death of Margaret Fuller,* by Faith Chipperfield (1957). Her famous book, *Woman in the Nineteenth Century,* was reprinted in paperback in 1971.

CHAPTER 3. The basic biography of Louis Agassiz is *Louis Agassiz, His Life and Correspondence,* edited by Elizabeth Cary Agassiz (1886). For modern studies, see *Louis Agassiz, A Life in Science,* by Edward Lurie (1960) and *Adventurous Alliance, The Story of the Agassiz Family of Boston,* by Louise Hall Tharp (1959). Mrs. Agassiz' story is more fully told in *Elizabeth Cary Agassiz, A Biography,* by Lucy Allen Patton (1919). As for their gifted son, see *Letters and Recollections of Alexander Agassiz, with a Sketch of His Life and Work,* ed. G. R. Agassiz (1913). An affectionate memoir of the Agassiz establishment, *The Agassiz House on Quincy Street,* was written by Charles W. Eliot and published in the *Harvard Alumni Bulletin* of March 29, 1917. The unpublished letters of Sarah Ellen Browne from the Agassiz School to her family are printed by permission of the Schlesinger Library at Radcliffe, and Mrs. Robert F. Bradford of Cambridge, Massachusetts.

There have been many recent histories of women in America, many of them unsatisfactory. On the education of women in the early nineteenth century, I am indebted to *Peculiar Institutions, An Informal History of the Seven Sister Colleges,* by Elaine Kendall (1976). See also *Perish the Thought, Intellectual Women in Romantic America, 1830–1860,* by Susan P. Conrad (1976).

CHAPTER 4. The bibliography of histories of the Civil War is, of course, enormous. For basic information, I have relied on *The Centennial History of the Civil War,* 4 volumes, by Bruce Catton (1963), *The Civil War, A Narrative,* 3 volumes, by Shelby Foote (1958–1974), and *The Oxford History of the American People,* by Samuel Eliot Morison (1965). On the literary history, *Patriotic Gore,* by Edmund Wilson (1962), is still unsurpassed, I think, and on the spirit of the capital, so is *Reveille in Washington,* by Margaret Leech (1941).

The great drama of Colonel Shaw at Fort Wagner is well told in *One Gallant Rush, Robert Gould Shaw and His Brave Black Regiment,* by Peter Burchard (1965). For details on the Saint-Gaudens monument, see *The Monument to Robert Gould Shaw, Its Inception, Completion, and Unveiling, 1865–1897,* Anonymous (1897).

As we now encounter the James family's involvement with Colonel

Shaw, we also encounter the enormous body of work by and about that family. The basic study of the novelist is Leon Edel's five-volume biography, published between 1953 and 1972: *Henry James, The Untried Years, 1843–1870; Henry James, The Conquest of London, 1870–1881; Henry James, The Middle Years, 1882–1895; Henry James, The Treacherous Years, 1895–1901,* and *Henry James, The Master, 1901–1916.* See also *Henry James, The Major Phase,* by F. O. Matthiessen (1944), and *The Question of Henry James,* a valuable collection of essays about James, edited by F. W. Dupee (1945).

James' own unfinished autobiography, written in the fullness of the later style, and therefore less valuable than it might have been, is in three volumes, the third a mere fragment: *A Small Boy and Others* (1913), *Notes of a Son and Brother* (1914), and *The Middle Years* (1917). Much more revealing are the sketchbooks and ruminations edited by F. O. Matthiessen and Kenneth B. Murdock under the title *The Notebooks of Henry James* (1947). And the letters, originally collected by Percy Lubbock in two volumes in 1920 and now being republished in a much more complete collection edited by Leon Edel. The first two of a projected six volumes were published in 1974 and 1975 and reach the year 1883.

On Henry's relatives, the best general account is *The James Family, Including Selections from the Writings of Henry James Senior, William, Henry and Alice James,* edited by F. O. Matthiessen (1948). On his older brother, see *William James, A Biography,* by Gay Wilson Allen (1967). And on his sister: *The Diary of Alice James,* edited by Leon Edel (1964).

Back to the Civil War. The story of the Sanitary Commission is perhaps best told in *Lincoln's Fifth Wheel, The Political History of the United States Sanitary Commission,* by William Quentin Maxwell (1956). For more detailed accounts of the Boston women's contribution, I have quoted from *Constitution and By-Laws of the New England Women's Auxiliary Association, Branch of the United States Sanitary Commission* (1864), and *Final Report of the Supply Department of the New England Auxiliary Association* (1865), both available at the Widener Library at Harvard. For a good general account, on the other hand, see *The Women and the Crisis, Women of the North in the Civil War,* by Agatha Young (1959).

Perhaps the fullest account of the experiment at Port Royal is *Rehearsal for Reconstruction,* by Willie Lee Rose (1964). See also *Port Royal Under Six Flags,* by Katherine M. Jones (1960), and *Letters from Port Royal, 1862–1868,* ed. Elizabeth Ware Pearson (1906, reprinted in 1969). On the black soldier's role in the war, the classic account is *Army Life in a Black Regiment,* by Thomas Wentworth Higginson, the commander of the first regiment of Southern blacks in the U.S. Army (1870, reprinted in 1960). And for a discussion of that account, see *Colonel of the Black Regiment, The Life of Thomas Wentworth Higginson,* by Howard N. Meyer (1967). A useful general survey is *The Negro in the Civil War*, by Benjamin Quarles (1953), and a valuable documentary collection is *The Negro's Civil War, How American Negroes Felt and Acted During the War for the Union*, by James M. McPherson (1965).

As for a number of other figures who make their appearances in this chapter on the Civil War, I should like simply to express my indebtedness to *FLO, A Biography of Frederick Law Olmsted*, by Laura Wood Roper (1973); *The Life and Letters of Henry Lee Higginson*, by Bliss Perry (1921); *Justice Holmes: The Shaping Years, 1841–1870*, by Mark DeWolfe Howe (1957); *Louisa May, A Modern Biography of Louisa May Alcott*, by Martha Saxton (1977); *James Russell Lowell*, by Martin Duberman (1966); and *The Life of Emily Dickinson*, by Richard B. Sewall (1974).

CHAPTER 5. An impressionistic but excellent account of the postwar mood of Boston may be found in *New England: Indian Summer, 1865–1915*, by Van Wyck Brooks (1940). For a more social version of the same scene, see *The Proper Bostonians*, by Cleveland Amory (1947). For a social version in the more serious sense of the word, see *The Problem of Boston, Some Readings in Cultural History*, by Martin Green (1966). The more physical details of Boston in transition may be found in *Boston, A Topographical History*, by Walter Muir Whitehill (1959). *The Early Years of the Saturday Club, 1855–1870*, by Edward Waldo Emerson (1918), provides affectionate sketches of the city's cultural leaders, including a rare one of Ephraim Whitman Gurney.

There have been many recent histories of the women's suffrage movement. I have relied mainly on *The Better Half, The Emancipation of the American Woman*, by Andrew Sinclair (1965); *Daughters of the Promised Land, Women in American History*, by Page Smith (1970); *The Ladies of Seneca Falls, The Birth of the Women's Rights Movement*, by Miriam Gurko (1974), and *Once Upon a Pedestal*, by Emily Hahn (1974).

The papers of Clover's aunt Caroline Sturgis Tappan are at the Houghton Library at Harvard. I have quoted from one letter and one poem, as well as two letters by Ellen Gurney, by permission of the library.

CHAPTER 6. Voluminous is too mild a word to describe the Adams Papers. Each reel of microfilm contains hundreds of documents, and John Adams' diary alone fills Reels 1–3, his letterbooks Reels 89–96 and 98–124. John Quincy's Diary fills Reels 4–48. The Harvard University Press has been dutifully publishing everything: John Adams' diary and autobiography in four large volumes, Charles Francis' diary in six volumes, with many more to come. Each volume is handsome and definitive.

There have been several collective histories of the Adams family. The best, I think, is *The Adams Chronicles, Four Generations of Greatness*, by Jack Shepherd (1975), a lavishly illustrated and very workmanlike production issued to coincide with the television series of the same name. See also

Adams, An American Dynasty, by Francis Russell (1976) and the much earlier *The Adams Family,* by James Truslow Adams (1930). The family genealogy is *Henry Adams of Somersetshire, England, and Braintree, Mass., His English Ancestors and Some of His Descendants,* compiled by J. Gardner Bartlett for Edward Dean Adams (1927).

The basic work on the family patriarch is the admirable *John Adams,* 2 volumes, by Page Smith (1962). A shorter, newer, and also admirable account is *The Character of John Adams,* by Peter Shaw (1976). Much inferior is *John Adams and the American Revolution,* by Catherine Drinker Bowen (1950), which suffers from the author's desire to imagine thoughts and conversations that are not actually known. Adams' wife suffers a similar fate in *Abigail Adams,* by Janet Whitney (1949). Abigail has her triumph, however, in the new tendency to print such original documents as her letters. See *The Book of Abigail and John, Selected Letters of the Adams Family, 1762–1784,* edited by L. H. Butterfield, Marc Friedlander, and Mary-Jo Kline (1975), and *New Letters of Abigail Adams, 1788–1901,* edited by Stewart Mitchell (1947, reprinted in 1973). (Note: Charles Francis Adams selected and published several collections of his grandparents' letters in 1840, 1841, 1848, and 1876, but they are now very difficult to find.)

John Quincy Adams' superb diary, too, was edited by Charles Francis and published between 1874 and 1877 in twelve volumes, a work that has long been out of print. Allan Nevins produced a condensation in one large volume in 1928, which was reprinted in 1969. Louisa Adams' miscellaneous writings can be found in Reels 264–279 of the Adams Papers, but the only printed version that I know is the fascinating manuscript entitled "Mrs. John Quincy Adams' Narrative of a Journey from St. Petersburg to Paris in February, *1815*," which her grandson Brooks Adams edited and published in *Scribner's Magazine* in 1903.

There is no biography fully worthy of John Quincy Adams. His public life is treated extensively in Samuel Flagg Bemis' two works, *John Quincy Adams and the Foundation of American Policy* (1950) and *John Quincy Adams and the Union* (1956). For a more intimate account, one can recommend *John Quincy Adams, A Personal History of an Independent Man,* by Marie B. Hecht. It should perhaps be noted that Adams is one of the heroes of John F. Kennedy's celebrated but rather sketchy work *Profiles in Courage* (1955). There is very little available on Henry Adams' other grandfather, the rich one who gave the children silver rather than bibles. For a few details, see *Memoir of Peter Chardon Brooks,* by Samuel G. Drake (1854).

Charles Francis Adams' interminable journal has already been cited. He was also the subject of a rather stiff and grudging biography entitled simply *Charles Francis Adams,* by his son, Charles Francis Adams, Jr. (1900). More recently, the same task has been undertaken, thoroughly but also a bit stiffly, in *Charles Francis Adams, 1807–1886*, by Martin B. Duberman (1960).

Charles Francis Adams, Jr., who took up history in his old age after a lifetime as a corporate executive, bequeathed to the Massachusetts Historical Society an unfinished manuscript published posthumously under the title, *Charles Francis Adams, 1835–1915, An Autobiography*. It was here that he concluded that the famous tycoons he had known were "a set of mere money-getters and traders. . . . essentially unattractive and uninteresting." The only recent biography of this embittered man is *Charles Francis Adams, The Patrician at Bay*, by Edward Chase Kirkland (1965).

Brooks Adams was no less embittered, but he had a far greater gift for expressing his anger. The best account of him, I think, is *Brooks Adams, A Biography*, by Arthur F. Beringause (1955). See also *Henry Adams and Brooks Adams, The Education of Two American Historians*, by Timothy Paul Donovan (1961). No understanding of the later Henry Adams is possible, of course, without a study of Brooks' great work *The Law of Civilization and Decay* (1896, reprinted in a paperback edition in 1955).

For the fifth generation's somewhat trivialized views of the fourth generation, see *Education by Uncles*, by Abigail Adams Homans (1966).

CHAPTER 7. My account of Henry's youth relies mainly on the masterful early chapters of the *Education*, augmented by the first volume of Samuels' biography.

CHAPTER 8. My version of *The Adams Chronicles* is based, obviously, on my own interviews with a number of the principal figures, to whom I am indebted for their cooperation.

On the darker side of William Dean Howells, see the excellent study by Kenneth S. Lynn, *William Dean Howells, An American Life* (1971).

CHAPTER 9. Clover's accounts of her wanderings in Europe are drawn from the Thoron edition of her letters and the unpublished letters in the Adams Papers.

On the enigmatic character of Francis Parkman, I have relied mainly on the biography by Howard Doughty, *Francis Parkman* (1962). See also *The Letters of Francis Parkman*, edited by William R. Jacobs (1960).

George Bancroft may best be viewed, outside his own *History of the United States*, in *Life and Letters of George Bancroft*, by M. A. DeWolfe Howe (1908). See also *George Bancroft, Brahmin Rebel*, by Russel B. Nye (1972). There are large collections of Bancroft's papers at the New York Public Library and at Cornell University.

The bumptious autobiography of Henry Cabot Lodge, who seems never to have realized how bumptious he was, not even when he was complaining that Dickens was not a gentleman, appeared under the title *Early Memories* (1913).

For the details of Ralph Waldo Emerson's appearance on the Nile, I have followed *The Life of Ralph Waldo Emerson*, by Ralph L. Rusk (1949). The scholarly publication of Emerson's journals has reached, I believe, 9 volumes, but his views on the Nile are still to come.

CHAPTER 10. Since Boston is exquisitely conscious of its own evolution, there are many valuable histories of the city. In addition to Whitehill's *Topographical History*, cited earlier, I have based my account of postwar developments largely on *Houses of Boston's Back Bay, An Architectural History, 1840–1917*, by Bainbridge Bunting (1967). For the description of life on Marlborough Street after Clover's departure, I am indebted to the *Hale House Newsletter*, January, 1977.

Harvard is, if possible, even more conscious of its own history than is Boston. The authorized biography, so to speak, is *Three Centuries of Harvard, 1636–1936*, by Samuel Eliot Morison (1946). For a few more informal views, see *Harvard, Through Change and Through Storm*, by E. J. Kahn, Jr. (1969). The best work on Eliot is the rather stately two-volume biography *Charles W. Eliot, President of Harvard University, 1869–1909*, by Henry James, a nephew of the novelist (1930). Howells provides a warm account of the Cambridge scene in *Literary Friends and Acquaintances, A Personal Retrospect of American Authorship* (1900, reprinted in 1968).

The description of the Adams cottage at Beverly Farms as "rather an ugly house" comes from the work of R. P. Blackmur, who devoted many years to an uncompleted study of Henry Adams. Two of his essays, "The Expense of Greatness: Three Emphases on Henry Adams" and "The Letters of Marian Adams," were published in the collection entitled *The Expense of Greatness* (1940, reprinted in 1958). But this was only a fragment of Blackmur's work, which was conceived during the 1930's as a kind of intellectual biography of Adams. Blackmur interviewed many people, studied many of the documents, and wrote about 450 pages out of a planned 750. The unpublished results may be found in eight large black boxes, numbered 16 to 24, in Blackmur's collected papers at the Princeton University Library.

On Henry Hobson Richardson's building of Trinity Church, the best early account, in fact the only early account, is *Henry Hobson Richardson and His Works*, by Mariana Griswold Van Rensselaer (1888, reprinted in 1969), which remained the unchallenged authority until the appearance of Henry Russell Hitchcock's admirable study *The Architecture of H. H. Richardson and His Times* (1936, reprinted in 1966). See also *Selected Drawings*, by Henry Hobson Richardson (1974). For a more general study of postwar architecture, see *The Brown Decades, A Study of the Arts in America, 1865–1895*, by Lewis Mumford (1931).

CHAPTER 11. In Washington, once again, I have relied largely on the published and unpublished letters of Henry and Clover.

The most colorful recent account of the great election fraud on behalf of Rutherford B. Hayes is *1876*, by Gore Vidal. For the unhappy winner's own account, see *Diary and Letters of Rutherford B. Hayes* (1922–1926), condensed from five volumes into one by T. Harry Williams in *Hayes: The Diary of a President, 1875–1881* (1964).

E. L. Godkin is not the most endearing of men, but he is central in this period, and his letters have recently been collected under the title *The Gilded Age Letters of E. L. Godkin* (1974), edited by William M. Armstrong, who is now at work on a biography of Godkin.

CHAPTER 12. To Europe again, with Clover's letters as the basic documents.

CHAPTER 13. Clarence King remains to this day a somewhat mysterious figure. After his death, his friends compiled and published an anthology of appreciations entitled *Clarence King Memoirs* (1904), with contributions by Henry Adams, John Hay, William Dean Howells, John LaFarge, and others, but they failed to explain the brilliance that seemed to have captivated a whole generation of his contemporaries. The same mystery shrouds the only recent study, *Clarence King, A Biography*, by Thurman Wilkins (1958). King's classic *Mountaineering in the Sierra Nevada* (1875) can still be found—I paid $20 for a copy in 1977—but it does not solve the mystery. King's personal papers, mostly scientific, are at the H. E. Huntington Library in San Marino, California.

John Hay, by contrast, enjoyed a thoroughly comprehensible success —best-selling books, a rich wife, and an appointment as Secretary of State. The tale is told, in the conventional nineteenth-century manner, in *The Life and Letters of John Hay*, 2 volumes, by William Roscoe Thayer (1915). I know of no searching modern biography of this dialect poet who, among other things, created the Panama Canal Treaty. His dreadful and fascinating novel *The Bread-Winners* (1884) was republished in 1973. His private papers are at the John Hay Library at Brown University.

For the social background on this postwar era, I have relied on *The Emergence of Modern America, 1865–1878*, by Allan Nevins (1927); *Political and Social Growth of the United States, 1852–1933*, by Arthur M. Schlesinger (1933); *The Growth of the American Republic*, by Samuel Eliot Morison and Henry Steele Commager (1938), and *The New Commonwealth*, by John A. Garraty (1968).

CHAPTER 14. The standard work on Garfield is *The Life and Letters of James Abram Garfield*, by Theodore Clarke Smith (1925). For the dark side of those same years, I have relied on Charles E. Rosenberg's interesting study *The Trial of the Assassin Guiteau, Psychiatry and Law in the Gilded Age* (1968).

I know of no books on either Simon or Donald Cameron, but a biogra-

phy of the beautiful Elizabeth Cameron is being written by Arline
Boucher Tehan, of West Hartford, Connecticut.

On Oscar Wilde's wanderings through America, I have followed Louis
Kronenberger's *Oscar Wilde* (1976).

On Chester Arthur, I have used *Chester A. Arthur, A Quarter Century of
Machine Politics*, by George Frederick Howe (1935, reprinted in 1966).

CHAPTER 15. I have already cited the main works on Henry Hobson
Richardson. For the details on the building of the Adams house, I am
much indebted to an excellent study by Marc Friedlander, "Henry Hobson Richardson, Henry Adams, and John Hay," published in the *Journal
of the Society of Architectural Historians* in October of 1970. See also "A
Tragic Circle," by James F. O'Gorman, in *Nineteenth Century*, August,
1976.

For some insights on the pioneers of photography, I have relied mainly
on *The History of Photography*, by Beaumont Newhall (1964). I have also
used the introduction by Margery Mann, of the San Fransciso Art Institute, to the catalogue entitled *Women of Photography*, *An Historical Survey*,
for a show that appeared in 1976 in San Francisco, Sante Fe, Milwaukee,
Wellesley, and New York.

For the details of Matthew Arnold's visit to America, I have used
Matthew Arnold, by Lionel Trilling (1949). Clover's version of the scene
comes, of course, from her letters. On the rise of Grover Cleveland, I
have relied on Allan Nevins' biography, *Grover Cleveland, A Study in Courage* (1932).

CHAPTER 16. This chapter comes almost entirely from the letters of the
principal characters. See also *The Letters and Journals of Nicholas Longworth
Anderson, 1854–1892*, edited by Isabel Anderson (1946).

The basic text on literary suicide is *The Savage God, A Study of Suicide*,
by A. Alvarez (1972). The literature on this subject is enormous, as can
be seen from Norman L. Farberow's *Bibliography on Suicide* (1969). See
particularly *The Cry for Help*, by Norman L. Farberow and Edwin S.
Shneidman (1961), and *Suicide*, by Jacques Choron (1972). Freud's essay
can be found in Volume IV of his *Collected Papers*. The statistics on American suicides during the 1880's come from the *World Almanac* of 1885. For
some exotic theories, see "The Incidence of Manic-Depressive Psychosis
in Certain Socially Important Families," by Abraham Myerson and Ros-
alie Boyle, in *The American Journal of Psychiatry*, July, 1941, and "Suicide
and Homicide in Their Relation to Weather Changes," by C. A. Mills, in
The American Journal of Psychiatry, November, 1934. Ernest Samuels' elaborate study of Mrs. Cameron's pregnancy, entitled "Henry Adams and
the Gossip Mills," appeared in *Essays in American and English Literature,
Presented to Bruce Robert McElderry, Jr.*, edited by Max F. Schulz *et al.*
(1967).

Ellen Gurney's last letters are in the Houghton Library at Harvard.

EPILOGUE. The sources here are all the basic ones, *Mont-Saint-Michel*, the letters, and the last volume of Samuels' biography. For an excessively critical study of this last period, see *Henry Adams on the Road to Chartres*, by Robert Mane (1971).

ACKNOWLEDGMENT

I am repeatedly impressed, as any historian must be, by the goodwill with which librarians search for documents, find obscure books, and answer questions. I am indebted to many of them, but particularly to Marc Friedlander and Celeste Walker of the Adams Papers at the Massachusetts Historical Society, the entire staffs of the New York Public Library and the Widener and Houghton Libraries at Harvard, Mrs. James H. Chadbourn of the Harvard Law School Library, Harley P. Holden and William W. Whalen of the Harvard University Archives, Elizabeth Shenton of the Schlesinger Library at Radcliffe, Mrs. Michael Sherman of the Princeton University Library, Marguerite J. Pack and Kathleen Jacklin of the Cornell University Library, Clifton Jones of the John Hay Library at Brown University, James Lawton of the Boston Public Library, Esmé Willis of the Sturgis Library at Barnstable, Massachusetts, Marian Gosling of the Marblehead Historical Society, Barbara Blundell of the Essex Institute in Salem, Lynne Calderone of the Hale House in Boston, and Norma Holmgren and her staff at the Locust Valley Public Library in Locust Valley, New York.

No less goodwill has been shown by the many scholars already at work in this field. Specifically, I should like to thank William N. Armstrong, Louis Auchincloss, Edward Chalfant, Leon Edel, Scott Fisher, Eugenia Kaledin, Stephen H. Kalish, Samuel Eliot Morison, Ernest Samuels, Elizabeth Stevenson, Arline Boucher Tehan, Louise Hall Tharp, Eleanor M. Tilton, Charles Vandersee, and Thurman Wilkins.

Finally, I must express my gratitude to the many Sturgis and Hooper descendants whom I have pursued with my questions. Thanks to Richard

ACKNOWLEDGMENT

Curtis, Greeley S. Curtis, Jr., Mrs. Thomas Hale Ham, Bayard Hooper, Gertrude Hooper, Robert C. Hooper, Mrs. Robert Knapp, Henry A. LaFarge, Francis B. Lothrop, Mrs. George McCandlish, Mrs. Edward W. Moore, Mrs. Curtis Prout, Mrs. John Swann, and Sturgis Warner.

And a final word of thanks to Jill Abramson for research assistance.

OTTO FRIEDRICH

Locust Valley, N.Y.
Aug. 13, 1978

INDEX

374